FOR COLLECTORS ONLY®

The Model 1911
and Model 1911A1 Military
and Commercial Pistols

by Joe Poyer

**edited by
Craig Riesch**

NORTH CAPE PUBLICATIONS®, INC.

A book such as this is more than the result of one person's labor. It could not have been written without the assistance of **Craig Riesch** and **Karl Karash**, both of whom spent many hours checking and rechecking facts, text, photographs, captions and providing advice and counsel. Their experience and suggestions made this book possible, and so it is dedicated to them.

Any mistakes or omissions are strictly the responsibility of the author.

The author wishes to thank all of the many collectors and shooters who, over the past five years, have helped with the preparation of this book; especially: Ken Catero; Bill Chachula; H.P. "Bud" Davey; John Domoslai; Chuck Doty; Ken Fladrich; Larry Gaertner; John Gangel, Little John's Auction Service; Horace Greeley IV; Brad Johnson; John Jordan; Roy Marcot; J. Michael Metzgar, Jr.; Lowell E. Pauli; Lee A. Rutledge; Mike Strietbeck; Gary Thomas; and Terry Tussey.

The cover photo is of the 115th Wyoming Cavalry conducting a pistol charge during field exercises sometime in the 1930s.

ISBN 978-1-882391-46-2

North Cape Publications®, Inc., P.O. Box 1027, Tustin, CA 92781
Phone: 800 745-9714 Fax: 714 832-5302
E-mail:ncape@ix.netcom.com
Website: http://www.northcapepubs.com
Printed in USA by Delta Printing Solutions, Valencia, CA 91355

Table of Contents

v

CHAPTER 3
SLIDE, PART BY PART 156

CHAPTER 5

CHAPTER 6

xiii

Appendices

List of Tables

xvii

Private Guy Dean Hughes, 92nd Division, U.S. Army, in France, 1918. Pvt. Hughes is wearing the Model 1910 Pistol Belt with the Type 5 Magazine Pocket. His Model 1911 .45 caliber pistol is carried in the Model 1916 Holster with the flap removed. Photo courtesy of Yvonne Williams.

A Marine fires his Model 1911 during target practice on Guam in 1923. Note the Model 1917 Cartridge Pouch on his belt. Photo by Charles Gibbons.

A paratrooper from the 505th Parachute Infantry Regiment, 82nd Airborne Division just before loading up for the combat jump into Sicily on July 9, 1943. He is armed with an M1 Carbine, M3 Combat Knife, and a Model 1911A1 .45 caliber pistol. U.S Army photo.

Ninth Air Force NCOs enjoy beers in the late August 1944 sunshine at the Hotel George V Cafe. The T/5 is wearing a Model 1911A1 in a Model 1916 holster. The NCOs are armed with M1 Carbines. U.S. Army Signal Corps photo.

American troops hunt for Japanese snipers above Holtz Bay on the island of Attu in the Aleutian Islands in late May 1943. U.S. Army photo.

Below, two soldiers struggle to put a track back on an armored amphibian tractor in the 1st Armored Amphibian Tractor Battalion command area in South Korea, July 1, 1953. Both are armed with the Model 1911A1 .45 caliber pistol. U.S. Army photo by TSgt W. G. Landers.

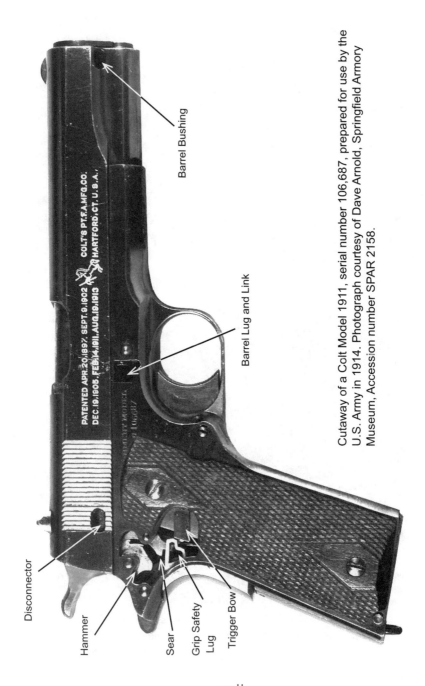

Cutaway of a Colt Model 1911, serial number 106,687, prepared for use by the U.S. Army in 1914. Photograph courtesy of Dave Arnold, Springfield Armory Museum, Accession number SPAR 2158.

INTRODUCTION

This book is not intended to be a definitive text on the development and history of the Model 1911/Model 1911A1 and its successors. Rather it is intended to allow collectors and shooters to identify specific models and determine whether or not all the parts of any particular pistol are original to its time of manufacture as determined by its serial number.

To that end, the organization of this book is somewhat different than others. A brief **history** of the development of the pistol and its manufacture and use is given in the first chapter. The second, third and fourth chapters provide a detailed, **part-by-part description of each part** of the receiver, slide and magazine, the three main components of the pistol—with dimensions where necessary—and illustrations, either photographs or drawings. Every change to each part is described, illustrated and provided with the serial number range of its introduction and range of use.

Chapter 5 provides tables of **serial numbers** for every variation of the pistol. The tables cover all Ordnance Department assigned serial number ranges for all contractors. All Colt commercial serial number ranges for every major variation in model and caliber that received its own serial number range are included. All known serial numbers of British military-acquired pistols, as well as all foreign contract pistols, are also included.

Chapters 6, 7, and 8 describe the **markings** found on the receiver, slide, and barrel, including factory model, address and factory inspection markings. U.S. Army Ordnance Department inspection markings for all military pistols are also given. Every change to the markings is related to its serial number range of use. Magazine markings are covered in Chapter 4.

Chapters 9, 10, and 11 provide detailed descriptions of all pistol **finishes, accessories, holsters, ammunition carriers,** and **belts** issued to the soldier, and **ammunition** developed for use with the Model 1911/1911A1 pistol.

Conventions
1) Following the editorial practice of North Cape Publications®, Inc., major changes to parts are classified as "**Types.**" Two kinds of receivers were developed for the Model 1911 and Model 1911A1. The first (Model 1911)

1

Model 1911, M1911A1

is referred to as "**Type 1**." The second for the Model 1911A1 is called the "**Type 2**." These are not Colt or Ordnance Department designations.

2) Within "types," minor changes were often made to parts during the manufacturing period or were made in slightly different ways by different manufacturers. These are referred to as "**Variations**." For instance, the Type 3 hammer was made in three variations.

3) Serial number ranges, unless known to be definite, are estimates and are preceded by the word "circa" or "ca.," meaning around or about. The range may be from a few hundred to a few thousand.

4) Dimensions given in the text, unless otherwise noted, reflect nominal or design measurements as taken from original engineering and production drawings. If the reader finds a part that varies more than a few thousandths from the dimensions given, consider replacing it as it may be unsafe.

5) When measurements are given from a point to a hole or other opening, that measurement is understood to be to the center of the hole or opening, unless otherwise noted.

6) All reference directions are given from the shooter's standpoint while looking over the sights toward the muzzle. Thus the left side refers to the side with the slide release and manual safety.

7) Line drawings may occasionally be used in preference to photographs for clarity or to emphasize certain aspects. But every effort was made to obtain photographs of original pistols.

8) The Model 1911/1911A1 was manufactured according to the English measurement system. All dimensions are given in decimal inches.

9) Information may be repeated in different parts of the text so that the reader does not have to page back and forth.

10) When period costs are given in the text, the equivalent in 2006 dollars are also given. For instance, a standard commercial Government Model

Military and Commercial Pistols

.45 in 1934 cost $22.00. The cost in 2006 dollars would be $314.03. The inflation calculator used was developed by S. Morgan Friedman. Cost information from before 1975 was based on information from the *Consumer Price Index Statistics from Historical Statistics of the United States* (USGPO, 1975). Those since 1976 are based on data from the *Annual Statistical Abstracts of the United States*. Mr. Friedman's calculator compares very favorably with other inflation calculators such as those developed by Robert C. Sahr of Oregon State University, Corvallis, Oregon, and the U.S. Department of Labor's Consumer Price Index Inflation Calculator.

According to the U.S. Department of Labor, the average annual salary in 1934 was $1,368. This encompassed largely the middle class: bus driver, $1,373; civil servant, $1,280; doctor, $3,382; electrical worker, $1,559; public school teacher, $1,227; and railroad conductor, $2,729, to name only a few categories. Thus, $22.00 in 1934 was around 1.61 percent of the average income; the current list price of the Colt Model 1991, the nearest equivalent, is $875. The average salary in 2008 is difficult to compare to 1934 because of the greatly increased middle class and the far larger list of middle-class jobs. But according to the Department of Commerce, the current middle-class average income in 2005 was $61,672. The sum of $875 is about 1.42 percent of the average income; not a great deal of difference between now and 1934. So basically, if you can afford to spend $875 for a Colt Model 1991 in 2008, you could probably have afforded to have spent $22 for a Government Model .45 in 1934—provided that you had a job, which 75% of the working population did, even at this point in the Great Depression.

11) All firearms shown in the illustrations in this book are from the collection of North Cape Publications®, Inc., and the author, unless otherwise credited.

PROPER NOMENCLATURE

The terms Model 1911 and Model 1911A1 are properly applied only to those pistols manufactured by Colt, Springfield Armory, Remington Arms-UMC, Singer, Remington Rand, Ithaca, and Union Switch & Signal, and purchased by the U.S. Government between 1911 and 1945. North American Arms Model 1911s were never accepted by the Ordnance Department. Those available today were probably assembled from parts after World War I. None are marked "1911" or "UNITED STATES PROPERTY."

Model 1911, M1911A1

The proper name for the commercial version of either the Model 1911 or Model 1911A1 as produced by Colt was "Government Model Automatic Pistol, .45 Calibre." Below are listed the proper military and commercial designations of Model 1911 and Model 1911A1 pistols by time period as manufactured by Colt.

U.S. Government Contract

1911-1926	Automatic Pistol, Caliber .45, Model of 1911
1924-1945	Automatic Pistol, Caliber .45, Model of 1911A1 (First delivery, January 1924)
1931-1936	Colt "ACE" Automatic Pistol, Caliber .22 Long Rifle
1936-1943	Colt "Service Model ACE" Automatic Pistol
1955-1968	National Match Pistols (U.S. Army, Navy, Air Force)

Commercial

Colt Government Model Automatic Pistol, .45 Calibre*
Colt "National Match" Automatic Pistol, Calibre .45
Colt "Super .38" Automatic Pistol
Colt "Super Match" Model, Calibre .38 Automatic
Colt "ACE" Automatic Pistol, Calibre .22 Long Rifle
Colt "Service Model ACE" Automatic Pistol
Colt Lightweight Commander, .45 ACP, 9 mm Luger, Super .38
Colt Commander, .45 ACP, 9 mm Luger, Super .38
Colt .22-.45 Service Model "Conversion Unit"
Colt .45-.22 "Conversion" Unit

Commercial, Post-1970

Colt Government Model Mark IV, Series 70 .45 ACP,
    9 mm Luger, Super .38
Gold Cup MK III .45 ACP, 9 mm Luger, Super .38
Government Model Mark IV/Series 80 .45 caliber,
    9 mm Luger, .38 Special
Officer's Model ACP MK IV/Series 80 .45 ACP
Mark IV/ Series 80 Combat Commander .45 ACP
Mark IV/ Series 80 Gold Cup .45 ACP
Colt 1991 Series
Colt 1911—World War I Replica Series
Colt XSE Government Model

Military and Commercial Pistols

Colt XSE Commander
Colt XSE LW Commander
Colt Defender
Colt .Super .38
Colt Super .38 Stainless
Colt Gold Cup Trophy
Colt Gunsite Pistol

* Colt used the spelling "calibre" for commercial pistols until about 1949.

SPECIFICATIONS

The following data was taken from *FM 23-35, Basic Field Manual, Automatic Pistol, Caliber .45 M1911 and M1911A1*, published under the direction of the Chief of Cavalry, in 1940.

Dimensions

General Data M1911 and M1911A1 (inches)	
Barrel	
Caliber of bore	0.45
Number of grooves	6
Twist in rifling	uniform L.H., one turn in 16 inches
Length of barrel	5.03
Pistol	
Overall length of pistol	8.593
Overall height of front sight above axis of bore	0.5597
Weights	
Weight of pistol with loaded magazine (pounds)	2.437
Weight of loaded magazine, 7 rounds (pounds, approximate)	0.481

Model 1911, M1911A1

General Data, cont. M1911 and M1911A1 (inches)	
Weight of empty magazine (pounds)	0.156
Trigger pull	
Pistols, new or repaired (pounds)	5 1/2 to 6 1/2
Pistols, in hands of troops (pounds)	5 to 6 1/2

Exterior Ballistics–Ball Ammunition

Accuracy with a Muzzle Rest		
Range	**Mean Radius**	**Mean Vertical Deviation**
Yards	Inches	Inches
25	0.86	0.62
50	1.36	0.91
75	2.24	1.42

Velocity with Striking Energy					
Range	**Velocity**	**Energy**	**Range**	**Velocity**	**Energy**
Yards	Feet per second	Foot-pounds	Yards	Feet per second	Foot-pounds
0	802	329	150	717	262
25	788	317	175	704	253
50	773	305	200	691	244
75	758	294	225	678	235
100	744	283	250	666	226
125	730	272			

Military and Commercial Pistols

Penetration in White Pine*			
Range	Depth	Range	Depth
Yards	Inches	Yards	Inches
25	6.0	150	5.2
50	5.8	200	4.6
75	5.6	250	4.0
100	5.5	—	—
* A penetration of 1 inch in white pine corresponds to a dangerous wound.			

Trajectory

The elevation required for 100 yards is 24 inches and for 200 yards about 1 degree. The elevation for 250 yards is about 1 degree 13 seconds, the maximum ordinate being approximately 130 yards distance from the muzzle and about 51 inches in height. The maximum range is approximately 1,600 yards at an angle of 30 degrees. The maximum ordinate for the maximum range is approximately 2,000 feet.

Study Aids

Chapter 5 contains a list of serial numbers for all major variations of the M1911/M1911A1 pistol as produced by all manufacturers. Also included are serial numbers for those purchased by the governments of Argentina, Great Britain, Norway, and Russia.

Appendix B matches Colt military and commercial production serial number ranges by year. Appendix F provides an annotated serial number list of U.S. Army Ordnance Department-purchased pistols by shipping date. This list can help to resolve differences between manufacturing dates and shipping dates.

Karl Karash has produced a portfolio of over 5,000 color photographs of Model 1911/1911A1 pistols, both military and commercial, which is available on CD from North Cape Publications®, Inc for $19.95. This collection is an invaluable tool for researching the M1911/M1911A1 Pistol. A total of 205 pistols are shown full size in right and left views, and in close-ups of all significant parts and markings. To obtain a copy of this CD, see the section, "Publications Available from North Cape Publications®, Inc.," at the end of this book.

7

CHAPTER 1
A SHORT HISTORY OF THE DEVELOPMENT, PRODUCTION AND USE OF THE MODEL 1911/1911A1 PISTOL

The late Dean of Science Fiction authors, Robert A. Heinlein, once wrote that "you cannot railroad until it is time to railroad." By this he meant, that until technology has developed all of the components—steam engines, hardened steel wheels, lengths of steel tracks, and so on—you cannot build a railroad system to carry passengers and freight.

And so it was with the development of the self-loading, self-cocking pistol. Early attempts to design such a weapon had foundered on the lack of a propellant that did not produce excessive fouling, cartridge cases too weak to contain the pressures needed to operate a self-loading mechanism, and a proper priming system to ignite the main propellant charge.

THE COMPONENTS COME TOGETHER
By the last decade of the 19th century, improved brass alloys and drawings techniques had been developed to the point where suitable rifle and pistol cartridge cases could be manufactured in bulk.

The First Self-Loading Pistols
The first practical self-loading pistol was the Schoenberger pistol developed by Joseph Laumann, who received his first patent in 1890. It used an 8 mm cartridge with a deep centerfire primer pocket. When the pistol was fired, the primer cup was forced 0.18 inch to the rear by gas pressure in the cartridge case. The energy produced was sufficient to unlock the breech, withdraw the expended cartridge case, cock the hammer and load and lock a new cartridge into the breech. The Schoenberger was not a commercial success but it did stimulate other designs.

Andreas Wilhelm Schwarzlose developed a self-loading pistol in the same year. Both the Schoenberger and Schwarzlose pistols are significant because they foreshadowed the designs of Borchardt, Luger, Mannlicher, and Browning that were to follow. All of these later designs operated

Military and Commercial Pistols

in somewhat the same manner: when fired, the barrel and/or bolt recoiled together along a track to open the breech and eject the fired case. The barrel or bolt was pushed forward by a return spring, stripping a new cartridge from a magazine and pushing it into the chamber. At the same time, the barrel or bolt locked shut in the breech, ready to fire the next round. A true self-loading pistol also cocks the hammer or firing pin.

The 7.65 mm Borchardt Model of 1893 was the first self-loading, or "automatic" pistol to gain true commercial success, see Figure 1-1. It employed a locked-breech recoil system with a jointed toggle similar to that developed by Smith & Wesson in 1854 for the Volcanic. This jointed toggle system was further refined by Hiram Maxim and used in his Maxim Machine Gun.

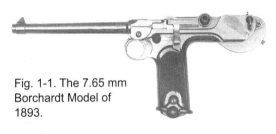

Fig. 1-1. The 7.65 mm Borchardt Model of 1893.

Theodor Bergmann followed with a self-loading pistol designed by Louis Schmeisser. The pistol employed the blow-back system in which the recoil force on the base of the cartridge moved the bolt back and residual gas pressure from the breech blew the case out of the chamber.

Fig. 1-2. Model 1903 7.65 mm Mannlicher Pistol. Illustration courtesy of John Batchelor.

Ferdinand Ritter von Mannlicher was a prolific and successful arms developer known primarily for his rifle designs. Mannlicher developed his first successful self-loading pistol in 1894 although it did not really qualify as an "automatic pistol." The hammer had to be cocked for each shot, see Figure 1-2. His 1896 design, known as the Mannlicher Model 1903, operated on the short recoil, locked breech principle which also cocked the hammer. It was chambered for the 7.65 mm Mannlicher cartridge.

9

Model 1911, M1911A1

Paul Mauser had developed a self-loading revolver which had failed to impress the German military authorities. He realized that if a self-loading pistol was to replace the revolver it would have to offer other definite advantages besides self-loading. Military revolvers of the period fired cartridges with large, heavy bullets ranging in size from 0.40 to 0.55 inch. Mauser realized that a smaller-caliber cartridge fired in a sealed breech could develop far more energy and striking power. Starting with Borchardt's Model 1893, he first changed the barrel and barrel extension, using the system invented by the Federle brothers so that the barrel/barrel extension rode on matching rails machined into the receiver. He convinced Hugo Borchardt to redesign his 7.65 mm cartridge into the 7.63 Mauser cartridge. While its caliber designation was smaller, the new bullet was actually 0.001 inch larger in diameter (0.307 to 0.308) and one grain greater in weight ahead of a heavier, compressed powder charge. The combination produced a more powerful cartridge which became the direct ancestor of the most widely used cartridge today, the 9 mm Parabellum. It also initiated a battle between proponents of light and fast bullets and heavy and slower bullets that affected the adoption of an automatic pistol for the United States military. That battle continues to rage to this day.

The C/96 Mauser Pistol

The Mauser C/96 was a great success commercially but not militarily. It was adopted by several countries, China, Persia, and Turkey among them, but not by any significant European military. It was, however, privately purchased in great numbers by military officers around the world, and this helped to popularize the self-loading pistol for military use.

One of its more famous users was Winston Churchill, then a young officer attached to the 21st Lancers in the Sudan, see Figure 1-3. In his autobiographical sketch, *My Early Life*, he wrote of his participation in the charge against the Maadi's forces on the plains of Omdurman in 1898.

The troop I commanded was, when wheeled into line, the second from the right of the regiment . . . Before we wheeled and began to gallop, the officers had been marching with drawn swords . . . On account of my shoulder (which had been dislocated in India) . . . I . . . use[d] a pistol and not a sword. I had purchased in

10

Military and Commercial Pistols

London, a Mauser automatic pistol, then the newest and latest design . . . I had first of all to return my sword into its scabbard, which is not the easiest thing to do at a gallop. I had then to draw my pistol from its wooden holster and bring it to full cock. I raised my pistol and fired, so close were we that the pistol actually struck him . . . I found that I had fired the whole magazine of my Mauser, so I put in a new clip of ten cartridges before thinking about anything else.

Churchill lost his pistol the following year in South Africa while serving as a war correspondent; he was captured when the armored train he was riding in was ambushed by the Boers, but quickly escaped and made his way through enemy territory to British lines. Churchill had left his Mauser pistol in the armored train coach when it was derailed and so was unarmed when captured; otherwise, he may well have been shot as an armed insurgent. The Boer horseman who reportedly captured him was none other than Louis Botha, who would later become the first Prime Minister of the Transvaal (1907) as well as first Prime Minister of the Republic of South Africa (1911), and later, a good friend of Churchill.

Fig. 1-3. Lieutenant Winston S. Churchill of the 21st Lancers, photographed on August 2, 1898, in Cairo wearing C/96 Mauser pistol as he was on his way to join Lord Kitchener's staff in the Sudan. *Illustrated Sporting and Dramatic News.*

During World War I, after being dismissed as First Lord of the Admiralty following the failure of the Dardanelles Campaign in late 1915, Churchill went on active duty as a Major, commanding an infantry battalion in France. Before departing England, he purchased a Colt Model 1911, serial number C15,566 in .45 Automatic Colt Pistol (ACP).

Georg Luger had served in the Austro-Hungarian Army both as a cadet and as an officer. After leaving military service, he worked as a railway engineer, and began designing rifles and handguns as a sideline.

11

Model 1911, M1911A1

In 1891, he joined the firm of Ludwig Löwe & Company, where he assisted Borchardt in the design of his pistol. In 1898, he redesigned Borchardt's pistol by shortening and improving the toggle system. Luger also improved the 7.63 Mauser cartridge by adding a heavier 93-grain bullet, see Figure 1-4. The cartridge was named the 7.65 mm Parabellum (the word "parabellum" translates to "for war" and was taken from the Berlin telegraph address of the Deutschen Waffen und Munitionsfabrik (DWM offices) which later absorbed Ludwig Löwe & Company. The eventual result was the direct ancestor of the first of the two most recognizable handguns in the world, the P.08 Luger. Georg Luger's pistol was one of those later in contention in the U.S. Army pistol trials.

Fig. 1-4. Model 1906 Swiss 7.65 mm Luger. Ian Shein collection.

While the military market in the early 1900s was huge, there was little interest among the major armies of the world for self-loading pistols. They were considered cranky, difficult to maintain, subject to breakage, and underpowered in comparison to the military revolvers of the day. But the commercial market was large and expanding. The economies of most of the world's nations had been growing rapidly, and the middle class was expanding and gaining in both wealth and leisure time. Crime was also spreading apace, creating a self-defense handgun market.

John M. Browning
John M. Browning had developed a machine gun for the U.S. Army, which was being manufactured by Colt. Browning also had a number of patents covering blow-back pistol designs directed at the commercial market, but Colt was only interested in developing and manufacturing a self-loading pistol that could be sold to the U.S. military; this required a large-caliber cartridge, one too powerful to use in a blow-back design.

Military and Commercial Pistols

Rebuffed in the United States, Browning traveled to Belgium and where he reached an agreement with Fabrique Nationale d'Armes de Guerre to develop his patents and market them in the Eastern Hemisphere. Fabrique Nationale was aware of the growing market for self-defense handguns and few countries then had serious restrictions regarding their ownership. By 1900, Browning and Fabrique Nationale had developed a medium-sized blow-back pistol that fired a Browning-designed 7.65 mm cartridge. The pistol was quickly adopted by the Belgian Army. In 1903 an improved version was also adopted by the Belgian and Swedish armies.

Browning next designed a "locked-breech" pistol firing a more powerful .38-caliber cartridge. And suddenly, Colt was interested. Browning's new design showed promise as the type of self-loading pistol for which the U.S. Army was searching.

The design employed a barrel mounted on two swiveling links pinned to the receiver. The top of the barrel and the underside of the slide had transverse grooves which allowed both parts to mate when in battery. When fired, the barrel and slide moved backward which caused the pinned barrel to pivot downward, separating the meshed grooves and allowing the slide to continue moving rearward until a recoil spring drove it forward again. As it did so, it stripped a new cartridge from the magazine and ran the barrel forward again on its pivoting link as the transverse grooves in the slide and on the

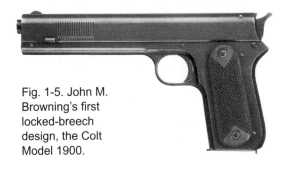

Fig. 1-5. John M. Browning's first locked-breech design, the Colt Model 1900.

barrel meshed, and forced a fresh cartridge into the breech.

The first of Browning's pistol designs to use this locked-breech system was the Model 1900, see Figure 1-5. Some 3,500 were made and the U.S. government bought 250 for trials. It was followed by the Model 1902 with several improved design features and an increased magazine capacity of eight .38 rimless cartridges, see Figure 1-6. A slide stop was added to hold the slide open after the last cartridge was fired. The front of the slide was checkered to make it easier to draw the slide back; later in

Model 1911, M1911A1

production, the check-
ered area was changed
to grooves and moved
to the rear of the slide.
It was tested by the
U.S. Army's Ordnance
Department but again,
was found to be not
quite suitable for mili-
tary use. Among other
objections was the small caliber of the cartridge.

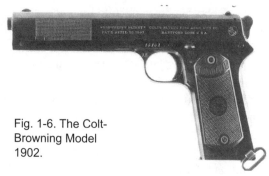

Fig. 1-6. The Colt-
Browning Model
1902.

The Spanish-American War, and in particular, the action in the
Philippines, had shown that the .38-caliber revolver cartridge adopted
by the Army in 1892 was relatively ineffectual as a "manstopper," see
Figure 1-7.

Fig. 1-7. The U.S. Army
Model 1901 Colt Double
Action Revolver and
holster.

THE ARMY'S REQUIREMENTS

Brigadier William Crozier
(Figure 1-8) was appointed
Chief of Ordnance by President Theodore Roosevelt
in 1901. One of the pres-
ident's admonitions was
to settle, and quickly, the
argument over which had
more killing power— fast,
small bullets or slower,
heavier bullets. General
Crozier ordered Colonel
John T. Thompson (Figure 1-9) to answer the question once and for
all. Thompson, who would later develop the Thompson submachine
gun, selected Colonel Louis A. LaGarde (Figure 1-10), a well-known
surgeon in the Medical Corps, to assist him. The two men carefully
developed their research plan.

They first interviewed soldiers who had been in combat about
their experiences with the current issue arms. Next, they conducted fir-

14

Military and Commercial Pistols

ing tests using a range of handgun calibers from .30 to .476 caliber on cadavers of cattle, horses, and on ten human bodies. The cadavers were suspended by their necks and the rounds fired from a standard distance. The distance the cadaver swung was plotted against weight to determine bullet effectiveness. The testing showed without equivocation the larger the bullet, the harder it hit.

Colonel LaGarde also dissected the wound channels to determine which bullet size, weight and shape had caused the most damage. Again, the results favored a large, round-nose bullet. The final round of testing involved shooting live cattle at a Chicago slaughterhouse. Once

Fig. 1-8. Brigadier William Crozier, Chief of Ordnance, 1901-1918.

more, the correlation between bullet size, weight, and knock-down power was demonstrated. The scales had tipped in favor of those who favored a large-caliber, heavy bullet for military sidearms.

Figs. 1-9 and 1-10. Left, Lieutenant Colonel John T. Thompson, U.S. Army; right, Lieutenant Colonel Louis A. LaGarde, M.D., U.S. Army.

Development and Testing

The Colt company and John M. Browning redesigned the Model 1902 semiautomatic pistol in .45 caliber and it entered production in 1905, designated the "Colt Automatic Pistol, Military Model, Calibre .45," see Figure 1-11. The Army tested the new pistol the same year.

In 1907, a total of 199 of the new automatic pistols were purchased by the Ordnance Department for field-testing and shipped to cavalry units: Troop K, Tenth Cavalry, Philippine Islands; Troop H, Sec-

Model 1911, M1911A1

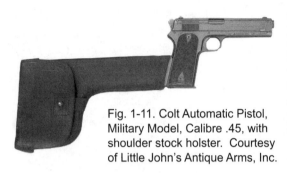

Fig. 1-11. Colt Automatic Pistol, Military Model, Calibre .45, with shoulder stock holster. Courtesy of Little John's Antique Arms, Inc.

ond Cavalry, Fort Des Moines, Iowa; Troop H, Fourth Cavalry, Fort Snelling, Minnesota; and the School of Musketry, Presidio, Monterey, California. The field tests did not go well. The pistols jammed, broke sears, went into uncontrollable automatic fire. The only thing that saved the Colt entry was the fact that pistols also entered in the field-testing by Savage Arms Company proved even more unreliable. The Savage pistols were built by hand and delivered eleven months after the Colt pistols.

Colt sold the Model 1905/07 pistol commercially during this time. There were few complaints about the pistol's reliability and performance—probably because in civilian hands, the pistols did not receive anything like the rough treatment they experienced in the hands of the military.

General Crozier insisted that Colt had the experience and design skills to provide the pistol to meet the Army's needs—although the Cavalry

Fig. 1-12. The U.S. Model 1909 .45 Revolver, top, Army Model; bottom, Navy Model. North Cape Publications collection.

was still very pro-revolver at this point. The Colt Model 1909 .45 Caliber revolver was considered by many cavalry and artillery officers and non-commissioned officers as the best sidearm the U.S. military had ever acquired (Figure 1-12).

16

Military and Commercial Pistols

A grip safety was added to the Model 1905/07 in 1908 to prevent accidental discharges, and the clip-type magazine release was changed to a button-activated release and moved from the butt to behind the trigger. Browning's original two-link system had used a slide block key to attach the slide to the receiver. But if the block broke or fell out, or if the shooter forgot to replace it, when the pistol was fired the slide could blow off the receiver directly back into the shooter's face. Browning developed a single link system in which the barrel was pinned to the receiver. A bushing in the slide through which the barrel protruded replaced the front barrel link. The magazine release was changed to the left side of the receiver.

A new test was arranged at Fort Myer, Virginia, on June 16, 1909. Lt. Colonel John T. Thompson supervised the testing and was so impressed when it was over that he arranged to have the 1907 tests repeated beginning on August 23, 1909, by a new Board. The modified Model 1905 pistol (M1905/09) was fired by John Browning and W.E. Hosmer of the Ordnance Department. The pistol functioned without misfires and produced a ten-round group of three inches at twenty-five yards.

Colt now manufactured a short run of twenty-two of the Model 1905/09 pistols, which underwent additional testing at the Springfield Armory on March 4, 1910. One of the pistols was fired one thousand times without a misfire or broken part. At the conclusion of the testing, the pistols were shipped to various Army posts around the country by Colt, often with a company representative in tow. This served both to acquaint Army officers with the new pistol and as a marketing ploy. Colt was confident that once Army officers and rank and file saw the new pistol, they would agitate for its adoption, and possibly purchase one for themselves.

Deutschen Waffen und Munitionsfabrik's Luger in .45 ACP and the Savage Arms Company .45 ACP pistol were both major contenders for the U.S. Army pistol contract as well. But neither pistol could match the improved Browning-Colt design for reliability, ruggedness, and accuracy. Savage did not have the deep pocket resources in design staff nor the ability to produce short runs of machine-made pistols for testing. DWM was more interested in selling their Mauser rifles designs around the world.

When the Savage Arms Company executives became concerned at the progress that Colt was making with the Ordnance Department, they tried to bring political pressure to bear by involving James S.

Model 1911, M1911A1

Sherman, the vice president of the United States. It was an unwise decision; from that time on, Savage received short shrift from the Ordnance Department.

On November 10, 1910, in what was hoped would be the final round of testing, both Colt and Savage submitted their latest designs. Browning had modified the safety system to include a thumb-operated safety on the left side of the receiver and a half-cock notch on the hammer. Both companies were represented by top executives and backed by qualified production personnel. A punishing 6,000 rounds were fired from the Colt and Savage pistols and from a Model 1909 revolver for comparison. Neither pistol lived up to the expectation of their respective companies nor the Ordnance Department. Thirteen parts on the Savage pistol broke and the recoil was reported to be excessive. Four parts, including two barrels, broke on the Colt. Worse, the barrels had both split at the bottom and the frames had cracked (Figure 1-13). Again, the Board concluded that neither pistol was ready for adoption.

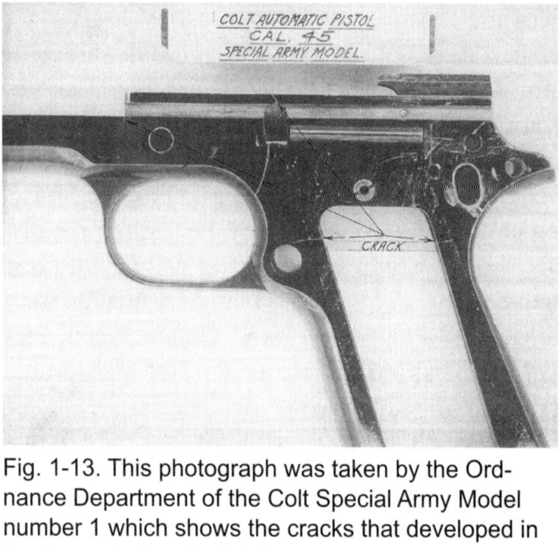

And again, another round of testing was set up at the Springfield Armory, this one on March 15, 1911. Colt and Savage both had worked hard to correct the defects in their designs. Colt had strengthened the frames and barrels of the test pistols designated the Special Army Models. Savage had struggled to correct the problems that the November 1910 testing had uncovered. When the new round of testing was completed, Colt was the clear winner. A total of 6,000 shots had been fired from each pistol. Not only was the Colt much more accurate, but not a single part had failed. Some thirty-seven parts had failed or malfunctioned on the Savage.

Fig. 1-13. This photograph was taken by the Ordnance Department of the Colt Special Army Model number 1 which shows the cracks that developed in the frame during the 6,000-round test on November 10, 1910.

Military and Commercial Pistols

The Model 1911 Pistol Is Officially Adopted

On April 21, 1911, Colt established a price for the U.S. government of $14.25 per pistol with one magazine ($282.12 in 2006 dollars). Additional magazines were priced at fifty cents each. At the same time, Colt allowed the Ordnance Department the right to manufacture the Model 1911 pistol subject to three conditions: 1) the payment of a royalty of $2.00 per pistol ($39.60 in 2006 dollars), from which Colt would pay the royalty due to John M. Browning, 2) production at a U.S. arsenal could not begin until the government had purchased 50,000 Model 1911 pistols from Colt, and 3) that manufacture by the Ordnance Department could not exceed one third of the pistols needed at any one time, with the other two-thirds being manufactured by Colt.

Colt Production

Events moved quickly. On the same day, April 21, the Ordnance Department issued the first purchase order for the new pistols plus spare parts, screw drivers, and arms chests for a total order of $459,988.77 ($9,106,795.73 in 2006 dollars). The War Department also requested some minor changes in the final design, which Colt promptly made: 1) the hammer spur was widened, 2) the recoil spring and plug were changed to remove the threads on the plug, 3) both ends of the recoil spring were crimped to hold it in the recoil plug, 4) the ejector shape was changed to improve its function, 5) the thumb piece on the slide stop was made slightly larger, and 6) the diamonds in the stock panels were cut larger to increase friction and make the pistol easier to control. The last three changes were made voluntarily by Colt.

The following weeks and months were taken up with the settlement of final details as production got underway. The wording, type style, size and location of the pistols' Ordnance Department–mandated markings were established including the serial number, caliber, and United States property markings. Major Walter G. Penfield of the Ordnance Department was assigned as the government inspector at the Colt plant.

In 1911, the Army numbered 450,000 including regulars, organized militia (at the time, the National Guard), and volunteers. Rearming the entire army with 120,000 new pistols was a huge undertaking and therefore, the contract terms concerning delivery schedules were exacting. But when, because of production problems with the new pistol, Colt was unable to make a complete delivery the first time on April 22, 1912, the Ordnance Department waived the penalty clause which would have deducted $1.50 per pistol ($29.70 in 2006 dollars). In spite of the fact that Colt employees went out on strike for thirteen days in December 1912, Colt was able to meet all further delivery schedules on time. By May 2, 1914, Colt had delivered every pistol contracted for between May 5, 1911 and December 5, 1912, a total of 72,570.

Springfield Armory Pistols

The Springfield Armory was founded in 1795 as the nation's major armory and arsenal and was charged with producing small arms for the United States Army. It was also the home of the Army's Ordnance Department at the start of the 20th century, see Figure 1-14.

Fig. 1-14. The Springfield Armory in a postcard photo taken prior to World War I.

The Army had estimated that they needed 120,000 Model 1911 pistols and because of the three-to-one production ratio between Colt and the government in the original contract, the Ordnance Department decided that 23,333 pistols would be manufactured at the Armory. When this was judged insufficient to establish a complete manufacturing center, a plan was submitted by Colonel S.E. Blunt, then Commanding Officer of the Springfield Armory, to use machinery and facilities in excess of

Military and Commercial Pistols

that needed for rifle production to build the pistol. Colonel Blunt's plan, which was adopted, called for pistol production to end if rifle production was required to run at full capacity of 500 per day.

The Ordnance Department felt sure that by producing the Model 1911 at Springfield, they would realize a great cost savings. The Government purchased the Model 1911 from Colt at the cost of $14.25 ($297.75 in 2006 dollars) each. But it was estimated that the Springfield Armory could manufacture the pistol at a cost of $7.50 each ($156.55). A royalty of $2.00 ($41.75) each would have to be paid to Colt, plus an overhead of $0.70 ($14.61) per pistol or a total cost for each pistol of $10.20 ($212.91), a savings of $4.05 ($84.54). This may not sound like much today but when multiplied by 23,333, it produced a savings of $94,498.00 ($1,972,512.52 in 2006 dollars).

The initial order given to Springfield for 11,285 pistols with one magazine plus 226 arms chests holding fifty pistols each was issued on December 27, 1912. The first serial number range issued by the Ordnance Department for Springfield's use was for 11,284 pistols and ran from 72,571 to 83,855. The serial number range was integrated with Colt's so that the serial numbers ran consecutively through the Colt/Springfield series.

Colt was unable to furnish a complete set of up-to-date drawings to the Springfield Armory. Colt production supervisors relied almost entirely on designated pistols for measurements, and gauges were produced using these pistols and their parts. Springfield Armory therefore produced their own set of drawings based on twenty sample Colt pistols. Each pistol was disassembled and all the parts measured. The drawings for each part were based on the averages of measurements taken. The variations from the average were assumed to be the manufacturing tolerances. Tools, fixtures and gauges were then manufactured according to these drawings. Due to a series of delays, the drawings were not completed until September 1914.

But production of parts, for which there were finished drawings, began in February 1914. The first thirty pistols were produced by hand to check the accuracy of tools, fixtures and gauges. The pistols were also submitted to interchangeability tests not only within the thirty produced, but also with randomly selected Colt pistols.

Model 1911, M1911A1

NOTE: The twenty sample Model 1911s purchased by Springfield Armory from Colt, to establish dimensions, were not serial numbered in the Colt range. At the end of the last Springfield production run, these pistols were stamped with serial numbers 125,567 to 125,586, inspected and accepted as part of the Springfield Armory series.

The next 100 pistols were made using standard production machinery. Minor adjustments were made to the manufacturing technique to avoid excessive hand fitting, and full production began. As succeeding batches of Model 1911s were manufactured, the Ordnance Department discovered that costs rose due to a variety of factors. The final cost of each Springfield pistol was estimated to be $13.26 ($276.52 in 2006 dollars), including the $2.00 ($41.75) royalty payment. This still amounted to a savings of $0.99 ($20.66) per pistol, or a total of about $23,099.67 ($482,169.73 in 2006 dollars). The difference between estimated and actual savings amounted to $87,732.08 ($1,831,270), 72 percent higher than the original estimate.

Production of the Model 1911 continued to April 17, 1917, at the Springfield Armory. As noted earlier, the Model 1903 rifle was considered a greater priority and required many of the same machines. Rather than add new machines, facilities, and employees, it was decided to end production of the Model 1911 pistol. A total of 25,767 Model 1911 pistols were manufactured between 1914 and 1917.

A further 400 Model 1911s were assembled at the Springfield Armory in 1921. The receivers had been serial numbered previously, leading some authorities to believe they may have been part of a batch of one thousand pistols which had never been listed in either the Colt or Springfield records.

Between 1919 and 1934, production of barrels and certain other spare parts for the Model 1911 was resumed at the Springfield Armory. While Armory personnel continued to repair and refurbish pistols throughout the rest of the decade, spare parts production ceased in 1934. Then, in 1940, when it became apparent that the U.S. would enter World War II sooner or later, spare parts production was again resumed and continued to mid-1943.

Some of the most sought-after collectible Model 1911s are those sold to civilians and shipped from the Springfield Armory between 1913

Military and Commercial Pistols

and 1917, and again between 1920 and 1922. They were processed through the Director of Civilian Marksmanship and sales were handled by the National Rifle Association. These Model 1911s were marked "**N.R.A.**" beneath the serial number or ahead of the slide stop pin, see Figure 1-15. Most, but not all, were manufactured at the Springfield Armory. The number of "N.R.A.-" marked pistols sold is unknown. Estimates vary from 150 to 1000, but unrecorded pistols continue to surface.

The U.S. Navy Model 1911s

Fig. 1-15. For short periods before and after World War I, the Ordnance Department sold Model 1911s to civilians through the National Rifle Association. They were marked "N.R.A." below or ahead of the slide stop pin. William Fairbairn collection.

All Model 1911s manufactured for the U.S. Navy, and so marked, were manufactured by Colt between 1912 and 1915 only. The U.S. Marine Corps Model 1911s and Model 1911A1s were never marked "U.S. Marine Corps."

Prior to World War I, the U.S. Navy's Bureau of Ordnance placed U.S. Navy orders for small arms through the Secretary of the Navy to the Secretary of War who directed the Army's Ordnance Department to supply the requested weaponry. Only if the arms were specific to the Navy and the Marine Corps, were they purchased through Navy channels.

On November 1, 1911, the Navy ordered 7,000 Model 1911 pistols with one magazine each and, presumably, the appropriate tools, spare magazines, parts, and maintenance equipment. The Ordnance Department instructed Colt to manufacture both the Army and Navy orders in alternating lots of 500 serial numbers for the first three orders, then in lots of 1,000. All manufacturing was done under Ordnance Department auspices, which meant that the Navy's pistols showed both Colt factory and U.S. Army Ordnance Department inspection and acceptance markings. The Navy requested, however, that the slides of their pistols be

Model 1911, M1911A1

Fig. 1-16. A U.S. Navy marked Model 1911 shipped to the General Store-keeper, Brooklyn Navy Yard, on July 25, 1913. Larry Gaertner collection.

marked "**MODEL OF 1911. U.S. NAVY.**" The finished pistols were delivered to the Brooklyn Navy Yard starting on March 1, 1912, see Figure 1-16. The Army charged the Navy $22.00 to make the roll die and an additional $0.22 each for the slide marking. The last Navy pistols to carry the "U.S. Navy" marking were shipped on March 15, 1915, serial numbered 109,501-110,000. All Navy pistols were subsequently marked "**U.S. ARMY**," see Figure 1-17.

Between 1912 and 1915, the Navy had ordered 15,037 Model 1911s throughout the serial number range 501 to 110,000, all marked on the slides, "**MODEL OF 1911. U.S. NAVY.**" These 15,037 pistols met the Navy's requirements until 1917. After the U.S. entered World War I, the Navy was unable to obtain all of the M1911s it requested. Several times, their orders were reduced by the need to supply the Army's combat troops with the pistol. As a consequence, the Navy had to take 8,100 Smith & Wesson Model 1917 revolvers and some eight thousand more .38-caliber revolvers and .32-caliber pistols in their stead. Only after the war ended was the Navy able to obtain their complete issue of the Model 1911 pistol.

When international tensions rose dramatically in the mid-1930s—the Japanese invasion of Manchuria, the Italian invasion of Ethiopia, and the German occupation of the Rhineland—the Navy, recognizing the lead

Military and Commercial Pistols

role they would play in the Pacific, began to rearm. They ordered and received a total of 1,580 Model 1911A1 pistols in 1937, 3,636 Model 1911A1s in 1939, and an additional 3,982 Model 1911A1s

Fig. 1-17. This U.S. Navy Model 1911 marked "U.S. ARMY" was one of 10,000 delivered to the Navy's Ordnance Depot, Bush Terminal, on August 19, 1918. Larry Gaertner collection.

in 1942. Post-World War I Navy pistols were marked with the legend, "**MODEL OF 1911. U.S. ARMY**" in 1937 only (due to a drawing error) and "**MODEL 1911A1 U.S. ARMY**" from 1939 on, saving at least $0.22 cents per pistol.

The U.S. Marine Corps 1911s

The U.S. Marine Corps ordered their first lot of 300 Model 1911 pistols through the Navy Department in May 1912. Due to a shortage of pistols received at the Springfield Armory, Colt was ordered to send the 300 pistols directly to the Marine Corps, which they did on June 6, 1912. A second order for 1,250 pistols with one magazine each, tools, 2,700 spare magazines and 300,000 rounds of ammunition was placed in April 1913. The Marine Corps did not require that the pistols be marked "U.S. Marine Corps," and so, with the exception of their serial number (and any markings that may have been applied by the Corps after receiving them), they are identical to their Army counterparts. The Marine Corps received 2,850 Model 1911 pistols between 1912 and the end of 1916 and a further 3,880 during World War I. A final delivery of 3,300 Model 1911s was received in December 1918, after the war had ended. This may seem like a small number of pistols but the Marine Corps in 1911 numbered only 9,620 men of which 328 were officers.

BRITISH CIVILIAN AND MILITARY CONTRACT PISTOLS

Sales of the Model 1911 to Great Britain, although slow to begin, were gratifying. Before our age of instant communication, international tele-

25

graph was the only means of fast communication. Shipping samples required at least a two-week steamship voyage plus shipping and receiving time on either end.

The Colt shipping records do not show any sales direct to the Colt's London office, but these records are not complete. And pistols may well have been shipped to individual purchasers throughout the British Empire. Most direct customer purchasers were listed in the shipping records only by name, and without addresses.

Pre-World War I Sales to Great Britain

The first British sale recorded in the Colt shipping records was serial number C4,513, sent to the London Armoury Company, Colt's agency from July 1913 on. Apparently fifteen more were shipped to the London Armoury in that year plus one Model 1911 shipped directly to a customer. All were .45 ACP caliber.

The new Colt automatic pistol was exhibited at the Bisley matches in September 1914 and stirred some interest. By the end of the year, a total of 550 Model 1911s had been sent to the London Armoury Company. It has long been assumed that all or most of these pistols were chambered for the .45 ACP cartridge as no caliber is listed for them in the Colt shipping records. But Clawson has stated that observation of several pistols in this range shows that they carried a "W" prefix and were thus chambered for the .455 Webley-designed cartridge.

Because the semi-rimmed .455 Webley was 0.476 inch in case diameter, 0.006 inch greater than the .45 ACP (0.470 inch) and had a rim 0.522 inch in diameter vs. the .45 ACP rim diameter of 0.476, it could not chamber in pistols built for the .45 ACP cartridge. So to distinguish between the different chamberings, Colt had replaced the "C" serial number prefix with a "W."

By 1915, the Model 1911 pistol was selling well in Great Britain; a total of 2,226 were shipped to the London Armoury Company, Colt's distributor, (including the author's Model 1911), of which it appears that around 224 were chambered for the .455 Webley cartridge (the author's is in .45 ACP). Again, these numbers cannot be taken as absolutely correct as we have no way of knowing how diligent the Colt shipping clerks were in recording the caliber of pistols shipped to Great Britain. The author's British Model 1911 was sold through the Army & Navy Store on the Pall Mall, see Figure 1-18.

Military and Commercial Pistols

Colt Model 1911, serial number 43, part of the first shipment of fifty Model 1911s to the U.S. Army on January 4, 1912. Karl Karash collection.

Colt Model 1911, serial #18,XXX, part of the third shipment on January 9, 1913, to Rock Island Arsenal. Model 1912 Mounted Holster, Model 1910, 3rd Variation Pistol Belt, Type 1 Magazine pocket. Craig Riesch collection.

Model 1911, M1911A1

Three World War I-era Model 1911s, clockwise from top: Remington Arms-UMC (Mike Strietbeck collection), Colt, Springfield Armory (North Cape Publications collection).

One of the last Colt commercial Government Models based on the Model 1911 pattern. This pistol, serial number C135,213, lacks the finger clearance cuts, retains the flat mainspring, long trigger, and Type 2 front sight, Type 2 rear sight. It was manufactured in 1924. North Cape Publications collection.

Military and Commercial Pistols

Three U.S. Navy Model 1911s. From the top down: 1912, 1913, and 1918. Larry Gaertner collection.

Model 1911, M1911A1

Colt Transition Model, serial number
700,5XX. Gary Thomas collection.

Singer Model 1911A1.
Karl Karash collection.

Military and Commercial Pistols

Pre-World War II Colt National Match Model 1911A1 with fixed rear sight. Karl Karash collection.

Post-World War II (1962) Springfield Armory National Match Model 1911A1. North Cape Publications collection.

Model 1911, M1911A1

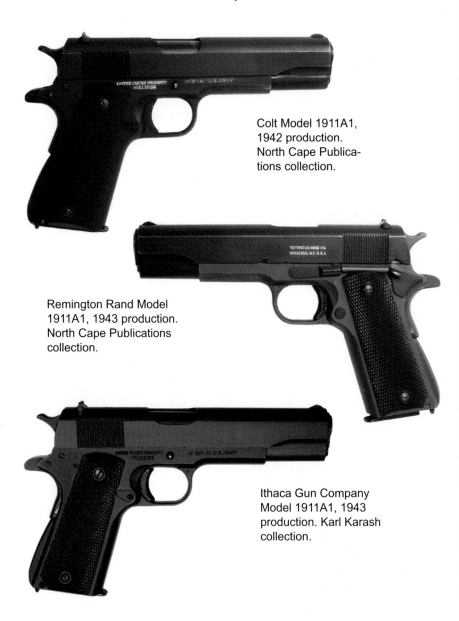

Colt Model 1911A1, 1942 production. North Cape Publications collection.

Remington Rand Model 1911A1, 1943 production. North Cape Publications collection.

Ithaca Gun Company Model 1911A1, 1943 production. Karl Karash collection.

Military and Commercial Pistols

Colt Lightweight Commander, 1950 production.

Colt Series 70 Gold Cup National Match.

Colt Officer's Model .45 caliber. Customized and accurized by Master Gunsmith, Terry Tussey. All from the North Cape Publications, Inc. collection.

Model 1911, M1911A1

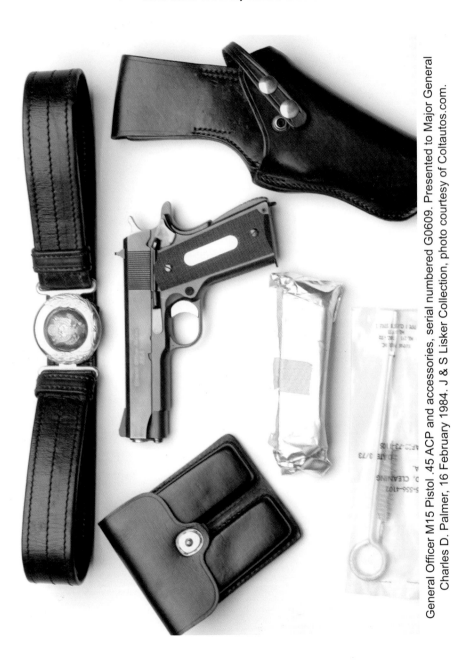

General Officer M15 Pistol .45 ACP and accessories, serial numbered G0609. Presented to Major General Charles D. Palmer, 16 February 1984. J & S Lisker Collection, photo courtesy of Coltautos.com.

Military and Commercial Pistols

World War I Sales to Great Britain

In 1914, the British Empire was at its peak. A map of the world showed colonies or Commonwealth countries colored in imperial red on every continent except the Antarctic. The British Navy was the most powerful in the world and had evolved to protect its sea lanes. But starting in the late 1880s, the nation had allowed other allied and friendly navies—particularly

Fig. 1-18. The author's Model 1911 manufactured in 1915 and shipped to the Army & Navy Store, Pall Mall, London. It is chambered in .45 ACP.

that of France and the United States—to help police the world's oceanic trade routes. Germany was not slow to notice and began its quest for world-wide empire in Africa, Asia and the Pacific by building its own powerful navy and army.

When Great Britain entered World War I, it was actually the British Empire that went to war. Virtually every corner of the Empire from Australia and New Zealand to Canada to India to the British East Africa Protectorate and South Africa to Hong Kong furnished troops. But the majority of weapons had to come from Great Britain as with the exception of small factories in Australia, India and Canada, few other members of the Empire had the facilities for manufacturing arms.

According to the late author, Charles R. Stratton, Great Britain manufactured a total of 2,620,162 Mk I and Mk III Enfield rifles during World War I. Australia manufactured 170,678, India 640,428, and Canada manufactured 342,040 Ross rifles. Some 1,243,515 new rifles, the Pattern 1914 Enfield, were manufactured in the United States by Remington and Winchester. But Britain was woefully short of handguns to issue to officers, machine gunners, and combat support personnel. To take up the slack, British purchasing commissions bought revolvers and pistols from Spain and the United States.

The British Navy had adopted the .455 Webley Self-Loading Pistol (see Figure 1-19). Its cartridge was the Self-Loading Pistol Car-

Model 1911, M1911A1

Fig. 1-19. Royal Naval Air Service officers are shown here at pistol practice with the .455 Webley Automatic Pistol in 1915. Photo courtesy of the Imperial War Museum.

tridge, Mark I" later redesignated the "Cartridge, Pistol, Self-Loading, .455 inch, Mark I or Mark II (nitrocellulose)." The British military establishment standardized the cartridge in that same year. The cartridge was designed by Webley, but as most were manufactured by the Eley company and so head-stamped, the designation, ".455 ELEY," is more commonly associated with the cartridge.

Between 1914 and 1916, the War Department submitted purchase orders to the London Armoury Company for the Model 1911 in .455 caliber. When a sufficient number for a decent order were accumulated, the pistols were shipped from Colt in Hartford to Great Britain. But after 1916, the London Armoury Company sold the majority of Model 1911s directly to the British government.

The British government issued two contracts for the Model 1911 to Colt. Contract number 94/P/952, on May 16, 1916, was for 500 pistols in .455 caliber. Contract number 94/P/1118 extended the order to 200 per month and increased the order again in January 1917 to 300 per month. A total of 12,009 Model 1911s in .455 Webley were procured under wartime contracts by 1918 and the end of the war. Besides the serial number prefix "**W**" these pistols can also be identified by the initial "**E**" for "English Contract" stamped near the disconnector hole in the receiver. The initial "E" can also be used to distinguish British military purchases from civilian sales.

The disposition of the Model 1911s shipped directly from Colt to the British government during World War I is not certain. Various authorities have attributed them to the Royal Flying Corps (RFC), Royal Horse Artillery (RHA), Royal Navy (RN), Royal Naval Air Service (RNAS), and Royal Marines (RM). We do know for certain that most

28

Military and Commercial Pistols

of them wound up in the Royal Air Force, organized on April 1, 1918, as an individual service by combining the Royal Flying Corps and the Royal Naval Air Service, see Figure 1-20. Model 1911s issued to the RAF were marked "R.A.F." by hand using individual stamps. British

Fig. 1-20. Model 1911 in .455 caliber. The serial number has a "W" prefix and it is marked "R.A.F." for the Royal Air Force on the left side as shown in the inset.

military firearms of this period will show the British broad arrow government ownership mark, crossed pennant proof mark and either the inspector's view mark or proof from the Royal Small Arms Factory at Enfield Lock which consisted of a crown over an initial and number over the letter "E." The initials include "F2," "T9," "FE," "U3," and "29." The letter "E" stands for Enfield and is usually vertical but can also be horizontal. Those "viewed" at the Colt factory in Hartford, Connecticut, by the British inspector, G.W.R. Steadman, show a crown over "G2" over "A" for America. See Appendix G for a more detailed description of British military markings.

After the formation of the Royal Air Force, the British inspector, G.W.R. Steadman, passed and stamped Model 1911s above W100,000 with his mark, "crown/G2/A." Other marks may have been used by other inspectors but Steadman was the principal British government inspector of Colt Model 1911s at the time and was stationed at the Colt factory. If the pistol with Steadman's marking also carries an Enfield mark, it was probably inspected later at that facility. Finally, pistols above W100,000 but without RAF markings were probably issued to other British military units. Some will also be seen with Canadian military markings, a "C" in a circle and a broad arrow.

Magazines for the British "W"-prefixed pistols will not fit pistols chambered for the .45 ACP as the cartridge was slightly wider; they are described in Chapter 4.

The "W"-prefixed RAF pistols remained in use through the end of World War II. In 1942, a large number were transferred to the Royal Navy. After the war, a small number were sold commercially. These, and early "W"-prefixed pistols sold commercially before World War I, will show the usual British commercial proof markings for the periods in which they were sold, see Appendix G.

The initials "JJ" are often found on the left front trigger guard of early, privately purchased commercial and some military "W"-prefixed pistols sold through Colt's London Agency and later, the London Armoury Company. Some authorities have suggested that these may be the initials of James Joseph Goodbody, the managing director at the time of Colt's London Agency. Others feel they are the initials of an inspector at Enfield Lock.

After World War I, there seem to have been few "W"-prefixed pistols shipped to Great Britain. The author could only identify three—two in 1929 and one in 1930. The lack of such sales may be a reflection of the increasing strictness of British gun-control laws.

Canadian Model 1911 Military Sales

Some 5,000 Model 1911s were also shipped to Canada in late 1914. These were in the circa serial range C5,400-C16,599. Some will show the Canadian "C" acceptance and the Broad Arrow government ownership marking while others will show no special Canadian markings.

FIRST COMBAT USE FOR THE M1911

The new Model 1911 .45 ACP pistol received its combat baptism in the Philippines during the closing days of the Moro Rebellion. Its use was noted during the battle of Bud Bagsak, June 11-15, 1913, when a combined American and Philippine Scout force led personally by Brigadier

Military and Commercial Pistols

General John J. Pershing defeated the last organized Moro resistance to the Philippine government. Four years later, the Model 1911, now nearing uniform distribution throughout the regular army, saw combat once again. During the early morning of March 9, 1916, revolutionary Mexican forces led by Francisco "Pancho" Villa attacked the small town of Columbus, New Mexico, and its detachment of the Thirteenth U.S. Cavalry. This, coming just two months after Villa's forces kidnaped and executed sixteen employees of an American company at Santa Isabel, Chihuahua, prompted President Woodrow Wilson to order the U.S. Army to lead an invasion force into Mexico to capture Villa and destroy his army. The Mexican Punitive Expedition, as it became known, was led by Brigadier General John J. Pershing.

The new Model 1911 received a real workout in the dust and heat of the Mexican summer. The most notable engagement in which the Model 1911 was used to advantage occurred when Congressional Medal of Honor recipient, Major Robert L. Howze, led six troops of the Eleventh Cavalry and a machine gun platoon against the Rancho Ojos Azules where Villa was believed to be hiding. The Villista soldiers saw the troopers approaching and opened fire. Without hesitation, Howze ordered a charge; troopers drew their Model 1911 pistols and attacked and killed sixty-two of the barricaded Villistas and wounded seventy-two more without a single loss to themselves. Villa had escaped earlier.

TRENCH WARFARE AND THE PISTOL

During World War I, trench warfare became the norm collectively on the Western, Eastern, and Southern Fronts, the latter extending from Italy through the Balkans. And, to a lesser extent, it was also the case in the Middle East. Opposing infantry forces faced each other in an elaborate series of trenches as close as twenty meters and as far apart as 1,000 meters, see Figure 1-21.

Trench warfare had been spurred by the invention of the cannon. By the 17th century, the digging of elaborate systems of ditches to shelter artillery, and more importantly, infantry, had become the premier development of the military sciences. Extensive trench works appeared both in Europe and North America during the Seven Years' War (French

31

Model 1911, M1911A1

Fig. 1-21. Canadian trench below Vimy Ridge, 1917.

and Indian War) when assaulting forts or cities, and during the American Revolution at the battles of Breed's Hill, Saratoga and Yorktown. During the Crimean War and the American Civil War massive trench works were dug at Sevastopol and Petersburg, respectively. Trench-to-trench raids preceded massive assaults in which hand-to-hand fighting became the norm.

During the Boer War in South Africa (1899-1902), the Boers were forced by superior British machine guns, artillery and reserves of manpower into trenches. Forced to resort to mounted guerrilla war, they were ultimately defeated by a combination of British fixed infantry and mobile cavalry forces. Similar circumstances prevailed during the Russo-Japanese War (1904-1905). Extensive trench lines were dug around Port Arthur and other Russian defensive positions along the Port Arthur-Harbin rail line and on the Liaodong Peninsula, but here they resulted in stalemate broken only by the defeat of the Imperial Russian fleet by the Japa-

Fig. 1-22. Russian soldiers in the trenches before Port Arthur, 1904. Photo by Burton Holmes.

32

Military and Commercial Pistols

nese Navy, see Figure 1-22. The same situation was repeated in the mountainous terrain of the Balkans during the wars which ravaged the area in 1912 and 1913.

The early wars of the 20th century were dominated by the machine gun and quick-firing, breech-loading artillery pieces which forced the opposing sides into miles of intri-

Fig. 1-23. U.S. soldiers in 1914 earned $13.00 a month in pay, the equivalent in 2006 dollars of $220.37. U.S. Signal Corps photo.

cate trench works. Even so, military planners around the world were surprised as trench raiding, even more than massive annual offensives, became the most common form of combat. Close-quarters weapons—the pistol, bayonet, knife, and club—dominated.

The Eve of War

In 1916, the United States was ill-equipped to wage a major war. The Army had less than 77,000 officers and enlisted men. The U.S. Army's equipment was obsolete—except for its small arms, the Model 1903 Springfield rifle and its new Model 1911 pistol. Its cannons were too small, its automatic weapons too few and largely based on the wrong European patterns. Its officer corps was distributed along the old regimental system and had never even participated in division-scale maneuvers.

A private was paid $13.00 a month ($220.37 in 2006 dollars), barely enough to sustain himself and certainly not a wife and family, see Figure 1-23. His food ration averaged twenty-eight cents a day ($4.75 in 2006 dollars) and if he had a high school education, he was considered above average in intelligence. The average age of non-commissioned officers was forty.

A lieutenant's pay was little more than double that of an enlisted man. Most officers were West Point graduates, and if they did not have an independent income, lived hardly better than many manual laborers. Combat experience was limited to the few remaining veterans of the Spanish-American War and the Philippine Insurrection as well as

33

Model 1911, M1911A1

the mostly Cavalry troopers who had participated in the Mexican Expedition. As that had been a fluid counterguerrilla war, their experience would prove of little value on the static European battlefield.

The United States entered World War I in April 1917 and the first American troops reached the trenches in the autumn of that year. The newly issued Model 1911 pistol proved to be a most effective

weapon in attacking and clearing enemy trenches, as exemplified by the exploits of Sergeant Alvin York and during the Battle of the Meuse River-Argonne Forest.

Fig. 1-24. The USS *New York* (BB-34) commissioned in 1914. She displaced 27,000 tons and was armed with ten 14-inch guns—and 100 Model 1911 pistols. U.S. Navy photo.

Status of the U.S. Navy on the Eve of World War I

In 1917, the U.S. Navy was the third most powerful in the world, behind Great Britain and Germany. Its fleet included thirty-nine battleships, sixteen of which had been built since 1910 (Figure 1-24) and seventy-two destroyers, fifty-two of which had been laid down since 1910. The destroyers were to prove more valuable than the battleships.

The U.S. Navy's tasks during the war were to provide escort services for American transport ships carrying troops to Europe, serve as convoy escorts, lay mines, conduct antisubmarine patrols, provide patrolling and scouting service with aircraft, and augment the U.S. Army ground forces with Marines and artillery support. The Marines were used primarily as infantry, see Figure

Fig. 1-25. A U.S. Marine fires his Springfield Rifle during the battle Chateau-Thierry in mid-July 1918. U.S. Marine Corps photo.

34

Military and Commercial Pistols

1-25. They also provided two aviation detachments: the 1st Marine Aero Company flying antisubmarine patrols from the Azores and the 1st Marine Aviation Force flying bombing missions against German positions in Belgium. The first Marine detachment from the 5th Marine Brigade arrived in France on June 16, 1917, and by mid-1918, the peak wartime strength of the Marine Corps had risen to 52,819, with 30,000 committed to the European front.

WARTIME PRODUCTION

It became clear that the Colt factory could not produce the required number of Model 1911 pistols needed by the three military services if the United States entered the war. At the start of 1917, just 68,533 Model 1911 pistols were in inventory and available for issue. Colt and Springfield Armory combined had under contract an additional total of 141,970 Model 1911 pistols. Clawson states that Colt delivered 112,875 more Model 1911 pistols as of April 5, 1917, and Springfield Armory, 25,767. Of these, 104,000 went to the Army, 15,037 to the Navy, 2,850 to the Marine Corps, and 16,110 to the Militia (National Guard) with the remainder held in stores.

The Springfield Armory had ceased production of the Model 1911 to concentrate on manufacturing the Model 1903 rifle. Congress, reflecting the Wilson Administration's determination to stay out of the European war, had allowed funding for the military to dwindle to the point where there were only 608 employees at the Springfield Armory at the start of September 1916. In the fiscal year just ended, only 13,285 Model 1903 rifles had been manufactured, far too few to support the massive army needed if the United States were to be dragged into the war.

Now, in the new fiscal year, the Springfield Armory was ordered to accelerate the production of small arms. New contracts were issued to Colt Firearms for the production of additional pistols, and the Ordnance Department sought other manufacturers for the Model 1911.

In June 1917, a contract was issued to Colt for 500,000 more Model 1911 pistols at $14.50 each, including one magazine. Colt immediately sought additional subcontractors to help them carry the load.

During the rest of 1917, Colt delivered an additional 48,800 Model 1911s. Then in January 1918, the Ordnance Department released a study indicating that a total of 2,473,354 pistols would be needed by

Model 1911, M1911A1

Fig. 1-26. Smith & Wesson Hand Ejector, Second Model produced for the British military. Note the crossed pennants ownership mark (arrow).

the end of 1918. Keep in mind that at that time, the war was expected to last well into the autumn of 1919.

To meet the perceived shortfall, Colt and Smith & Wesson were ordered to increase the manufacture of their large-caliber revolvers. Colt was already manufacturing the commercial New Service Revolver in .45 Colt and had produced 21,933 of them as the U.S. Model 1909 for the Army, Navy and Marine Corps. Smith & Wesson had been manufacturing its .45-caliber Hand Ejector, Second Model in .455 caliber for the British government, see Figure 1-26. The company also worked with the Springfield Armory to produce a variation of

Fig. 1-27. The U.S. Model 1917 Service revolver was a modified Model 1909 based on the Colt New Service. The cylinder was modified to use the half-moon clips for the .45 ACP cartridge.

the revolver that would function with the .45 ACP cartridge. They developed a "half-moon" clip that held three .45 ACP rounds. One stroke of the ejector rod emptied the clipped cartridges from the cylinder and allowed the soldier to reload quickly by dropping in two more clips, see

Military and Commercial Pistols

Figure 1-27. Smith & Wesson produced a total of 163,476 U.S. Service Model of 1917 Revolvers.

Colt had also manufactured their New Service revolver in .455 Webley caliber for the British military. The Ordnance Department now ordered the company to produce the revolver in .45 ACP, capable of being charged with the half-moon clips. The New Service-based U.S. Model 1909 revolver was reworked into the U.S. Model 1917 revolver with a shorter cylinder and a tapered barrel. A total of 151,700 were manufactured at the same time as production continued on the Model 1911. But still the projected quantities were deemed insufficient.

Remington Arms-UMC

The Ordnance Department sought new production resources for the Model 1911. The first of these was the Remington Arms-UMC Company which was issued contract, WAR-ORD No. R-296, on December 29, 1917, to manufacture a total of 150,000 Model 1911 pistols.

Production took place at the new Remington Arms-UMC plant in Bridgeport, Connecticut, one of the largest firearms manufacturing plants in the world at that time. It had originally been built to produce the Model 1908 Mosin-Nagant rifle for Russia. Production of the Model 1911 was delayed by incorrect or incomplete drawings, difficulty in obtaining machinery, and the scarcity of experienced workmen in the booming war industries.

Colt was to have supplied six sets of drawings plus three sample pistols and three sets of master gauges to Remington Arms-UMC. The gauges were received but the drawings lacked tolerances and so were not complete enough for production work. When a second set was sent, it was discovered that they did not agree with the first. Colt did send ten pistols to be used for an interchangeability test and from these Remington Arms-UMC undertook to make their own drawings. Remington Arms-UMC drawings produced "perfectly functioning pistols" but they would not interchange with the Colt pistol . . .," according to then Lt. Colonel, Julian Hatcher of the Ordnance Department.

(The author interchanged parts from four Remington Arms-UMC pistols with two Model 1911s and two Model 1911A1s, one made by Remington Rand with only one sear and one magazine release assembly that did not fit the Remington Rand. Lt. Colonel [later General] Hatcher

Model 1911, M1911A1

Fig. 1-28. Remington Arms-UMC produced 21,677 Model 1911 pistols before the contract was ended. Mike Strietbeck collection.

may have been referring to a complete interchangeability of parts between Colt, Springfield Armory and Remington Arms-UMC pistols.)

In spite of these problems, on March 21, 1918, the Ordnance Department issued WAR-ORD No. P-4537-11338SA which superseded the December 1917 contract and increased the order to 500,000 Model 1911 pistols, see Figure 1-28.

Production began in August 1918 but less than four months later, the Armistice was signed and the fighting ended. By then, Remington Arms-UMC had produced 13,152 M1911s. Another 8,001 were manufactured after the Armistice and delivered by February 1919. A final 156 plus five additional were delivered a few months later. In all, Remington Arms-UMC produced and delivered 21,677 Model 1911 pistols according to a letter from Remington Arms-UMC to the Ordnance Department, dated July 26, 1923 (see Chapter 5). It is doubtful that few, if any, reached combat troops in the front lines before the fighting ended. A few additional pistols were manufactured and may have been sold commercially.

Other World War I Production Contracts

Four contracts for Model 1911 manufacture were let in 1918. On March 4, an order was placed with Winchester Repeating Arms Company for 500,000 Model 1911 pistols under Contract No. P-7388-1564SA. Again, the prob-

38

Military and Commercial Pistols

lem of production drawings and the shortage of machine tools delayed manufacture of the pistol, designated G19P for internal purposes. The company was also producing the U.S. Model of 1917 Enfield Rifle and the Model 97 Trench Shotgun, which required their entire current work force, and company executives estimated that handgun production could not begin until December 1918. An inspection by Elbert H. Searle, of the Bridgeport Ordnance District, found that any pistol production was unlikely before March 1919. The war ended on November 11, 1918, and the contract was terminated December 4, 1918.

Fig. 1-29. An A.J. Savage slide mounted on a Colt Model 1911 receiver. Savage only managed to manufacture slides and springs before their contract was terminated. Kark Karash collection.

On July 1, 1918, WAR-ORD P-11-92-1953SA was issued to North American Arms Company, Ltd., Quebec, which had leased the premises of the former Ross Rifle Company. On July 20, 1918, WAR ORD P-12303-2078SA was issued to A. J. Savage Munitions Company of San Diego, California. On July 22, WAR ORD P-12408-2091SA was also issued to the National Cash Register Company. All three contracts were an attempt to decentralize the manufacture of the pistol.

Only the A. J. Savage Company managed to produce any parts that were accepted by the Ordnance Department and these were limited to an estimated 68,000 springs and an unknown number of slides. Although no confirming records have yet been located, the Ordnance Department is known to have accepted an unknown number of the A.J. Savage finished slides which were subsequently used for repairs, see Figure 1-29.

Complete pistols manufactured by Savage have been reported from time to time but have never been verified, to the author's knowledge. If you are offered the opportunity to inspect such a pistol, keep this in mind: there are no known records of the Ordnance Department

Model 1911, M1911A1

accepting complete A. J. Savage Model 1911s and there are no known documents providing the company with the authorization to apply U.S. government markings to slides or receivers. This is borne out by the fact that all A. J. Savage slides examined by the author and others are marked only on the left side with the Colt patent information and "**MODEL OF 1911. U.S. ARMY**" on the right when used as military replacements.

The North American Arms Company, Ltd., of Quebec was, like the A. J. Savage Company, admitted to the game too late to have produced finished pistols accepted by the Ordnance Department. The company was formed in early 1918 and took over part of the premises of the Dominion Rifle Factory, formerly the Ross Rifle Factory, in which the Canadian Ross bolt-action .303-caliber rifle had been manufactured.

On September 1, 1918, North American Arms Company, Ltd., obtained an eighteen-month lease on the factory to manufacture the Model 1911 pistol for the U.S. Army Ordnance Department. But with the abrupt end of the war, the contract was suspended in December 1918. North American Arms apparently managed to produce some parts and even entire pistols. Somewhere around fifty North American Arms M1911 pistols have been observed and recorded by various collectors and researchers over the years. But it should be emphasized that none of these are "military" pistols delivered to and accepted by the Ordnance Department.

Fig. 1-30. The Canadian company, North American Arms, did not begin production of the Model 1911 before WWI ended. Fifty or so of their pistols extant are thought to be commercial models assembled after the war. Photo courtesy of Little John's Auction Service.

Military and Commercial Pistols

None have the U.S. Ordnance Department-ordered model and property markings or inspection markings. They are thought to have been completed in 1919 or later and sold commercially, see Figure 1-30. It is known that a North American Arms Model 1911, serial #46, was submitted to a U.S. Government Claims Board in early 1920 for inspection, but this is as close as the North American Arms Model 1911 got to official U.S. attention. Other serial numbers listed by various researchers are 22, 51, 67, 68, 94, 111, 222, and 555. Two other North American Arms pistols inspected by the author were not numbered, although the trigger of one was marked "32" on the left side. This company is in no way related to the current company, North American Arms of Provo, Utah.

TRANSITION TO THE MODEL 1911A1

During World War I, certain minor annoyances had been reported with some regularity to the Ordnance Department and to Colt. The hammer spur was too long and often bit the web of the shooter's hand. The front sight was too narrow to pick up quickly against a dark background or in low-light situations. The flat back of the mainspring housing allowed the pistol to rock up in the hand during firing. The trigger was too long for soldiers with small hands to obtain a proper grip on the pistol. And dirt often found its way into the receiver through the gap between the bottom front of the slide and the receiver. Plus the slide stop was so narrow that it was difficult for the soldier to release it under combat conditions, particularly when wearing gloves. Accordingly, changes were made to the Model 1911 during the serial number range 700,001 to 710,000, see Figure 1-31.

The receiver recoil spring housing was lengthened by 0.031 inch to 6.431 inches (arrow A) to eliminate any possibility of a gap between the receiver and the recoil spring housing when the slide was mounted. The receiver rail width was reduced by 0.001 inch to 0.120 inch to improve the fit.

The original thumb piece on the Model 1911 slide stop was parallel with the top of the thumb piece and the bottom of the slide. To increase friction between the thumb and the thumb piece, the thumb piece was angled upward slightly (arrow B). The serrations remained parallel with the bottom of the slide, but in effect were angled upward, front to rear, on the new slide stop.

Model 1911. M1911A1

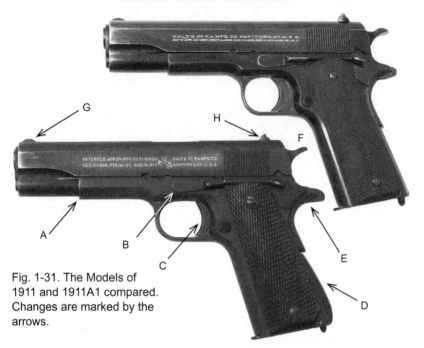

Fig. 1-31. The Models of 1911 and 1911A1 compared. Changes are marked by the arrows.

A shorter, checkered trigger (arrow C) replaced the original plain, long trigger. The mainspring housing was arched and checkered (D). The grip safety spur (arrow E) was lengthened from 0.614 to 0.704 inch to prevent "hammer bite." The hammer (arrow F) was bobbed in early 1939 to further reduce hammer bite and in 1943, a wider front sight (arrow G) was installed and the rear sight notch widened to 0.080 inch (arrow H). Model 1911A1 pistols between 700,001-710,000 were manufactured in fourteen batches by Colt and delivered to the U.S. Army in 1924. In June 1926, the Ordnance Department ordered that ". . . as a means of ready distinction between the two models . . . all pistols bearing serial numbers under 700,000 should be designated M1911 pistols, while pistols bearing serial numbers beginning at 700,001 should be designated M1911A1 pistols." However, military pistols purchased in 1924 and 1937 were marked **MODEL of 1911. U.S. ARMY**.

PRELUDE TO WORLD WAR II

The rise of Fascist Italy, Germany, and Japan was largely ignored in the United States during the 1930s. Between 1922 and 1936, the Army was restricted to 144,000 enlisted men, officers and Philippine Scouts. Not until

42

Military and Commercial Pistols

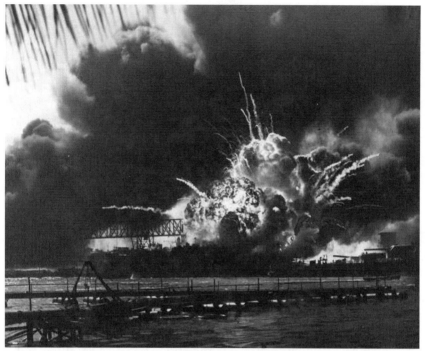

Fig. 1-32. Japan attacked the United States on December 7, 1941, at Pearl Harbor, Hawaii. The following day, President Roosevelt asked Congress to declare war on Japan. War was declared on Germany and Italy on December 11. U.S. Navy photo.

1940 and the Japanese occupation of French Indochina in September, did it finally become clear to Congress and the Administration that the United States could not avoid being dragged into what had until then been considered " . . . another of Europe's interminable wars and no business of ours." Slowly, over the next year, the nation began to rearm, reluctantly and with a great deal of opposition from both the minority Republican Party and a very large number of Democrats. When Pearl Harbor was bombed, the nation was shocked from its isolationist mood, see Figure 1-32.

Singer Manufacturing Company
Although Singer was known principally as a manufacturer of sewing machines, the company's capabilities extended to anything requiring precision manufacturing techniques applied to small parts. Singer was granted Educational Order W-ORD-396 on April 17, 1940, to manufacture a

Model 1911, M1911A1

Fig. 1-33. Model 1911A1 produced by Singer Manufacturing Company under an Educational Order before World War II. Karl Karash collection.

demonstration lot of five hundred Model 1911A1 pistols. The cost was set at $278,875.67 ($3,711,025.12 in 2006 dollars) with the equipment involved remaining the property of the U.S. government.

Singer manufactured 500 Model 1911A1 pistols which were shipped to the U.S. Army Air Force (reorganized in June 1941) after December 5, 1941. The company was granted an additional contract for 15,000 pistols but felt that its manufacturing capabilities were better utilized by building shipboard and artillery fire control directors. The Ordnance Department agreed and the contract was withdrawn.

The serial number range S800,001-S800,500 was assigned to the Singer educational order pistols. All Singer Model 1911A1s were extremely well made, highly polished, and finished with the Du-Lite black oxide process, see Figure 1-33.

At the conclusion of the educational contract, the production machinery was shipped to Remington Rand in Syracuse, New York. Some of it was made available to other contractors and subcontractors on the Model 1911A1 production project, but most was used by Remington Rand.

The five hundred Singer Model 1911A1s are a sought-after example of the pre-World War II Model 1911A1 and so the collector should be extremely careful of any "Singer" Model 1911A1 he or she is offered. Examine the markings as listed in Chapters 6, 7 and 8 with a magnifying glass. They should be stamped through the blued finish and not etched. Any Parkerized Singer Model 1911A1 has been refinished.

Singer stock panels were made of plastic by the Keyes Fibre Company. Their distinguishing feature is a lightening recess on the inside of the panel 0.8 inch wide of the top, 1.0 inch wide at the bottom and 2.57 inches long. Keyes later manufactured a similar stock panel for Remington Rand and Union Switch and Signal which has a cross-shaped reinforcement in the recess. Some have been made into counterfeit Singer stock panels by removing the reinforcement and polishing the interior. For more information, see the section on stock panels in Chapter 2.

Harrington & Richardson Arms Company
On April 23, 1940, H&R Arms Company was awarded an Educational Order, W-ORD-395, to prepare for the manufacture of the Model 1911A1 pistol. The contract price was set at $192,497.50 ($2,561,582.58 in 2006 dollars), somewhat less than the Singer contract. Colt sent H&R Arms a skeletonized pistol, C106,686, and the manufacturing drawings were received from the Springfield Armory. H&R Arms Co. is reported to have produced at least ten pistols but none were acceptable to the Ordnance Department for a variety of reasons. The problem was traced to the fact that the Springfield drawings were not up-to-date and did not always contain correct dimensions. The contract was canceled on June 24, 1942, and the government's production equipment was shipped to Remington Rand for distribution among other companies who would soon be working on Model 1911A1 contracts and subcontracts. Most of the equipment appears to have wound up at the Ithaca Gun Company.

WORLD WAR II PRODUCTION
Colt Patent Firearms Manufacturing Company
As a good percentage of this book is devoted to the Colt company's development of the Model 1911/1911A1, only a brief review will be given here of the company's production during World War II. Minor changes were made by Colt to the Model 1911A1 as described below and in succeeding chapters, primarily to the sights, mainspring housing, stocks, trigger, hammer, and the finish. Model 1911A1s were blued to circa serial #s 734,001 to 735,000. From that point to circa serial #s 1,700,000 to 1,710,000 they were Parkerized. Parkerizing as used at the time required a light sandblasting which produced a slightly rough or grainy surface to the

steel. A variation on the phosphate finish called Parco-Lubrite was applied by Colt from serial #s1,700,001 to 1,710,001 to the end of production. Parco-Lubrite pistols were sandblasted very lightly before finishing.

Congress enacted legislation in 1938—Educational Orders Act, Public Act No. 639—which provided funds for American industry to prepare for war production. Colt took advantage of the act and by December 1941, was producing 5,000 Model 1911A1s per month.

During World War I, Colt had been the major producer of service pistols; Colt fell to second place during World War II. The company's production of machine guns was deemed more important to the future war effort and so the Ordnance Department issued educational contracts to Singer, Harrington & Richardson Arms (as discussed above) and the Ithaca Gun Company. By the time Ithaca had decided to reject the contract offer and concentrate on other war production work, the program had been canceled.

Colt later issued a contract to Ithaca to refurbish numerous spare parts, mostly left over from Remington Arms-UMC's World War I production contract, but these were later found not to be salvageable. Ithaca, Remington Rand, and Union Switch & Signal received Model 1911A1 production contracts after the United States entered the war in late 1941, as described below. The three companies produced almost sixty percent more Model 1911A1s than did Colt between 1941 and 1945. Nevertheless, Colt produced an estimated total of 629,000 Model 1911A1s during World War II.

Colt also experimented with faster production methods such as sheet-metal stampings, manufacturing some twenty or more test pieces. Colt developed at least two variations of a select-fire Model 1911A1, one based on William Swartz's safety patent under instructions from the U.S. Army Ordnance Department.

With the development of the M1 Carbine, there was an attempt within the Armed Services to eliminate the pistol altogether. Reacting to the threat, Colt developed and submitted for testing a Model 1911A1 modified with an 11-inch-long barrel inside a slotted shroud, a buttstock attachment somewhat reminiscent of that developed for the Model 1860 Colt revolver except that it was flat on both sides, a twenty-round magazine that extended eight inches below the grip, and a long-range rear sight. The mainspring housing was modified to allow for the attachment of the stock.

Military and Commercial Pistols

The "Colt Cal. .45 Automatic Pistol with Long Barrel and Stock," as it was designated, was tested at Aberdeen Proving Ground in early November 1941. It was found to be more accurate than the Model 1911A1, but not as accurate as the M1 Carbine and very awkward to use. The sample was returned to Colt with no further action required. The next year, the requirement for the pistol carbine was ended.

Fig. 1-34. Ithaca Gun Company was the only other regular firearms manufacturer besides Colt to manufacture the Model 1911A1 during World War II. John Domoslai collection.

Ithaca Gun Company, Inc.

Ithaca, the manufacturer of a well-known series of shotguns including the famous Model 37 pump action, received a contract from the U.S. Ordnance Department to manufacture the Model 1911A1 pistol during World War II, see Figure 1-34.

Ithaca encountered problems procuring and installing sufficient equipment to manufacture the pistol and so did not begin actual production with their own parts until July 1943. In the meantime, they received 6,200 surplus receivers from the Springfield Armory. These were a mix of unfinished and refurbished receivers that had been accumulated by the Ordnance Salvage Board in the early 1920s. Most were of Colt manufacture and can be identified by the initial "H" for Ordnance Inspector Frank Hosmer on the top rear of the receiver adjacent to the disconnector hole. Many can also be further identified by the lightening cuts under the

47

stocks which were scalloped at top and bottom, indicating their original manufacture by Colt between circa serial #s 375,501-630,000.

Ithaca also purchased some 7,000 additional newly manufactured receivers and 2,200 slides from Colt in late 1942 and early 1943 to meet their quotas. Both slides and receivers were not marked by Colt but the slides can usually be distinguished by the small radius (0.13 inch) of the curve at the front top corner of the ejection port (see Chapter 3, Table 3-1). The radius of the top left corner of the ejection port on slides manufactured by Ithaca will be 0.23 inch.

Ithaca received five contracts in all from the Ordnance Department between 1942 and 1945 and produced a total of 335,466 Model 1911A1 pistols, plus spare parts.

Remington Rand

Many beginning collectors of the Model 1911A1 make the mistake of thinking that the Remington Rand Company was a part of the Remington Arms Company. In fact, the typewriter division had been spun off from E. Remington & Sons in 1886 to become a separate company called the Remington Typewriter Company. The Rand Kardex Company acquired the Remington Typewriter Company in 1927 and the name of the combined companies became Remington Rand.

In 1942, the company received government tools and machines to produce the Model 1911A1 pistol, see Figure 1-35. By the end of production in 1945, the company produced the majority of parts but depended on High Standard for barrels, Keyes Fibre for stock panels, and other subcontractors for minor parts such as triggers, mainsprings, and stock screw bushings, etc. Remington Rand also made extensive use of its other divisions to produce parts.

Remington Rand did not get off to a smooth start. The results of a weekly interchangeability test in February 1943 brought production to a halt by order of James Rand, Jr., the company president. An investigation revealed that inspections were not being performed properly or in an efficient manner. Management personnel were replaced and an employee retraining program was instituted. Production resumed in May and all pistols and parts in inventory were reinspected before being shipped.

To show that new procedures and management were in place, the serial number prefix was changed from "**Nº**" to "**NO.**" During previous production, the serial number had been stamped on the receiver before

Military and Commercial Pistols

Fig. 1-35. The Remington Rand Company manufactured over 877,700 Model 1911A1s between 1943 and 1945.

the pistol was assembled, and finished. This made it difficult to maintain track of the finished receiver and slide during subsequent stages of production and testing. After the management/inspection change which took place circa serial #s 955,000-1,015,499, all Remington Rand Model 1911A1 serial numbers were stamped after (through) the applied Parkerized finish as a final production operation. The metal surrounding the indentations made by the number dies may be lighter in color than the surrounding metal. The same system was adopted at Ithaca later in the year. Colt and Union Switch & Signal continued to stamp the serial number into the receiver before finishing.

The changes in management and inspection techniques reduced the rejection rate to less than 5 percent by the end of 1943.

In addition to the Model 1911A1s contracted for by the Ordnance Department, Remington Rand produced a limited number of pistols (estimated at 145) for various tests. These pistols were serial numbered in their own series and prefixed with the letters "**ERRS**," reported to stand for "Experimental Remington Rand Series." It is thought that after the war, functioning pistols in this series were given to various officials and company employees, but no documentation for this exists.

Model 1911, M1911A1

Fig. 1-36. Remington
Rand "preproduction"
Model 1911A1, serial
number 72, see inset.

Another series of pistols are thought to be preproduction pistols. These were also numbered in their own series but without a prefix. Figure 1-36 shows Remington Rand Model 1911A1, serial number 72, as an example. The pistol has a thin, very light green-gray Parkerizing, a milled instead of stamped trigger, narrow front sight and early rear sight, and no Ordnance Department inspection markings. The barrel was manufactured by Colt. Most have some late features that make the idea of "preproduction" pistols unclear.

Remington Rand introduced several new production and metal treatment techniques that reduced the time and cost to manufacture the 1911A1. By the end of the war, Remington Rand Model 1911A1s had attained nearly the quality of the Colt-manufactured Model 1911A1s. The company had also managed to reduce the price to the government below that of Colt.

Remington Rand manufactured a total of either 877,744 or 877,751 (depending on how the factory and Ordnance Department figures are read) Model 1911A1s during World War II.

Military and Commercial Pistols

Union Switch & Signal

Union Switch & Signal had been founded in 1881 by George Westinghouse to consolidate a number of companies that manufactured various types of railroad track circuits, switches and other equipment. In 1917, it became a subsidiary of Westinghouse Air Brake. The company was approached by the Ordnance Department in early 1942 to manufacture the Model 1911A1 pistol. Contract W-ORD-2211 was signed in early May, see Figure 1-37. The company reorganized two floors of one of their buildings in Swissvale, Pennsylvania, for production and developed a firing range for testing finished pistols.

Fig. 1-37. Union Switch & Signal manufactured 55,000 Model 1911A1 pistols in 1943. John Domoslai collection.

Production began in earnest in January 1943, when the first 102 pistols were accepted by Lt. Colonel Robert C. Downie (R.C.D.), the ordnance inspector for the Pittsburgh Ordnance District. But relations with the Ordnance Department proved hectic. Within days, the company was notified that their contract would be canceled as of March 8, 1943, as the requirement for the Model 1911A1 had been reduced. The company was asked if they wished to participate in the production of receivers, operating slides and bolts for the M1 Carbine. A contract to that effect was signed on February 11, 1943, and the company began setting up equipment and retraining workers. But on June 26, 1943, the company was notified that they were now to produce an additional 25,000 Model

Model 1911, M1911A1

1911A1s with a contract effective from July 9, 1943. In spite of the confusion and lack of personnel and equipment much of which was devoted to the M1 Carbine contract, US&S delivered their contractual total of 55,000 M1911A1s by November 27, 1943.

The US&S pistol was of very high quality, and so acknowledged by the Ordnance Department. All were finished using the Du-Lite black oxide process. Any that have been Parkerized, have been refinished. None of the US&S pistols were stamped with the Ordnance Department Crossed Cannon acceptance mark and the pistols were not marked with the "P" proof until two-fifths of the production run had been completed—at circa serial #1,060,000.

With the exception of the barrel, barrel bushing, lanyard loop, recoil spring guide, stocks, and trigger, the US&S company manufactured all other parts in their own facilities. Barrels were purchased from High Standard throughout production, although a few Colt barrels may have been used in the very early stages. The slide stop was purchased as a forging and finished by US&S.

US&S went on to manufacture M1 Carbine bolts, receivers, and operating slides which were furnished to M1 Carbine prime contractors Quality H.M.C., Rock-Ola, and National Postal Meter. They also manufactured a wide range of

Fig. 1-38. British troops wade from the beaches at Dunkirk to a waiting destroyer in late May 1940. Photo courtesy of the U.S. National Archives.

equipment for various wartime contracts ranging from fuses to artillery shells and from coding devices to bomb assemblies.

WORLD WAR II—LEND-LEASE

The British retreat from Dunkirk, between May 26 and June 4, 1940, left the British Army very short of weapons, see Figure 1-38. With the Western Desert Force already engaged in Egypt and Libya, and other elements scattered to the outposts of the British Empire from Kenya to

Military and Commercial Pistols

Hong Kong, they had barely enough equipment for two divisions. The Neutrality Act prevented the United States from selling weapons directly to Great Britain and France for military use but did not restrict commercial sales. The British Purchasing Commission established itself in New York City in September 1939 and accumulated over 14,000 pistols and revolvers, primarily from Colt inventory. These were paid for in cash and exported to Great Britain by the Winchester Repeating Arms Company through Canada. Other commercial channels were used as well. See Chapter 8 and Appendix G for details on identifying both British Purchasing Commission and Lend-Lease pistols sold to Great Britain.

In June 1940, the U.S. government established the United States Steel Export Corporation, which purchased obsolete (and not-so-obsolete) American military equipment and then resold it to France and Great Britain. In the first shipments to reach Great Britain, by July 1, 1940, were 500,000 U.S. Model of 1917 Enfield rifles. Later shipments included M1903 Springfields, M1 Garands, machine guns, and field guns.

With Great Britain quickly running short of cash, the Roosevelt Administration persuaded Congress to pass the Lend-Lease Act. This landmark law which allowed the President to "from time to time, when he deems it necessary . . . to sell, transfer title to, exchange, lease, lend, or otherwise dispose of to any such government any defense article . . . ."

Great Britain, and other allied nations, could now place orders directly with the U.S. Government which then arranged for production and shipment of the needed goods. Most of the weapons were transferred directly from current military production in the beginning, but were newly manufactured as the war dragged on. Payment for equipment purchased was to be made in fifty annual installments at two percent interest, starting in 1950. The last payment was made in 2006. Equipment and arms that were "lent" remained the property of the U.S. Government.

Among the weapons transferred under the Lend-Lease Act were 39,592 Model 1911 and Model 1911A1 .45 ACP pistols and ammunition to Great Britain. Another 12,977 were shipped to the Soviet Union, 19,325 to the Free French forces, 1,515 to Canada, 2,266 to Nationalist Chinese forces, and 2,890 to various South American countries according to *United States Army in World War II, Special Studies, The Ordnance Department: Planning Munitions for War*, Office of the Chief of Military History.

Model 1911, M1911A1

NOTE: Lend-Lease-supplied Model 1911A1s in .45 ACP should not be confused with those acquired by the British Purchasing Commission, which were largely commercial pistols in both Super .38 ACP and .45 ACP. Most of those were inspected and so marked as British military property. Many arms transferred under Lend-Lease remained U.S. property and so will not show the property or inspection marking of the receiving country but may show British military release or commercial markings.

Post-World War II Firearms Imports

Virtually all commercial small-arms manufacture had ceased in the United States by early 1942. For the thirty-nine months that the United States was at war, a large percentage of hunters, target shooters, plinkers, and collectors were in uniform using rifles, shotguns, and handguns to end the Axis menace. As nearly 12 million servicemen returned home and took up their lives again, the demand for small arms overwhelmed the nation's commercial firearms manufacturing capability.

A number of entrepreneurs, most of them returned veterans, saw an opportunity in the millions of obsolete military rifles and handguns lying around in arsenals in Europe, Africa, and Asia. Within a very few years, a lucrative trade had developed centered on London. Small arms purchased for pennies on the dollar were shipped to warehouses in England, Belgium, France, and Italy where they were given a minimum of cleaning and refurbishment and resold to wholesalers in the United Kingdom, United States, Canada, and Australia. Later the trade was extended to West Germany, France, Italy, the Scandinavian countries, and Latin America.

When it became apparent to American commercial firearms manufacturers that the sale of foreign military arms, most of which could easily be converted to sporting arms, was a threat to their continued existence, they lobbied Congress to restrict their sale. On August 16, 1954, President Eisenhower signed into law the Firearms Excise Tax (26 USC Sec. Title 26 - INTERNAL REVENUE CODE, Subtitle D - Miscellaneous Excise Taxes, Chapter 32 - Manufacturers Excise Taxes, Subchapter D - Recreational Equipment, Part III - Firearms). The law imposed an eleven percent excise tax on all imported firearms. But, as it turned out, this did little to slow their sales.

Military and Commercial Pistols

By the time President Lyndon Johnson signed the Gun Control Act of 1968 (Chapter 44 of Title 18, United States Code), it was possible for a collector, target shooter, or hunter to purchase a World War I or earlier, or World War II rifle or handgun used by virtually any nation except the United States. Most American small arms such as the M1 Garand, M1 Carbine, and the Model 1911A1 pistol were not only still in service in the U.S. military, but were not eligible for reimportation and sale as most had been sent to foreign governments as part of the World War II Lend-Lease program. They were considered to still be U.S. government property.

A number of these small arms, particularly the Model 1911A1, which were surplus to U.S. government requirements and had not been "military aid supplies," were sold starting in the late 1950s through the Director of Civilian Marksmanship in conjunction with the National Rifle Association.

Not until 1986, did Congress again allow the importation of surplus military small arms under certain conditions. This time, any American military weapon manufactured before the end of 1945 was also eligible for importation providing it could be proved that it had not been a part of a Lend-Lease shipment. As a so-called crime preventive measure, the Clinton Administration banned the further importation of American military arms in 1994.

In the 1930s, most commercial manufacturers had barely managed to remain solvent. Increasing urbanization, and particularly the Great Depression and the recessions that followed, had reduced sales of commercial small arms. More people had hunted than ever before but the lack of jobs and money meant that they had to keep using the same old rifle that Dad, and in many cases, Granddad, had used.

But following World War II, the age group twenty to forty-five years once again had jobs and spending money, and they knew how to shoot, courtesy of the U.S. armed forces. As fast as small arms could be manufactured or imported, they were snapped up in gun shops, department stores, hardware shops, and the 1930-1950s big-box stores—Sears, Roebuck & Co. and Montgomery Ward. In 1962, for $29.95 ($184.95 in 2006 dollars), you could purchase through the U.S. mail, a German or Swedish Mauser rifle, a German Luger pistol or a .455 Webley revolver and many others. Later came the Remington Rolling Blocks for as low as ten cents a pound.

Model 1911, M1911A1

Robert Brenner, one of the principals in Golden State Arms, the largest of the 1950s arms importers, once recalled to the author that his company had purchased 12,690 unissued Model 1911s and Model 1911A1s in their original U.S. Quartermaster cartons from the British government. As required by British law, they were inspected, and proof marked at the Birmingham proofing facility, then shipped aboard the *Queen Mary* to the United States. Golden State Arms sold them for $39.95 ($274.57 in 2006 dollars), far below today's current price of $800 plus for the Government Model.

THE COMMERCIAL GOVERNMENT MODEL

At almost the same time that Colt began shipping the Model 1911 to the U.S. Army Ordnance Department, they also began shipping the commercial model. The first fifty military 1911s were shipped on January 4, 1912. The first commercial 1911, serial number C1, was shipped on April 13, 1912. Commercial models were serial numbered in their own series and prefixed with a "C." Otherwise, the commercial model was identical to the military model in most every respect except for the U.S. Property markings, the absence of government inspector's markings, and after Parkerization began, finish. The 1912 Colt catalog carried the first advertisement for the new pistol, see Figure 1-39.

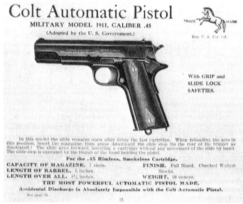

A total of 1,899 commercial models of the Government Model Automatic Pistol, Caliber .45 were sold that first year for $22.00 each (the equivalent of $435.00 in 2006); it is probable that sales would have been even higher if the Ordnance Department contracts had not had higher priority. In 1915, when the Ordnance Department contracts were well underway, Colt produced and sold a third more commercial models than they had in the first two years. The following year commercial sales increased by

Fig. 1-39. Colt's 1912 catalog listing of the Model 1911 pistol. Roy Marcot collection.

Military and Commercial Pistols

more than sixty percent and in 1917, sales tripled. From 1917 to 1919, war production took the major portion of all Colt Model 1911s manufactured. Even so, by the end of 1919, nearly 121,000 commercial pistols had been manufactured, 22,000 of them during the war years.

Starting in October 1923, Colt began shipping the Government Model Automatic Pistol, Calibre .45 with changes which were inspired by the U.S. Army Ordnance Department and would become the commercial Government Model equivalent of the Model 1911A1. The changes first appeared in the commercial serial number range circa C135,000-C139,999 and included relief cuts on the receiver behind the trigger, an arched and checkered mainspring housing, and fully checkered walnut stocks.

American small-arms manufacturers know that there are two benefits to be derived from military acceptance of their products. First, the majority of development costs can be charged to government contracts. Secondly, once the arm is in use with the military, civilians will naturally wish to buy it because its quality and dependability has been proven under the harshest conditions.

Colt had a third advantage on which they capitalized. With only one exception, the Colt Government Model Automatic Pistol, .45 Calibre, was the only large-caliber semiautomatic pistol available on the commercial market at the time. Other pistols manufactured by Savage, DWM in Germany, and Webley in Great Britain were for sale in the United States during and after World War I, but the first two were smaller calibers; the Webley automatic, besides being somewhat ungainly, was chambered for the .455 ACP Webley, a cartridge which was not widely available in the U.S. And, many ex-soldiers who had carried the Model 1911 during the war (and had not managed to liberate one) also sought to buy the commercial model.

In nearly every respect, any changes made to the military pistol were also made to the commercial pistol at the same time, more for reasons of efficient production and reduced inventory than for any great demand on the part of commercial owners. See Appendix B for a comparison of U.S. military and commercial serial numbers.

NATIONAL MATCH PISTOLS

As early as 1915, Springfield Armory, through the auspices of the National Rifle Association, offered the Model 1911 for sale to civilians so

Model 1911, M1911A1

that they could compete in the National Matches on an equal footing with military personnel.

As sales grew in the 1920s, Colt began to receive requests for a target-grade version of the Colt Government Model Automatic Pistol, prompted in part by the growing popularity among target shooters at the National Matches. Right from the beginning, civilian as well as military shooters sought to make the pistol "shoot better." The Colt factory, for a small extra fee, would hand-fit barrels and bushings.

The first "National Match" pistols appeared in 1930 at the National Matches at Camp Perry, Ohio. They were the result of a combination of service requests for a special target model of the 1911 pistol and the efforts of Henry "Fitz" FitzGerald, a Colt employee, who was willing to accurize pistols for anyone attending the National Matches.

Fig. 1-40. A prewar Colt National Match with a fixed rear sight. Many match shooters preferred this to the Stevens Adjustable Rear Sight that was also offered but was hard to adjust. Karl Karash collection.

In 1932, Springfield Armory personnel began to prepare pistols especially for the National Matches with a "hand-honed target action" and a "match barrel." The first commercial National Match Pistols appeared in the Colt catalog in 1933 with the standard fixed service sights, see Figure 1-40. In 1935 the "Stevens Adjustable Rear Sight" was added which allowed the shooter to make windage and elevation adjustments. The Stevens rear sight was matched with a Patridge-type front sight that had a serrated rear edge and was known as a "fixed ramp with a ser-

Military and Commercial Pistols

rated face." This pistol, when manufactured by Colt, was known as the "National Match Automatic Pistol." The National Matches continued to be held every year at Camp Perry, Ohio, until World War II intervened. Some of the last pre-World War II National Match pistols produced by Colt were shipped to the U.S. Coast Guard in April 1940. They were numbered from C201,070 to C201,075 and marked "**U.S. COAST GUARD**" on the receiver's right side, forward of the trigger bow.

When the National Matches were resumed in 1953, Springfield Armory was directed to select Model 1911A1s from inventory, clean and repair them as necessary, and make them available for use by military personnel. In February 1954 under "TA 20-2, Change 2," the Ordnance Department was directed to develop and make available a specific National Match Model 1911A1. From 1955 to 1968, the National Match Pistol was also available to civilians through the Director of Civilian Marksmanship Program, see Figure 1-41.

Fig. 1-41. This National Match Model 1911A1 was produced at the Springfield Armory in 1962.

The development and production of the National Match 1911A1 pistol was conducted at the Springfield Armory with assistance from Rock Island Arsenal and the Watertown Arsenal.

Model 1911, M1911A1

Fig. 1-42. The post-WWII Gold Cup National Match Pistol production began in 1957 with an adjustable trigger, Elliason rear sight and an "Accurizor" bushing.

The production of the commercial National Match Pistol was resumed at Colt in 1957. The pistol had several new design and manufacturing features that provided a very accurate production pistol with less hand-fitting than the pre-World War II model, see Figure 1-42.

An "Accurizor" bushing with "fingers" replaced the solid and beveled bore bushing used previously to guide the barrel to the same point of aim with each shot. An adjustable trigger stop on a wide, grooved trigger was added. The grasping grooves on the slide were angled to provide a better grip. The top of the slide was flattened, grooved, and sandblasted to improve sight visibility.

The new "Gold Cup National Match Pistol" was equipped with an adjustable rear sight manufactured by Micro until 1965 when Colt introduced the Colt-Elliason adjustable rear sight. Windage and elevation adjustments could be made more accurately on the new sight.

The Gold Cup National Match Pistol was manufactured in both .45 and Super .38 ACP starting in 1957 and 1960, respectively. The Super .38 Special ACP was re-released as the "Mark III Gold Cup 38 Special" as part of the Series 70. The barrel's chamber was shortened by 0.002 inch, the rifling diameter tightened, the barrel-to-slide fit tightened, and the magazine lips improved.

Serial number ranges of National Match Pistols manufactured by both Springfield Armory and Colt will be found in Chapter 5. A complete

Military and Commercial Pistols

description of the pre-World War II National Match Pistol will be found in Appendix D.

Super .38 Automatic Pistols

When Colt introduced its "Super .38" caliber in the Government Model series in 1929, it was aiming for two kinds of customers: those who found the hard recoil of the .45-caliber pistol too much to handle, and at the law enforcement market. Also in Colt's marketing sights were countries like Mexico and Italy which had forbidden their citizens to own military-cali-

Fig. 1-43. Colt Super .38, serial number 1. Robert Petersen collection.

ber handguns. The Super .38 proved very popular south of the border. Until the advent of the .357 Magnum cartridge in 1935, the Super .38 was considered the most powerful handgun cartridge available.

The Super .38 was given its own serial number range and finished in either blue or nickel plate, see Figure 1-43. From 1929 to the start of World War II when commercial production ended, some 34,450 Super .38s were produced.

After World War II, Colt struggled to get back into commercial production with a limited work force that had endured devastating layoffs. Postwar Super .38s were assembled from a variety of prewar, wartime and some new commercial parts through circa serial #37,834 in 1946.

Model 1911, M1911A1

When commercial production resumed in earnest in 1947, the Super .38 was arbitrarily jumped to serial number 40,001 and continued until 1969 at serial number 202,188. The serial numbering procedure was changed in 1969 and restarted at CS001,001; the receiver was stamped with the Colt address as required by the 1968 Gun Control Act.

In 1971, the .45, 9 mm, and .Super .38 production lines were combined and all were designated as the Series 70. A new designation, Series 80, appeared in 1980 to indicate that the Government Model pistol now included a safety system that prevented the pistol from discharging if dropped on its muzzle—although most pistols were not so equipped until 1983. In 1985, the Accurizor bushing was dropped and was replaced by the solid bushing.

The Commander Series

The development of a lightweight pistol by Colt was motivated in part by a U.S. Army requirement for a smaller, lighter .45 ACP pistol in the immediate post-World War II years. The Army published its requirements in 1947 and among other specifications was the requirement that the pistol be no more than seven inches long and weigh no more than 25 ounces (compared to the 39 ounces of the 1911A1).

Walther in Germany had developed a duraluminum receiver for some of its pistols before World War II. Colt had also begun to develop a smaller Model 1911A1-type pistol in 1941, but the war had put that project on hold. Colt began working with the Aluminum Company of America (ALCOA) to develop an aluminum receiver in 1947. Later that year, the first aluminum receivers were delivered to Colt. They were given a serial number prefix, "GX" and designated as "Pistols, Lightweight B." All commercial markings were applied. The receivers were 0.75 inch shorter than the standard Government model receiver. A new steel slide 6.6 inches long and a 4.5-inch barrel were fitted to the aluminum receivers, which the factory called "Coltalloy." The mainspring housing was made of aluminum and a new hammer with a pierced, rounded and serrated thumb piece was fitted. Full checkered plastic stocks with the Colt logotype molded in were used. The slide was given a commercial Du-Lite finish and the receiver was anodized in blue.

Colt introduced the new pistol commercially in 1949-50 with the serial number suffix of "LW" and a separate serial number sequence beginning with "001," see Figure 1-44. Slides were initially marked

Military and Commercial Pistols

Fig. 1-44. Production of the Lightweight Commander pistol with an aluminum receiver began in 1949-50.

"**GOVERNMENT MODEL**" but that was quickly changed to "**COMMANDER/MODEL COLT AUTOMATIC/CALIBER .45.**" The Lightweight Commander was available in .45 ACP, Super .38, and 9 mm calibers. Colt also experimented in the early 1950s with a full-size commercial .45 ACP Government Model pistol with an aluminum receiver.

Lightweight Commanders required hand-fitting prior to finishing and final assembly. As a result, all major parts of the Lightweight Commander will show a fitting number scratched in with a scribe or electric pen: receiver, magazine catch, trigger, slide release, grip safety, manual safety, mainspring housing, extractor, slide, barrel, bushing, recoil spring plug.

In 1970, Colt introduced a new Commander series of pistols but with a steel rather than an aluminum receiver. The new steel Commanders used the same slide and parts as the Lightweight Commander and were available in blued as well as nickel and satin-nickel finishes. The aluminum receiver Lightweight Commander morphed over the years into the Colt Defender series today.

The .22-Caliber Government Models

In 1889, the U.S. Navy had one hundred Model 1870 Remington Rolling Block Rifles converted from .50-70 centerfire to .22-caliber rimfire for target practice aboard Navy ships. In 1905, the Pennsylvania National Guard asked the Springfield Armory to convert some U.S. Model 1898

63

Model 1911, M1911A1

Krag Rifles to .22 caliber for indoor or "gallery" practice. The intention was to both provide equipment for use on indoor firing ranges and to reduce the cost of ammunition for target practice. In 1907, the U.S. Army adopted the "U.S. Gallery Practice Rifle, Caliber .22, Model of 1903 (Hoffer-Thompson)" and later, the "Model 1922 Gallery Rifle, Cal. .22" series of rifles for the same reason. The army had also shown an interest in a .22-caliber Model 1911, and the Springfield Armory had converted a small number of existing .45 ACP pistols to that caliber beginning in 1913. Steel cartridge holders resembling the .45 ACP cartridge but holding the .22 rimfire cartridge were fabricated. The slide had to be operated manually. These pistols were designated "Gallery Practice Pistols."

Colt had been experimenting with a .22-caliber Government Model for a number of years, trying to convert it to a blowback design. After a survey conducted in the *American Rifleman* magazine produced a positive response, a new pistol, the "Colt ACE .22 Long Rifle Automatic Pistol" was marketed in 1931, see Figure 1-45. The new pistol was aimed at target shooters, police of-

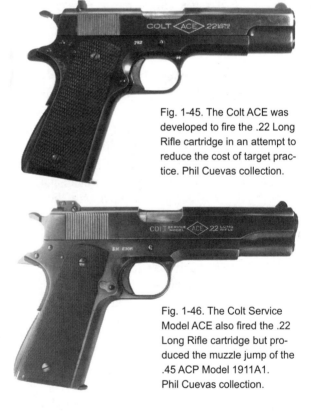

Fig. 1-45. The Colt ACE was developed to fire the .22 Long Rifle cartridge in an attempt to reduce the cost of target practice. Phil Cuevas collection.

Fig. 1-46. The Colt Service Model ACE also fired the .22 Long Rifle cartridge but produced the muzzle jump of the .45 ACP Model 1911A1. Phil Cuevas collection.

ficers, and the military. It had a ten-round magazine, a rear sight adjustable for elevation and windage and a slightly higher blade front sight. The .22-caliber pistols were serial numbered in their own series.

Military and Commercial Pistols

Some 11,000 ACE pistols were sold between 1931 and 1941 but only 206 to the U.S. Army. The problem lay in the fact that the .22 rimfire cartridge could not produce sufficient recoil impulse to operate the slide. The lighter slide and spring allowed the pistol to function but it did not have the feel or muzzle jump of the standard Government Model .45 ACP pistol.

David Williams, a North Carolina firearms designer, developed a "vibrating chamber" that allowed the .22-caliber rimfire pistol to simulate the recoil and muzzle jump of the larger caliber. A separate chamber held the cartridge and was positioned to leave a short gap between it and the back of the barrel. The barrel was fastened to the receiver with a solid lug. When the pistol was fired, gas from the burning powder expanded into the space between the barrel shoulder and the separate chamber, thrusting it back against the face of the slide and which simulated the recoil and muzzle jump of the full .45 ACP cartridge.

Colt called the "vibrating chamber" a "floating chamber" and the new "Colt Service Model ACE Automatic Pistol" appeared in the 1937 catalog, although ten had been produced starting in 1935. It was serial numbered in its own system beginning with "SM1." By 1944 when "original" production ended, more than 13,000 had been manufactured with most sales to the U.S. military, see Figure 1-46. It should be noted that the last original Service Model ACEs were not shipped until 1945 or possibly later.

In June 1938, Colt began marketing just the .22-caliber slide and barrel in kit form, see Figure 1-47. The kit also included the ejector, slide lock, recoil spring, and magazine. The kit converted any .45 ACP Government Model to fire the .22-caliber cartridge. A few months later in September, a .45-.22 kit was offered to convert the Service Model ACE to a standard Government model pistol.

The Colt .22 conversion kit with the floating chamber—but not the .45-.22 conversion kit—was offered again beginning in 1947. The complete Colt .22 pistol with the floating chamber (renamed the Colt ACE) was not sold again until 1978.

THE END OF THE LINE?

In 1985, the Beretta M9 9 mm pistol replaced the Model 1911A1 as the standard sidearm of the U.S. armed forces. The change was made partly due to pressure from NATO to standardize military weapons and systems within the Alliance, and partly to the idea that the "old slabside" was too

Model 1911, M1911A1

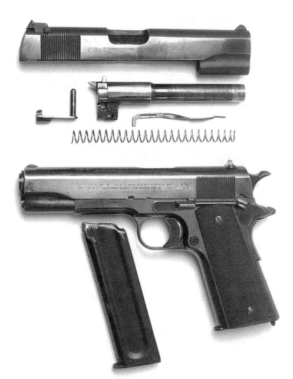

much pistol for most soldiers to shoot, too old a design, and inaccurate as well. Even though 417,448 Model 1911A1s remained in inventory according to the Comptroller General's report (PLRD-82-42) dated March 8, 1982, the decision was made to adopt a new, 9 mm pistol.

Then a strange thing happened. Interest in the .45 ACP cartridge and pistol quickened. Police departments around the country began to adopt the .45 ACP cartridge and Model 1911A1-type pistols. At the same time, the increase in interest in target

Fig. 1-47. A kit (above) to convert a .45 ACP Government Model to .22 Long Rifle was available both before and after World War II. This example was made in 1948.

shooting of all types placed the spotlight on the reliable old Government Model. Today, a quick survey of advertisements in any publication devoted to firearms will reveal that an amazing number are devoted to the Government Model, accessories for the Government Model, or clones of the Government Model.

We started off this chapter with a quote from Robert Heinlein (an ex-Navy man) and we will end with another of his observations. In his 1948 science fiction novel, *Beyond This Horizon*, a man from the 20th century who had taken part in a suspended animation experiment wakes up in the 23rd century. He discovers that his new friend and guide is carrying a Colt Model 1911 for self-defense! The Government Model may not last another three hundred years, but the author is willing to bet that it will still be around by at least the year 2111.

CHAPTER 2
THE RECEIVER, PART BY PART

MODEL 1911/1911A1 SUBASSEMBLIES

The Model 1911/1911A1 can be divided into three subassemblies: A) Receiver, B) Slide, and C) Magazine. An exploded view of the entire pistol will be found in Appendix A.

RECEIVER ASSEMBLY

The Receiver Assembly shown in the exploded view below consists of: A-1) trigger, A-2) sear, A-3) disconnector, A-4) sear and disconnector pin, A-5) sear, trigger, grip safety spring, A-6) hammer, A-7) hammer strut, A-8) hammer strut pin, A-9) hammer pin, A-10) mainspring housing, A-11) mainspring housing pin, A-12) lanyard loop, A-13) mainspring, A-14) mainspring cap, A-15) mainspring cap pin, A-16) mainspring housing pin retainer, A-17) safety lock, A-18) grip safety, A-19) stock panels (2), A-20) stock screw bushings (4), A-21) stock screws (4), A-22) magazine catch spring guide, A-23) magazine catch spring, A-24) magazine catch housing, A-25) plunger tube, A-26) slide stop plunger, A-27) plunger spring, A-28) safety catch plunger, A-29) slide stop, A-30) ejector, A-31) receiver or frame.

The pistol's finish depended on the period of manufacture and the customer for which it was destined. Types of finish included: heat, and later, chemical bluing, Du-Lite (another chemical bluing process), or two phosphate coatings called "Parkerizing" and "Parco-Lubrite."

U.S. Model 1911/1911A1 pistols were blued from 1911 to 1941. They were Parkerized by Colt from circa serial #s 734,001-735,001 in May 1941 to circa serial #s 1,700,000 to 1,710,000 in late 1944. From that point to the end of production, they were finished using the Parco-Lubrite process, which provided a smooth finish as less preliminary sandblasting was required. The collector should also be aware that many M1911 pistols in service when the United States entered World War II were rebuilt and Parkerized.

Ithaca and Remington Rand used the Du-Lite process for most of their first serial number assignments (serial #s 856,405 -916,404 for Ithaca and serial #s 916,405-995,499 to 1,015,499 for Remington Rand). There was overlap for both manufacturers at the changeover to Parker-

Model 1911, M1911A1

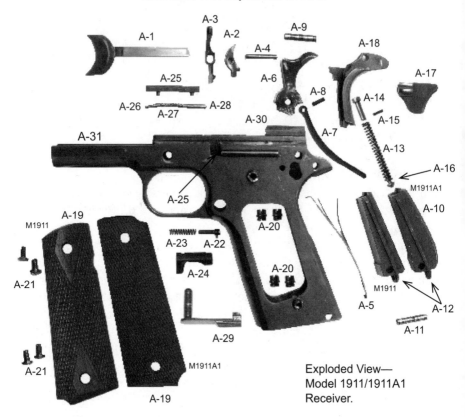

Exploded View—
Model 1911/1911A1
Receiver.

izing. All Union Switch & Signal Model 1911A1 pistols received the Du-Lite finish over a light sandblasting during their entire production run.

The five hundred Model 1911A1s manufactured by Singer received the Du-Lite finish also. Because the metal surfaces were not sandblasted as was done on Parkerized Ithaca and Remington Rand pistols, the Singer pistols, when new, had a very deep, lustrous blue, leading many collectors to believe that Singer pistols had been heat-blued.

Colt commercial finishes were limited to bluing until the 1930s when nickel plate became available. Not until the advent of the 1991A1 series was Parkerizing applied to production commercial Colt pistols.

Of course, various other finishes were available from the Colt Custom Shop or its predecessor, including royal blue, and gold and silver plating. See Chapter 6 for an explanation of Receiver Markings and Chapter 9 for Finishes.

Military and Commercial Pistols

NOTE: All Remington Rand parts, such as the sear, were finished with the Du-Lite black oxide process in the early months of production (to June 1943). These parts may also be found in very early Ithaca Model 1911A1s as they received some parts from Remington Rand while their manufacturing process was ramping up. And of course, some parts with a Du-Lite finish may have been used at a later date until they were used up.

The receiver was manufactured in two basic types. The Model 1911 receiver (**Type 1**) is easily identified by its lack of the half-moon-shaped clearance cuts on either side behind the trigger guard, see Figure 2-1A and B, arrow 1.

Fig. 2-1A. Receivers, Model 1911 (above) and Model 1911A1 (below), right side.

The Type 1 or Model 1911 receiver measured 6.40 inches from front to back, 0.760 inch wide (at the slide stop pin hole) and 4.5 inches high (toe of grip to top of rail when held vertically). The center of the slide stop pin hole is the base from which all measurements of the receiver are

69

Model 1911, M1911A1

made. From the slide stop pin hole to the front of the receiver, the distance is 2.660 inches. From the slide stop pin hole to the rear of the receiver, the distance is 3.750 inches. The receiver rails were 0.121 inch wide.

Starting at Colt serial #s 700,001 - 710,000 (circa serial #s C135,000-C139,999) to the end of

Fig. 2-1B. Receivers, Model 1911 (above) and Model 1911A1 (below), left side.

production, the **Type 2** or Model 1911A1 receiver was lengthened at the front by 0.031 inch for an overall length of 6.431 inches. The receiver rail width was changed to tighten the fit between receiver and slide and the finger clearance cuts were added to either side behind the trigger guard, see Figure 2-1A and B, arrow 2.

Trigger Guard

The trigger guard was an integral part of the receiver. Its shape was a rectangle with a rounded, lower front corner, 1.6 inches long by 1.05 inches high by 0.37 inch wide. The ends of the trigger guard faired into the receiver in short curves. The shape of the trigger guard remained unchanged on both the Model 1911 and Model 1911A1 to the end of production, see Figure 2-2.

Fig. 2-2. The trigger guard on the Model 1911 and Model 191A1 remained the same to the end of production.

Trigger Slot

A nearly vertical slot was cut at the rear of the trigger guard for the trigger. It was 0.2 inch wide and 0.95 inch high. Di-

70

Military and Commercial Pistols

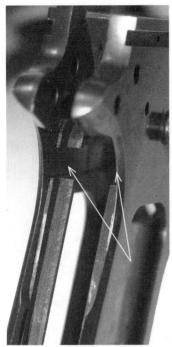

Fig. 2-3. Trigger slot (arrows) showing the twin grooves in which the trigger bow rode.

rectly behind the slot were twin rectangular grooves 0.233 inch high by 0.1 inch wide by 1.6 inches long in which the trigger bow rode, see Figure 2-3. The shape and dimensions of the trigger slot did not vary from manufacturer to manufacturer and remained unchanged throughout production. Any variation noted will be an artifact of the various manufacturing processes and will be so minor that they will not interfere with the interchangeability of two types of trigger.

Grip

The grip section of the Model 1911/1911A1 receiver was perhaps the finest ever designed for instinctive aiming. Its 74-degree slant and width, length and thickness make the pistol a natural pointer no matter the size or shape of the shooter's hands. In the pistol's nearly one-hundred-year history, the only change to the grip was actually made to the mainspring housing. A hump or curve was added to the rear of the mainspring housing at serial #700,001 to allow the pistol to ride back in the hand under recoil in a more controllable manner during rapid fire.

Figure 2-4 shows the various holes and openings at the rear of the receiver: A) stock screw bushing, B) lightening cuts, C) grip safety, D) mainspring housing opening, E) hammer pin hole, F) disconnector/sear pin hole, G) mainspring housing pin hole, H) slide stop pin hole, I) magazine well, and J) magazine catch assembly.

The grip dimensions without stock panels or mainspring housing in place are: 1) from the rear edge of the spring tunnel housing to the bottom, 3.9 inches as measured vertically, 2) a uniform 0.750 inch in thickness (side-to-side), and 3) the width is 1.875 inches when measured horizontally from a point below the grip safety cutaway, flaring to 2.02 inches at the bottom.

The grip was drilled on the right and left sides for the four stock panel screw bushings. Lightening cuts removed a section of steel from the center of the grip to save weight. The holes for the grip safety, hammer and disconnector/sear pins were drilled. At the bottom rear of the grip, a hole was drilled for the mainspring housing pin. The rear of the grip area was milled away for the mainspring housing, mainspring and grip safety. The front of the grip was curved from side-to-side so that when held properly, the first joint of the average shooter's trigger finger pointed toward the muzzle when the finger was placed on the trigger. The bottom of the grip offered entry to the magazine well.

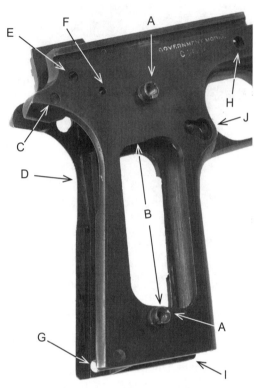

Fig. 2-4. The grip section of the receiver contains the A) stock screw bushing, B) lightening cuts, C) grip safety, D) mainspring housing opening, E) hammer pin hole, F) disconnector/sear pin hole, G) mainspring housing pin hole, H) slide stop pin hole, I) magazine well, and J) magazine catch assembly.

Stock Screw Bushings

Four stock screw bushing holes, two on each side of the receiver, held the stock panel bushings which held the stock panels in place, see Figure 2-5. The top bushing hole on either side was 0.431 inch below a line with the front, upper flat of the receiver and 1.937 inches behind a vertical line down from the slide stop hole. The bottom bushing hole was 3.018

Military and Commercial Pistols

Fig. 2-5. Stock screw bushing holes.

inches behind a vertical line drawn down from the slide stop hole and 0.286 inch above the center of the mainspring housing pin. The holes were 0.219 inch in diameter, tapped with .2360"-60NS-2 threads.

Clearance Cuts

In late November 1922, the Ordnance Department approved the addition of crescent-shaped clearance cuts on both sides of the receiver at serial # 700,001 to the receiver behind the trigger guard to prevent the receiver from interfering with the trigger finger, see Figure 2-6 (arrow) and compare to Figure 2-1A and B. The change was made to commercial pistols at circa serial #s C135,000-C139,999.

NOTE: In 1924, the Ordnance Department ordered 10,000 pistols and required a number of improvements that would result in the change in designation to "Model 1911A1." Collectors refer to these 10,000 pistols —as well as the 2,349 pistols of 1937— as the "Transitions" partly because the Army had not officially adopted the designation "Model 1911A1" and also because these pistols were still marked "MODEL OF 1911." as the drawings had not been updated. In 1938, starting with serial #712,350, the receiver marking was changed to read "M1911A1 U.S. ARMY."

Fig. 2-6. The clearance cuts behind the trigger guard were added at serial #700,001 to the Model 1911A1 series.

Model 1911, M1911A1

Lightening Cut

In order to reduce the weight of the pistol, an area under the right and left stocks was milled away. From the beginning of production to circa serial #375,000 the metal was cut away in the shape of a trapezoid. The top and bottom and sides of the cut formed straight, horizontal lines, see Figure 2-7, arrows.

From circa serial #s 375,001-629,500, the area cut away was roughly the same but the top and bottom edges were scalloped with a point in the center, see Figure 2-8. The milling machine was drawn from top to bottom without the side-to-side cuts that finished the top and bottom edges in a straight line. This procedure was thought to save time. Clawson has estimated that only some 60-70% of all receivers made during this period show the scalloped cuts.

Fig. 2-7. Lightening cuts (arrows) were made in the grip area of the receiver to remove unneeded metal and reduce the weight of the pistol. Shown here are the lightening cuts in the Springfield Model 1911 (top) and Colt Model 1911 (bottom) grip.

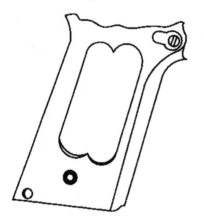

Fig. 2-8. From ca. serial # 375,001-629,500, perhaps as many as two-thirds of all lightening cuts were cut with scalloped edges top and bottom.

From circa serial #700,001 to the end of production, the trapezoid milled cut was again finished with straight edges. Table 2-1 summarizes the shape and dimensions of the receiver lightening cuts under the stocks for selected manufacturers.

Military and Commercial Pistols

Manufacturer	Width (midpoint)	Length (longest point)	Top and Bottom Edge Shape
Table 2-1 Receiver Lightening Cuts under the Stocks (inches)			
Colt (1 to circa 375,000)	1.30	2.35	Straight
Colt (circa 375,001 to 629,500)	1.30	2.35	Scalloped (60-70%)
Colt (circa 700,001 to EOP)	1.30	2.35	Straight
Colt Officers Model	1.00	1.80	Straight
Springfield Armory	1.38	2.38	Straight
Singer	1.38	2.38	Straight
Remington Arms-UMC	1.03	2.38	Straight
Remington Rand	1.30	3.40	Straight
Ithaca	1.00	2.35	Straight
US&S Co.	1.02	2.35	Straight

Magazine Catch Opening

The magazine catch opening was located on either side of the receiver slightly above the bottom edge of the trigger guard. On the right side, it was a keyhole-shaped opening 0.585 inch long. The forward part of the opening was a circle 0.308 inch in diameter and 0.280 inch deep. The after part was a slot 0.20 inch wide with a rounded end. The left side was a circular hole 0.285 inch in diameter, see Figure 2-9.

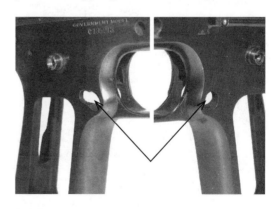

Fig. 2-9. Magazine catch opening (arrows).

Model 1911, M1911A1

The magazine catch was held in the magazine catch opening by a tab on the magazine catch lock which swivelled into the larger-diameter, slotted portion of the magazine catch opening.

NOTE: While no changes were made to the magazine catch opening during the production life of the Model 1911/1911A1, a functional change was made when the Type 1 (Colt nomenclature Type "O") magazine catch was replaced with the Type 2 magazine catch. See also the section entitled "Magazine Catch," below.

Safety Lock Opening

The opening for the safety lock took the form of a slot with rounded ends with an additional hole formed by the arc of a circle on the forward side at the middle, see Figure 2-10. The opening was tipped forward at 70 degrees. The hole was so located that a stud on the inside of the manual safety lock protruded through the opening. When the hammer was drawn back to full cock, the safety lock could be rotated upward so that its stud blocked both the sear and hammer and prevented their movement.

Fig. 2-10. The safety lock opening (arrow).

The opening was 0.405 inch long and 0.276 inch wide at its widest point. No change was made to the safety lock opening during the production life of the Model 1911/1911A1.

Grip Safety and Mainspring Housing Opening

The grip safety opening was a slot at the rear of the receiver into which were fitted the sear spring, hammer strut, mainspring housing, and grip safety, see Figure 2-11. The slot was 3.5 inches high by 0.542 inch wide. The grip safety was pivoted in the grip safety slot by the pin (arrow A) on the safety lock.

76

Military and Commercial Pistols

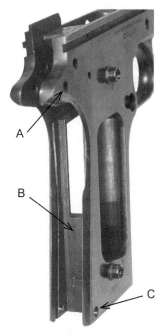

Fig. 2-11. Grip safety and Mainspring Housing Opening. Note the pin hole for the grip safety (A), the channel for the mainspring housing (B), and the mainspring housing pin hole (C).

This same opening also held the mainspring housing in a channel cut on either side of the opening (arrow B). The mainspring housing was secured by the mainspring housing pin which passed through a hole in both sides of the receiver (arrow C). The pin hole was 0.157 inch in diameter. The mainspring housing pin was held in place by a point on the mainspring follower riding in the center groove of the mainspring pin.

No changes were made to the grip safety opening during the production life of the Model 1911/1911A1.

Pin Holes

Ten kinds of pin holes were located in the receiver: 1) slide stop pin hole, 2) sear/disconnector pin hole, 3) hammer pin hole, 4) safety lock pin hole, 5) mainspring housing pin hole, 6) forward plunger tube and 7) rear plunger tube pin holes (not visible), 8) the ejector cross pin hole (not visible), 9 and 10) the ejector mounting pin holes (not visible), see Figure 2-12. Holes 1-5 and 8 penetrated both sides of the receiver, holes 6 and 7 penetrated one side of the receiver and holes 9 and 10 were blind holes.

The slide stop pin hole (1) served three purposes: a) it held the slide stop which secured the barrel to the receiver, b) it allowed the slide to be locked open and released, and c) its center was the point from which all other features on the receiver were located for machining operations.

The slide stop pin hole was 0.201 inch in diameter and penetrated both sides of the receiver 2.656 inches behind the front of the receiver, and 0.450 inch below the top of the rails. The hole on the left side of the receiver had a slight countersink of 60 degrees.

Model 1911, M1911A1

Fig. 2-12. The receiver, showing the location of all ten kinds of pin holes.

Military and Commercial Pistols

The ten pin holes are summarized below in Table 2-2, which provides their individual diameters and relation, in inches, to the slide stop pin hole. J. Browning established the center of the slide stop pin hole as the point of reference for these and other measurements.

Table 2-2
Location of Pin Holes in the M1911/M1911A1 Receiver
in Relation to the Slide Stop Pin Hole
(inches–nominal)

Dimension/ Location	Diameter	Horizontal Plane (a)	Vertical Plane (a)	Countersink (Degrees)
Sear Pin Hole	0.110	-2.602	-0.252	60 (left)
Hammer Pin Hole	0.157	-2.973	+0.016	60 (left)
Safety Lock Pin Hole	0.157	-3.368	-0.210	60 (left)
Mainspring Housing Pin Hole	0.157	-3.750	-3.595	None
Plunger Tube Pin Holes (b)	0.099	-1.402 and -2.203	+0.760	none
Ejector Pin Holes				
Forward	0.124	-2.412	N.A	none
Rear	0.096	-2.97	N.A.	none
Cross Pin Hole	0.063 (b)	-2.26	+0.300	none

a. Negative values (-) indicate that the pin hole is below or behind the slide stop pin hole; positive values (+) indicate that it is above.
b. The cross pin hole penetrates through the left slide rail groove, then through a groove cut through the forward ejector pin to hold it in place.

Receiver Rails and Grooves
The slide assembly of the M1911/1911A1 was propelled back and forth along the top of the receiver by the recoil forces generated from the

Model 1911, M1911A1

fired cartridge. The slide and receiver had matching grooves and rails which were rectangular in cross section, see Figure 2-13A.

The dimension of the receiver rails and grooves (and the slide rails and grooves) changed once during production. The **Type 1** receiver rails were in use from the start of production to circa serial #629,500.

Fig. 2-13A. The Model 1911 receiver rails and grooves, arrows.

They were 3.510 inches long. The top of both the right and left rails was 0.460 inch above the center of the slide stop pin hole. The front, outside edge of each rail was slightly radiused and the rails were lightly polished so that when lubricated, the slide passed with a minimum of friction.

Immediately beneath the receiver rail was a groove or slot 0.121 inch high by 0.075 inch deep. The rail above the groove was 0.101 inch high. The left rail was 0.195 inch wide at the front and 0.95 inch wide at the rear. The corresponding groove in the slide was about 0.104 inch wide. The groove was slightly longer than the rail as both were cut vertically at a slight forward angle. The groove was also slightly polished.

Starting at serial #700,001 (circa serial #s C135,000-C135,999) with the **Type 2** receiver, certain rail dimensions were changed for all subsequent production at the start of Model 1911A1 production. The height of the rails was lowered by 0.001 inch to 0.120 inch high to improve the fit between the slide and receiver. The receiver rails remained at 0.066 inch wide and 3.510 inches long but were now reduced by 0.001 inch to 0.100 inch high. The groove was reduced in height also by 0.001 inch.

The measurements noted above were obtained by measuring the rails and grooves of five M1911 and five M1911A1 pistols and averaging the results.

Military and Commercial Pistols

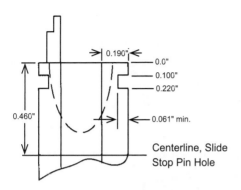

Fig. 2-13B. The receiver slide rails and grooves. Measured dimensions for the M1911/1911A1 prior to and after ca. serial #700,001.

Figure 2-13B shows the receiver rail and groove dimensions for the M1911 and M1911A1.

Ejector

The ejector was a rectangular fixture mounted on the top left side of the receiver slightly behind the magazine well, see Figure 2-14. Its function was to intercept the edge of the fired case and knock it loose from the grasp of the extractor and deflect it out through the ejection port in the slide. John Browning designed the firing cycle so that when a cartridge was fired, the breech face of the slide would be just behind the magazine well and no longer pressing down on the next round in the magazine. As that round rises from the magazine, it strikes the rim of the fired case at the moment it encounters the ejector and is knocked loose from the extractor. The added momentum of the new cartridge helps propel the expended case out through the ejection port. For the ejection cycle to function properly, a properly functioning magazine is a necessity.

NOTE: If a Model 1911/1911A1 does not eject properly, always examine the magazine first for dents, bent feed lips, or a kinked spring. Likewise, an extractor hook that is too long will fail to eject the last cartridge case.

Fig. 2-14. Ejectors. The Type 1 is mounted on the receiver. The inset shows a post-WWII commercial Type 3 ejector before the ejector nose angle is cut.

81

Model 1911, M1911A1

The ejector had two pins extending from the bottom: the forward pin was 0.320 inch long and 0.124 inch in diameter. The rear pin was 0.090 inch long and 0.096 inch in diameter. Both pins were inserted into pin holes in the top of the receiver. The forward ejector pin was secured by a cross pin 0.063 inch in diameter through the left rail groove. All three pins had a 45-degree chamfer of 0.010 inch on their ends.

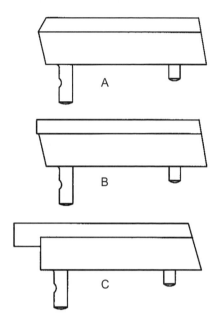

Three types of ejector were used: The **Type 1** ejector had a nose angled 20 degrees to the rear from its center line, see Figure 2-15, A. Samples measured ranged from 0.920 to 0.964 inch long and 0.220 to 0.240 inch high. The rear was angled right to left 10 degrees and bottom to top, 10 degrees forward.

Fig. 2-15. Types 1, 2 and 3 ejectors compared. Note the angle of the nose for Types 1 and 2. The Type 3 nose is custom cut by a gunsmith.

The Type 1 ejector was in use throughout the Colt, Springfield, Remington Arms-UMC, Singer, Ithaca, Remington Rand and Union Switch & Signal production ranges.

The **Type 2** ejector was not used by any World War II manufacturer and is probably a post-World War II replacement or commercial part. It lacked the angle cut at the nose and was nearly vertical instead. It was slightly longer, averaging 0.990 inch in length for the samples measured, refer to Figure 2-15, B.

The **Type 3** ejector was developed after World War II and installed on National Match pistols. It proved to work so well that it was widely copied by aftermarket manufacturers. The nose extended forward at least 0.170 inch to provide consistent ejection with non-service ball ammunition, refer to Figure 2-15, C.

Military and Commercial Pistols

Magazine Well

The magazine well was 0.555 inch wide by 1.40 inch long and 4.35 inches deep. The magazine opening ran from the base of the grip to the top of the rails and was angled eight degrees toward the muzzle. Commercial pistols chambered in Caliber .455 Webley had a slightly larger magazine well. A .455 magazine will usually jam in a .45 ACP magazine well.

No changes were made to the magazine well from start to the end of production, see Figure 2-16. Some late (1980s-1990s+) competition pistols had their magazine well beveled to make it faster and easier to change magazines during competition.

Fig. 2-16. The magazine well for the .45 ACP magazine was 0.555 inch wide.

Ramp

The ramp angle was important to the proper functioning of the Model 1911 pistol, see Figure 2-17, arrow. The ramp was the first point on the receiver the bullet nose contacted when the cartridge was moved into the breech. The ramp's slope was originally calculated to function optimally with round-nose, full-jacketed bullets and was tilted 26 degrees toward the muz-

Fig. 2-17. The bullet ramp (arrow) was designed originally to function with a round-nose, jacketed bullet.

zle and polished. The ramp angle and shape did not change from the start to end of production.

Model 1911, M1911A1

Parkerized receivers had their ramps reground after finishing and left in the white to eliminate friction that might cause misfeeds. From circa serial #s 1,700,000-1,710,000 to the end of military production, Model 1911A1s manufactured by Colt were Parco-Lubrite finished. Because only a mild sandblasting was required prior to the application of the Parco-Lubrite finish, the feed ramps did not have to be remachined and so will show the same color as the rest of the receiver (see Chapter 9). Some Ithaca Parkerized feed ramps were not machined in some mid-range shipments.

NOTE: Any Model 1911 or Model 1911A1, with only the exceptions noted immediately above, that have Parkerized feed ramps, have been refinished. The feed ramps were not remachined after refinishing.

Plunger Tube

The plunger tube was fastened to the left side top of the receiver above the stock screw bushing, see Figure 2-18. It held a spring which had two round metal follower caps; each rode against the cam actions of the slide stop (front) and the safety lock (rear) to hold them in position.

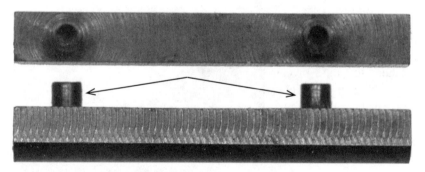

Fig. 2-18. The plunger tube was attached to the left side of the receiver with studs (arrows) which were upset against the interior wall.

The plunger tube (A) was 0.158 inch wide by 0.158 inch high and 1.28 inches in length, see Figure 2-19. The outermost surface was rounded and the bottom surface was flat to fit tightly against the receiver. Two legs or pins 0.104 inch long by 0.98 inch in diameter extended from the side of the plunger tube. These slipped into the two plunger tube pin holes in the left side of the receiver. The inside of each leg was drilled with a 0.050-inch hole, 0.062 inch deep. The plunger tube was placed

Military and Commercial Pistols

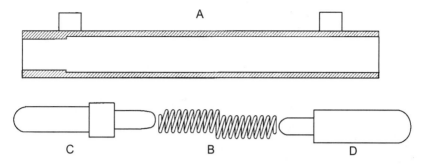

Fig. 2-19. The plunger tube assembly including the (A) plunger tube, (B) plunger tube spring, (C) slide stop plunger, and (D) safety lock plunger.

against the side of the receiver with the legs protruding through the wall. The ends of the legs were upset to stake the tube in place.

The interior of the tube was 0.109 inch in diameter for 1.1 inch, then narrowed to 0.091 inch in diameter at the forward end. The reduction in diameter prevented the plunger spring and its plunger cap from protruding so far beyond the end of the tube, when the slide stop was removed, that it would be difficult to replace the slide stop.

The plunger spring (B) was a coil spring 0.106 inch in diameter. It had seventeen coils and was kinked slightly in the middle so that it would remain firmly in the tube. Each end of the spring was capped with a plunger.

The forward plunger (C) that pushed against the slide stop was 0.392 inch long with a stem 0.10 inch long. Its forward portion was 0.091 in diameter for 0.18 inch. This allowed the plunger cap to go forward far enough to control the movement of the slide stop but not so far that it would interfere with its reassembly. The after end formed a collar 0.107 inch in diameter. The forward end of the plunger spring captured the plunger by a groove in its stem.

The after plunger (D) was 0.107 inch in diameter and 0.572 inch long with a stem 0.10 inch long and controlled the movement of the safety lock. The end of the coil spring was captured by a groove in its stem.

85

Model 1911, M1911A1

No substantial or visible changes were made to the plunger tube assembly during the course of production.

Disconnector Port

The disconnector port was a round opening in the top of the receiver between the magazine well and the hammer slot through which the tip of the disconnector protruded. The port was 0.155 inch in diameter and centered 0.20 inch behind the rear lip of the magazine well, see Figure 2-20, arrow.

At Colt, the assembler's mark (number or initial) was stamped near the disconnector hole and on the trigger guard from the start of production to circa serial #460,000; after to the end of production a number only was used. See Chapter 6, Markings—Receivers, Colt Assembly Marks.

Hammer, Colt Types

The hammer underwent a number of changes during the production life of the Model 1911/1911A1. The changes concerned the shape of the spur and its checkering, and the weight of the hammer, and are described below and in Table 2-3.

Fig. 2-20. The disconnector port is on top of the receiver, forward of the hammer well (arrow). Note the inspector's initial "O" which indicates that this receiver (s/n C135,351) was manufactured by Colt for the commercial market.

Hammer, Colt Type 1

The original **Type 1** hammer had a short, wide spur 0.430 inch wide and exactly 0.800 inch long from the hammer face to the after end of the spur. The Type 1 hammer was in use from the start of production to serial #89,800. Note the sharp end of the spur in Figure 2-21.

NOTE: All hammers had a half-cock safety notch so that the pistol could be carried cocked with a cartridge in the chamber. In practice this proved unsafe if the pistol was dropped on the hammer.

86

Military and Commercial Pistols

Hammer, Colt Type 2

Concern was expressed by the Ordnance Department that the hammer was hard to cock but they also insisted that maximum mainspring pressure be maintained to prevent misfires. The Springfield Armory disagreed with their assessment but the Ordnance Department persisted. As a result, the **Type 2** hammer was designed and approved on February 5, 1914. Its hammer spur was lengthened by 0.092 inch to 0.892 inch. The width remained the same at 0.430 inch. This change

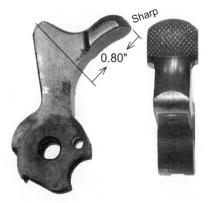

Fig. 2-21. The original Type 1 hammer was developed by Colt and is characterized by the short, wide spur.

in length increased the hammer's weight which required a corresponding change in the mainspring. The Type 2 hammer was in use by Colt only from serial #s 89,801 to 108,600, see Figure 2-22.

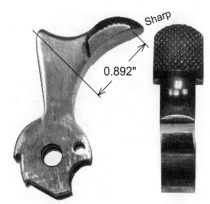

Fig. 2-22. The Type 2 hammer was ordered by the Ordnance Department with a lengthened spur. It was used only by Colt.

Hammer, Colt Type 3

As the rear edge of the Type 2 hammer spur was rather sharp and overhung the rear of the grip safety enough to pinch the skin of the shooter's thumb web, Colt's designers rounded the edge of the spur which shortened it slightly to a nominal 0.890 inch. This **Type 3** hammer was in use on Colt Model 1911s and Model 1911A1s from serial #s 108,601-714,000, see Figure 2-23. The author has chosen to call this the **1st Variation** of the Type 3 hammer.

The Type 3 hammer was also manufactured by two other contractors, Remington Arms-UMC (**2nd Variation**) and Singer Manufacturing Company (**3rd Variation**). Both the 2nd and 3rd Variations were identical to

Model 1911, M1911A1

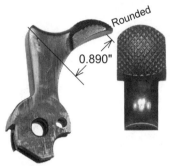

Fig. 2-23. The Type 3/1 hammer with the rounded rear edge of the spur.

the Colt Type 3, 1st Variation and were not marked. The fact that both were also blued makes it difficult to tell them apart, see Figure 2-24. One way to differentiate some, but not all Type 3, 2nd Variation hammers made by Remington Arms-UMC is to examine the first row of checkering. On many of these hammers, the first row of "X's" was often cut in half or otherwise obscured during the final polishing process, refer to Figure 2-24.

Hammer, Colt Type 4
The limited production of the General Officer Pistol M15 by Rock Island Arsenal used the Type 3 hammer, polished bright. The author has chosen to call this the **Type 4** Colt hammer.

When viewed in profile, this hammer is similar in shape to the original Type 1 Colt Hammer except that the rear portion is rounded and turned up slightly. This design brought the hammer full circle to its original design.

Hammer, Colt Type 5
The Colt **Type 5** hammer had a slightly shorter spur. It measured 0.781 inch long from the front face of the hammer to the rear edge of the spur. It was in use from circa serial #s 714,001-1,700,000.

Fig. 2-24. Remington Arms-UMC hammers (Type 3, 2nd Variation) were almost identical to the Colt/Springfield Type 3 hammer (1st Variation). The front row of checkering (arrow) on the Remington Arms-UMC hammer was often cut in half by the final polishing technique.

The Springfield Armory hammers followed the three design changes of the Colt hammers. There are slight differences in dimensions and hammer

Military and Commercial Pistols

knurling between Colt and Springfield production. Springfield knurling was noticeably coarser and extended over the end of the hammer spur to the edge on all variations. Springfield hammers were usually marked "S."

Hammer, Springfield Armory Type 1

The Springfield **Type 1** hammer was identical to the Colt Type 1 hammer except that the Armory's was slightly narrower at 0.425 inch instead

of 0.430 inch wide. It was the same length as the Colt hammer, 0.800 inch. The Springfield hammer had a thicker inside profile than did the Colt Type 1 and 2 hammers. It was in use from the start of Springfield production to circa serial #77,000, see Figure 2-25.

Hammer, Springfield Armory Type 2

The Springfield **Type 2** hammer spur was lengthened at the behest of the Ordnance Department. It was nominally 0.892 inch from the hammer face to the after edge of the spur and 0.425 inch wide. The spur edge was sharp and this hammer was only used for a short time from circa serial #s

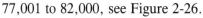

Fig. 2-25. The Type 1 Springfield hammer was similar to the Colt Type 1 hammer except that it was slightly narrower and marked "S."

77,001 to 82,000, see Figure 2-26.

Hammer, Springfield Armory Type 3

The Springfield **Type 3** hammer spur was rounded slightly (like the Colt Type 3 hammer) to eliminate the sharp edge of the Type 2 hammer beginning at circa serial #82,001, see Figure 2-27, arrow. This

Fig. 2-26. The Type 2 Springfield hammer was slightly longer and the rear edge was rather sharp.

Fig. 2-27. The Type 3 Springfield hammer spur (arrow) was shortened slightly and rounded to prevent hammer bite. Most were marked "S."

shortened the length to a nominal 0.890 inch. It remained in use to the end of production.

NOTE: Although most but not all Springfield Armory hammers were marked "S," they can be identified by the distinctive profile, refer to Figures 2-27 and 2-28, arrows.

Hammer, Type 6

The **Type 6** hammer was adopted during World War II as a way to simplify manufacturing. Colt received approval on July 30, 1942, to eliminate the flanges, or wings, on the side of the hammer. This reduced the width of the Type 6 hammer to 0.305 inch. At the same time, the length of the hammer from the front face to the after end of the spur was 0.785 inch. Five variations of the Type 6 hammer were manufactured, see Figure 2-29.

The **1st Variation** was manufactured by Colt and was used from circa serial #1,700,001 to the end of their production. The hammer knurling was 0.245 inch long. It can also be identified by the fact that it had eight rows of pointed dia-

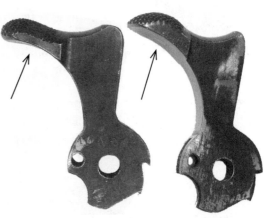

Fig. 2-28. The Springfield Armory hammer is also identifiable by its shape. The Springfield Type 3 (left) is compared to the Colt Type 3, 1st Variation hammer (right). Note that the Springfield hammer spur is thinner while the Colt spur is blockier.

monds (counting the first row of full diamonds along the left side), and

Military and Commercial Pistols

the knurling ended in a straight line at the bottom, see Figure 2-30.

The **2nd Variation** was manufactured by Remington Rand and was used on all of their production. They can be identified by the fact that the diamonds in the knurling have flat tops for the most part. The knurling follows the curve of the hammer at the bottom and was 0.300 inch long front to back, refer to Figure 2-30, arrow.

The **3rd Variation** hammer was manufactured and used by

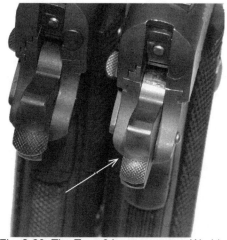

Fig. 2-29. The Type 6 hammer was a World War II expedient to save labor. The spur flanges (arrow) were eliminated, reducing the width and also the length slightly.

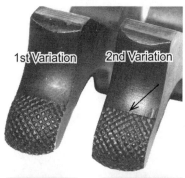

Union Switch & Signal. It was similar to the Type 6, 1st Variation hammer used by Colt except that the knurling was not as sharply cut and it had only six rows of diamonds. With the exception of a possible few Type 5 hammers procured from Colt early in their contract, US&S used the Type 6, 3rd Variation hammer. Original, unrefinished US&S hammers can be identified by their six rows of diamonds across the hammer width and their blue-gray to blackish, Du-Lite finish, refer to Figure 2-30.

Fig. 2-30. Variations of the Type 6 hammer can *sometimes* be identified by the type of "diamonds" created by the knurling process. The Type 6, 1st, 2nd, 3rd and 4th Variations are compared.

Model 1911, M1911A1

Note: At most, only a few hundred US&S pistols would have had the Colt Type 5 hammer—most observers believe they were never used.

The **4th Variation** was used by Ithaca. It was similar to the Type 1, 1st Variation hammer except that the knurling only extended for 0.18 inch over the hump of the spur rather than the 0.245 inch of the Colt Type 6, 1st Variation. This hammer was used by Ithaca for nearly half of its production with the exception of those Type 6, 1st Variation hammers procured from Colt at the start of their first contract (serial #s 856,405-916,404). Ithaca Type 6, 4th Variation hammers are easy to recognize. They show diamond checkering only four rows deep and six wide, refer to Figure 2-30.

Fig. 2-31. Ithaca used the Type 6, 5th Variation hammer from ca. serial #1,816,642 to the end of their production. To save labor, the knurling was replaced by five grooves.

The **5th Variation** was used only by Ithaca. Colt had obtained approval in late 1943 for a hammer cut with five longitudinal grooves or serrations rather than the diamond checkering to speed production. Only Ithaca actually used this hammer for the remainder of their production, beginning at circa serial #1,816,642, see Figure 2-31.

Hammer, Type 7

The **Type 7** hammer was developed for the Lightweight Commander model and used on the Commander and (commercial) Officer's series, and some special orders. The spur was replaced by a round thumb piece with a hole, see Figure 2-32.

Fig. 2-32. Round spur hammer for the Lightweight Commander pistol.

NOTE: The grooves applied to hammers may vary somewhat depending on how the hammer was set into the fixture.

Military and Commercial Pistols

Type/ Variation	Manufacturer	Serial # Range	Characteristics
	Table 2-3		
	Model 1911/1911A1 Hammers		
	(inches)		
1	Colt	1-89,800	Spur 0.430 x 0.800
2	Colt	89,001-108,600	Spur 0.430 x 0.892, sharp rear edge
3/1	Colt	108,601-714,000	Spur 0.430 x 0.890, rounded rear edge
3/2	Remington-Arms-UMC	All production	Spur 0.430 x 0.890, rounded rear edge
3/3	Singer	All production	Spur 0.430 x 0.890, rounded rear edge
4	Officer Model M15 (RIA)	All production	Similar in profile to Colt Type 1, but with turned-up spur, polished bright
5	Colt	714,001-1,700,000	Face to back of hammer spur, 0.781 inch long
1	Springfield Armory	72,571-77,000	Spur 0.425 x 0.800, marked "S"
2	Springfield Armory	77,001-82,000	Spur 0.425 x 0.892, sharp rear edge, marked "S"
3	Springfield Armory	82,001-EOP	Spur 0.425 x 0.890, rounded rear edge, marked "S"
6/1	Colt	1,700,001-EOP	OA Length, 0.785 inch, width 0.305 inch. 8 rows of *pointed* diamonds, knurling length 0.245 inch. Knurling ends in straight line
6/2	Remington Rand	916,405 - EOP	OA Length, 0.785 inch, width 0.305 inch. 8 rows of *flat-topped* diamonds. Knurling ends in curved line

Model 1911, M1911A1

Table 2-3, cont. Model 1911/1911A1 Hammers (inches)			
Type/ Variation	Manufacturer	Serial # Range	Characteristics
6/3 (1)	US&S	All production	6 rows of diamonds, Du-Lite "blue" finish
6/4	Ithaca	856,405-1,471,430	4 x 6 rows of diamonds, knurling length 0.18
6/5		1,816,642-EOP	5 longitudinal grooves on spur
7	Colt	Commander/ Officer's production	Round thumb piece, center hole
1. A few Colt Type 5 hammer possibly used at start of contract			

Hammer Pin

The hammer revolves on the hammer pin. It was 0.157 inch in diameter and 0.786 inch in length. The left end of the pin was flared at a 60-degree angle to a diameter of 0.182 inch. This prevented the pin from pushing through and out of the right side of the receiver. It was held in position on the left by the safety lock. The hammer pin was unchanged throughout production, see Figure 2-33.

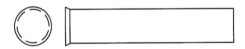

Fig. 2-33. Hammer pin.

Hammer Strut

The hammer strut (B) was attached by the hammer strut pin (C) to the base of the hammer (A). The mainspring/mainspring cap pushed against the base of the hammer strut to drive the hammer when released by the sear, see Figure 2-34.

The hammer strut was 0.107 inch wide by 2.015 inches long overall. It had a shallow curve that was 0.664 inch wide (center of the hammer strut pin hole to the bottom of the strut). The pin hole was 0.100 inch in di-

Military and Commercial Pistols

ameter. The strut was rectangular in cross section to 0.630 inch from the bottom; the remainder was round.

All Colt hammer struts and pins were blued until May 1941 (circa serial #s 734,001-735,000). After, all Colt hammer struts were Parkerized.

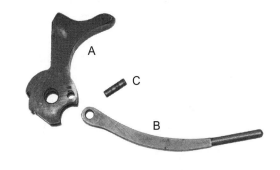

Fig. 2-34. Hammer assembly: (A) hammer, (B) strut, and (C) hammer strut pin.

All hammer struts manufactured by Springfield, Remington Arms-UMC, and Singer were blued.

Early Remington Rand and Ithaca hammer struts were Du-Lite finished; after they were Parkerized. Union Switch & Signal hammer struts were blued using the Du-Lite process. See Chapter 9 for additional details on finishes.

The hammer strut was machined from bar stock and not punched from sheet metal. It remained unchanged during the course of manufacture except for its finish. During World War II, hammer struts were manufactured under subcontract by Hartford Screw Machine Company for Ithaca.

Hammer Strut Pin

The hammer strut pin served to attach the hammer strut to the hammer and also to act as the pivot point for the two parts. It was 0.096 inch in diameter and 0.305 inch long. Each

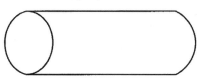

Fig. 2-35. Hammer strut pin.

end was beveled for 0.01 inch at a 45-degree angle. No changes were made to the hammer strut pin throughout production, see Figure 2-35.

95

Model 1911, M1911A1

Sear

The sear was a crescent-shaped piece of steel pivoted on the sear pin and it controlled the hammer's release. When the trigger was pulled back, the

rear of the trigger bow pushed against the base of the sear, causing it to rotate out of the hammer notch. The mainspring, acting through the hammer strut, snapped the hammer forward to strike the rear of the firing pin.

The sear was 0.309 inch wide. The portion of the sear above the sear pin hole was the critical measurement. It must be 0.4045 ± 0.0030 inch long. The top edge was squared off at 90 degrees to provide proper contact in the hammer notch, see Figure 2-36. The lower part of the sear below the pin hole is often referred to as the "sear hook."

Fig. 2-36. Sear

Sears were manufactured by all makers of the Model 1911 and 1911A1 but as none (except Springfields) are proofed or marked in any way; it is difficult to tell which sears were made by what company. Those manufactured by Springfield Armory were marked "S." Broadly speaking, Colt sears manufactured before serial number #s 734,001-735,000 (May 1941) were blued; after, they were Parkerized.

Remington Arms-UMC manufactured its own sears and they were blued and unmarked. Since they were not highly polished except for the contact surfaces, they were dark blue, almost black and may show machine marks on the sides.

Remington Rand manufactured sears at its Elmira, NY, plant. They were blued using the Du-Lite black oxide process to circa serial #s 995,000-1,015,499; after, they were Parkerized.

Ithaca manufactured its own sears. From the start of the contract at serial #856,405 to circa serial #900,000, the sears were blued using the

Military and Commercial Pistols

Du-Lite black oxide process. From circa serial #900,001 to the end of production, they were Parkerized.

NOTE: The first 60 to 100 sears used by Ithaca were obtained from Colt and may have been Parkerized.

Singer and Union Switch & Signal sears were blued, using the Du-Lite black oxide process.

Disconnector

The disconnector acts to "disconnect" the trigger, hammer and sear so that the pistol can only fire one cartridge until the action is recocked and the trigger is pulled again. The disconnector plays a vital role in the firing sequence and therefore must meet strict dimensional specifications, see Figure 2-37.

The disconnector is nominally 1.302 inches long. It can be divided into two parts: the top portion is 0.826 inch long and is raked backward at a slight angle. The lower portion is 0.476 inch long and is exactly vertical. The top portion has a round cap 0.155 inch in diameter, 0.312 inch long and has two bevels, front and rear. The front bevel is cut at a 42-degree angle and the rear bevel at a 44-degree angle. The apex is rounded to a 0.15-inch radius.

Fig. 2-37.
Disconnector

The lower portion has a flat plate-like surface 0.285 inch wide and 0.169 inch high. The bottom of the plate is beveled rear to face at 48 degrees and rests against the rear of the trigger bow. This surface is usually referred to as the trigger bow contact surface. Opposite the trigger bow contact surface is the sear spring contact surface (48-degree bevel).

The disconnector pivots on the disconnector pin, which passes through an oversized-square hole in the disconnector. The hole is 0.174 inch on each side and the corners are rounded.

97

Model 1911, M1911A1

For the disconnector to function properly over the life of the pistol, Colt Firearms and the Ordnance Department originally specified that it be made of a material comparable to 1060-1074 steel, heat-treated to Rockwell Hardness 43.5 ~ 50. All sharp edges were broken and the top, or cap, of the disconnector was lightly polished at the apex as was the trigger bow contact surface and the sear spring contact surface.

The disconnector was unchanged during its production life. Originally blued, it received the same finish at the same time period as the sear.

Sear Spring

The sear spring is a sheet of spring steel divided into three leaves which operate three separate mechanisms, see Figure 2-38. The entire sear spring was 2.985 inches long and 0.532 inch wide. The bottom end of the spring was rebated 0.10 x 0.10 inch on either side. The 0.780-inch tab thus formed was bent inward 0.15 inch to fit into a slot in the receiver that held it in place.

Fig. 2-38. Sear Spring

The left leaf was longest at 2.985 inches and 0.175 inch wide, and drove the sear.

The center leaf was 2.855 inches long and 0.185 inch wide. It drove the disconnector and returned the trigger by pressing against the back of the trigger bow.

The right leaf was the shortest at 2.510 inches long and 0.10 inch wide, and drove the grip safety.

The sear spring was bent inward to apply the proper tension. When the base of the spring was pressed against a flat surface each leaf tip came to rest above the horizontal plane as follows: the tip of the sear leaf was 0.65

Military and Commercial Pistols

inch above; the disconnector leaf tip, 0.415 inch above; and the grip safety tip, 0.135 inch above. The disconnector and grip safety leaves had compound curves and the grip safety leaf had to press backwards (in relation to the muzzle) against the disconnector and grip safety.

The tips of the disconnector and grip safety springs were beveled slightly to reduce friction against the disconnector and grip safety.

Two types of sear spring were developed, see Figure 2-39.

The **Type 1** sear spring does not have a right-angle tab on the sear leaf and was used in the first one thousand or so pistols manufactured. The tip of the sear leaf was straight and 0.175 inch in width.

The **Type 2** sear spring had a forward-pointing right-angle tab 0.155 inch long and 0.90 inch wide on the end of the sear leaf. The tab was added to prevent the sear leaf from sliding under the sear during reassembly, where it could not press the sear out of engagement with the disconnector when the slide was retracted. Under this circumstance, allowing the slide to go forward with a loaded magazine in place could result in an accidental discharge. The Type 2 sear spring was used in all pistols from circa serial #1,000 until the end of production.

Fig. 2-39. The Type 1 and Type 2 sear springs compared. Note the straight sear leaf on the Type 1 (A) compared to the right-angle bend on the Type 2 (B), arrows.

As the Type 1 sear spring was considered unsafe, they were recalled by the military and the Colt company and presumably, destroyed. Very few survived. The Type 1 sear spring shown in Figure 2-39 was found in a commercial Model 1911, serial #C82X.

99

Model 1911, M1911A1

Trigger

The trigger consists of a finger piece, a flat piece of metal curved at the front to take the shape of the finger, and the bow which is a rectangular rail extending from the finger piece that when pushed to the rear to fire, trips the sear and allows the hammer to fall, see Figure 2-40. The finger piece protruded through the trigger slot and the bow rode in the two rectangular grooves milled inside the grip.

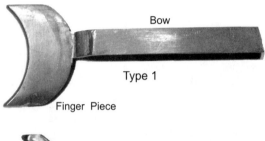

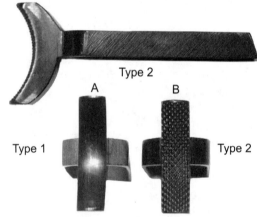

Fig. 2-40. Two types of triggers were used on the Model 1911/1911A1: left, Type 1, right, Type 2. Notice the difference in the finger piece width and surface treatment.

All Model 1911 triggers were blued. All Colt Model 1911A1 triggers to circa serial #s 734,001-735,000 were blued; after, they were Parkerized. All Remington Rand and Ithaca triggers, throughout their respective first contracts, were blued — actually a Du-Lite finish over a light sandblasting. After, both Remington Rand and Ithaca triggers were intermittently blued or Parkerized to the end of their production. All Singer and Union Switch & Signal triggers were polished and received a Du-Lite finish.

Two major types of triggers were designed and manufactured in two variations. The **Type 1** was distinguished by its smooth face and long finger piece (refer to Figure 2-40, A). The Type 1 trigger was made in two variations.

The Type 1, **1st Variation** trigger was manufactured and used by Colt and by Remington Arms-UMC. The finger piece was 0.445 inch long,

Military and Commercial Pistols

0.235 inch thick, and 0.905 inch high. The bow was 0.223 inch high and 1.741 inches long. Both the finger piece and bow were milled from a single piece of steel. The Type 1 was blued and used from the start of production to circa serial #s 700,001-710,000 at the start of the Model 1911A1 series.

The **Type 1, 2nd Variation** was manufactured and used on all Springfield Armory Model 1911s and closely resembled the Colt 1st Variation, differing only in dimensions. The Springfield trigger was 0.395 inch long, 0.238 inch thick, and 0.902 inch high. Like the 1st Variation, it was milled from a single piece of steel and blued. Most were marked "S" on the bottom of the finger piece, see Figure 2-41.

The **Type 2** trigger had a shorter finger piece. The front of the finger piece was knurled to provide a better grasp, refer to Figure 2-40, B. The Type 2 was manufactured in three variations.

The finger piece and bow of the **Type 2, 1st Variation** were milled from a single piece of steel. The finger piece was much shorter than the Type 1 finger piece at 0.30 inch long, 0.230 inch thick and 0.900

Fig. 2-41. The Springfield Type 1 trigger differed only slightly in dimensions from the Colt Type 1, but was usually marked "S" on the bottom of the finger piece.

inch high. The 1st Variation can be identified by the fact that there were no welded or brazed joints between the bow and finger piece, see Figure 2-42 (arrow A).

Colt-manufactured Type 2, 1st Variation triggers can be distinguished from Singer and early Remington Rand triggers only by their sharp, deep checkering. Singer and Remington Rand checkering is dull, see Figure 2-43. The Type 2, 1st Variation trigger was in use by Colt from serial #700,001 until it was replaced by the Type 2, 3rd Variation during World War II. See

101

Model 1911, M1911A1

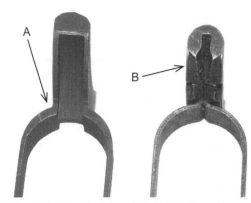

Fig. 2-42. Type 2, 1st and 2nd Variation triggers compared.

Table 2-4 for specific periods of use by manufacturer. Remington Rand also used the Type 2, 1st Variation trigger from circa serial #s 916,405-930,000.

The **Type 2, 2nd Variation** finger piece and bow were stamped separately from sheet steel and brazed together as a cost-savings and wartime production expedient. The finger piece was 0.280 inch long, 0.240 inch thick and 0.890 inch high.

The 2nd Variation can be identified by looking at the back of the finger piece. The trigger bow was inserted into the hollow finger piece, crimped and brazed in place, refer to Figure 2-42, arrow B. The Type 2, 2nd Variation trigger was manufactured exclusively by Yawman Metal Products in Rochester, New York. These triggers were used by Remington Rand from circa serial #s 930,000-1,500,000 and overlapped with the 3rd Variation. Ithaca used the Type 2, 2nd Variation during its first production run, serial #s 856,405-916,404.

Fig. 2-43. The Colt-manufactured Type 2, 1st Variation trigger (left) with sharper, deeper checkering than the Singer or early Remington Rand (right) triggers.

The **Type 2, 3rd Variation** was identical to the 2nd Variation except that the back of the trigger bow was relieved at the top 0.010 inch deep and 0.356 inch long to prevent any possible interference with the sear, see Figure 2-44. The Type 2, 3rd Variation trigger entered production in late September/October 1943 at Yawman Metal Products, Inc.

102

Military and Commercial Pistols

All late Colt Model 1911A1s from circa serial #1,160,001 to the end of production were equipped with this 3rd Variation trigger and obtained them from Yawman Metal Products. Note that Yawman also provided Type 2, 1st, 2nd, or 3rd Variation triggers to all manufacturers, as shown in Table 2-4, until the end of wartime production.

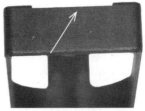

Fig. 2-44. The Type 2, 3rd Variation trigger bow was modified at the rear top with a narrow rebate (arrow) to avoid possible interference with the sear.

Table 2-4		
Model 1911 and 1911A1 Triggers by Manufacturer		
User/Type	Manufacturer	Estimated Serial Number Range
Colt – Type 1, 1st Variation	Colt	1 to 700,001-710,000
Remington Arms-UMC, Type 1, 1st Variation	Remington Arms-UMC	1-21,677 (all)
Springfield – Type 1, 2nd Variation	Springfield Armory	72,571-127,978 (all)
Colt – Type 2, 1st Variation	Yawman Metal Products	700,001-710,000 to 1,160,000
Colt – Type 2, 3rd Variation	Yawman Metal Products	1,160,001-EOP
Remington Rand – Type 2, 1st Variation	Remington Rand	916,405-930,000
Remington Rand – Type 2, 2nd Variation	Yawman Metal Products	930,000-1,500,000+
Remington Rand – Type 2, 3rd Variation	Yawman Metal Products	1,500,000-EOP
Ithaca – Type 2, 2nd Variation	Yawman Metal Products	856,405-916,404

Table 2-4, cont.		
Model 1911 and 1911A1 Triggers by Manufacturer		
User/Type	**Manufacturer**	**Estimated Serial Number Range**
Ithaca – Type 2, 3rd Variation	Yawman Metal Products	1,441,431 to EOP
Union Switch & Signal – Type 2, 3rd Variation	Yawman Metal Products	Entire Production Run
NOTE: Serial number ranges are approximate and based on a relatively small number of observations in relation to the total manufactured.		

Safeties

The Model 1911/1911A1 had four safeties: 1) hammer half-cock notch, 2) the disconnector which prevented the hammer from being released until the slide/barrel were in battery (both discussed above), 3) a manual thumb safety lock that could be moved up to the "on" position to block the sear when the hammer was cocked, and 4) a grip safety that was automatically depressed by the palm of the shooting hand when the pistol was held in the proper position, both discussed below. The safety system is shown in Figure 2-45.

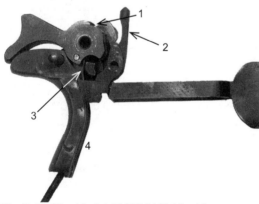

Safety Lock

The manual thumb-activated safety was referred to as the "Safety Lock." The safety lock could only be applied when the hammer was fully cocked. This, in combination with the other safety features of the Model 1911/Model 1911A1, enabled the pistol to be carried in combat in a "cocked and locked" position, i.e., with the hammer fully

Fig. 2-45. The Model 1911/1911A1 had four safeties: 1) hammer half-cock notch, 2) disconnector, 3) manual thumb safety lock, and 4) grip safety.

cocked but the movement of the sear blocked by the safety lock. It should

Military and Commercial Pistols

be noted that if dropped on the muzzle in this condition, the pistol may discharge.

Fig. 2-46 The spring-loaded plunger in the plunger tube (arrow) held the safety lock in the position selected. Safety shown in "off" position.

The safety lock was held in the "on" or "off" position by the rear spring-loaded plunger in the plunger tube, see Figure 2-46. The safety lock consisted of four main segments: 1) the safety plate, 2) the safety lock pin, 3) the sear stop surface, and 4) the thumb piece, see Figure 2-47.

The 1) safety plate was an irregularly shaped plate of steel 0.712 inch high, by 1.022 inches long by 0.046 inch thick. It had a round pin projecting at a right angle to the interior surface on which the safety lock pivoted in the receiver. 2) The safety lock pin passed through the receiver and was the axis on which the safety lock pivoted. 3) A lug on the interior forward surface carried the sear stop surface which blocked the movement of the sear when the hammer was cocked and the safety lock in the "on" position (up). It did so by rotating the sear stop surface against the back of

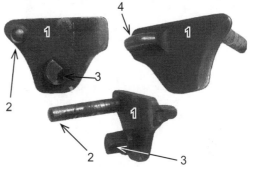

Fig. 2-47. The safety lock (exterior and interior views): 1) safety plate, 2) safety lock pin, 3) sear stop surface, and 4) thumb piece.

the sear (the lower part called the sear hook). When the safety lock was rotated into the "off" position (down), the sear stop surface on the lug was withdrawn and the sear was allowed to move to release the hammer. 4) The thumb piece projected at right angles to the safety plate and was used to move the safety lock up into the "on" or safe position, or down into the "off" position.

105

Model 1911, M1911A1

Six types of safety locks were used in the Model 1911 and Model 1911A1. The top and bottom surfaces of the thumb piece of all types were machined in a checkered or a ridged pattern to increase contact with the shooter's thumb.

The **Type 1** safety lock was 0.075 inch thick with a sharp, square edge and a perfectly flat side. It was made in two variations, see Figure 2-48.

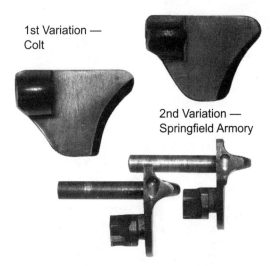

1st Variation — Colt

2nd Variation — Springfield Armory

The **1st Variation** was manufactured by Colt and was used from the start of production to circa serial #6,000

Springfield Armory manufactured the **2nd Variation** (0.075 inch thick) and installed it on all of its limited production, but rounded the edges slightly, refer to Figure 2-48.

Fig. 2-48. Type 1 Safety Lock. Left, 1st Variation by Colt. Notice the sharper edges and flat plate. Right, 2nd Variation by Springfield Armory. Notice the rounded edges.

Shortly after the Model 1911 began to be issued to the troops, controversy concerning the safety lock began. It was reported that in drawing a cocked and locked pistol from the issue holster, the safety lock could be inadvertently pushed down into the off position. This was obviously dangerous as the soldier was now holding a pistol ready to fire when he thought it was on safe. Not withstanding the fact that the Army trained the soldier not to carry the pistol in the holster in the cocked and locked mode, it was deemed sufficiently dangerous that Colt was asked to modify the safety lock. They did so by increasing the thickness of the **Type 2** thumb piece to 0.105 inch and rounding it off so that the friction of the thumb piece edge against the leather holster would not push it into the off position, see Figure 2-49. After circa serial #6,001, a small shelf

Military and Commercial Pistols

of material was present on all Colt Type 1 and 2 safety locks where the thumb piece joined the plate (arrow). As noted above, Springfield Armory chose to continue making the Type 1 safety, but did round the edges slightly to prevent rubbing the safety lock off against the holster.

Remington Arms-UMC used the Colt-style Type 2 thumb piece.

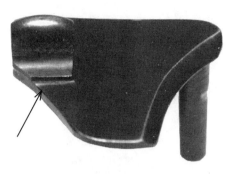

Fig. 2-49 Type 2 Safety Lock. Notice the "shelf" of material left by the machinist (arrow).

At circa serial #375,000, the "shelf" of excess material was eliminated. Instead, the machinist simply milled a contour under the thumb piece shelf, see Figure 2-50, arrow. This **Type 3** thumb piece was adopted as a cost- and time-saving measure and was retained to the end of M1911 production at Colt. The Type 3 safety lock was also used by Singer, Remington Rand to circa serial #1,441,430, Ithaca from circa serial #s 1,208,674 -1,279,673, and by Union Switch & Signal for their entire production run.

By stretching the definition a bit, a **Type 4** safety lock can be identified. This was essentially the Colt Type 3 safety lock, but where previously the entire surface had received the same even polish, now the rear top surface from the thumb piece back was polished in a different

Fig. 2-50. Type 3 Safety Lock. Notice that the "shelf" (arrow) around the thumb piece has now been eliminated and replaced by a smooth contour.

direction and provided an almost two-tone finish, see Figure 2-51. The change appears to have occurred at circa serial #s 700,001-710,000 and was used only by Colt. Some were used on post-war commercial production to circa 1949.

Model 1911, M1911A1

Fig. 2-51. Type 4 Safety Lock. Notice the "two-tone" effect created by polishing around the thumb piece at right angles.

NOTE: This so-called "two-tone" polish is more or less visible depending on the individual doing the polishing. Interestingly enough, the author has not seen this effect on safety locks manufactured by Singer, Remington Rand, Ithaca, or Union Switch & Signal. It is important only in identifying Colt-manufactured safety locks after circa serial #s 700,001-710,000.

A **Type 5** safety lock was developed and used by Ithaca from circa serial #1,208,674 to the end of production. The Type 5 safety lock thumb piece had three serrations or ridges and grooves running front to back instead of checkering, see Figure 2-52. The change was adopted as a wartime cost- and time-saving measure. The Type five *may* also have been used in very late production by Remington Rand.

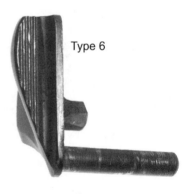

Fig. 2-52. Types 5 and 6 Safety Locks. Grooves were authorized on the Type 5 thumb piece and was used by Ithaca. The Type 5 (left) had a tab thumb piece but the Type 6 (right) was extended for more positive control and used on commercial pistols from 1949 on.

Military and Commercial Pistols

A **Type 6** safety lock was used by Colt on postwar commercial production starting at circa serial #C238,000. It had two or three grooves along the top surface. Instead of the "tab"-type thumb piece used earlier, the thumb piece surface was extended both front and rear for a more positive grip, refer to Figure 2-52.

Type/Variation	Manufacturer	Characteristics	Estimated Serial Number Range
Table 2-5 **Safety Lock Types**			
1/1	Colt	0.075 inch thick, sharp edge, high polish, bright blue, no shelf	1-6,000
1/2	Springfield Armory	0.075 inch thick, rounded edge, high polish, chemical blue. Most marked "S"	72,571-EOP (all production)
2	Colt	0.105 inch thick with "shelf" on thumb piece	6,001-374,999
2	Remington Arms-UMC	0.105 inch thick with "shelf" on thumb piece	All production
3	Colt	Smooth contour under thumb piece	375,000-629,500
3	Singer	Smooth contour under thumb piece	All production
3	Remington Rand	Smooth contour under thumb piece	916,405-1,441,430 (1)
3	Ithaca	Smooth contour under thumb piece	1,208,674-1,279,673 (1)
3	US&S	Thumb piece contour, Du-Lite finish	All production
4 (2)	Colt	Two-tone caused by polishing	700,001-710,000 to 734,001-735,001
4 (2)	Colt	Parkerized	734,001-735,001 to EOP
5 (3)	Ithaca	Three serrations on thumb piece replaced checkering	1,208,674-EOP
6	Colt	Two or three serrations on extended thumb piece. Commercial use	C238,000-EOP

1. An overlap of Type 3 and Type 5 Safety Locks will be observed at the start of the serial number range.
2. Were also used (not Parkerized) on post-WWII commercial production to circa 1949.
3. May have been used in very late production, if at all, by Remington Rand.

Model 1911, M1911A1

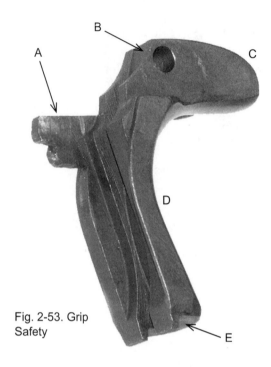

Fig. 2-53. Grip
Safety

Grip Safety

The grip safety blocked the trigger and prevented it from being pulled unless the pistol was held properly in the firing hand, see Figure 2-53. A horizontal lug on the interior of the grip safety (arrow A) pressed against the rear of the trigger bar until the base of the grip safety was depressed. When depressed, the grip safety rotated about the axis of the grip safety pin hole (arrow B), lifting the lug out of engagement with the trigger bar. When the safety lock was in the off position and the slide was locked into battery, the pistol could be fired.

The grip safety was 0.619 inch wide at its widest point and 1.777 inches high overall. The top section protruded to the rear to protect the web of the shooting hand from the hammer spur during recoil (C). The lower section (D) was curved to match the slant of the grip. A notch or ledge at the end (arrow E) was captured by a lip on the top of the mainspring housing.

The grip safety pin hole was centered 0.143 inch below the top of the grip safety and was 0.156 inch in diameter,

The lug which contacts the trigger bar was 0.309 inch wide and 0.675 inch long. The tip was machined to match the slant of the rear of the trigger bar when the grip safety was not depressed.

Seven types of grip safety were used. They are described below and summarized in Table 2-6.

Military and Commercial Pistols

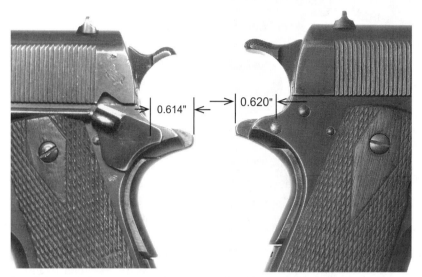

Fig. 2-54. Colt ,Type 1 grip safety.

Fig. 2-55. Springfield Armory, Type 2 grip safety.

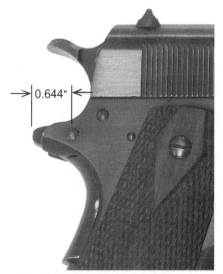

Fig. 2-56. The Type 3 grip safety used by Remington Arms-UMC can be identified by its "blunt"-ended tang. Mike Strietbeck collection.

Fig. 2-57. Type 4 grip safety. The tang was extended to protect the hand from "hammer bite."

Model 1911, M1911A1

The **Type 1** grip safety tang was manufactured by Colt and protruded 0.12 inch beyond the rear shoulder of the receiver (0.614 inch from the center of the grip safety pin hole to the end of the tang), see Figure 2-54. The tang was carefully rounded. The bottom edge of the Colt grip safety was beveled slightly. It was in use from the start of production to circa serial #629,500 and the end of Model 1911 production.

The **Type 2** grip safety was used by the Springfield Armory. It differed from the Type 1 grip safety in that the tang extended 0.18 inch beyond the receiver's rear shoulder (0.620 inch from the center of the grip safety pin hole to the end of the tang), see Figure 2-55. The tang curved to an almost flat base. The bottom edge was left sharp in contrast to the beveled bottom edge of the Colt Type 1 grip safety. Most were marked "S."

The **Type 3** grip safety was used by Remington Arms-UMC. It extended 0.15 inch beyond the rear shoulder of the receiver (0.644 inch from the center of the grip safety pin hole to the end of the tang) and was slightly blunt at the rear, see Figure 2-56. The bottom edge was also beveled slightly similarly to the Colt Type 1.

The tang of the **Type 4** grip safety was lengthened to protect the web of the hand from "hammer bite" to 0.30 inch (0.704 inch from the center of the grip safety pin hole to the end of the tang), see Figure 2-57. It was in use from serial #s 700,001-710,000 on all Model 1911A1 production pistols by all manufacturers.

Singer manufactured its own grip safeties under their Educational Contract #W-ORD-396. All were blued using the Du-Lite process.

Ithaca, Remington Rand, and Union Switch & Signal used Colt-manufactured grip safeties very early in their own production but manufactured their own for the balance of their World War II production. US&S grip safeties were Du-Lite finished after a light sandblasting. Ithaca (serial #s 856,405-916,404) and Remington Rand (serial #s 916,405-1,041,404) were also Du-Lite finished. After, both companies' grip safeties were Parkerized.

All Type 4 grip safeties were unmarked. Minor differences in shape will be observed between manufacturers.

Military and Commercial Pistols

The **Type 5** grip safety was a replacement part manufactured by Colt from 1949 to replace worn parts on all the Model 1911A1s. They can be identified by a "C" inside a box stamped on the left side, see Figure 2-58. The Type 5 grip safety will also be seen on many post-World War II National Match Pistols prepared by the Springfield Armory.

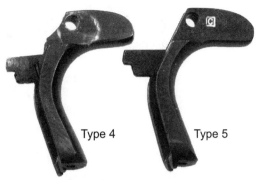

Type 4   Type 5

Fig. 2-58. Grip safeties marked "C" in a box were Colt post-World War II replacement parts.

NOTE: Colt began using the "C" in box marking late in World War II, and some 1945-made parts may be so marked.

The Type 5 grip safety was also used on all post-World War II commercial Government Model pistols until the advent of the Series 70 in 1970.

The **Type 6** grip safety was manufactured by Colt for all commercial Government Model pistols made in the Series 70, 80 and the Model 1991 series standard pistols. During the late 1960s, early 1970s Colt switched to injection molding for certain parts like the grip safety. They can be identified by mold marks and a slight pebbly surface on unpolished sides.

The **Type 7** grip safety was manufactured for the Lightweight Commander, Commander series and special-order pistols. Because the Type 7 hammer with the round thumb piece was used in this series, the grip safety tang could be made shorter at 0.589 inch than the grip safety used on the full-size Government model made with the hammer spur.

NOTE: Some slight variation in the length of grip safety tangs can be expected.

Model 1911, M1911A1

Table 2-6
Grip Safety Types (inches)

Type	Manufacturer	Serial Number Range	Center of Safety Pin Hole to Rear Edge Dimension
1	Colt	1-629,500	0.614
2	Springfield Armory	All	0.620
3	Rem. Arms-UMC	All	0.644
4	Colt	700,001-710,000 to EOP*	0.704
4	Singer, Remington Rand, Ithaca, US&S	All	0.704
5	Colt	Post-WWII U.S. Government contract replacement parts	0.704
6	Colt	All post-WWII commercial	0.782
7	Colt Commander series	All	0.589

* U.S. Government contract Model 1911A1 pistols.

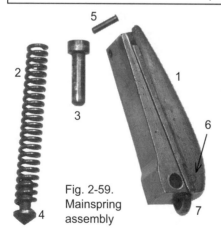

Fig. 2-59. Mainspring assembly

Mainspring Housing Assembly

The mainspring was contained in the mainspring housing at the rear of the grip and consisted of seven components: 1) mainspring housing, 2) mainspring, 3) mainspring cap, 4) mainspring housing pin retainer, 5) mainspring cap pin, 6) lanyard loop pin, 7) lanyard loop, see Figure 2-59.

114

Military and Commercial Pistols

Mainspring Cap

The function of the mainspring cap was to provide a platform through by which the hammer strut could drive the hammer through the force of the main-spring. The mainspring cap re-

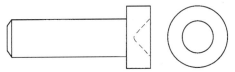

Fig. 2-60. Mainspring Cap.

sembled a flathead rivet 0.75 inch long overall, see Figure 2-60. Its cap was 0.279 inch in diameter and had a cone-shaped depression 0.064 inch deep in the head to seat the end of the hammer strut. The shaft was 0.174 inch in diameter and 0.61 inch long and beveled slightly at the end to enter the spring easily. The cap was heat-treated to harden it. No changes were made to the mainspring cap during its production life.

Mainspring

The mainspring was a coil spring contained within the mainspring housing and drove the hammer, see Figure 2-61. It was anchored in the housing by the mainspring housing pin retainer and acted on the hammer strut through the mainspring cap. The outside diameter of the mainspring was nominally 0.273 inch.

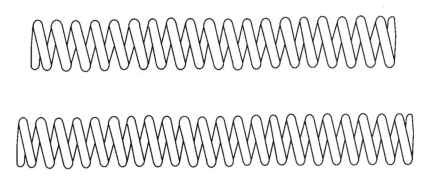

Fig. 2-61. Mainsprings: Type 1 above, Type 2 below.

Two types of mainspring were used during the production life of the Model 1911/1911A1, refer to Figure 2-61. The **Type 1** mainspring was made of spring steel wire 0.0458 inch in diameter and wound into 19 coils. It was in use from the start of production to circa serial #108,261 (C1-17,500).

115

Model 1911, M1911A1

When the slightly heavier Type 2 hammer was adopted, the **Type 2** mainspring was substituted for the Type 1. It was made of spring steel wire 0.045 inch in diameter and wound into 22 coils. It was used from circa Colt serial #108,262 to the end of production (C17,501-EOP).

Starting at Colt serial #s 700,001-710,000, the wire used to produce the mainspring was reduced to 0.4140 inch in diameter. It was quickly discovered that the new mainspring did not produce a sufficient hammer blow to ignite the primers used in the 1924 National Match .45 ACP ammunition. The change order was rescinded and the 0.0450-inch Type 2 mainspring was returned to service.

Mainspring Housing Pin Retainer

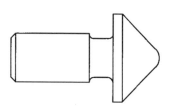

Fig. 2-62. Mainspring Housing Pin Retainer.

This pin (also called lock plunger) was seated in the end of the mainspring and was pressed downward both to prevent the mainspring from wobbling and to lock the mainspring housing pin in place, see Figure 2-62. The cap end of the pin somewhat resembled a pointed mushroom and it was this end, slightly rounded, that bore against the 0.06-inch radius in the mainspring housing pin to lock it in place. The mainspring housing pin retainer was 0.53 inch long overall. The cone-shaped cap (45-degree slope) was 0.270 inch in diameter and 0.16 inch high. It was heat-treated to harden it. No changes were made to it throughout production.

Mainspring Cap Pin

The function of this pin was to retain the mainspring and mainspring cap in place in the mainspring housing, see Figure 2-63. It was 0.36 inch long by

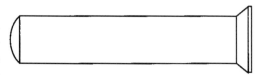

Fig. 2-63. Mainspring Cap Pin.

0.085 inch in diameter with a slightly flared head and a rounded end. The flared head prevented it from being driven too deeply into the mainspring housing. The pin was heat-treated to harden it. No changes were made to it throughout production.

Military and Commercial Pistols

Mainspring Housing

The mainspring housing contained the main-spring, also called the hammer spring. It slid onto rails at the rear of the pistol grip and was held in place with the mainspring housing pin. The mainspring housing was 0.622 inch wide (including the rails which were 0.538 inch wide) and 1.704 inch high from the center of the main-spring housing pin hole to the top of the housing (rear of the slant). All but the Type 4 had a steel attaching point in the shape of a "U" for the lanyard loop, see Figure 2-64.

Two types of mainspring housing were used, the Model 1911 and Model 1911A1, and are distinguished by whether or not the back surface was flat or arched, see Figure 2-65.

The various types of mainspring housing are described below and in Table 2-7.

The **Type 1** mainspring housing had a flat,

Fig. 2-64. The mainspring housing with a "U"-shaped steel wire loop for attaching a lanyard. This photo shows an M1911 mainspring housing.

smooth back surface, see Figure 2-66. It was in use from the start of production to circa serial #700,001 (C135,000) by Colt, and by Springfield, and Remington Arms-UMC. All were blued.

1st Variation Colt-manufactured mainspring housings were unmarked. The bottom rear edge was beveled.

Type 1

Type 2

Fig. 2-65. Mainspring Housings, right to left: Type 1, flat; Type 2, arched.

Model 1911, M1911A1

2nd Variation Springfield Armory mainspring housings were marked "S." The lower rear corners of the Springfield-manufactured mainspring housings were left sharp.

3rd Variation Remington Arms-UMC mainspring housings were marked on the bottom with an "E" in sans serif type for Walter H. Evans, Provisional Inspector. His marking appears from serial #1 to circa serial #15,000. After serial #15,000, the "E" provisional inspection marking on the mainspring housing are said by some authorities to have

Fig. 2-66. Type 1 Mainspring Housings, l-r: Colt, 1st Variation; Springfield Armory, 2nd Variation.

been phased out, after which the mainspring housing was left unmarked. But pistols with serial #s 18,449 and 21,512 do retain the "E" marking.

The **Type 2** mainspring housing was curved, or arched, as well as checkered or grooved, to allow the pistol to roll back in the hand rather than lift the wrist. This allowed the shooting hand to recover more quickly from the muzzle lift produced by recoil.

Type 2 mainspring housings were blued to between circa serial #s 734,001-735,000 (Colt production); after, they were Parkerized. All World War II mainspring housings from 1943 on were Parkerized except for those manufactured by Union Switch & Signal, which finished their production using the Du-Lite black oxide process. Early first contract Ithaca and Remington Rand Type 2 mainspring housings were also finished with the Du-Lite process. Singer mainspring housings were Du-Lite finished.

Military and Commercial Pistols

Five variations of the Type 2 mainspring housing were manufactured.

NOTE: Other authorities have counted rows of diamonds to distinguish mainspring housings by manufacturer. The system is inaccurate, leading different observers to obtain different results. The knurling pattern used on M1911A1 mainspring housings and the tools that made them are specified by "pitch" and measured in "knurls per inch." The knurl pitch can accurately and easily be measured using a standard SAE thread pitch gage available in hardware and auto parts stores. Using one of the thread gages' fold-out leaves and aligning it with the knurls, or diamonds, along the center row of the mainspring housing, the user will obtain very repeatable results.

Fig. 2-67. Type 2 Mainspring Housing, 1st Variation by Colt. 14 knurls per inch.

Throughout production of knurled mainspring housings, Colt used a pitch of 14, Ithaca 13, and US&S, 16 knurls per inch. Remington Rand used 20 knurls per inch for the first 20,000 or so pistols and thereafter, used 18 knurls per inch.

A Springfield Armory Ordnance Drawing dated 1944 set the knurling pattern at 16 knurls per inch (the Ordnance Department was never shy about telling Colt how to build pistols) but Colt continued to use 14 knurls to the end of military production.

Both the knurls per inch and the number of diamonds per row (for traditionalists) are included in the text and in Table 2-7.

The **1st Variation** pattern used by Colt had raised diamonds and was manufactured from circa serial #s 700,001-2,248,000 (C135,000-C220,000) with 14 knurls per inch (26 diamonds top to bottom, four per row), see Figure 2-67.

The **2nd Variation** was manufactured by Singer throughout their production run. It can be identified by its very fine checkering with twenty kmurls per inch or 39 full diamonds top to bottom, center, and 5 diamonds per row, see Figure 2-68, left.

119

Model 1911, M1911A1

Remington Rand manufactured the **3rd Variation** mainspring housing and used it from circa serial #s 916,405-1,609,528 in early 1944. The first 20,000 had 20 knurls per inch; later ones had 18 (37 x 4 and 35 x 4 diamonds), refer to Figure 2-68, right.

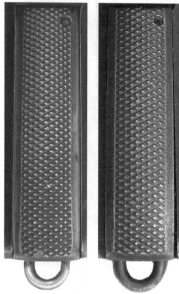

NOTE: Early Remington Rand mainspring housing checkering is nearly identical to the Singer mainspring housing checkering, as Remington Rand received much of the tooling needed to produce the Model 1911A1 from Singer. The Remington Rand variation was in use from circa serial #s 916,405-1,609,528, refer to Figure 2-68.

Fig. 2-68. Type 2 Mainspring Housing, 2nd Variation by Singer (left) and 3rd Variation by Remington Rand (right) compared. Karl Karash collection.

Ithaca manufactured the **4th Variation** mainspring housing from circa serial #s 856,405-1,220,000 to 1,279,673 with 13 knurls per inch (27 x 3 diamonds), see Figure 2-69.

Union Switch & Signal manufactured the **5th Variation** mainspring housing throughout their World War II production run. It had 16 knurls per inch, (37 x 4 diamonds) see Figure 2-70. US&S mainspring housings were finished originally with the Du-Lite black oxide process.

Fig. 2-69. Type 2 Mainspring Housing, 4th Variation by Ithaca. 13 knurls per inch. Karl Karash collection.

The **Type 3** mainspring housing was manufactured in two variations during the latter part of World War II. Instead of diamond checkering, longitudinal

120

Military and Commercial Pistols

grooves were machined on its back surface as a cost- and time-saving feature.

The **1st Variation** was manufactured by Cayuga Motors and was installed on Colt and Ithaca pistols. It had eight vertical grooves, see Figure 2-71.

Colt used the 1st Variation mainspring housing from circa serial #2,248,001 to the end of production.

Ithaca used the 1st Variation mainspring housing from circa serial #1,441,431 to the end of production.

Remington Rand manufactured a **2nd Variation** of the Type 3 mainspring housing and used them from circa serial #1,743,847 to the end of production. This 2nd Variation had nine vertical grooves instead of eight, see Figure 2-72.

Fig. 2-70. Type 2 Mainspring Housing, 5th Variation by US&S—16 knurls per inch. Karl Karash collection.

The **Type 4** mainspring housing without a lanyard loop was installed on many, but not all commercial pistols—including those purchased by the Ordnance Department—i.e., the Colt "Super .38" Automatic Pistol, Colt "Super Match" Model, Calibre .38 Automatic, Colt "ACE" Automatic Pistol, Calibre .22 Long Rifle, and Colt "Service Model ACE" Automatic Pistol and all pre-World War II National Match pistols. The Type 4 2st Variation mainspring housing was identical to the Type 2, 1st Variation mainspring housing but without the lanyard loop and holes which would have been drilled for it.

Fig. 2-71. Type 3 Mainspring Housing. The 1st Variation was manufactured by Cayuga Motors and had eight vertical grooves.

121

Model 1911, M1911A1

There were three variations of the Type 4. The **1st Variation** was used from 1924 to late 1942 on many, but not all of the models mentioned in the preceding paragraph. Consult the serial number tables in Chapter 5 for the model in question. The **2nd Variation** (ridged) was installed on all post-World War II Model 1911A1s, and Series 70 and Series 80 pistols. The **3rd Variation** (ridged) was used on the Lightweight Commander.

NOTE: A mainspring housing with depressed, or inverted, checkering is of Argentine manufacture, see Figure 2-73.

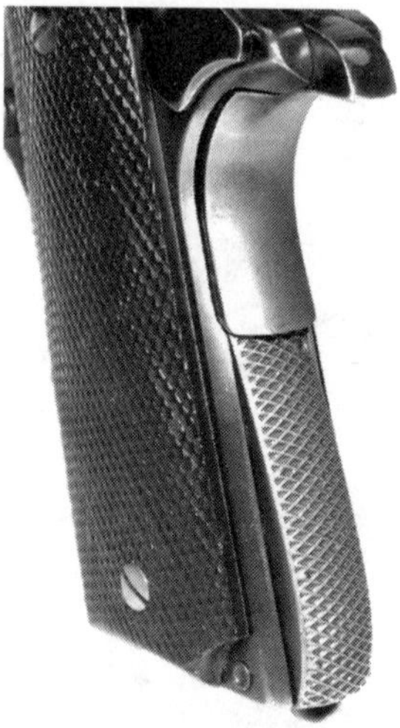

Mainspring Housing Pin

The mainspring housing pin held the mainspring housing in the receiver. The pin was 0.765 inch long, 0.156 inch in diameter with a 0.06-inch-radius center groove. Two types were used, see Figure 2-74.

Fig. 2-72. Type 3, 2nd Variation Mainspring Housing. It had nine vertical grooves.

Fig. 2-73. Mainspring housings with depressed checkering may be of Argentine manufacture.

The **Type 1** mainspring housing pin had a slight convex radius on both ends. This made it difficult to center a punch on the pin when removing it and often resulted in damage to the finish around the pin hole. It was in use from serial #s 1-6,499.

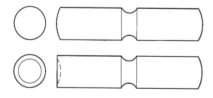

Fig. 2-74. Mainspring Housing Pin. Top: Type 1; bottom, Type 2.

In June 1912, the Ordnance Department approved a minor change. The **Type 2** mainspring housing pin was made with a 0.06-inch concave radius in the left end, which allowed a punch to center itself. The change was made at circa serial #6,500.

Military and Commercial Pistols

Table 2-7
Mainspring Housing Types

Type	Variation	Manufacturer	Identification	S/N Range (1)
1	1	Colt	Flat, unmarked	1 to 700,001
	2	Springfield Armory	Flat, marked "S"	All production
	3	Remington Arms-UMC	Flat, marked "E"	1-15,000+
			Flat, probably marked "E"	15,001+-EOP
2	1	Colt (2)	Arched, raised diamonds 14 kpi (26 x 4)	700,001-2,248,000
	2	Singer (2)	Arched, raised diamonds 20 kpi (39 x 5)	All Production
	3	Remington Rand (2), (3)	Arched, raised diamonds 20 kpi and 18 kpi (37 x 4 to 35 x 4)	916,405-1,609,528
	4	Ithaca (2)	Arched, raised diamonds 13 kpi (27 x 3)	856,405-1,220,000 to 1,279,673
	5	US&S (2)	Arched, raised diamonds 16 kpi (37 x 4)	All Production
3	1	Cayuga Motors	8 vertical grooves	Colt: 2,248,001-EOP Ithaca: 1,441,431 to EOP
	2	Remington Rand	9 vertical grooves	1,743,847-EOP

123

Model 1911, M1911A1

Table 2-7, cont.
Mainspring Housing Types

Type	Variation	Manufacturer	Identification	S/N Range (1)
	1	Colt "Super .38" Automatic Pistol, Colt "Super Match" Model, Calibre .38 Automatic, Colt "ACE" Automatic Pistol, Calibre .22 Long Rifle, and Colt "Service Model ACE" Automatic Pistol	Arched, raised diamonds 14 kpi (26 x 4)	1924-1942
4	2	All post-WWII models	Arched, 7 vertical grooves	1945+
	3	Lightweight Commander	Arched, 7 vertical grooves, aluminum	1949+

1. All serial number ranges are approximate.
2. KPI = knurls per inch. To count diamonds, first count top to bottom down the center, then across the center.
3. Remington Rand used three different checkering patterns, each progressively coarser until changing to the Type 3, 2nd Variation ridges mainspring housing.

The Type 2 pin was used to the end of production by every manufacturer.

Lanyard Loop and Pin

The lanyard loop was attached to the bottom of the mainspring housing. A mounted soldier attached a lanyard to the pistol using the lanyard loop to prevent its loss while on horseback. Rarely did dismounted soldiers use the lanyard loop although it remained a feature on the pistol to the end of military Model 1911/1911A1 production.

124

Military and Commercial Pistols

The lanyard loop was a steel wire nominally 0.107 inch in diameter bent into a "U" shape. Each side of the "U" was notched 0.090 inch from the end and inserted into holes in the mainspring housing base and held in place by the steel lanyard loop pin (0.090 inch in diameter and 0.5 inch long). The leading edge of the lanyard loop pin was beveled and the trailing end rounded. No design changes were made to the lanyard loop or pin during Model 1911/1911A1 production.

Fig. 2-75. Lanyard Loop examples. Left: Colt Model 1911 (mfg. 1912); right, Remington Rand (mfg. 1944).

The size and diameter of the steel wire varied from manufacturer to manufacturer, see Figure 2-75 and Table 2-8. Use care with these dimensions when identifying a mainspring housing: height and diameter of the wire varied within production runs by various manufacturers.

Table 2-8
Lanyard Loop Dimensions by Manufacturer
(inches)

Manufacturer	Loop Size (1)	Width (2)	Wire Diameter (3)
Colt, pre-700,001-710,000	0.226	0.435	0.107
Springfield Armory	0.226	0.432	0.107
Rem. Arms-UMC	0.252	0.421	0.104
Colt, post - 700,001-710,000	0.186	0.417	0.106
Singer	0.260	0.432	0.107
Ithaca	0.200	0.417	0.112
Remington Rand	0.250	0.421	0.104
US&S	0.256	0.417	0.108

1. Size of loop from base of mainspring housing to outside bottom edge of loop.
2. Outside width.
3. Measured at base.

Model 1911, M1911A1

NOTE: Pre-World War II ACE Model .22, Service Model ACE, Super .38, National Match, and some special-order pistols did not have a lanyard loop—although it could be added, also by special order. All post-World War II production Colt pistols do not currently have the lanyard loop with the exception of the Model 1911—World War I Replica.

Magazine Catch

When the magazine is inserted into the bottom of the grip, a rectangular cut in the front, right side of the magazine is engaged by the magazine catch. When the protruding button on the left side of the catch is depressed, it is withdrawn from the rectangular cut and the magazine is released to fall out of the well.

The magazine catch assembly (Figure 2-76, A) is composed of three parts: 1) magazine catch housing, 2) magazine catch spring, and 3) the magazine catch lock. All parts were blued or Parkerized to match the finish on the receiver. Springs were either polished after heat-treating or left with the heat-blue-black finish. Three types of magazine catches were used, see Figure 2-77.

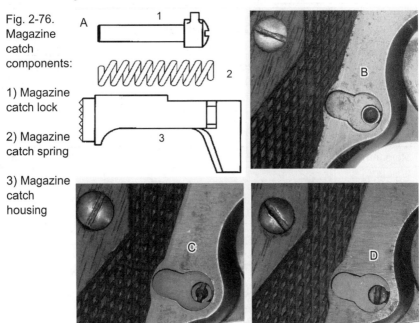

Fig. 2-76. Magazine catch components:

1) Magazine catch lock

2) Magazine catch spring

3) Magazine catch housing

Military and Commercial Pistols

From serial #s 1-3,188, according to Colt records, the **Type 1** magazine catch is easily identifiable by its concave, or dimpled head, refer to Figure 2-76, B. It had to be removed from the receiver with a tool that depressed the magazine catch housing from the left side. This forced the magazine catch into its slot in the left side of the receiver, allowing it to protrude past the right side of the receiver. Meanwhile, the magazine catch lock remained stationary with its protruding tab in the groove cut in the receiver. The magazine catch was then turned clockwise (from the left side) by grasping with thumb and index finger, until the tab on the magazine catch lock traversed the groove in the receiver and popped free—often a great distance and into a mud puddle. Installing the magazine catch required that the dimpled head be depressed with the standard takedown tool while turning the magazine catch body so that the lock tab engaged the groove in the receiver cutout; again very hard to do without burnishing the edge of the receiver cutout. This was not one of Mr. Browning's better ideas.

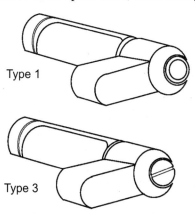

Type 1

Type 3

Fig. 2-77. Top, Type 1 magazine catch (ca. serial numbers 1-3,188); bottom, Type 3 magazine catch (ca. 6,501 to EOP).

Springfield Armory suggested a flat magazine catch lock head slotted for a flathead screwdriver be substituted. This change was implemented at serial #3,188 (according to Colt records). Along with slotting the magazine catch lock head, the magazine catch housing also had to be slotted for the Types 2 or 3 magazine catch lock to function.

Any pistol below serial number 3,188 with a slotted magazine catch body is a poor restoration as the Type 1 magazine catch (serial #s 1-3,188) did not have a slot in the housing.

The **Type 2** magazine catch with a slotted, concave head was made from the remaining inventory of Type 1 magazine catches. They were modi-

Model 1911, M1911A1

fied at the Colt factory by cutting a screwdriver slot in the head. The Type 2 slotted, concave head magazine catch lock also required a slot to be cut in the magazine catch body as the previously made magazine catch bodies lacked the slot. They were installed on pistols from serial #3,189 to *circa* serial #6,500, refer to Figure 2-76, C.

The **Type 3** magazine catch was similar to the Type 1 but the concave head was replaced by a round head with a screwdriver slot. The dismounting technique for the Types 2 and 3 magazine catch was far easier than the Type 1. Press the magazine catch from the left far enough that a screwdriver inserted into the slot in the magazine catch lock will turn counterclockwise until the lock tab is captured in the magazine catch body slot. The assembly can be removed without danger of parts flying everywhere. The Type 3 was used from circa serial #6,501 to the end of production, refer to Figure 2-76, D.

Magazine Catch Housing

The magazine catch housing (refer to Figure 2-76, A1) contained the magazine catch spring and catch lock and held the magazine in place. It was 0.861 inch long and 0.192 inch in its major diameter. The left side ended in a round, checkered button 0.284 inch in diameter. The checkering was composed of rows of four-sided pyramids.

The right side of the housing had a tunnel 0.091 inch in diameter for the magazine catch spring and catch lock. The back end was contoured to match the front contour of the magazine. The following serial number ranges are estimates.

Five types of magazine catch housing were used and are identified by the button release checkering, see Figure 2-78 and Table 2-9. The **Type 1** had eight full diamonds at the widest point of the diameter and was used by Colt and Springfield Armory to circa serial #s 110,000 and 81,750, respectively. The Type 1 magazine catch was blued. Springfield magazine catch housings were marked "S," see Figure 2-79.

Springfield Armory used the **Type 2** magazine catch housing button release with seven horizontal diamonds for their 1915 production, circa serial #s 81,751-120,566 Singer used the Type 2 as well. Some later Springfield

Military and Commercial Pistols

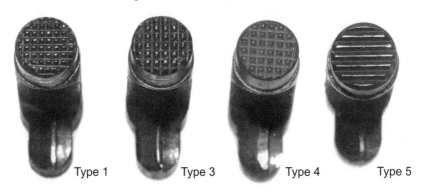

Type 1   Type 3   Type 4   Type 5

Fig. 2-78. Magazine catch housings, l-r: Type 1, eight diamonds; Type 3, six diamonds; Type 4 was Parkerized; and the Type 5 had six grooves.

production (125,567-EOP) had six diamonds. Some observed Colt Model 1911s manufactured in late 1917-1918 have the Type 2 magazine catch housing with seven diamonds. The Type 2 magazine catch was blued except for those made by Singer (Du-Lite finish)

The **Type 3** magazine catch housing button release had six full diamonds diagonally across the widest point of the diameter and was in use by Colt interchangeably with the Type 2 from circa serial #s 110,001-735,000 and by Remington Arms-UMC for all of their production. The Colt magazine catch housings were blued to circa serial #s 734,001-735,000 and Parkerized after; the Remington Arms-UMC were blued.

Fig. 2-79. Springfield Armory-manufactured magazine catch housing marked "S."

The Type 3 magazine catch housing was blued by Colt to circa serial #s 734,001-735,000 (commercial magazine catches were always blued). Early Ithaca (856,405-916,404 1943) and early Remington Rand (916,405-1,041,404) production were Du-Lite finished; after to the end of production, both companies' magazine catch housings were Parkerized. Union Switch & Signal Type 3 magazine catch housings were Du-Lite finished.

The **Type 4** magazine catch housing was similar to the Type 3 but was first Parkerized and later given the Parco-Lubrite finish. The button release had

129

Model 1911, M1911A1

	Table 2-9 Magazine Catch Housing Types		
Type	**Manufacturer**	**Identification**	**Serial Number Range**
1	Colt	8 diamonds, blued	1-110,000 (1)
	Springfield Armory	8 diamonds, blued	72,571-81,750 (2)
2	Springfield Armory	7 diamonds, blued	81,751-120,566 (2)
	Colt	7 diamonds, blued	Some in late 1917, early 1918
	Singer	7 diamonds, Du-Lite	All
3	Colt	6 diamonds: Colt, blued to s/n 734,001-735,000	110,001-735,000
	Springfield		125,567-EOP
	Remington Arms-UMC	6 diamonds, blued	All
	Ithaca	Ithaca; Du-Lite to s/n , Parkerized after. Remington Rand; Du-Lite to US&S; all Du-Lite finished.	All
	Remington Rand		916,405-1,041,404
	US&S		All
4	Colt	6 diamonds, Parkerized to s/n 1,700,000 to 1,710,000, Parco-Lubrite to EOP	734,001-735,001-EOP
	Remington Rand	Parkerized	1,041,405-EOP
5	Colt	6 grooves	Post-World War II commercial production
1. Unslotted s/n 1-3,188; slotted 3,189 to EOP.			
2. Most Springfield Armory magazine catch housings were marked "S."			

six diamonds across its point of widest diameter and was in use at Colt from circa serial #s 734,001-735,001 to the end of production. It was used by both Colt (on military orders only) and Remington Rand.

Military and Commercial Pistols

The **Type 5** magazine catch housing was used on all Colt post-World War II production. The cut diamonds on the button release were replaced with six grooves, refer to Figure 2-78. Its finish matched that of the receiver.

Magazine Catch Spring

The magazine catch spring was a coil spring made of spring steel wire. It was fitted into a tunnel in the magazine catch housing and pressed against a shoulder of the catch lock. It had an outside diameter of 0.149 inch and was 0.7 inch long with 16 coils. Only one type of spring was used during the entire production run, refer to Figure 2-76, A2.

Magazine Catch Lock

The magazine catch lock was 0.51 inch long overall. Its head was 0.154 inch in diameter with a tab extending from the head 0.140 inch long, refer to Figure 2-76, A3. The tab rotated into and out of a slot in the receiver to retain the magazine catch assembly. The right side of the magazine catch lock contained a screw slot or a dimple for takedown. The magazine catch lock and spring fitted inside the magazine catch housing.

Three types of magazine catch locks were used and all were unmarked, see Table 2-10, Magazine Catch Lock.

The **Type 1** had a concave head and was in use from serial #s 1-3,188. It was used only by Colt with the Type 1 magazine catch, refer to Figures 2-76, B and 2-77, Type 1.

The **Type 2** was the Type 1 with a screwdriver slot cut into it and was used from serial #3,189 to circa serial #6,500, refer to Figure 2-76, C. A slot had to be cut into an original housing (pre-serial #3,188) if the Type 2 lock was used.

The **Type 3** had a rounded head and a screwdriver slot. It was used from circa serial #6,501 to the end of production, refer to Figures 2-76, D and 2-77, Type 3. The Type 3 was used by all manufacturers.

Slide Stop

The slide stop was an "L"-shaped pin with a thumb piece and lug attached at a right angle, and which passed through the receiver and the barrel link.

131

Model 1911, M1911A1

Table 2-10 Magazine Catch Assembly Types		
Magazine Catch Lock	**Magazine Catch Spring**	**Magazine Catch Housing**
Type 1-Concave Head, unslotted ca. 1-3,188 Colt Only		Type 1, 8 diamonds Colt, ca. 1-110,000 Springfield Armory, ca. 72,571-81,750
Type 2-Concave Head, Slotted, made from Type 1 magazine catch locks ca. 3,189-6,500 Colt Only	OD=0.149 inch Coils = 16 Nominal Length 0.700 inch	Type 2, 7 diamonds, Springfield Armory, 81,751-120,566. Colt, some late in 1917, early in 1918. All Singer
Type 3-Round Head, Slotted Colt, ca. 6,501-EOP. All other manufacturers, all production		Type 3, 6 diamonds, Colt, ca. 110,001-735,000. All Remington Arms-UMC. All Ithaca. All US&S All Remington Rand
		Type 4, 6 diamonds, Colt, ca. 734,001 to 735,001-EOP. All Remington Rand
		Type 5, 6 grooves. All Colt post-World War II Commercial production

The slide stop had two functions. The first was to lock the slide in the rear position. When the slide was drawn to the rear, the slide stop was either raised by the magazine follower if the magazine was empty, or it could be raised by the operator by pushing up on the thumb piece. Either way, the lug on the other side of the thumb piece entered the slide stop notch on the left side to hold the slide open. Pushing down on the thumb piece disengaged the lug and allowed the recoil spring to push the slide forward into battery.

The second function was to secure the barrel to the receiver via the link. The cross-pin of the slide stop serves as an axle on which the barrel/link rotates through a short arc to lock and unlock the barrel in the slide.

Military and Commercial Pistols

The slide stop was 0.344 inch wide (widest point) and 1.356 inches long. Its pin was 0.867 inch long. The thumb piece was checkered in a raised diamond pattern on all M1911s and M1911A1s until 1944 when they were replaced by grooves. The lug on the inside rear of the thumb piece was 0.197 inch long by 0.204 inch wide and 0.236 inch high. A channel 0.085 inch wide by 0.075 inch deep was cut into the top of the lug, which allowed it to slide into the dismount notch on the left side of the slide. Slide stops for U.S. Army Ordnance Department contracts were not manufactured by subcontractors. See Table 2-11 for slide stop use by serial number range by manufacturer.

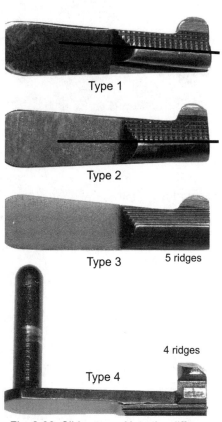

Four types of slide stop were used. The **Type 1** slide stop can be identified by the fact that the lines of checkering were parallel with the top of the slide stop arm. The Type 1 was manufactured by Colt, Springfield Armory, and Remington Arms-UMC, see Figure 2-80.

The **1st Variation** slide stop was manufactured by Colt and the thumb piece was checkered, which formed fourteen diamonds along its lower edge. It was used from the start of production to the end of Model 1911 production, by Colt, circa serial #s 700,001-710,000.

Fig. 2-80. Slide stops. Note the difference in orientation of the line of checkering between the Type 1 and Type 2. In the Types 3 and 4, the checkering was replaced by 5 and 4 parallel ridges, respectively.

Remington Arms-UMC also used the Type 1, 1st Variation with fourteen rows of diamonds along its lower edge throughout its production run.

Model 1911, M1911A1

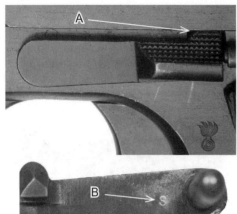

The Type 1, **2nd Variation** slide stop was manufactured by Springfield Armory; the thumb piece checkering had twelve diamonds on its lower edge. The checkering goes to the top of the tab on the Springfield slide stops, see Figure 2-81, A. Most Springfield-manufactured slide stops were marked on the interior surface with the letter "S." Refer to Figure 2-81, B.

Fig. 2-81. Springfield Armory Type 1 slide stops were checkered to the top of the tab (arrow A) and marked "S" (arrow B).

The **Type 2** slide stop was designed for easier manipulation. The thumb piece was angled upward so that the checkering was no longer parallel with the top of the arm. The Type 2 was used by Colt from circa serial #s 700,001-710,000-1,668,999, refer to Figure 2-80. The checkering formed fourteen diamonds along the lower edge. See Table 2-11 for the serial number ranges by manufacturer.

The **Type 3** slide stop was similar to the Type 2 except that five parallel grooves replaced the checkering on the thumb piece at circa serial # 1,669,000, refer to Figure 2-80, Type 3.

The **Type 4** slide stop was used on all postwar commercial Colt Model 1911A1s. It had four parallel ridges on the thumb piece, refer to Figure 2-80.

Table 2-11				
Slide Stop Types				
Manufacturer	**Type 1**	**Type 2**	**Type 3**	**Type 4**
Colt, Military	All M1911s (1st Variation)	ca. 700,001-ca. 1,668,999	ca. 1,669,000-EOP	
Remington Arms-UMC	All production, 1st Variation			

134

Military and Commercial Pistols

Table 2-11, cont. Slide Stop Types				
Manufacturer	**Type 1**	**Type 2**	**Type 3**	**Type 4**
Springfield Armory	All (2nd Variation)			
Colt, Commercial	C1-ca. C120,999 (1st Variation)	ca. C120,999-C220,001	C220,001-EOP (Intermittent)	
Singer		All production		
Ithaca		856,405-ca. 900,000	ca. 900,001-EOP	
Remington Rand		916,405-ca. 930,000	ca. 930,000-EOP	
Union Switch & Signal		All production		
Colt				Post-WWII commercial production (Intermittent with Type 3)

Recoil Spring Shroud

The recoil spring shroud (dust cover) is the forward portion of the receiver which is shaped like a trough. It serves to protect the recoil spring assembly in the slide, see Figure 2-82.

Three types of recoil spring shroud have been observed. The downward curve on the scallop at the end of the **Type 1** recoil spring shroud has a 50-degree radius curve.

Fig. 2-82. Recoil Spring Shroud.

135

Model 1911, M1911A1

The **Type 2** recoil spring shroud is observed on Springfield Armory-manufactured Model 1911 receivers. The rear curve of the housing was much sharper than on Colt or other Model 1911 or Model 1911A1 receivers. The radius of the curve on the scallop at the end of the recoil spring shroud was 55 degrees. In Figure 2-83, the Type 1 and Type 2 recoil spring shrouds have been photographed to allow a direct comparison of the rear curve.

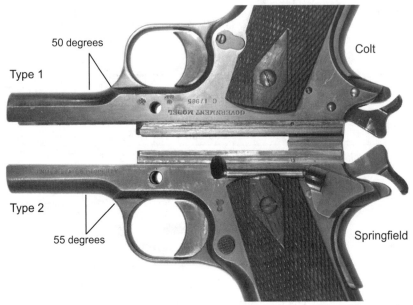

Fig. 2-83. Type 1 and Type 2 recoil spring housings compared. The difference in the radius of the curve at the end of the recoil spring housing is subtle but real.

At serial circa #s 275,000-285,000, the **Type 3** recoil spring shroud on the Colt receiver was lengthened by 0.031 inch to 2.631 inch. The change was made to eliminate a gap that sometimes developed between the end of the recoil spring shroud on the receiver and the recoil spring tube on the slide which allowed the entry of dirt and grit. This gave the scallop a 20-degree radius curve, see Figure 2-84.

The Type 3 recoil spring shroud was used on military Model 1911 and 1911A1 pistols by Colt starting at circa serial #s 275,000-285,000 through the end of production and on commercial Government Model

Military and Commercial Pistols

pistols at circa serial #s C99,001 to the end of production, and by Remington Arms-UMC. Singer, Ithaca, Remington Rand and US&S all used the Type 3 recoil spring shroud as well.

Walnut Stocks, Truncated Diamond Pattern

The stocks (also referred to as grip panels) for the Model 1911 and Model 1911A1 average 1.25 inches wide at the top, 1.50 inches wide at the bottom and 4.055 inches long.

The original stocks designed for the Model 1911 were made of American black walnut. They were checkered to improve friction between the stock and the hand. The stocks had a re-

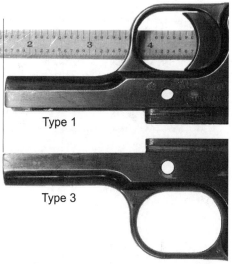

Type 1

Type 3

Fig. 2-84. Type 1 and Type 3 recoil spring housings compared. Note the slight additional length of the Type 3.

inforcement in the shape of a large, truncated diamond around the top and bottom screw holes. The term "truncated" is used as the top (or bottom) of the diamond was cut off parallel to the top or bottom of the stock.

The truncated diamond pattern stock was manufactured by Colt, Springfield Armory and Remington Arms-UMC, see Figure 2-85. This pattern stock was used by Colt to circa serial #s 700,001 (C130,000), the start of the so-called "transition model." Springfield Armory and Remington Arms-UMC used the diamond stock during their entire production run.

NOTE: As with the mainspring housing knurling, the system of counting diamonds to identify a manufacturer may be inaccurate. Measurement using a thread gage may provide more reproducible results. Unfortunately, reproduction stocks can, and often are, made with identical checkering, and so a combination of methods may be the best solution, coupled with a study of wood grain, orientation, delicacy of cuts, etc. As with the mainspring housing, both methods and results are included here.

137

Model 1911, M1911A1

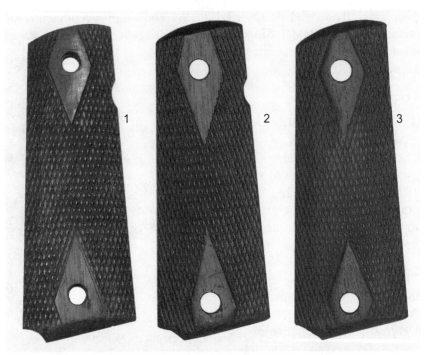

Fig. 2-85. Walnut stocks, truncated diamond pattern, were installed on Model 1911s made by Colt (1), Springfield Armory (2), and Remington Arms-UMC (3).

Colt stocks were cut with 14 diamonds per inch. All appear machine cut and as such are very consistent. **Remington Arms-UMC** stocks were cut with 13 to 13.5 diamonds per inch. The evenness of the lines was not as consistent as Colt. **Springfield** stocks had finer checkering and 15 diamonds per inch. This suggests that stocks can be identified to their manufacturer—or as a good counterfeit.

To identify stocks by manufacturer, begin by measuring the size of the large diamonds (if any) and confirm by counting the small diamonds. Count the full diamonds in the horizontal row immediately above the lower truncated diamond's point. To further check, count the rows of diamonds top and bottom as they alternate left and right in a straight line.

Exercise caution in your measurements and compare samples to known originals whenever possible.

Military and Commercial Pistols

Walnut Stocks, Truncated Diamond Pattern, Colt

Colt walnut stocks, with the large truncated diamonds at the stock screw holes, were used from start of production to circa serial #700,001 (start of the "transition" models) and had 14 diamonds per inch (thread gage measurement). The top and bottom large diamonds averaged 0.62 inch wide and 1.28 inches high measured in the longest dimension through the screw hole. The Colt-manufactured stocks had twenty full, raised diamonds across their width. There were either fourteen to sixteen full rows of diamonds in the vertical row between the top and bottom points of the large diamond which were 1.42 or 1.55 inches apart, respectively. The collector should keep in mind that each stock was held in a fixture and the pattern cut with a knurling tool. Slight variances can be expected in the number of small diamonds between the large truncated diamonds. See Figure 2-86.

Colt pistols sold to the government of Argentina before circa serial #C120,000, including the Argentine Navy (Marina Argentina, C86,000-C120,000) wore the truncated diamond pattern walnut stocks.

Walnut Stocks, Truncated Diamond Pattern, Springfield Armory

Springfield Armory–manufactured walnut stocks also had a truncated diamond pattern with 15 diamonds per inch (thread gage). The top diamond averaged 0.66 inch wide and 1.66 inches long while the bottom diamond averaged 0.65 inch wide and 1.30 inches long when measured from the top or bottom of the diamond through the screw hole, see Figure 2-87. Post-WWII Springfield stocks for National Match pistols were also cut with 15 diamonds per inch but without the truncated diamonds.

The Springfield-manufactured stocks were twenty-one diamonds wide above the lower truncated diamond's point with ten to eleven diamonds vertically between the truncated diamonds which were 1.0 to 1.1 inches apart.

Walnut Stocks, Truncated Diamond Pattern, Remington Arms-UMC

The top truncated diamond on Remington Arms-UMC–manufactured stocks averaged 0.59 inch wide and 1.26 inches long from the top to bottom of the diamond through the screw hole. The bottom truncated diamond was 0.57 inch wide, 1.08 inches long and 1.30 inches apart.

Model 1911, M1911A1

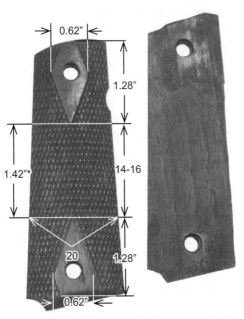

Fig. 2-86. Walnut stocks, truncated diamond pattern — Colt. 14 diamonds/inch.

* Dimension is 1.42" if 15 small diamonds, or 1.55" if 16 small diamonds.

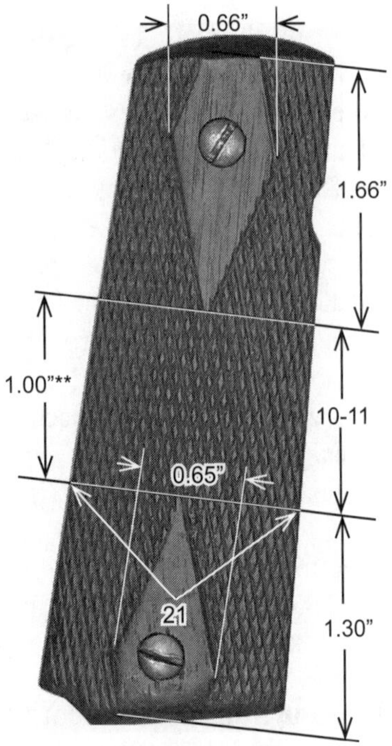

Fig. 2-87. Walnut stocks, truncated diamond pattern — Springfield Armory, 15 diamonds/inch.

** Dimension is 1.00" if 10 small diamonds, or 1.10" if 16 small diamonds.

Fig. 2-88. Walnut stocks, truncated diamond pattern — Remington Arms-UMC, 15 to 15.5 diamonds/inch.

NOTE: There may be a slight difference in dimensions between left and right stocks.

All dimensions are ± 0.02 inch.

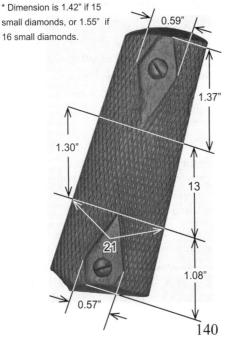

140

Military and Commercial Pistols

The stocks had fifteen to fifteen and one-half diamond points per inch or thirteen rows of diamond points in a vertical row between the upper and lower truncated diamonds, see Figure 2-88.

Table 2-12 Truncated Diamond Stocks (inch)					
Manufact-urer	Diamond Dimensions (averages–inches)		Horizontal Count	Vertical Count	Diamonds per inch
	Top	Bottom			
Colt	0.62 x 1.28	0.62 x 1.28	20	14-16	14
Springfield Armory	0.66 x 1.66	0.65 x 1.30	21	10-11	15
Remington Arms-UMC	0.59 x 1.37	0.57x1.08	21	13	15-15.5

WALNUT STOCKS, PLAIN

Walnut Stocks, Plain, Colt Manufacture
Only Colt manufactured walnut stocks (also called "plain" or "full check-ered" walnut stocks) without the truncated raised diamonds reinforcing the screw holes. The new pattern came into use on civilian models in late 1923 at circa serial #C130,000. The first full checkered walnut stocks installed on the U.S. Army pistols occurred in the 1924 contract at serial #'s 700,001-710,000, the first of the post-World War I contract purchases.

Originals of Colt manufacture can be identified by the fact that they have 14 diamonds per inch or 20 diamonds in the row immediately above the lower screw hole and 30 diamonds in a vertical line between the top and bottom screw hole, see Figure 2-89. Collectors should exercise caution as many aftermarket copies as well as reproduction plain checkered walnut stocks were sold in the post-World War I period to the present. Many were close copies.

Walnut Stocks, Plain, Argentina
After 1925, all pistols manufactured by and shipped from Colt to Argentina, other than for sales to the Argentine Army, were equipped with commercial plain checkered walnut stocks with 14 diamonds per inch. These are found in the range circa serial #s C150,000-C178,000.

141

Model 1911, M1911A1

Fig. 2-89. Walnut stocks, plain checkered, as manufactured only by Colt. They have 14 diamonds per inch.

Fig. 2-90. Stocks for Model 1911A1s manufactured by FMAP in Argentina were made in two types. Shown here are Type 1 stocks which can be distinguished by their flat interiors.

Fig. 2-91. Type 2 FMAP-manufactured stocks have a hollowed interior. All Argentine grips for the Model 1927 have 14 diamonds per inch.

Military and Commercial Pistols

In 1927, the Argentine Army (*Ejercito Argentino*) signed a contract with Colt to purchase 10,000 Model 1911A1 pistols. They were to be manufactured at the Colt facility in Hartford, Connecticut. These were equipped with commercial plain checkered walnut stocks. These pistols were from the commercial series and were numbered in their own serial number range from 1 to 10,000. The serial number was stamped on top of the slide, under the mainspring housing, and on top of the barrel, but not on the right side of the receiver.

The second batch of ten thousand Model 1911A1s were manufactured and assembled in Argentina and were equipped with black hard rubber stocks that were very similar to the Colt plain checkered walnut stocks. A raised diamond pattern was used with 14 per inch. The horizontal row immediately above the lower stock screw hole had nineteen diamonds. There were thirty-eight rows of diamonds between the two stock screw holes.

NOTE: Some of the first Argentine-made pistols were equipped with walnut stocks, before hard rubber stocks became available.

Two types of black hard rubber stocks were manufactured by FMAP; the **Type 1** hard rubber stock was solid on the interior and formed a flat surface. A thin reinforcing ring encircled the screw hole, see Figure 2-90.

The **Type 2** black hard rubber stock panel interior surface had a hollow space in the shape of a rectangle with rounded ends on the inside. They also had a reinforcing ring around the screw hole, see Figure 2-91.

Walnut Stocks, Great Britain

All Model 1911 and Model 1911A1 pistols purchased by the British government for their military forces, or which were imported for sale, were equipped with the type of stocks appropriate to their manufacture date as determined by the serial number.

No Model 1911 or Model 1911A1 pistols were ever manufactured in Great Britain.

Model 1911, M1911A1

Walnut Stocks, Norway

Norwegian Model 1912 and Model 1914 pistols, whether manufactured in the United States by Colt or in Norway by Kongsberg Vapenfabrik, were issued with the commercial pattern walnut stocks with the truncated diamond reinforcing the screw hole. Colt-manufactured walnut stocks with the truncated diamond had twenty diamonds in the horizontal row immediately above the lower stock screw hole and fourteen diamonds between the upper and lower stock screw holes.

Norwegian-manufactured walnut stocks were made of birch, which is lighter and finer grained than American black walnut. Norwegian stocks were painted black through 1941-42, and originally had a fine checkering pattern with small truncated diamonds (top: 0.61 x 1.35 inch; bottom 0.60 x 1.25 inch) around the stock screws. The truncated diamonds on stocks made after 1924 vary slightly in dimensions. Dimensions are averages from seven samples. Norwegian-made stocks were painted black using a water-based stain and so appear dark, even when worn. Early Norwegian-manufactured stocks had nineteen diamonds in the horizontal row immediately above the lower stock screw hole; later stocks had 22 diamonds.

Fig. 2-92. The left stock panel for the Norwegian Model 1914 pistol had a semicircular cut in the top, left edge for the extended slide stop.

The Norwegian Model 1914 pistol after serial #900 had a recess cut into the top left corner (nearest the muzzle) of the left stock panel to accommodate the extended slide stop installed on that pistol, see Figure 2-92, arrow.

Walnut Stocks, Russia

Like all other components of the 51,000 finished Model 1911 pistols purchased by Russia through a purchasing commission called the "Russian Government Committee In London," the stocks were standard Colt commercial walnut stocks with the truncated diamond reinforcement about the screw holes.

Military and Commercial Pistols

Other Stocks

Over the past century, the Model 1911 and Model 1911A1 were manufactured or remanufactured in a number of countries, usually without the formality of licensing from Colt. Unknown numbers of pistols were manufactured in China between the two World Wars, and underground in the Philippines during World War II, and in North Vietnam during the 1950s and 1960s. Most were equipped with wooden stocks made from a variety of woods and it is impossible to qualify them further.

PLASTIC STOCKS
Plastic Stocks, Colt

As the inevitable American entry into World War II drew nearer, surveys of raw materials that would be needed for the war effort revealed potential shortages in several materials, one of which was American black walnut. After World War I, walnut had replaced mahogany and oak as a popular wood for furniture. The art deco furniture designs of the period used immense quantities of the wood. Native groves of American black walnut which had long been considered the ideal source for gun stocks had, by the mid-1930s, been thinned considerably. Projections of the amount of walnut wood needed for rifle stocks and pistol stocks to equip a military force large enough to fight a two-front war raised concern in the Ordnance Department.

As the price of walnut had risen, Colt had been experimenting with various plastics for both gunstocks and pistol stock panels. The first Colt design drawings were approved on January 15, 1936, at the Rock Island Arsenal. The stock panels were to be made of a phenolic resin designated Type CFI-20, Color No. 20045, 20059 or 20062, a semigloss brown. They were originally assigned the part numbers C5564062 and C5564063.

By 1939, Colt felt they had perfected a proprietary phenolic resin they called Coltrock. Stock panels made from Coltrock were approved in November 1939 and were installed intermittently on some of the Model 1911A1s starting at circa serial #718,000. Coltrock was manufactured in a molding process by impregnating cloth with resin and was reddish-brown in color. All Colt stocks had 14 diamonds per inch.

NOTE: There will be minor variations in measurements among plastic stock panels due to small dimensional differences among various molds.

Model 1911, M1911A1

The **Type 1** Coltrock stocks had twenty-five diamonds between upper and lower screw holes. All had concave reinforcing rings 0.05 inch wide, see Figure 2-93.

The early Coltrock stocks cracked easily and additional cloth fiber was added in an effort to strengthen the panel and reduce its brittleness. This additional cloth fiber is sometimes visible on the inside surface. Mold numbers may have been added on the interior surface about this time. It is thought they were only used intermittently on military contract pistols from circa serial #s 718,000-728,000 along with the standard issue plain checkered walnut stocks.

Even so, the Coltrock stocks proved to be too brittle for service. In March 1941 at circa serial #728,001, a new stock made from an improved formula called Coltwood was introduced.

Coltwood stocks proved more durable and became the standard plastic resin used on military Model 1911A1s to the end of World War II. Coltwood stocks can be identified by their dark brown color and by a mold mark, usually a single digit, on the interior surface. Molds were updated during manufacturing. It is likely that the same molds used for the Coltrock stocks were used to make Coltwood stocks.

Three variations of the **Type 2** Coltwood stocks were manufactured and are easily identified.

The **1st Variation** Coltwood stock had no strengthening ribs on the interior. The reinforcing rings around the screw holes were slightly concave and 0.05 inch wide. There were twenty-five diamonds in a vertical line between the two stock screws. They were in intermittent use from circa serial #728,001 to circa #795,000.

A small number of **2nd Variation** Coltwood stocks without strengthening ribs on the interior and with flat reinforcing rings (0.070 inch wide) around the screw holes were made starting sometime before circa serial #795,001 and used intermittently to about circa serial #845,000. There were twenty-five diamonds between the two stock screws.

Military and Commercial Pistols

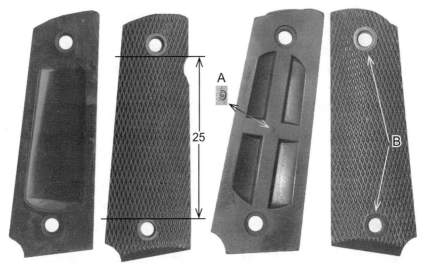

Fig. 2-93. Coltrock (plastic) Type 1 stocks (above) can be identified by their reddish brown color, hollow interior with rounded end, and 14 diamonds per inch. Coltrock stocks had a reinforcing ring around the screw hole.

Fig. 2-94. Coltwood Type 2, 3rd Variation stocks (above) have reinforcing ribs on the interior, 14 diamonds per inch, and will show a mold mark (arrow A). They also have a reinforcing rim 0.07 inch wide around the screw holes (arrows B).

Coltwood Type 2, 3rd Variation

Keyes Fibre Type 3, 2nd Variation

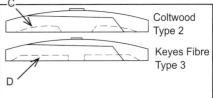

Coltwood Type 2

Keyes Fibre Type 3

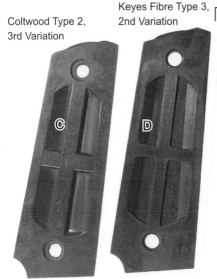

Fig. 2-95. The Coltwood Type 2 stock panel, 3rd Variation (left) compared to the Keyes Fibre Co. Type 3, 2nd Variation stock panel (right). Notice the difference in rib thickness and the stepped hollows in the Keyes stock panel (D) vs. the sloping sides of the Coltwood stock panel hollows (C). Colt stocks have 14 diamonds per inch, Keyes stocks have 16 . The inset shows cross-section drawings of the same Coltwood and Keyes Fibre stock panels. See also Fig. 2-96.

Model 1911, M1911A1

The **3rd Variation** Coltwood stock was improved by the addition of a cross-shaped reinforcing rib on the interior surface of the stock. The flat reinforcing ring around each screw hole remained 0.07 inch wide. The larger reinforcing rings reduced the number of diamonds between the screw holes to twenty-four. Measurements of several samples showed that the flat of the vertical reinforcing rib averaged 0.265 inch across and the flat of the horizontal rib 0.245 inch across. The rims of the reinforcing ring averaged 0.075 inch wide, see Figure 2-94. They were used from circa serial #795,001, overlapping the 2nd Variation, to the end of production.

Both Coltrock and Coltwood stocks reproduced the diamond pattern of the plain walnut stocks. Both types of stock were produced in-house by Colt's Plastic Division.

Plastic Stocks, Remington Arms-UMC

As point of interest, in early February 1918 as Remington Arms-UMC found they were short the machines required to produced the checkered wood panels. They were given permission to produce checkered stock panels of Bakelite. Bakelite was an early phenolic resin made from formaldehyde, carbolic acid and wood pulp. It was invented by Dr. Leo Baekeland and patented in 1910. The Ordnance Department allowed the use of Bakelite stocks only until the proper machinery for producing the walnut stock panels could be procured. The machinery was found and the Bakelite stocks were never installed on Remington Arms-UMC Model 1911s accepted by the Ordnance Department.

NOTE: Bakelite stock panels were tested again in 1932-1933, found satisfactory and approved as a substitute standard on November 16, 1933. But again, the Bakelite stock panels were never used. Bakelite is a very brittle plastic and would probably have proven unsatisfactory if actually used in production.

Plastic Stock Panels, Remington Rand, Ithaca, and Union Switch and Signal

The **Type 3** stock panel was used for all production by Remington Rand, Ithaca, and Union Switch & Signal for their Model 1911A1 pistols. They were manufactured for all three companies by Keyes Fibre Co., located in New York City. The stock panels were made of a plastic composi-

Military and Commercial Pistols

tion that was very similar to that used by Colt but was a darker brown in color. The Keyes stock panels were made with 16 diamonds per inch (thirty rows of diamonds between the upper and lower screw hole reinforcing rings).

The shape of the cross-shaped reinforcing ribs on the interior surface of the Keyes Fibre stock panels (described below) differs from that of the Colt Type 3 stock panel, refer to Figure 2-95. In the Colt Type 2, the reinforcing ribs slant outward from the top of the rib to the base (arrow C) and then curve upward again to the sides. In the Keyes Fibre Type 3 design, the ribs have square sides and there is a flat or step in the area between the rib (arrow D) and where the plastic slants upward to the edges.

The reinforcing rings around the screw holes on the Keyes Fibre stock panels were 0.054 inch wide. The company's model mark, "K" within a five-pointed star, plus a mold mark or numbers such as 9, 10, 11, 12, 21, 22, 27, 28, were molded into the lower quadrant, see Figure 2-96.

Three variations of the Type 3 stock panel were manufactured. The **1st Variation** did not have a reinforcing ring around the screw holes.

The **2nd Variation** had reinforcing rings around the screw holes with rims 0.054 inch wide. The company's model mark, "K" within a five-pointed star, was molded into the lower quadrant at the 5 o'clock position.

Fig. 2-96. Type 3, 2nd Variation Keyes Fibre Co.-manufactured stocks show the Keyes logotype—"K" within a five-pointed star.

The **3rd Variation** stock panels are distinguished by the Department of the Army part number (5564062 and 5564063), left and right (respectively) molded into the upper quadrant at the 1 o'clock position. These were manufactured after World War II as replacement stocks, see Figure 2-97.

Model 1911, M1911A1

Plastic Stocks, Singer

Stocks for Singer pistols were subcontracted to Keyes Fibre Company and were the approved Model 1911A1 stocks with a checkered surface but made of a phenolic resin. The author has chosen to refer to these as the **Type 4** plastic stock. Singer stocks had sixteen diamonds per

Fig. 2-97. Plastic stock panels showing the part numbers 5564062 or 5564063 are post-World War II replacement stocks.

inch. There were thirty rows of diamonds between the top and bottom unreinforced screw holes. One other distinguishing feature of the Singer stocks is found on the interior. The lightening recess was 0.8 inch wide at the top, 1.0 inch wide at the bottom and 2.57 inches long. The recess was hollow, that is, without any reinforcing ridges. See Figure 2-98.

NOTE: Counterfeit Singer stocks have been made from Keyes Fibre Co. Type 3, 1st Variation stocks by removing the reinforcing rings and ribs and polishing the interior. Examine the lightening hollow carefully for signs of tool work.

Fig. 2-98. Singer stocks were manufactured by Keyes Fibre Company. Look carefully with a magnifying glass for tool and polishing marks to identify counterfeit Singer stocks.

The **Type 5** stock was made for the Commander series in four variations. The **1st Variation** was made of plastic with the Colt logotype molded in, see Figure 2-99. The stocks were chocolate brown in color and the interior was hollowed without reinforcing ribs, very much like the Singer stocks. The narrow reinforcing rings around the screw holes were 0.03 to 0.04 inch in diameter. The checkered surface had fourteen diamonds running horizontally immediately above the bottom stock screw hole and thirteen diamonds between the Colt logo and the bottom stock screw hole. See Table 2-13 for plastic and wood stock types and variations.

Military and Commercial Pistols

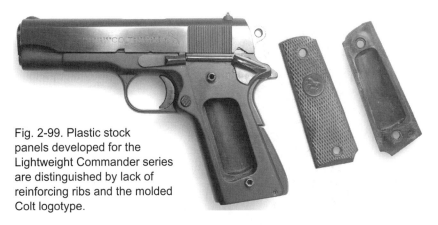

Fig. 2-99. Plastic stock panels developed for the Lightweight Commander series are distinguished by lack of reinforcing ribs and the molded Colt logotype.

Colt Commanders in the 70 series (**2nd Variation**) were produced with non-checkered wood stocks with the Colt logo medallion inset. Series 80 Commanders (**3rd Variation**) were furnished with plastic, checkered stocks. Late Series 80 and Series 91 stocks (**4th Variation**) used the truncated diamond pattern. All have 14 diamonds per inch.

Fig. 2-100. Polyester-impregnated wood stocks have been used on Series 70/80 and some current-production Colt Government Model pistols as standard.

NOTE: Collectors should be careful when removing the early post-World War II plastic stocks. They tend to shrink with age and crack above and below the screw holes.

Commercial Stocks

The **Type 6** stock used as standard on all Colt commercial Model 1911A1s in the Series 70 and 80 is a polyester-impregnated checkered stock with a gold-colored plastic medallion, see Figure 2-100.

The **Type 7** stock is in current use. It is a copy of the original truncated diamond stock used on

Model 1911, M1911A1

Fig. 2-101. The current Colt 1911 Replica Series stock panels are copies of the original truncated diamond stocks. John Domoslai collection.

the Colt Model 1911 and the 1918 replicas of the original Model 1911, see Figure 2-101. In most instances, the wood has a reddish oil finish. It has 14 diamonds per inch, 12 diamonds in a vertical line between the top and bottom truncated diamonds and alternating rows of 18 and 19 nineteen across. The diamonds are evenly cut with a laser where original stocks were cut by a rotary cutter and are not quite as even.

NOTE: Stocks for the Government Model are also available in Rosewood, Ebony, Walnut, Ivory, and Mother-of-Pearl from the Colt Custom Shop. Rubber stocks are also available in a variety of styles. See www.coltsmfg.com.

Stock Screw/Bushing Assembly
Stock Screw Bushing
Four stock screw bushings were threaded into the receiver's grip area, two on either side, to hold the stocks in place. The stock screw bushing provided the extra length necessary for the stock screws to hold the stocks securely in the receiver.

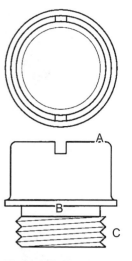

Fig. 2-102. Two types of stock screw bushings were used. At s/n 3,000, the screw head was thickened to prevent burring.

152

Military and Commercial Pistols

Used By	Type	Variation	Characteristics (1)
		Table 2-13	
		Plastic and Wood Stocks, Model 1911/1911A1	
Colt	1	1 718001-728000	Coltrock: reddish-brown, hollow interior, concave reinforcing rings–0.05 in. wide, 14 diamonds/inch, 25 diamonds between screw holes. More cloth fiber added later, 14 diamonds/inch, 25 diamonds between screw holes
	2	1 728001-795000	Coltwood: brown, hollow interior, concave reinforcing rings–0.05 in. wide, mold numbers, 14 diamonds/inch, 25 diamonds between screw holes
		2 795001-845000	Coltwood: brown, no strengthening ribs, flat reinforcing rings–0.07 in. wide, mold numbers, 14 diamonds/inch, 25 diamonds between screw holes. Used intermittently
		3 795,001-EOP	Coltwood: strengthening ribs, flat reinforcing rings–0.07 in. wide, mold numbers, 14 diamonds/inch, 24 diamonds between screw holes
Ithaca	3	1 All production	Dark brown: no reinforcing ring, "K" in 5-pointed star logo, 16 diamonds/inch. 30 diamonds between screw holes. Keyes Fibre Co.
Remington Rand		2 All production	Dark brown: flat reinforcing ring 0.054 in. wide, "K" in 5-pointed star logo, 16 diamonds/inch. 30 diamonds between screw holes. Keyes Fibre Co.
US&S		3	As above but with mold marks 5564062 (left), 5564063 (right). 16 diamonds/inch. 30 diamonds between screw holes. Keyes Fibre Co. Post-WWII
Singer All Production	4		Brown: made by Keyes Fibre Co., no reinforcing rings, 16 diamonds/inch, 30 diamonds between screw holes, hollow lightening recess

153

Model 1911, M1911A1

Table 2-13, cont.
Plastic and Wood Stocks, Model 1911/1911A1

Used By	Type	Variation	Characteristics (1)
Colt	5	1 1950-1970	Chocolate brown: Colt logotype molded into stock, no reinforcing ribs, 0.03–0.04 inch wide flat reinforcing rings, 14 diamonds/inch, 13 diamonds between Colt logo and screw hole
		2 1970 Series (2)	Varnished wood, inset Colt medallion, 14 diamonds/inch
		3 Early 1980 Series	Plastic, checkered, no medallion, 14 diamonds/inch
		4 Late 1980, 1991A1 Series	Plastic, truncated diamond pattern, 14 diamonds/inch
Colt	6		Polyester-impregnated checkered stocks, gold-colored logotype, 14 diamonds/inch (2)
Colt	7		Reddish oil finished wood: copy of original truncated diamond stock, 14 diamonds/inch (2)

1. Both diamonds per inch and diamonds between screw holes or logo are included.
2. Although these stocks are wood, they are included here for chronological reasons.

The bushing (Figure 2-102) had three sections: A) the top which was threaded internally for the stock screw, B) the base ring which bottomed against the receiver to prevent the bushing from being screwed too far into the receiver, and C) the bottom which was threaded externally to screw into the receiver. The diameter of each part was: top, 0.235 inch; base ring, 0.282 inch; and bottom, 0.230 inch. The interior of the bushing was threaded .1500-50 NS-2 for the stock screw. The exterior was threaded .236-60 NS-2 to thread into the receiver.

Two types of stock screw bushings were used. The **Type 1** was 0.300 inch long overall. The top section was 0.148 inch long. The base ring was 0.05 inch thick and the bottom was 0.102 inch long. The Type 1 stock screw bushing was in use from the start of production to circa serial #2,999.

Military and Commercial Pistols

At circa serial #3,000 to the end of production, the **Type 2** stock screw head was thickened to allow a deeper slot in the stock screw bushing to prevent burring. The overall length of the stock screw bushing was shortened to 0.279 inch to prevent the stock screw head from protruding too far past the stock. The base ring and bottom section measurements were unchanged.

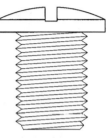

Stock Screws
The stock screws secured the stocks to the receiver, see Figure 2-103. The stock screw was 0.355 inch long overall. The screw heads were slotted for a flat head screwdriver. Two types of stock screws were used and the shanks were threaded .1500-50 NS-2.

Fig. 2-103. The stock screw head was thickened at s/n 3,000 and the shank was shortened.

From serial #1 to circa serial #2,999 the **Type 1** stock screw head was 0.275 inch in diameter and 0.08 thick. The shank was 0.280 inch long. The screwdriver slot in the thin head was easily deformed; a change was approved in March 1912 to make the head thicker and the slot deeper.

The **Type 2** stock screw head was made thicker (0.10 inch) to deepen the screwdriver slot. The bushing was shortened by 0.02 inch to prevent the screw heads from protruding against the shooter's hand. To prevent the shank from protruding into the magazine well, it was shortened to 0.255 inch. The Type 2 stock screw was used from circa serial #3,000-EOP.

Colt stock screws through circa serial #2,400 were "fire blued" to a bright, iridescent color, sometimes called "peacock blue." After circa serial #s 2,401 to circa 734,000, stock screws were not as highly polished and were a dull blue. Starting at circa serial #s 734,001-735,001 to 1,700,000-1,710,000 they were Parkerized. After, to the end of production, they received the Parco-Lubrite finish.

All Ithaca and Remington Rand stock screws were Du-Lite finished to circa 1,208,674 (Ithaca) and 1,015,001 (Remington Rand). They were Parkerized thereafter. Singer stock screws were Du-Lite finished. US&S stock screws were lightly sandblasted before Du-Lite finishing. Singer stock screws were polished without sandblasting and so appear bright.

CHAPTER 3
SLIDE, PART BY PART

John Browning's design for the Model 1911 pistol encompassed three main assemblies: receiver with trigger mechanism and receptacle for the magazine; the slide with firing pin and barrel, and the magazine.

The Model 1911/1911A1 slide houses the barrel, firing pin, and front and rear sight assemblies. Figure 3-1 shows the slide and its component parts: 1) Barrel bushing seat, 2) breech face, 3) ejection port, 4) center slide rail, 5) disconnector cam timing recess, 6) extractor passage, 7) firing pin port, 8) firing pin retainer plate or stop, 9) firing pin retainer plate guide, 10) hammer recess, 11) safety catch notch, 12) front sight and seat, 13) rear sight and dovetail, 14) recoil spring housing, 15) slide dismount cut, 16) slide locking lugs, 17) slide rails, 18) slide stop detent, 19) barrel, 20) link, 21) link pin, 22) barrel bushing, 23) recoil spring plug, 24) recoil spring, 25) recoil spring guide, 26) firing pin, 27) firing pin spring, 28) extractor, and 29) slide.

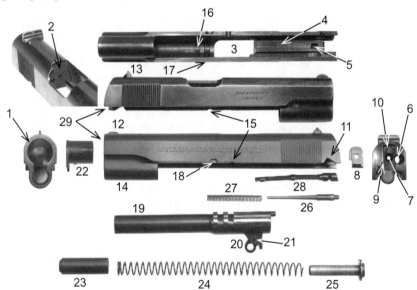

Fig. 3-1. The Model 1911 and 1911A1 slides and their component parts and areas.

156

Military and Commercial Pistols

SLIDE, PHYSICAL DESCRIPTION

The Model 1911 or 1911A1 slide is 0.903 inch wide by 7.4 inches long by 1.0 inch high (not including the recoil spring housing), and 1.425 inches high when the recoil spring housing is included, see Figure 3-2.

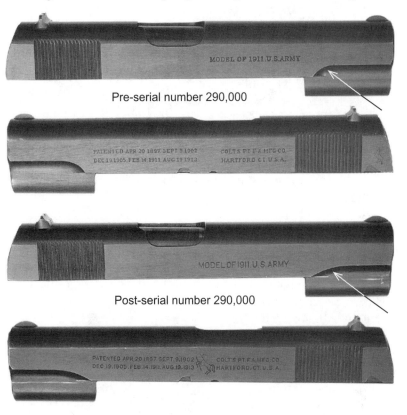

Pre-serial number 290,000

Post-serial number 290,000

Fig. 3-2 . Right and left views of the Model 1911 and Model 1911A1 slides.

Beginning at the front, the recoil spring housing is nominally 0.640 inch wide and 1.698 inches long (in fact, actual measurements show that the recoil spring housing can vary from 1.685 to 1.710 inches long).

NOTE: The arc of the recoil spring housing was extended at circa serial #290,000, refer to Figure 3-2, arrows.

Model 1911, M1911A1

Fig. 3-3. The front sight is mounted in a slot cut in the top of the slide.

The front sight is mounted in a slot at the top along the center line of the slide, see Figure 3-3. On M1911 pistols, a round hole was drilled through the slot for the stem on the bottom of the front sight. The stem was upset against the underside of the slide to hold it in place. The slot was 0.056 inch wide by 0.315 inch long. On the Model 1911A1, starting at serial number 700,001, the hole was made rectangular (0.56 inch wide by 0.124 inch long). The center point of the sight mounting cut was 0.205 inch behind the muzzle face of the slide.

The front sight on the Springfield Armory slide was machined from the slide stock, rather than added as a separate piece.

The rear sight was mounted in a dovetail 0.650 inch ahead of the rear of the slide, see Figure 3-4. The dovetail was 0.346 inch long and 0.115 inch deep. The rear sight dovetail and corresponding sight dovetail tapered from right to left and therefore, the rear sight must be installed from the right and removed by using a punch to push it out from the left to the right.

Fig. 3-4. The rear sight was mounted in a dovetail at the back of the slide.

The forward part of the slide (1.75 to 2.0 inches long) was heat-treated to prevent wear and damage from circa serial #s 710,001 to the end of production. At circa serial #880,000, the slide stop detent was also hardened. These hardened areas can be detected by a slight discoloration, usually darker than the surrounding area. It is more noticeable in

Military and Commercial Pistols

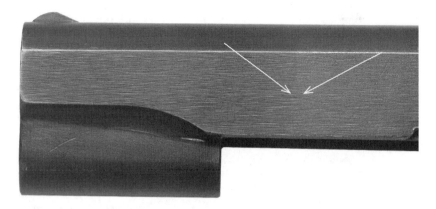

Fig. 3-5. After ca. serial #710,001, the front of the slide was hardened (arrows). This is most noticeable in original Parkerized slides. After ca. serial #880,000, the slide notch release was also hardened. Photo enhanced slightly for clarity.

original Parkerized-finished-slides than blued slides. And of course, it is not visible at all in plated slides, see Figure 3-5.

NOTE: In some slides manufactured by Remington Rand, these hardened areas may be lighter in color than the surrounding finish. It is thought that these slides were hardened excessively and did not accept the Parkerized finish as well.

Fig. 3-6. Barrel Bushing Seat.

SLIDE, PARTS
Barrel Bushing Seat
This is the area at the front, inside of the slide immediately above slide recoil assembly housing. The seat for the barrel bushing was 0.699 inch in diameter, see Figure 3-6.

Breech Face
The breech face is the vertical portion of the slide's breech which the cartridge case strikes under the recoil force imparted by the bullet, driving the slide back. It contained the firing pin tunnel opening in the center. At circa serial #710,001, a hardened steel bushing was installed

Model 1911, M1911A1

Fig. 3-7. Breech Face. Note the hardened bushing (arrow) installed after circa serial #710,001 to the end of production.

which surrounded the firing pin tunnel opening, see Figure 3-7.

Center Slide Rail

The center slide rail was machined along the bottom of the slide at the rear, see Figure 3-8. At the front was the breech face and at the rear was the opening for the firing pin stop plate. The center slide rail was 0.241 inch higher than the bottom edges of the slide rails. The disconnector timing recess was near the rear of the center slide rail.

Disconnector Cam Timing Recess

This was a semicircular cut (0.375-inch radius) in the bottom of the center slide rail at the rear, see Figure 3-9. When the slide is in the full forward position (in battery), the disconnector slot in its underside is in position to allow the spring below to force the disconnector

Fig. 3-8. The center slide rail (arrow) is on the bottom, center rear of the slide.

up so that its top end is in the disconnector slot. The lower end of the disconnector makes a connection between the trigger stirrup, tail of the sear, and the hammer, allowing the pistol to be fired.

When the pistol is fired, the slide is thrust backward. As the slide begins to move, the disconnector is forced down by the beveled disconnector cam timing recess acting on its rounded head, pushing the tail of the sear out of engagement with the trigger stirrup until the slide stops its rearward movement and is pushed forward into battery by the recoil spring.

Military and Commercial Pistols

Two types of disconnector cam timing recess were used. The **Type 1** is found on all Model 1911 pistols and measured nominally 0.160 inch wide by 0.268 inch long. The **Type 2** disconnector cam timing recess on the Model 1911A1 was enlarged to nominally 0.160 inch wide by 0.400 inch long. The change took place at serial number

Model 1911

Model 1911A1

Fig. 3-9. Disconnector Cam Timing Recess (arrows). Note the difference in size between the M1911 and M1911A1.

710,001 for military models and circa serial #C135,000 for commercial models.

Fig. 3-10. Ejection Port, Remington Rand.

Ejection Port

The ejection port was a rectangular opening cut in the top right side of the slide 3.733 inches behind the front of the slide and through which the fired cartridge case was ejected, see Figure 3-10. The port was nominally 0.424 inch wide and 1.157 inches long The front and rear vertical sides of the ejection port were curved downward to reduce the opening on the right side to 1.15 inches at midpoint.

Slides by different manufacturers can often be distinguished by measuring the length, width and radius of the ejection port as shown in Table 3-1 and Figure 3-11. Note that the Ithaca slide after circa serial #870,000 has a

Colt

Ithaca

Fig. 3-11. Colt and Ithaca Model 1911A1 ejection ports compared. Note the larger radius on the corner on the Ithaca slide.

161

Model 1911, M1911A1

Manufacturer	Top Left Corner Radius	Length (1)	Width (2)
Table 3-1 Ejection Port Dimensions (inches—nominal)			
Colt	0.13	1.313	0.615
Springfield	0.20	1.290	0.598
Remington Arms-UMC	0.24	1.330	0.698
Singer	0.13	1.313	0.615
Ithaca	0.23	1.318	0.717
Remington Rand	0.18	1.324	0.615
US&S	0.18	1.329	0.687

1. Measure from center of rear to center of front.
2. Measure from inside center to inside center at midpoint.

radius of 0.23 inch. Slides on Ithaca pistols before circa serial #870,000 may have been manufactured by Colt, Springfield or Remington Arms-UMC. The Remington Arms-UMC slides were reclaimed World War I-era manufacture.

Extractor

The extractor was machined from spring steel and heat-treated. Its forward end was shaped into a claw that grasped the cartridge rim and drew it from the chamber after it was fired. The claw was held in the slide by the firing pin retainer plate. The extractor was 2.674 inches long overall with a slight curve. The hook was 0.150 inch wide by 0.099 inch long with a radius of 0.22 inch at the bottom

Fig. 3-12. The extractor slides into a tunnel on the left side of the slide.

edge of the hook that first encounters the case rim. The bend or curve in the extractor should be 0.02 inch above the centerline. The extractor was held in the slide by the right edge of the firing pin retainer plate, see Figure 3-12. Springfield extractors were marked "S."

162

Military and Commercial Pistols

Extractor Tunnel

The extractor rested in a tunnel drilled through the top right-hand side of the center slide rail. The tunnel was straight, which forced the slightly curved extractor claw to bend to the left to grip the cartridge rim, see Figure 3-13, arrow.

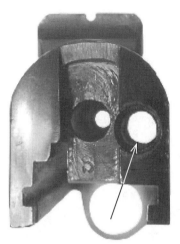

Fig. 3-13. The extractor tunnel, arrow. The tunnel is straight, which forces the curved extractor to bend and serve as a spring.

Firing Pin Tunnel

The firing pin tunnel was a round passageway from the rear of the slide to the breech face, or recoil, plate of the slide. The firing pin tunnel was 0.219 inch in diameter with a shoulder (arrow) near the firing pin port at the front to contain the firing pin spring. This spring maintained rearward pressure on the firing pin to keep it pressed back into the tunnel to prevent accidental strikes against the chambered primer, see Figure 3-14.

Fig. 3-14. The firing pin tunnel, arrow.

Firing Pin

The firing pin was machined from steel and hardened, see Figure 3-15. It was 2.295 inches long. The forward end or tip (A) was 0.089 inch in diameter and 0.55 inch long and was rounded to prevent primer punctures. The firing pin was a tapered cylinder for 1.550 inches behind the tip, before forming a shoulder 0.193 inch in diameter and 0.393 inch long (B). The firing pin spring rested against this shoulder. A second shoulder 0.214 inch in diameter and 0.150 inch long began (C). The rear of this shoulder pressed against the firing pin retainer plate. The rear of the firing pin was called the anvil and was 0.149 inch in diameter and 0.165 inch long (D). The anvil protruded

163

Model 1911, M1911A1

A   B   C   D

Fig. 3-15. Firing Pin.

through the firing pin retainer plate. When the anvil was struck, the firing pin was thrust forward to protrude through the firing pin port in the breech face and strike, and ignite, the cartridge primer.

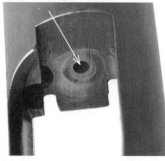

Fig. 3-16. The firing pin port, (arrow). Compare to Figure 3-22.

Firing Pin Port

The firing pin rested in a tunnel drilled along the axis of the slide and exited in the center of the breech face. The front of the firing pin tunnel narrowed abruptly to the firing pin port, which was 0.094 inch in diameter, see Figure 3-16. See also Recoil Plate, below.

Firing Pin Retainer Plate

Also called the "firing pin stop," the firing pin retainer plate was 0.458 inch wide, 0.138 inch thick and 0.643 inch high. The hole for the anvil of the firing pin was 0.155 inch in diameter, see Figure 3-17.

The two types have been observed, see Figure 3-18. The early **Type 1** firing pin retainer plates showed a lower curve (arrow A) at the bottom with a radius of 0.078 inch. It was used by Colt from the start of production to circa serial #240,000 when a change to the radius of the curve was made.

Fig. 3-17. The firing pin retainer plate.

The **Type 2** firing pin retainer plate had a far higher curve at the bottom with a radius of 0.22 inch (arrow B). It was originated by

164

Military and Commercial Pistols

Springfield Armory to make it easier for the slide to cock the hammer during recoil and was used on all their production as well as by Remington Arms-UMC, Singer, Remington Rand, Ithaca, and Union Switch and Signal.

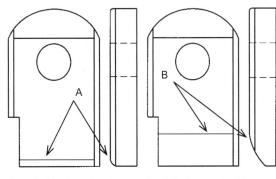

Fig. 3-18. The drawing on the left shows the Type 1 and that on the right, the Type 2 firing pin retainer plates.

Most Springfield Armory-manufactured firing pin stops were marked "S" on the front and have a rounded upper rear edge, see Figure 3-19. All others were unmarked. Those Colt slides that were serial numbered (circa serial #s 710,001-1,138,000) will usually show a ghost image of the serial number reversed on the front of the firing pin retainer plate.

Firing Pin Retainer Plate Guides

The firing pin retainer plate was inserted into guides at the rear of the hammer recess, see Figure 3-20, arrows. The rear of the firing pin protruded through the retainer plate to receive the hammer strike. The rearward pressure of the firing pin spring on the firing pin pressed its rear shoulder against the retainer plate to hold the retainer plate in place. The slot was 0.476 inch wide by 0.10 inch deep.

Fig. 3-19. Springfield Armory-manufactured firing pin retainer plates were marked "S" on the front.

Fig. 3-20. Firing pin retainer plate guides.

165

Fig. 3-21. Firing pin spring and firing pin.

Firing Pin Spring

The firing pin spring served to retract and hold the firing pin inside the firing pin tunnel until it was struck by the hammer. It had sixty-three coils and was made of 0.022-inch-diameter spring wire. The spring had an outside dimension of 0.150 inch and was nominally 1.7 inches long, see Figure 3-21. No changes were made to the firing pin spring throughout production.

The Colt firing pin spring has a smaller diameter at one end (arrow) to hold the firing pin captive.

Recoil Plate

From the start of production to serial #710,001, the recoil plate, or face, was not heat-treated. After World War I, Colt engineers noticed a number of slides in which the firing pin hole had been reduced in size. The problem was traced to peening, caused by the cartridge cases battering the recoil plate. It was not possible at the time to harden the recoil plate without warping the surrounding thinner areas. Starting at serial #710,001, a separate hardened recoil plate bushing was machined and threaded into the breech face, see Figure 3-22. All subsequent Model 1911A1s by any manufacturer used the separate recoil plate bushing,

Fig. 3-22. After serial number 710,001, a separate hardened steel bushing (arrow) was threaded into the breech face to prevent peening of the firing pin hole. Compare to Figure 3-16.

Military and Commercial Pistols

including post-World War II commercial Colt pistols until the hard slide was developed with the Series 70.

NOTE: All Model 1927 slides manufactured by Colt in the United States for Argentina, or manufactured in Argentina, have the hardened steel recoil plate threaded into the breech face.

Hammer Recess

The hammer recess was the vertical rectangular opening at the rear of the slide into which the hammer fell, see Figure 3-23. It also allowed access to the extractor, firing pin retainer plate, and firing pin. The recess was 0.320 inch wide and 0.351 inch deep and the opening of the firing pin tunnel was 0.212 inch wide.

Safety Catch Notch

The safety catch notch was a triangular cut at the left rear of the slide, see Figure 3-24. The lug on the safety catch entered this notch to prevent the slide

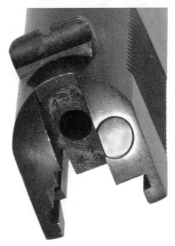

Fig. 3-23. Hammer Recess.

from moving. The notch was nominally 0.380 inch long and 0.140 inch high.

Slide Dismount Cut

The slide dismount cut allowed the slide stop to rise high enough that its lug disengaged from the receiver and it could be pushed out to the left, see Figure 3-25. This released the slide and allowed it to be moved off the receiver. The cut was 0.190-0.200 inch long by 0.050 inch high.

Fig. 3-24. Safety Catch Cut.

167

Model 1911, M1911A1

Fig. 3-25. Slide Dismount Cut.

Slide Locking Grooves

The slide locking grooves are on the inside of the slide and follow its contour, see Figure 3-26. The barrel is attached to the receiver by the barrel link assembly. When in battery, the barrel locking lugs engage the slide locking lugs. When the slide moves back out of battery, the rotary motion imparted by the barrel link assembly causes the barrel and slide locking lugs to disengage (0.125-inch movement), allowing the slide to move to the rear.

Ordnance Department dimensions for the lugs are given in Figure 3-27 and are used with permission from Jerry Kuhnhausen's *The U.S. M1911/M1911A1 Pistols.*

Slide Rails

The slide rails are located on the inside of the slide, along the bottom. They match similar rails on the receiver and allow the slide to move back and forth on the receiver, see Figure 3-28.

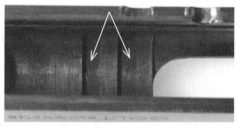

Fig. 3-26. Slide Locking Grooves.

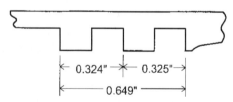

Fig. 3-27. U.S. Army Ordnance Department slide locking groove dimensions.

Ordnance Department dimensions for the slide rails are shown in Figure 3-29. The drawing is exaggerated for clarity.

Slide Stop Detent

The slide stop detent allowed the slide stop to rise and hold the slide to the rear. The detent was nomi-

Military and Commercial Pistols

nally 0.15 inch long with a slight slant to the rear, see Figure 3-30, arrow.

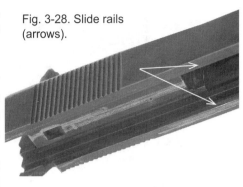

Fig. 3-28. Slide rails (arrows).

NOTE: Beginning in early 1943, the slide stop cut and the barrel bushing seat were also hardened. The process began at Colt circa serial #1,100,000; Ithaca circa serial #s 860,000 to 900,000; Remington Rand circa serial #s 950,900 to 1,020,000; and all Union Switch & Signal pistol production. Often these areas show darker against the finish. It is most visible in original Parkerized finishes.

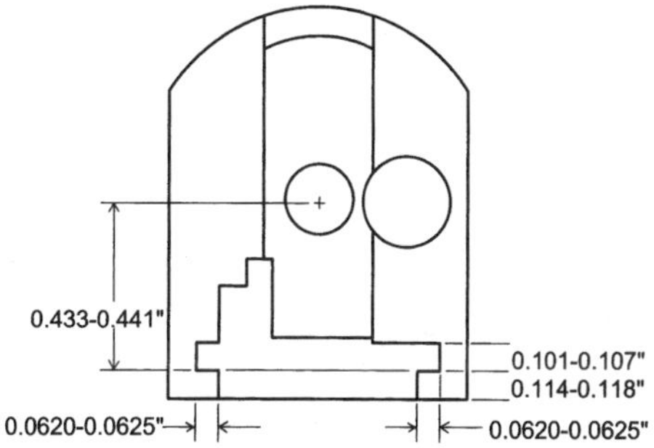

0.433-0.441"

0.101-0.107"
0.114-0.118"

0.0620-0.0625"

0.0620-0.0625"

Fig. 3-29. U.S. Army Ordnance Department slide rail dimensions.

NOTE: In some slides manufactured by Remington Rand, these hardened areas may appear lighter in color than the surrounding finish.

Recoil Spring Assembly

The recoil spring assembly served to store the recoil energy that returned the slide to battery after a shot was fired. It consisted of the A) recoil spring, B) recoil spring plug, and C) recoil spring guide. The assembly rested beneath the barrel and was contained by the receiver recoil spring housing and the receiver's recoil spring shroud, see Figure 3-31.

Recoil Spring

The recoil spring supplied the force to return the slide to battery after recoil from the fired cartridge drove it to the rear. The recoil spring was made of spring steel wire

Fig. 3-30. Slide stop detent cut with slide stop in the "up" or locked position holding the slide to the rear.

169

Model 1911, M1911A1

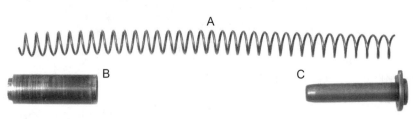

Fig. 3-31. Recoil Spring Assembly: (A) recoil spring, (B) recoil spring plug, and (C) recoil spring guide.

0.044 inch in diameter. The coil spring was 0.430 inch in diameter, see Figure 3-32.

Fig. 3-32. Top, the Type 1 recoil spring. Bottom, the Type 2.

Two types of recoil spring were used. The original **Type 1** recoil spring had 33 coils and was 6.9 inches long when not under tension. Two variations were made.

The **1st Variation** was in use from serial #1 to circa #150,000 in early 1917. Both ends of the spring were slightly crimped to fit tightly on the recoil spring guide. It was feared that if only one end of the spring was crimped and the uncrimped end of the spring was placed on the recoil guide, the pistol might malfunction.

The **2nd Variation** was used from circa serial #s 150,001-710,000. Only one end of the spring was crimped so that the other end of the recoil spring could fit more securely under the recoil spring plug tab.

Military and Commercial Pistols

The **Type 2** recoil spring was identical to the Type 1 spring except it was reduced to 30 coils and was 6.55 inches long when not under tension. The change was made at serial #710,001 (the first military contract after World War I) to make it easier to retract the slide, refer to Figure 3-32.

Recoil Spring Plug

The recoil spring plug captured the front end of the recoil spring and together with the barrel bushing, held the recoil spring and recoil spring guide in alignment. The plug, a hollow tube closed at the front end, accepted the forward end of the recoil spring. It was 1.51 inches long by 0.498 inch in diameter. The front end was rebated 0.106 inch leaving a round projection 0.392 inch in diameter which entered the cutout in the flange of the barrel bushing. Recoil plug checkering had 10 diamonds (counted through the center) for all Model 1911/1911A1 pistols.

Three types of recoil spring plug were used, see Figure 3-33. The **Type 1** recoil spring plug had no provision for fixing the recoil spring in place. It was found that during disassembly, unless the recoil spring plug was held firmly, the tension of the recoil spring could propel it out of the hands of the person disassembling the pistol with enough force to cause injury. The Type 1 was in use from serial #s 1 to circa 6,500.

Fig. 3-33. Three types of recoil spring plug were used. L-r: (A) Type 1, no tab. (B) Type 2, square tab. (C) Type 3, rounded tab.

A Colt inspector suggested that a tab be punched into the side of the recoil spring plug near the top to hold the recoil spring. The tab in the **Type 2** recoil spring plug was nominally 0.08 by 0.08 inch and used from circa serial #s 6,501 to 42,500.

To ease production and increase the tab's holding power on the spring, it was changed from a square tab to a rounded tab at circa serial #42,501. This **Type 3** recoil spring plug was used to the end of production.

171

Model 1911, M1911A1

Barrel Bushing

The barrel bushing was a hollow tube with a flange at the front. A stud on the tube meshed with a groove in the slide's muzzle to secure it. The bushing centered the barrel when in battery and retained the recoil spring plug. Three types were used, see Figure 3-34A.

The **Type 1** barrel bushing was made in two variations: the **1st Variation** was blued, the **2nd Variation** was Parkerized. The Type 1 was used by Colt, Springfield, Remington Arms-UMC, Singer, Ithaca, and Remington Rand. The **Type 2** barrel bushing was used by Union Switch & Signal and can be identified by concentric circles on the face (arrow) caused the machining operation. The

Fig. 3-34A. Barrel bushings, clockwise from top, Type 1, Type 2 (US&S only), Type 3, Colt Accurizor bushing.

Type 3 was used Series 70 and into the Series 80 and on post World War II National Match Gold Cup pistols. The "Accurizor" bushing had "spring" fingers to center the muzzle for improved accuracy. The Type 1 "solid" bushing is currently in commercial use.

Barrel Assembly

The barrel is fastened to the receiver with a pin passing through its lug and the hole in the top of the toggle link which in turn is fastened to the barrel with the slide stop pin. When the barrel and slide are in battery, their lugs are meshed. Because the barrel is fixed in place with respect to the receiver, it can only rotate through a short arc of less than 0.2 inch. Figure 3-34B shows the barrel assembly: A) Barrel, B) link, C) link pin.

Barrels

The nominal dimensions for the Model 1911 and Model 1911A1 barrels were 5.031 inches long from muzzle to the end of the barrel hood. The diameter was 0.577 inch at the muzzle and 0.695 inch at the rear.

Military and Commercial Pistols

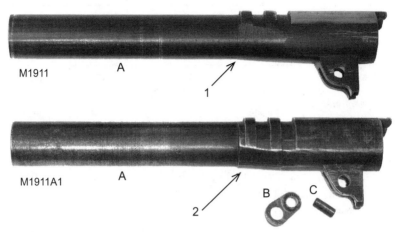

Fig. 3-34. The Model 1911 and 1911A1 barrels showing the link assembly common to both. Note the added extra metal (compare area at arrows 1 and 2) ahead of the chamber on the bottom of the M1911A1 barrel.

Chamber depth was nominally 0.900 inch. The barrel was rifled with six grooves having a twist of one in sixteen (1:16) inches to the left.

Table 3-2 provides nominal barrel dimensions as established by the Ordnance Department. These dimensions were applied to commercial barrels as well.

Table 3-2 Model 1911/1911A1 Nominal Barrel Dimensions (inches)				
Area	**1911**	**1923**	**1942**	**1943**
Diameter, grooves	0.455	0.454	0.454	0.454
Diameter, lands	0.451	0.450	0.450	0.450
Depth, grooves	0.0030	0.0035	0.0040	0.0040
Width, grooves	0.1522	0.1522	0.1470	0.1470
Chamber, taper nominal	0.0022	0.0022	0.0022	0.0080

173

Model 1911, M1911A1

Table 3-2, cont. Model 1911/1911A1 Nominal Barrel Dimensions (inches)				
Area	**1911**	**1923**	**1942**	**1943**
Chamber, taper measured	0.0018	0.0018	0.0018	0.006

The barrel had two locking lugs on the top surface of the barrel just ahead of the chamber area, refer to Figure 3-34B. The center of the first lug was located exactly 1.0 inch ahead of the forward end of the chamber. Each lug was nominally 0.059 inch deep at the top, center and 0.148 inch wide. Actual measurements of a wide assortment of barrels throughout the production period showed that the width of each lug varied between 0.146 and 0.151 inch wide. All barrels measured were from working Model 1911s or Model 1911A1s and functioned properly.

Fig. 3-35. The barrel is fastened to the receiver through the barrel link (arrow).

The barrel lug was on the bottom of the barrel beneath the chamber. The lug was slotted into two halves, see Figure 3-35 and refer to Figure 3-34B. The barrel link rode between the two split halves and was attached to the barrel by a barrel link pin. The barrel lug was 0.358 inch wide overall. Each half was 0.106 inch wide with a space 0.146 inch between. The lug was 0.542 inch long where it extended below the barrel and protruded 0.52 inch below the barrel. The link pin hole was 0.151 inch in diameter and was located 0.507 inch ahead of the rear of the barrel, not including the hood.

The hood on the top breech end of the barrel was 0.152 inch long and formed a segment of an arc 0.418 inch long. The left side of the hood was offset to the right by six degrees.

Military and Commercial Pistols

The bottom rear of the chamber was cut at an angle to ease the passage of the round-nose bullet into the chamber. The angle of entry was sixty-four degrees. The matching angle in the bottom of the hood was also 0.464 inch in diameter.

From the start of production to circa serial number 24,000, barrels were inspected for dimensions, rifling and chamber sizes, and obvious defects.

Model 1911 barrels have lugs that extend not quite halfway over the top of the barrel ahead of the chamber. The barrel flares smoothly on the bottom beneath the lugs, refer to Figure 3-34B, arrow 1.

The Model 1911A1 barrel lugs extend over approximately two-thirds around barrel diameter. The area beneath the lugs is reinforced with additional metal, leaving a slight ledge where the barrel joins the chamber area, refer to Figure 3-34, arrow 2.

All barrels manufactured under contract to the U.S. Army's Ordnance Department before 1941 were heat-blued. From 1941 on, all barrels were finished with the proprietary chemical finish called Du-Lite. The difference between heat-blued and chemically blackened barrels is difficult to discern if the barrel is worn. Heat-blued barrels in near-new condition will show a brighter black color with shadings of blue in strong light. Du-Lite barrels are uniformly darker in strong light.

A Parkerized military M1911/M1911A1 barrel has been refinished.

All blued or Parkerized Colt receivers after circa serial #s 710,000 to circa 1,700,000-1,710,000 had their bullet ramps remachined after finishing.The bullet ramp will present a bright appearance in contrast to blued or dull, Parkerized finish of the rest of the interior. Colt switched to the Parco-Lubrite finish at that point, which produced a smooth enough finish that the bullet ramp did not need to be remachined. It will therefore match the color and finish of the rest of the receiver.

Colt and Springfield Armory Military Barrels
Colt (1911-1970) and Springfield Armory (1914-1933, 1941-1943) manufactured the Government Model barrels with only the minor changes to

dimensions and markings as listed in Table 3-2. The same barrel specifications for Ordnance Department–contracted barrels were applied to commercial barrels.

The changes to Colt-produced barrels that identify them by serial number range are primarily in their markings which are described in detail in Chapter 8.

During World War II, Colt manufactured all the barrels used in their own production. In addition, they provided 5,000 barrels to Remington Rand in August 1942 and smaller shipments to Ithaca, Remington Rand, and Union Switch & Signal from December 1942 to May 1943. These barrels were mixed in with barrels supplied by Springfield Armory and High Standard. Union Switch & Signal used very few, if any, of the barrels made available by Colt, depending instead of timely deliveries of barrels from High Standard.

Some military barrels have been reported used in Colt commercial Government Models manufactured and sold in the immediate post-World War II period.

A.H. Fox Gun Company Barrels
Colt contracted with the A. H. Fox Gun Company of Philadelphia, Pennsylvania, in November 1917 to provide barrels for the Model 1911 at the rate of 2,500 daily. Colt also agreed to provide all the tools, fixtures, cutters and gages. The A. H. Fox barrels are not readily identifiable until the end of the contract period when, it is thought, they began to stamp an ampersand (&) on the bottom of the barrel, ahead of the lug. See Figure 8-F in Chapter 8, "Barrel Markings."

Springfield Armory Interwar Barrels
In the years between World War I and World War II, both Colt and the Springfield Armory produced barrels for the Model 1911 and Model 1911A1 under contracts from the U.S. Army Ordnance Department. According to the reports of the Chief of Ordnance to the Secretary of War, between 1919 and 1933, the Springfield Armory manufactured at least 153,486 replacement barrels.

Military and Commercial Pistols

In 1941, the Springfield Armory was directed to again produce replacement Model 1911A1 barrels. But during the changeover to new equipment in the late 1930s, the original barrel rifling equipment had been removed. Two screw-type broaching machines were modified for barrel production and between July 1, 1941, and June 30, 1943, a total of 143,098 replacement barrels were produced. These can be identified by the sans serif letter "S" and the heat lot number stamped on the left barrel lug. The following markings have been noted: AG1, AG-1, BF1, BH1, PX-1, PX-8, and REP 1, REP 2 and REP 3. When the heat lot number marking was discontinued in late 1943, the Ordnance Department's crossed cannon acceptance mark was stamped on the right lug, see Figure 8-2G in Chapter 8, "Barrel Markings.

All barrels made by any manufacturer under contract to the Ordnance Department were blued before 1941. During World War II, the Du-Lite black oxide process was used instead of heat or furnace bluing.

Remington Arms-UMC Barrels

The barrels made by Remington Arms-UMC are identical to Colt and Springfield Armory barrels in every respect. Some early barrels have been observed with a single marking, a sans serif "P" proof mark struck on the forward part of the right barrel lug, at about the two o'clock position above the link pin hole. Most production barrels have a single sans serif "P" proof mark on top of the barrel visible through the ejection port. A number of identical barrels have been observed in Colt Model 1911 pistols during the World War I period. These barrels may have been supplied as replacements.

NOTE: No other Model 1911 or Model 1911A1 barrel maker struck the sans serif "P" proof mark by itself on the right barrel lug.

Singer Barrels

Singer barrels complied with the dimensions authorized for use in 1923 (see Table 3-2). The barrels were blued and can be identified by the single sans serif "P" proof mark stamped on the left barrel lug at the two o'clock position above the link pin hole.

Model 1911, M1911A1

High Standard Barrels

It was determined that the Model 1911A1 subcontractors Ithaca, Remington Rand, and Union Switch & Signal would manufacture the pistol receiver, slide and most of their parts, but not barrels or magazines. A subcontract was awarded to the High Standard Manufacturing Company of New Haven, Connecticut, in March 1942 to manufacture barrels. High Standard had a difficult time gathering the needed equipment and so production did not begin until November 1942. And continuing shortages of equipment played havoc with production and delivery.

In December 1942, the Ordnance Department canceled the subcontract and issued a prime contract to High Standard. Barrels manufactured to that point had been shipped to Ithaca and US&S. To make up for the shortages, Colt sent 5,000 barrels to Remington Rand in August 1942 and additional shipments later. It has been estimated by observation that approximately the first ten thousand Remington Rand Model 1911A1s had Colt-supplied barrels.

Some 18,000 new barrels from Springfield Armory were also sent to Remington Rand and Ithaca, but many were rejected because the area above the chamber was out of tolerance. Many of these were re-machined and used mostly for field replacement parts. High Standard reached full barrel production in July 1943 and from then on supplied most of the barrels used by the three subcontractors, Remington Rand, Ithaca and US&S, to the end of the war.

High Standard barrels were manufactured according to the Ordnance Department specifications published in 1942 and 1943 (refer to Table 3-2).

Barrels were not marked by Remington Rand, Ithaca or US&S; only by High Standard. The sans serif "P" proof mark was stamped on the left barrel lug at the two o'clock position above the link pin hole. The sans serif initials "HS" for High Standard were stamped on the right barrel lug, at the eleven o'clock position above the link pin hole.

Flannery Bolt Company Barrels

To take up the slack when the Springfield Armory discontinued Model 1911A1 barrel production in July 1943, Flannery Bolt Company, Brid-

Military and Commercial Pistols

geville, Pennsylvania, was awarded a barrel contract; most of the Springfield Armory barrel-making machinery was transferred to them. Flannery barrels were manufactured according to the Ordnance Department specifications published in 1942 and 1943 (refer to Table 3-2). Most Flannery production were used on late Ithaca Model 1911A1s and as replacement barrels.

The sans serif "P" proof mark was stamped on the left barrel lug at the two o'clock position above the link pin hole. The sans serif initial "F" for Flannery was stamped on the right barrel lug, at the eleven o'clock position above the link pin hole.

Post-World War II Replacement Barrels
After World War II, Colt continued to make replacement barrels for the Model 1911A1 under government contract. These were manufactured according to the dimensions published in 1942 and 1943 (refer to Table 3-2). They can readily be distinguished from previous Model 1911 and Model 1911A1 barrels by the Federal part number "7791193" which was stamped on the top of the barrel and visible through the ejection port. Other postwar barrels were supplied with different 779XXXX numbers by Colt and other manufacturers as replacement parts and for National Match barrels.

During the 1960s, chrome-lined barrels were manufactured for the Model 1911A1. The barrels themselves were unmarked and the only identification was on the packaging, which included the contract and government part number.

Barrel markings are described fully in Chapter 8.

Post-World War II Commercial Barrels
Colt manufactured new barrels for commercial sale starting in late 1946. These barrels were made according to the U.S. Army specifications published in 1942-1943 (see Table 3-2).

Post-World War II commercial barrels were finished with the Du-Lite process as standard unless plated.

Model 1911, M1911A1

Postwar commercial barrels were marked "**COLT 45 AUTO**" on top of the barrel, visible in the ejection port. They may or may not have been marked "**P**" on the left side of lug and "**C**" in a box with rounded corners on the right side of lug. See Chapter 8, Table 8-1 for a complete discussion of Colt barrel markings.

Barrel Link

The barrel link connects the barrel to the frame. It is an ellipse with one end larger than the other. The smaller end is pierced with a hole for the barrel link pin and the other with a hole for the slide stop which holds the barrel to the receiver, refer to Figure 3-34, B. The slide stop pin passing through the link allows the rear end of the barrel to describe a short arc when the slide is moved backward or forward in relation to the receiver.

The barrel link was nominally 0.605 inch long. The barrel link pin hole was 0.156 inch in diameter; the slide stop hole was 0.204-0.210 inch in diameter. The barrel link hole was slightly countersunk at 60 degrees on both sides on later production. Model 1911 barrel links will show no signs of countersinking other than deburring.

The thickness of barrel links varied between about 0.130 to 0.136 inch in width due to normal manufacturing tolerances. Most Model 1911 barrel links are at the narrower width while the Model 1911A1 pistol barrel links tend toward the wider width.

NOTE: Some barrel links appear to have the edges chamfered on only one side. These are aftermarket barrel links stamped from sheet steel. Colt-manufactured, and all aftermarket barrel links that are precision made, are cut from bar stock and machined to final shape. World War II non-Colt manufacturers used barrel links from subcontractors. None were marked nor are uniquely identifiable.

Barrel Link Pin

The barrel link pin was nominally 0.155 inch in diameter and 0.358 inch long. Two types were made, refer to Figure 3-34, C.

Military and Commercial Pistols

The **Type 1** barrel link pin ends were chamfered up to 0.01 inch by 45 degrees at each end according to specifications. That said, many observed link pins show little chamfer. These were in use to the end of Model 1911A1 production in 1945. Like the barrel links, none of the barrel link pins were marked nor are uniquely identifiable.

The **Type 2** barrel link pin was manufactured after 1945. The ends of these pins were rounded slightly.

SIGHTS

The Model 1911/1911A1, as issued, was equipped with fixed, non-adjustable sights mounted on the top of the slide, see Figure 3-36. These sights would be considered rudimentary by today's standards, when many semiautomatic pistols are equipped with adjustable sights. The front sight was in the shape of a section of an arc and raised just high enough above the slide to center the aim point at fifty yards, the traditional aim point of U.S. military handguns. The rear sight was

Model 1911

Model 1911A1

Fig. 3-36. The rear sights on the Model 1911 or 1911A1 would be considered rudimentary by today's standards. Craig Riesch collection.

simple, non-adjustable, and machined from bar stock. Its aperture was originally a "U"-shaped notch, later changed to a square notch, through which the front sight presented as a post to the shooter's eye. The sights were designed for use by the mounted soldier. Firing with the pistol was expected to be done at close quarters with little time to aim, and usually from horseback. In a combat situation the soldier was expected to sight along the top of the slide to orient the pistol. If the situation allowed, or the soldier was on foot, he could use the sights to align the weapon.

Model 1911, M1911A1

Since the early 1990s, the Colt factory has supplied both fixed and adjustable "ramp-style" rear sights through the Custom Shop, but these are beyond the scope of this text. The reader is referred to the Colt's Web site (www.coltsmfg.com) for the latest information.

Starting in 1935, the Colt factory began to equip, as an option, National Match pistols, target pistols in Super .38 and .45 ACP caliber, as well as the .22-caliber Service ACE with a "Stevens Adjustable Rear Sight" and a variety of front sights to match.

Sight, Front

The front sight was manufactured in nine basic types ranging from an arc of a circle to a bar of metal rounded at the top front and either sloping upward or forming a vertical post. The designer's intent was to provide the shooter's eye with a vertical black rectangle in the aperture of the rear sight with sufficient light on either side to force the eye to center it. The goal was also to provide a front sight that would not snag on clothing or holsters. All production front sights were non-adjustable, except by filing or grinding. All dimensions given below are **nominal** unless otherwise stated.

The **Type 1** front sight was issued from the start of Colt production to the adoption of the M1911A1 at circa serial #700,001. It was also used by Remington Arms-UMC. The front sight formed an arc of an oval with a stem extending from the bottom. The lower part of the oval rested in a slot cut into the top of the slide. The stem protruded through a hole drilled in the slide and was staked in place against the underside. The Type 1 front sight was nominally 0.400 inch long and 0.10 inch high, 0.058 inch wide at the bottom and tapered

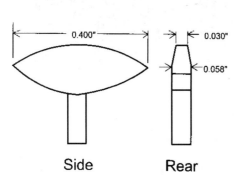

Side   Rear

Fig. 3-37. Type 1 Front Sight, exaggerated for emphasis.

to 0.03 inch wide at the top, see Figure 3-37. Actual measurements of several pistols in this serial number range showed an average length of 0.410 inch and a height of 0.120 inch.

Military and Commercial Pistols

NOTE: Early Model 1911 front sights have a noticeable taper bottom to top, but starting at circa serial #217,000, the taper is no longer apparent.

The Type 1 front sight tended to work loose, as the round stem did not have sufficient metal to hold it in place when staked. The narrow sight was also difficult for the shooter to "pick up" in the rear sight, particularly when the target was moving, or in low-light conditions.

At circa serial #700,001 (C135,000) and the changeover to the M1911A1, the **Type 2** front sight was adopted, see Figure 3-38. Its stem was rectangular in cross section and when staked, provided more metal to hold the front sight securely. The tapered sides were eliminated and the front sight was nominally 0.058 inch wide from top to bottom and remained nominally 0.400 inch long and 0.10 inch high. Again, actual measurements of several pistols in this serial number range showed an average length of 0.410 inch and a height of 0.120 inch.

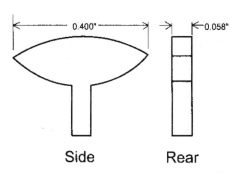

Side   Rear

Fig. 3-38. Type 2 Front Sight, exaggerated for emphasis.

The Type 2 front sight was in use from circa serial #s 700,001-893,000 (March 1943) for Colt and Singer production. Remington Rand, Ithaca, and Union Switch and Signal may have used the Type 2 front sight in combination with the Type 3, 1st and 2nd Variation rear sights for very brief periods after production began in 1943 but it is doubtful. All quickly switched to the Type 3 front and rear sight. See Type 3, Rear Sights.

The **Type 3** front sight was developed by Colt and approved by the Ordnance Department to be used when the "Type 3 rear sight" with a square aperture was adopted, see Figure 3-39. The oval shape was modified with a straight, serrated slope at the rear. The sight was nominally 0.416 inch long by 0.10 inch high by 0.08 inch wide with no bottom-to-top taper.

Model 1911, M1911A1

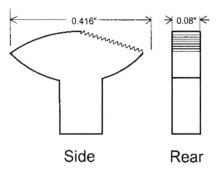

Side   Rear

Fig. 3-39. Type 3 Front Sight, exaggerated for emphasis.

It was used from circa serial #893,001 to the end of production by Colt. Remington Rand, Ithaca, and Union Switch and Signal used it throughout production.

The Type 3 front sight was also installed on all Lightweight Commander, Commander, and Combat Commander pistols through the Series 70 pistols.

The **Type 4** front sight was developed at the Springfield Armory, see Figure 3-40. The front sight was machined from the steel billet used to make the slide, i.e., it was an integral part of the slide. The front sight was shaped like the arc of a circle. It was nominally 0.060 inch wide at the base tapering to 0.050 inch at the top. The front sight was nominally 0.400 inch long by 0.10 inch high.

The **Type 5** front sight was installed on the pre-World War II ACE pistols. It was similar to the Type 2 front sight but formed a larger segment of an arc and was 0.218 inch high, see Figure 3-41.

Fig. 3-40. Type 4 Front Sight as manufactured at the Springfield Armory, 1914-1917. It was integral to the slide and milled from the steel ingot from which the slide was cut.

The **Type 6** front sight was installed on National Match pistols equipped with the Stevens Adjustable Rear Sight (Type 1), starting in 1935 and on the Service Model ACE from the start of production in 1937 through 1954. It was called the High Ramp Front Sight (Colt Part #CPA 69). The front half of the sight was rounded while the rear half was cut in a straight slope and serrated horizontally, see Figure 3-42.

Military and Commercial Pistols

The **Type 7** was a "Patridge" front sight and similar to the King's Vertical Face Front Sight. Dimensions were nominally 0.125 inch wide and 0.488 inch long. Height was

Fig. 3-41. The Type 5 front sight was higher than the Type 2 and installed on ACE and Service ACE pistols. Phil Cuevas collection.

superfluous as the top was filed down to center the point of aim. It was installed on request and standard on Gold Cup match pistols equipped with the Bo-Mar BMC series of adjustable rear sights, see Figure 3-43.

Sight, Front, National Match

Pre-World War II National Match pistols were either the "Service" model or the "National Match Government Model" purchased from the Colt company. Civilian shooters used the few service models available from the Director, Civilian Marksmanship Program through the Na-

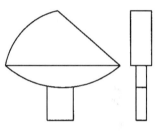

Fig. 3-42. The Type 6 Front Sight was usually installed on pistols equipped with the Stevens Adjustable Rear Sight.

tional Rifle Association or commercial Model 1911/1911A1s "customized" by themselves or gunsmiths to improve accuracy. When it became available in the 1930s, many top civilian shooters purchased the Colt commercial National Match pistol.

A variety of front sights were installed on the commercial National Match pistol, depending on the needs of the owner and what he was willing to pay. If purchased from the Colt company or one of its dealers, the shooter had a choice of the standard Type 1, 2, or, after 1935, the Type 6 front sight. Front sights were also fitted by custom gunsmiths and could be anything from a variation on the standard Colt Type 2 to the "Vertical Face Front Sight" (King's Patent).

Model 1911, M1911A1

Front sights developed for post-World War II National Match pistols are grouped together as the **Type 8** and divided by their variations.

Fig. 3-43. The Type 7 Front Sight installed on a USAF Premium Grade Hardball Match Pistol. North Cape Publications collection.

The **1st Variation** National Match Vertical Face Front Sight was a rectangular block of steel usually between 0.120 and 0.125 inch wide, rounded at the top front and sloping up slightly to a flat, vertical back. The sides and top were carefully machined to present a solid black image in the open, "U" aperture rear sight. The width could be adjusted by filing to allow the proper amount of light on either side to suit the shooter. The top was intended to be filed down to zero the sights at the distance desired, refer to Figure 3-43.

The **2nd Variation** of the Type 8 front sight installed on the National Match Model 1911A1s built in 1956 retained the shape and configuration of the Type 2 front sight but was 0.130 inch wide. Height and length remained 0.120 inch and 0.410 inch, respectively.

For the 1957 production of the National Match Model 1911A1, a new, "Patridge"-type front sight (**3rd Variation**) was introduced, see Figure 3-44. It was nominally 0.125 inch wide but was cut away on the top to produce a vertical component 0.295 inch high. This sight was designed to work with the 0.395-inch-high fixed rear sight, and later with a variety of adjustable rear sights. The top could be filed to center the point of aim.

The **4th Variation** front sight installed on the National Match Model 1911A1 in 1958 was identical to the 3rd Variation front sight except that it was nominally 0.358 inch high, refer to Figure 3-44, and again, intended to allow the pistol to be zeroed by filing down the front sight as

186

Military and Commercial Pistols

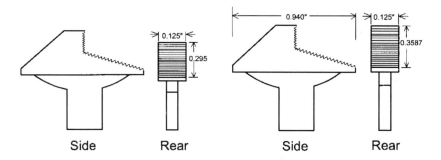

| Side | Rear | | Side | Rear |

Fig. 3-44. Patridge-style Type 8, 3rd and 4th Variation front sights installed on Army, Air Force, and Navy match pistols from 1959 to as late as 1978.

necessary. Front sights on the 1957 and 1958 National Match pistols will therefore vary in height.

The 3rd and 4th Variation front sights were installed on all National Match Model 1911A1 pistols from 1959 through 1968, when the National Match Pistol building program ended at the Springfield Armory and Rock Island Arsenal (refer to Figure 3-43). They were also installed on some "Premium Grade" hardball or wadcutter Model 1911A1 pistols built at the USAF Marksmanship Gunsmith School at Lackland AFB, San Antonio, Texas. They were commonly installed on U.S. Navy .45 Caliber, M1911A1 Centerfire Match Pistols built at the Small Arms Training Unit at the Naval Training Center, San Diego, California, from 1957 through 1978 and on most mid-range (Super .38 caliber) Government Models for the military services as well as civilian target and match shooting.

Fig. 3-45. This M15 General Officer pistol with the Type 9 ramp front sight was issued to Major General Charles D. Palmer, U.S. Army, retired. Sam Lisker collection.

Model 1911, M1911A1

The **Type 9** front sight (Figure 3-45) was developed for the M15 General Officer Pistol. It was a Patridge-style sight with a vertical front and top flat 0.25 inch long. The back of the sight was 0.7 inch long, was knurled and sloped to the top of the slide. The sight was nominally 0.125 inch wide and 0.255 inch high above the top of the slide. It did not have a stem, but rather a "V"-shaped base that was brazed into a groove in the top front of the slide.

Sight, Front—U.S. Marine Corps Match Pistols

The U.S. Marine Corps Model 1911A1 match pistols built in the pre-World War II years generally were equipped with the standard Type 2 front sight. In the post-World War II period, a variation on the Vertical Face Front Sight or the King's Patent-type front sight was installed on many competition pistols built by the Marksmanship Unit at Camp Matthews, California (1956 to 1961), or Quantico, Virginia, from 1962. Today, it is known as the Weapons Training Battalion and remains at Quantico.

Sight, Front—U.S. Coast Guard Match Pistols

The U.S. Coast Guard first purchased match-grade pistols from Colt in late December 1931 for use in the 1932 National Matches. These were catalog items but fitted with a ramp front sight or a modified Vertical Face Front Sight. In the post-World War II period, small-arms training was de-emphasized as the Coast Guard resumed its emergency services and in February 1960, the small-arms training program was canceled. Coast Guard members firing in the National Matches were subsequently required to pay their own way and provide their own equipment.

Table 3-3 Front Sights (1) (inches—actual measurements)					
Type/ Varia- tion	Shape	Size (2) (width x length x height)	Serial Number Range	Comment	Manufacturer
1	Oval	0.058-0.030 x 0.400 x 0.100	1-700,000	Tapered bottom to top: more before 1918, less after	Colt, Remington Arms-UMC

Military and Commercial Pistols

Table 3-3, cont. Front Sights (1) (inches—actual measurements)					
Type/ Varia- tion	Shape	Size (2) (width x length x height)	Serial Number Range	Comment	Manufacturer
2	Oval	0.058 x 0.400 X 0.100	700,001 to 710,001- 893,000	Flat sides	Colt, Singer (all)
3	Oval, serrated rear slope	0.08 x 0.416 x 0.10	Colt: 893,001- EOP Others: all	Flat sides	Colt Singer, Ithaca, Remington Rand, US&S
4	Oval	0.060-0.050 x 0.400 x 0.100	All	Integral, tapered, bottom to top	Springfield Armory
5	Oval	0.058 x 0.410 x 0.218	All	Flat sides, higher arc than previous types	Colt ACE
6	Post, serrated rear slope	0.058 x 0.40 (3)	Pre-WWII National Match, Service ACE, also on request	Used with Stevens Adjustable Rear Sight	Colt
7	Patridge, rounded top front, vertical back	0.125 x 0.488 (3)	Installed on request, usually with an adjustable rear sight such as the Bo-Mar	Height filed to adjust point of aim	Colt, Gold Cup and others
8/1	Vertical Face	0.120-0.125 x 0.930+ (3)	Installed on request, post-1952	0.120 and 0.125 widths available	Colt/Springfield Armory Match

Model 1911, M1911A1

Type/Varia-tion	Shape	Size (2) (width x length x height)	Serial Number Range	Comment	Manufacturer
		Table 3-3, cont. **Front Sights (1)** **(inches—actual measurements)**			
8/2	Oval. Similar to Type 2 but wider	0.130 x 0.410 x 0.120 (3)	1956	U.S. Army National Match Pistols	Springfield Armory
8/3	Modified Patridge, ramp with vertical back	0.125 x 0.940 x 0.295 (3)	1957	U.S. Army National Match Pistols	Springfield Armory
8/4	Similar to 3rd Variation	0.125 x 0.940 x 0.358 (3)	1958-1968	U.S. Army National Match Pistols; U.S. Air Force and U.S. Navy Match Pistols	Springfield Armory; USAF Marksmanship School, Lackland AFB; Naval Small Arms Training Unit, San Diego
9	long sloping trailing edge to rear	0.125 x 0.250 x 0.255	All	M15 General Officer Pistol	Rock Island Arsenal

1. Colt, Springfield Armory, USAF Marksmanship Gunsmith School and the U.S. Navy's Small Arms Training Unit "production" front sights only are included. Other U.S. military small-arms units often installed other commercial sights or sights of their own design on match pistols. Due to their variety and number, they cannot be included here.
2. All sizes listed are actual measurements. See text for nominal dimensions.
3. Front sight adjusted by shooter by filing to center point of aim.

SIGHT, REAR ASSEMBLY—FIXED

The rear sight was mounted in a dovetail at the top, rear of the slide, see Figure 3-46. The rear sight was a simple notch in a machined bar of steel. Specifications called for the rear sight to be 0.626 inch wide and 0.245 inch high. Measured front to back it was 0.346 inch at the base and 0.06 inch across at the top. The sight notch was first a "U"-shape,

Military and Commercial Pistols

then a square, depending on the type of front sight blade installed. Slight variations from the nominal dimensions given below will be noted when actual rear sights are measured. The variations are due to manufacturing tolerances, wear, and replacements. Four types of rear sight were employed.

Fig. 3-46. Model 1911 and 1911A1 Rear Sight.

NOTE: The rear sight dovetail in the slide (and the dovetail on the rear sight itself) is wider on the right than on the left. The rear sight must be inserted from the right and driven out from the left to right.

The **Type 1** rear sight was used from the start of production to circa serial #62,000. The top surface was rounded to form an arc from the edge of the notch to the base like the M1909 revolver sight. The sight notch was "U"-shaped and nominally 0.06 inch wide by 0.04 inch deep, see Figure 3-47.

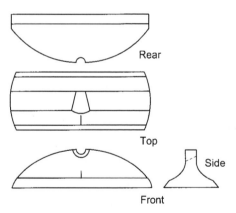

Fig. 3-47. Rear Sight, Type 1.

It was suggested that if the top of the rear sight was made flat, it would help the shooter to hold the pistol level and thus improve aim. The Ordnance Department approved the change on September 15, 1913. The top of the **Type 2** sight was to be machined flat across the top of the sight bar, leaving corners with a nominal radius of 0.06 inch, see Figure 3-48.

Two variations of the Type 2 rear sight are seen. As manufactured by Colt from circa serial #62,001 to circa serial #958,100, Remington Arms-

Model 1911, M1911A1

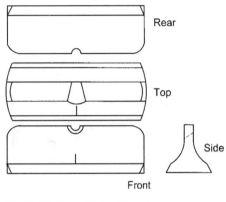

Rear

Top

Side

Front

Fig. 3-48. Rear Sight, Type 2.

UMC and Singer for all of their production, the **1st Variation** rear sight had a corner radius that was closer to 0.10 inch than 0.06 inch and the shoulders were slightly rounded. Its sight notch was 0.07 inch wide by 0.05 inch deep.

The Springfield Armory manufactured a **2nd Variation** of the Type 2 rear sight that was also flat across the top of the sight bar but had corners with a nearly exact 0.06-inch radius, which gave the sight bar a squared appearance. It was used on all Springfield Armory Model 1911 pistols.

The **Type 3** rear sight was developed and used on later Colt World War II Model 1911A1 pistols and by Remington Rand, Ithaca, and Union Switch & Signal. Its use was approved on April 2, 1942, as Drawing No. 4, but subsequently underwent two additional revisions as listed below which delayed its installation until mid-1943. The Type 3 can instantly be identified by its square sight notch, see Figure 3-49.

The Type 3 sight dimensions were nominally 0.626 inch wide by 0.245 inch high and 0.346 inch front to back. The square notch was 0.080

Fig. 3-49. Typical Type 3 Rear Sight as used during World War II.

inch wide. The edges of the base were rounded to a radius of 0.312 inch. All Type 3 rear sights had the bevel leading from the front (side away from the shooter's eye) of the aperture that opened outward (arrow in Figure 3-49). Three variations of the Type 3 that were developed and used are as follows.

192

Military and Commercial Pistols

The **1st Variation** (Drawing No. 4) rear sight can be identified by the straight, angled edges to the bevel at the front of the sight notch, see Figure 3-50, arrow A. The front of the sight was also stepped (arrow B). It was used by Ithaca and Remington Rand from the start of their production at serial #s 856,405 and 916,405 respectively in mid-1943, but was soon replaced with the Type 3, 3rd Variation rear sight.

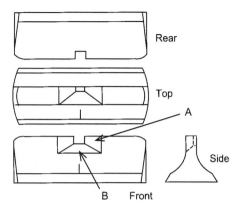

Fig. 3-50. Type 3 Rear Sight, 1st Variation.

The **2nd Variation** (Drawing No. 5) rear sight retained the straight, angled edges to the bevel but the front of the aperture was curved, see Figure 3-51, arrow. It was used by Union Switch and Signal from the start of its production at serial #1,041,405 in mid-1943 to circa serial #1,080,000.

The **3rd Variation** (Drawing No. 6) rear sight changed the bevel on the front of the sight notch to a wide curve (0.20 inch across), see Figure 3-52, arrow. It was used by Colt from circa serial #1,088,726-EOP; Ithaca from serial #1,441,431-EOP; Remington Rand from serial #1,609,528-EOP and US&S from serial #1,080,001-EOP.

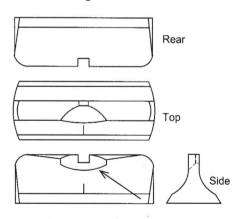

Fig. 3-51. Type 3 Rear Sight, 2nd Variation.

NOTE: Some collectors have suggested that Remington Rand, Ithaca, and Union Switch & Signal used the Type 3, 1st and 2nd Variation rear sights in combination with the Type 2 front sight for brief periods after beginning production in 1943. It is doubtful that they did.

Model 1911, M1911A1

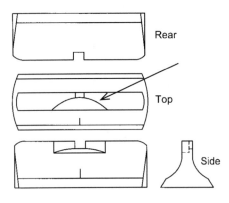

Fig. 3-52. Type 3 Rear Sight, 3rd Variation.

NOTE: Collectors should be aware that some Type 1 and Type 2 rear sights may have square notches; these were usually filed either by owners or gunsmiths. Look for file marks and unevenness.

The **Type 4** fixed rear sight was developed and used on the M15 General Officer Pistol. It had a square notch and was higher at 0.395 inch to compensate for the shorter sight line of the 5.25-inch sight line. The front of the aperture had curving sides that ended in a straight line, see Figure 3-53. See Table 3-4 for fixed rear sights.

NOTE: Do not mistake the M15 General Officer Pistols manufactured at the Rock Island Arsenal for any of the custom-built pistols manufactured by the commercial firm, Springfield Armory, Inc., of Geneseo, Illinois, or others.

Fig. 3-53. The M15 General Officer Pistol fixed rear sight, Type 4.

Sights, Rear Assembly— Adjustable

The first adjustable rear sight (**Type 1**) developed and supplied by Colt as a production item appears to have been the Stevens Adjustable Rear Sight. It was developed for and installed as optional on National Match pistols starting in 1935, see Figure 3-54.

It consisted of a fixed base held in the rear sight dovetail in the slide, and a separate center and rear plate which could be adjusted up and down and side to side for elevation and windage by two screws. It was usually installed with the Type 6 front sight (High Ramp Front Sight).

194

Military and Commercial Pistols

Table 3-4
Fixed Rear Sights
(inches)

Type/ Variation	Manu- facturer	Top Surface	Circa S/N Range	Sight Notch Shape	Sight Notch Nominal Dimensions (width x height)	Comments
1	Colt	Rounded	1-62,000	"U"	0.626 x 0.245	Corner radius 0.06
2/1	Colt	Flat	62,001-893,000	"U"	0.626 x 0.245	Corner radius, 0.10
2/1	Remington Arms-UMC, Singer	Flat	All	"U"	0.626 x 0.245	Corner radius, 0.10
2/2	Springfield Armory	Flat	All	"U"	0.626 x 0.245	Corner radius, 0.06
3/1	Ithaca (1)/ Remington Rand (1)	Flat	856,405-1,471,430/ 916,405-1,041,404	Square	0.626 x 0.245	Front of aperture has straight, angled bevel
3/2	US&S (1)	Flat	1,041,405- 1,080,000	Square	0.626 x 0.245	Front of aperture bevel is curved

195

Model 1911, M1911A1

Table 3-4, cont.
Fixed Rear Sights
(inches)

Type/Variation	Manufacturer	Top Surface	Circa S/N Range	Sight Notch		Comments
				Shape	Nominal Dimensions (width x height)	
3/3	Colt/Ithaca/Remington Rand/US&S	Flat	1,088,726-EOP (2)/ 1,441,431-EOP/ 1,609,528-EOP/ 1,080,001-EOP	Square	0.626 x 0.245	Front of aperture has wide curve
4	Rock Island Arsenal	Flat	All	Square	0.626 x 0.395	M15 General Officer Pistol

1. It has been suggested that Remington Rand, Ithaca, and US&S used Type 2, 1st Variation rear sight in combination with the Type 2 front sight for a short period at the start of production in 1943. This is very doubtful.
2. Colt obtained approval in early 1942 but did not actually begin to use the Type 3/3 rear sight until mid-1943, ca. 1,088,726.

Military and Commercial Pistols

The **Type 2** adjustable rear sight was the short-lived Coltmaster adjustable rear sight introduced in 1948 on the Woodsman .22-caliber pistol. It was also available on the few Service Model ACE pistols and .22-45 conversion kits manufactured

Fig. 3-54. The Stevens Adjustable Rear Sight mounted on a 1942 production Colt Service Model ACE. Phil Cuevas collection.

before World War II but assembled after, which were sold by the end of 1950, see Figure 3-55.

The **Type 3** adjustable rear sight was the Accro rear sight that provided a more positive click stop, see Figure 3-56. It was installed on the National Match and Service Model ACE Pistols from 1955 to 1957, when it was replaced by the Micro Sight.

The **Type 4** adjustable rear sight was purchased from the Micro Sight Company. It allowed windage and elevation changes to be made by turning a single screw for each. The sight was 0.715 inch wide by 0.720 inch long. The aperture bar was 0.319 inch high, see Figure 3-57.

Fig. 3-55. Coltmaster adjustable rear sight on a Colt .22 ACE, first installed in 1948.

The Type 4 adjustable sight was installed on the Gold Cup National Match Pistols in .45 and the Super .38 ACP, from its introduction in 1957 through mid-1965.

197

Model 1911, M1911A1

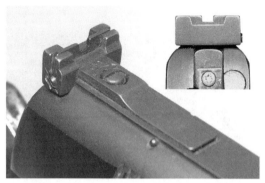

Fig. 3-56. Colt Accro adjustable rear sight on the post-World War II ACE. The inset shows the shooter's-eye view of the aperture.

Fig. 3-57. The Micro adjustable rear sight supplied from 1957 through mid-1965.

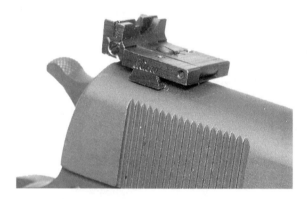

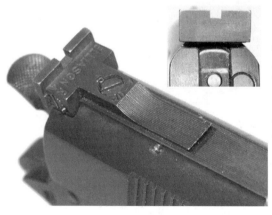

Fig. 3-58. Colt began to install the Elliason adjustable rear sight on the Gold Cup National Match Pistol in mid-1965. The inset shows the shooter's-eye view of the aperture. Compare to Fig. 3-56.

Military and Commercial Pistols

The **Type 5** adjustable rear sight was the Colt-Elliason, see Figure 3-58. It was installed on all Gold Cup National Match and Service ACE pistols from mid-1965 until superseded by the **Type 6** Bo-Mar adjustable rear sight from the late 1980s to 2007.

NOTE: Shooters, check the transverse pin on your Elliason rear sights from time to time. They tend to shoot loose and back out to the right. If you lose it while shooting, you will also lose the tiny spring that presses against the forward tongue. The pin is easily replaced; the spring is not.

Fig. 3-58. Type 6 Bo-Mar adjustable micrometer rear sight. Photo courtesy of Bo-Mar Tool and Manufacturing Company.

CHAPTER 4
MAGAZINES

DESIGN

The concept of the detachable box magazine holding individual cartridges that were fed one by one into the firing chamber was not new to American arms. In fact, the first successful box magazine was developed by an American, James Paris Lee, as early as 1879 for the U.S. Model 1879 Lee Rifle manufactured by the Sharps Rifle Company and later by the Remington Arms Company. Its best-known use was in the British Lee-Metford bolt-action rifle with a ten-round Lee-designed box magazine and bolt action.

By the introduction of the Model 1911 in 1912, the detachable box magazine had been in use in pistols for some fourteen years, most notably in the FN Browning Model 1900 and the Borchardt-Luger Model of 1898. Over 110 different copies of the Browning Model 1900 were in production by 1912, some licensed, some not.

The U.S. Model 1892, 1896 and 1898 rifles and the Model 1896, 1898 and 1899 carbines had used a fixed box magazine, as had the U.S. Model 1903 rifle. The detachable box magazine for a pistol was first introduced into U.S. service with the Colt Model 1900 .38-caliber Automatic Pistol, two hundred of which were purchased for trials. Through the succeeding models designed by John M. Browning that led to the adoption of the U.S. Model 1911 .45 ACP pistol, the magazine design had been refined. After the Model 1911 was adopted, the only changes made to the magazine had to do with production methods and the elimination of the lanyard loop on the base.

The magazine developed for use in the Model 1911 pistol and its successors initially consisted of 1) a magazine body, 2) follower, 3) spring, and 4) non-detachable base plate with a lanyard loop, see Figure 4-1.

All Model 1911, Model 1911A1, Series 70, Series 80 and Model 1991A1 magazines have, as a common feature, five round holes on both sides to allow the shooter to count remaining cartridges.

It should be noted that if John Browning's Government Model design can be said to have one weak spot, it is the magazine. To function

Military and Commercial Pistols

properly, the magazine sides must not be dented, the spring must retain its tension and the lips must be properly angled to present the tip of the bullet at the correct angle to the chamber. Gunsmiths have long attributed the vast majority of "failures to fire" or jams to damaged magazines, or to those too poorly manufactured to function properly.

LANYARD LOOP

The lanyard loop was first proposed to be added to the Army's handguns by the Army Trial Board meeting at the Springfield Armory in November 1894. The board suggested that the then current issue Model 1892 .38 double action revolver be provided with both a "lanyard and a loop." But the lanyard loop was not actually installed until the first of the Model 1901 .38 double action revolvers were manufactured in that same year.

The Model 1902 Automatic Pistol was the first automatic pistol to use the lanyard loop swivel. The

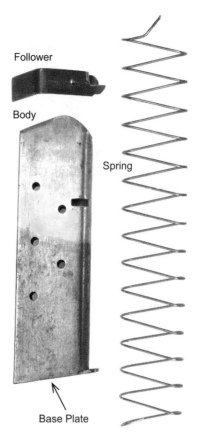

Fig. 4-1. The Model 1911/1911A1 magazine without lanyard loop, disassembled.

Model 1902 (Military) Automatic Pistol was the first to have the lanyard loop on the magazine as well. Interestingly enough, the reason for adding it to the automatic pistol was not only to prevent the trooper from losing his pistol, but from losing the magazine also, see Figure 4-2. Captain James A. Cole was concerned that if a cavalry trooper lost his magazine while on horseback, he would be reduced to a single-shot pistol.

It was intended that any lanyard issued for use with the semi-automatic pistol and worn by cavalry troopers have an extra attaching line added for the magazine. Although the lanyard loop was added to

201

Model 1911, M1911A1

Model 1911 Type 1 through 3 magazines manufactured by Colt and the Type 1 magazine manufactured by Springfield, the two-loop lanyard was never issued. The lanyard loop was officially eliminated from the Model 1911 magazine on March 20, 1916, but the lanyard loop on the butt of the pistol has remained a standard feature on all U.S. military pistols intended to be used in combat to the present day. For more information about the lanyard, see Chapter 10.

Fig. 4-2. The lanyard loop was installed on Types 1, 2 and 3 magazines.

The last Model 1911 shipped by Colt with the lanyard loop magazine is believed to have been serial #125,566. Springfield Armory probably shipped their production subsequent to January 1, 1916, with lanyard loop magazines.

MAGAZINES FOR THE MODEL 1911

Four types of Colt, two types of Springfield Armory, and one type of Remington Arms-UMC magazines were developed and issued for the Model 1911. They are described below and summarized in Tables 4-1, 4-2 and 4-3 with serial number ranges for military and commercial pistols.

Type 1 Colt Magazine

The **Type 1** magazine was made of seamless steel tubing imported from Germany. Five "witness" holes were punched in either side to allow a quick check of the number of cartridges remaining in the magazine. A rectangular slot was cut into the right side of the magazine body for the magazine catch. The base plate's edges were exposed, i.e., the sides of the magazine body ended above the base plate. Two visible rivets on either side penetrated the bottom of the magazine wall to hold the base plate in place. The rivets were centered 0.15 inch above the bottom of the base plate. The forward rivet was 0.3 inch from the front of the magazine body and the after rivet was centered 0.2 inch ahead of the rear wall. The base plate was equipped with a lanyard loop.

Military and Commercial Pistols

Three variations of the Type 1 magazine will be found, all with lanyard loops. The entire **Type 1A** magazine was heat-blued after tempering. The magazine lips were weak and did not feed well, see Figure 4-3.

The upper-one-inch section of the **Type 1B** was hardened using a cyanide process. This restored the spring temper after the magazines were heat-blued. Because the cyanide removed the blue color from the metal, the magazine had a two-tone appearance: the upper one inch was steel gray and the rest of the magazine remained blue, see Figure 4-4, arrow.

In the **Type 1C** magazine, the hardened section was extended down to include the magazine catch area using the cyanide process after the magazines were heat-blued. Because the cyanide removed the blue color from the metal, the magazines had a two-tone appearance: blue below the magazine catch slot and a mottled steel gray above, see Figure 4-5, arrow.

NOTE: The distinction between the three variations of the Type 1 magazine is usually difficult to determine as most Type 1 magazines show considerable blotchiness and the temper line is often hard to see, especially when worn.

Any true Type 1A magazine with insufficient spring in the lips, which would prevent proper functioning, would probably have long been discarded. Most Type 1 magazines observed today are likely to be Type 1B or Type 1C. The most common problem seen in all Type 1 magazines was cracks in the rear corners.

The Type 1 magazine was issued to circa serial #4,500 in the U.S. military series. Very few, if any, were issued with commercial pistols.

Type 2 Colt Magazine

The **Type 2** magazine was made from seamless steel tubing obtained from a domestic source and with a higher carbon content, which made it more brittle. During use, the rear corners of the magazine lips had a tendency to crack. Experimentation showed that by punching an oblong hole 0.4 inch below the top rear of the magazine wall (Figure 4-6) and cutting a thin vertical slot below (arrow), the magazine lips could flex properly and cracking was nearly eliminated. At the same time, the two top corners of the magazine were rounded slightly. Colt termed this the

203

Model 1911, M1911A1

Fig. 4-3. The lip area of the Type 1A magazine was not hardened (arrow 1). The base plate was visible from the sides and attached with two rivets (arrow 2).

Fig. 4-4. The lip area of the Type 1B magazine was hardened for one inch or so down from the top (arrow), creating the characteristic two-tone effect.

Fig. 4-5. The top third of the Type 1C magazine was hardened down to include the magazine catch slot (arrow).

"punch and slot" method of manufacturing the magazine. The Type 2 magazine walls were also lowered to cover the sides of the base plate, which was attached with two rivets.

Two variations of the Type 2 magazine were made, both with lanyard loops. Because the magazine steel was so hard, it was difficult to push the magazine past the magazine catch. A slight indentation was made on the

Military and Commercial Pistols

top right-side wall just past the middle of the top curve to allow the magazine to slide past the catch more easily, see Figure 4-7, arrow. The indentation was retained in subsequent magazine designs. The Type 2 magazine was in use from circa #s 4,501-42,000.

The **Type 2A** magazine did not have the indentation but the **Type 2B** did. The majority of "punch and slot" magazines were the Type 2B.

They were heat-treated to harden the magazine, quenched, and finished in the same manner as the Type 1C magazines. The Army accepted the new magazine on August 30, 1912.

The punch and slot (saw cut) in the Type 2 magazine did not entirely fix the cracking problem as the carbon content of the steel was still too high. In order for the magazine lips to flex properly when

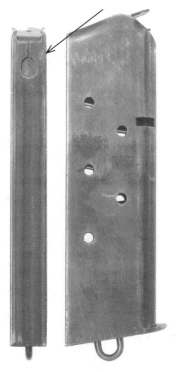

Fig. 4-6. The Type 2 magazine with the "punch and slot" (arrow) to prevent cracking in the corners. Craig Riesch collection.

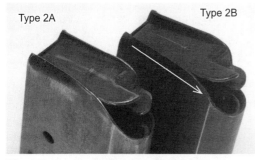

Type 2A   Type 2B

Fig. 4-7. The Type 2B magazine (right) had a slight indentation in the top right-side wall (arrow) to allow it to easily pass the magazine catch. The earlier Type 2A magazine on the left did not.

feeding cartridges, the lips themselves needed to be hardened. The bluing process tempered the metal too much if the magazines were allowed to cool slowly. If quenched, the high-carbon center hardened too much despite the considerable de-carbonization of the surface. Simply put, it was impossible to achieve consistent results with the technology of the day.

Type 3 Colt Magazine

The **Type 3** magazine was manufactured from domestically obtained, cold-rolled sheet steel. The sheets were formed and folded to the shape of the body and welded together. The magazines were first blued using an

oven-bluing process as described in Chapter 9. The upper portion of the magazine was heat-treated by soaking in a solution of molten cyanide for three minutes to allow carbon atoms to diffuse into the surface to a depth of several thousandths of an inch. The magazines were then immediately quenched in oil. The result was a carefully controlled case-hardening of the magazine lips and the rear corners. The outer surface was hard and springy while the center remained tough and flexible. The amount of spring in the lips could be controlled by adjusting the cyanide soak time.

Because the carbon content was lower (0.12% to 0.20%), the factory could dispense with the "punch and slot" method of preventing the magazine lips from cracking. Instead, the sides of the indent at the top rear of the magazine were rounded, see Figure 4-8, arrows A.

Fig. 4-8. Type 3 magazine. Karl Karash collection.

The Type 3 was issued from circa serial #s 42,001-125,566 (see Table 4-1) and had a lanyard loop (B), refer to Figure 4-8. The bottom right and left sides of the base plate were covered by the magazine walls (arrow C). Two rivets were again used on either side of the magazine

Military and Commercial Pistols

to hold the base plate in place (D). The rivets were centered 0.1 inch above the bottom of the base plate and magazine wall. The forward rivet was 0.315 inch behind the front wall and the after rivet was 0.2 inch ahead of the rear wall.

The **Type 4** magazine was also made from cold-rolled sheet steel, folded and welded. The Type 4 magazine did not have the lanyard loop. The magazine walls covered the base plate, which was riveted in place with two solid-steel rivets, see Figure 4-9.

The Type 4 magazine was heat-treated, tempered and finished as the previous magazines and showed the characteristic two-tone coloration, blue below the magazine catch slot and steel gray above. For all intents and purposes, this was the Type 3 magazine but without the lanyard loop.

The Type 4 magazine was issued for all subsequent military contracts as well as commercial models from circa serial #s 125,567 to 629,500 and through circa serial #s 700,000-735,000 (transition models) to the M1911A1.

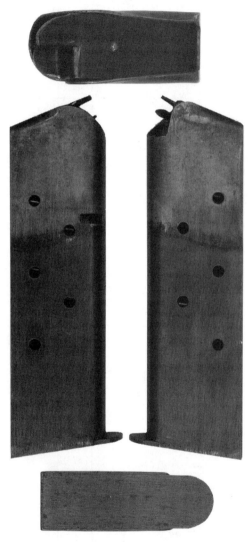

Fig. 4-9. The Type 4 magazine was essentially the Type 3 magazine without the lanyard loop. Karl Karash collection.

207

Model 1911, M1911A1

Table 4-1
Pre-World War II Model 1911/1911A1 Magazine Types

Characteristics	Type 1			Type 2		Type 3	Type 4
	1A	1B	1C	2A	2B		
Magazine Body	Seamless Tube			Seamless Tube		Folded and Welded	Folded and Welded
Base Plate	Exposed on sides and rear			Covered		Covered	Covered
Base Plate Fastening	Rivets			Rivets		Rivets	Rivets
Indent for Magazine Catch	No			No	Yes	Yes	Yes
Lanyard Loop	Yes			Yes		Yes	No
Top, Rear	Sharp Corners			Punch and Slot		Rounded Corners	Rounded Corners
Finish	Blue	Two-tone, one inch		Two-tone above and below magazine catch			
Serial Number Range	1-4,500			4,501-42,000 C1-C5,000		42,001-125,566 C5001-C27,699	125,567-629,500 700,000-735,000 C28,000-C139,999

Military and Commercial Pistols

During World War I, Colt was given two contracts, WAR ORD No. 14671 and WAR ORD No. P5662-1412SA for 1,000,000 and 9,531,244 magazines, respectively. To meet these requirements, Colt subcontracted the manufacture of some of the magazines to four companies. Each company marked their production with an identifying letter on the top of the base plate toe. The author has chosen to classify these as **Type 4 Variations 4A** through **4E**, as shown in Table 4-2 and Figure 4-10.

Table 4-2
World War I Colt Subcontracted Model 1911 Magazines

Manufacturer	Variation	Marking
Colt	Type 4A	None
American Pin Company	Type 4B	A
Barnes & Kobert Manufacturing Co.	Type 4C	B
M.S. Little Manufacturing Co.	Type 4D	L
Risdon Tool and Machine Co.	Type 4E	R

A total of 4,605,884 magazines were produced by the four subcontractors to Colt under both World War I contracts.

COLT MAGAZINES FOR THE COMMERCIAL MODEL 1911

Starting in the 1930s, Colt **Type 4** commercial magazines were marked on the base, "**COLT/.45 AUTO**" using an extended type face. Some commercial magazines so marked may have been shipped with 1911A1 military pistols during the years 1937-1943.

Fig. 4-10. A Type 4B World War I-period contract magazine marked "A" for American Pin Company.

Depending on the period of manufacture (compare the serial number on the receiver to Table 5-13, and Appendix B) the magazine would have been the same as those manufactured for U.S. military contracts.

209

Model 1911, M1911A1

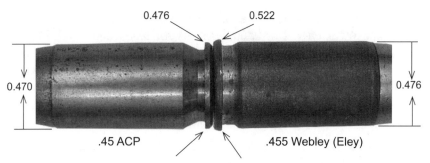

Fig. 4-11. The rimless .45 ACP and the semi-rimmed .455 Webley, as manufactured by Eley, compared. The .45 ACP has a case diameter of 0.470 and a rim diameter of 0.476 inch; the .455 is 0.476 and 0.522 inch, respectively.

.455 Caliber Colt Magazines

The only deviation from the above rule would have been those magazines manufactured for sale in Great Britain in .455 caliber. The points of difference for those made in Great Britain from standard commercial magazine manufactured for the U.S. market would have been: 1) Marked on the base plate "**.455 ELEY**" and 2) magazine bodies 0.025 inch wider to accept the wider semi-rimmed .455 cartridge, see Figure 4-11. Commercial magazines for either the .45 or .455 caliber Model 1911 sold in Great Britain will not show British commercial proof marks.

NOTE: The .45 ACP cartridge is a "rimless" design with a case diameter of 0.470 inch with a rim diameter of 0.476 inch. The .455 Webley cartridge is semi-rimmed with a case diameter of 0.476 inch but the semi-rim has a diameter of 0.522 inch.

Other World War I Magazine Subcontractors

The Ordnance Department issued contracts to five manufacturers during World War I to produce magazines for the Model 1911, all based on the Colt Type 4 magazine. The subcontractors and their markings, if any, are shown in Table 4-3. For convenience, the author has chosen to continue his arbitrary Type/Variation classification from Table 4-2, above.

The **Remington Arms-UMC**—manufactured Type 4 magazine can sometimes be identified by its base which averaged 1.603 inches long. Colt and other subcontracted magazine bases averaged 1.609 inches long, see Figure 4-12.

Military and Commercial Pistols

Table 4-3 World War I Ordnance Department Subcontracted Model 1911 Magazines (Other than through Colt)		
Manufacturer	**Variation**	**Marking**
Remington Arms-UMC*	Type 4F	None
Raymond Engineering Corp.	Type 4G	R (bottom of base)
Ferro Stamping & Mfg. Co.	Type 4H	None delivered
International Silver Co.	Type 4I	None delivered
* Remington Arms-UMC magazines can be identified by their base which is 0.06 inch shorter than the Colt Type 4 base.		

Springfield Magazines

Two types of magazines were produced at the Springfield Armory from May 1913 to April 15, 1917.

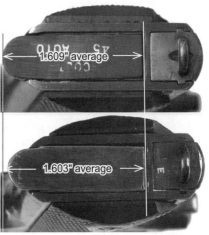

Fig. 4-12. Remington UMC magazine bases (below) are 0.06 inch shorter than Colt or other Type 4 bases (above).

The Springfield Armory **Type 1** magazine was made of sheet steel, gas welded at the left corner, see Figure 4-13 (A). Flanges were formed from the magazine walls which were then folded over and welded to the magazine base (B). A lanyard loop (C) was installed in the base. This manufacturing technique formed an extremely strong magazine. The upper rear one inch, including the corners, of the magazine body underwent copper-plating for three minutes to act as a carbon diffusion barrier, then the upper part of the magazine down to the magazine catch slot was soaked in cya-

211

Model 1911, M1911A1

nide at 1,600 degrees F for four minutes and quenched in sperm oil. This provided a carefully controlled case-hardening similar to the process used at the Colt factory. Next, the magazine lips were tempered in lard oil at 430 degrees F. This greatly increased the toughness and ability of the feed lips to flex without cracking. Finally, the bottom portion of the magazine was sandblasted, then degreased and finished. The finished magazine was cleaned in gasoline and oiled. The foregoing procedure was outlined in "Ordnance Office file 474.6/3491, 3rd Ind, WNRC."

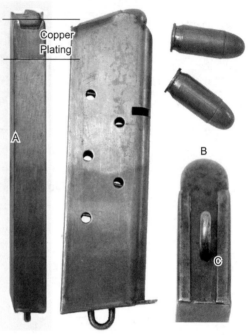

Fig. 4-13. The Springfield Armory magazine is readily distinguishable by its folded and welded base.

The Springfield Armory **Type 2** magazine was exactly like Type 1 but was made without the lanyard loop. It was approved March 20, 1916, but due to the large number of Type 1 base plates in inventory at the time, only a few were made before pistol manufacturing was suspended at the Springfield Armory in April 1917.

NOTE: Springfield Armory magazines were not marked with the "**S**" mark that is stamped on other parts of the Springfield Armory Model 1911.

During World War I National Blank Book Co. of Holyoke, MA, manufactured three 25-round magazines for Ordnance Department testing. It is not known how they were marked and no photograph could be found. See also the section on "British Magazines."

212

Military and Commercial Pistols

MAGAZINES FOR THE MODEL 1911A1
Colt Magazines
Colt continued to manufacture their **Type 4** magazine after World War I until mid-1940 for both commercial and military use. Prior to mid-1940, all magazines produced by Colt were Type 4. The heat-treating process provided the characteristic two-tone appearance.

NOTE: Field service reports complained that the early World War I magazines often did not activate the slide stop. A directive was therefore issued to scrap all World War I-era magazines.

NOTE: Starting in the 1930s, Colt commercial magazines were marked on the base "**COLT/.45 AUTO**" in a sans serif, elongated type. Some of these magazines may have been shipped with military 1911A1 orders between 1937 and 1943. Type 4 commercially marked magazines have been observed in some blued military 1911A1s circa serial #s 710,000-735,000 but it is not known if they were original to the pistol. Starting at circa serial #735,001, Type 4 commercially marked magazines have been intermittently observed with the Du-Lite finish (sandblasted). The remainder of the magazine was polished except for a slight sandblast overspray. Use of these magazines continued to at least 1943. There is no unanimity of agreement concerning Type 4 commercially marked magazines with the elongated type face marking. Some collectors believe they were only issued with the "commercial" to "military" conversion pistols circa serial #s 756,000-870,000. Others point out that far too many of these magazines have been observed to be accounted for only by these conversions, and that they were probably used intermittently throughout the period.

World War II Type 5 Magazines
Magazines made by Colt to mid-1940 were Type 4 magazines which were heat-blued. After, the heat bluing was replaced with a low temperature "black oxide" process. Two similar processes were used, "Du-Lite" and "Penetrate" (proprietary, trademarked processes of the Du-Lite Chemical Corporation and the Heatbath Corporation, respectively). Either allowed the magazine body to be blued after heat treatment without any effect on the heat-treated metal. All Type 5 magazines were blued top to bottom. In April 1942, to meet the need for more magazines, a contract was awarded to the M.S. Little Company, which had produced magazines

213

Model 1911, M1911A1

during World War I. M.S. Little formed a cooperative with the now Risdon Manufacturing Company and the Scovill Manufacturing Company. Scovill had merged with American Pin Company and so all three partners in the cooperative had previous experience during World War I manufacturing Model 1911 magazines. They produced the magazine that the author has chosen to call the **Type 5**, see Figure 4-14.

Magazines were manufactured both for the four Model 1911A1 manufacturers—Colt, Ithaca, Remington Rand, and Union Switch & Signal—and as spare parts for various military and government agencies in the Type 5 series. Singer had manufactured its own magazines.

Scovill   Risdon   M.S. Little   Colt

Fig. 4-14. Type 5 magazines can often be identified by the deep stress relief cut at the top rear. Compare to Figure 4-8.

Colt continued to manufacture magazines but in addition, Colt Type 5 magazine parts were obtained from the subcontractors in the cooperative. Colt received the assembled magazine body and base plate, which was delivered for final production and finishing, and added the follower and spring. These Type 5 magazines can be distinguished by their markings: "**C-X**" on the bottom of the base plate lip, see Figure 4-15. The "C-" stands for "Colt" and the "X" signifies the manufacturer of the magazine body: "**L**" for M.S. Little; "**R**" for Risdon Manufacturing; "**S**" for

Military and Commercial Pistols

Scovill. The manufacturer's single initial was also marked on the top of the toe.

Those magazines intended for direct shipment from the cooperative's manufacturing company to the military, other pistol contractors, or other government agencies were marked on the top of the base plate lip only with the initial of the manufacturer in the cooperative: "**L**" for M.S. Little; "**R**" for Risdon Manufacturing; "**S**" for Scovill. Magazines wholly manufactured by Colt were unmarked, see Figure 4-16.

NOTE: The collector must be careful here as not all magazines that appear to be Type 5 and are unmarked were manufactured by Colt. Many post-World War II unmarked aftermarket copies have been observed. If the magazine does not have all of the characteristics of a Type 5 magazine as described below, then it was not manufactured by Colt.

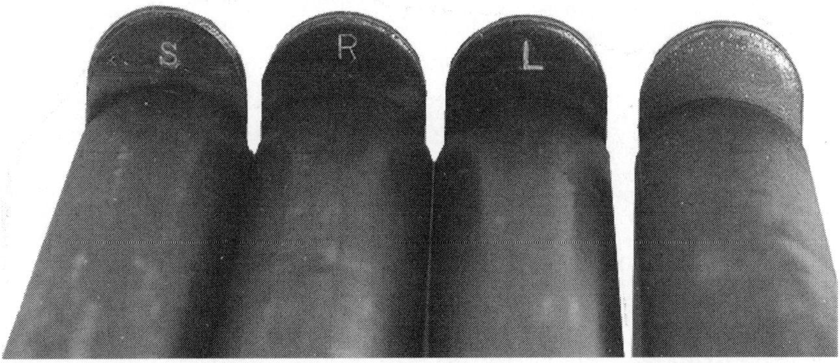

Fig. 4-15. Colt purchased magazine bodies with attached base plates from various companies and finished them in-house. These were marked on the bottom of the base plate lip, "C-" for Colt and "X" for the subcontractor, in this case, "R" for Risdon.

Fig. 4-16. Magazines sent directly to the U.S. Military during World War II were marked on the toe, "S," "R," or "L" for Scovill, Risdon, or M.S. Little, respectively. Those left unmarked were manufactured by Colt.

The **Type 5A** magazine was manufactured by the Colt factory. It was made from steel tubing with riveted base plates, blued, and unmarked.

Model 1911, M1911A1

The **Type 5B** was manufactured by M.S. Little as part of the cooperative and made from seamless steel tubing. The base plate was riveted on in the same manner as the Colt Type 4. The magazine was blued. The base plate was marked "**L**, " as shown in Table 4-4.

The **Type 5C** magazine was manufactured by Risdon Manufacturing Company as part of the M.S. Little cooperative but from sheet steel gas welded into a tube. The base plate was riveted and the magazine was blued. The base plate was marked "**R**," as shown in Table 4-4.

The **Type 5D** magazine was made by the Scovill Manufacturing Company as part of the M.S. Little cooperative from sheet steel welded into a tube but from mid-1943 on, the base plate was surface welded to the tube. The magazine was blued. The base plate was marked "**S**," as shown in Table 4-4.

General Shaver Magazines

In addition to the three companies in the M.S. Little cooperative, the Model 1911A1 magazine was also manufactured by the General Shaver Division of Remington Rand. These magazines were produced under subcontract to the U.S. Army Ordnance Department. They were made of sheet steel, folded into a rectangular tube and spot welded down the back, see Figure 4-17. Base plates were first riveted on as in the Colt Type 4 magazine and later, spot welded in such a manner that rectangular indentations were created. The top of the toe was marked "**G**" (arrow) with the "**G**" partially obscured by the magazine wall. It is generally believed that most, if not all, of General Shaver's 1.5 million production were used by Remington Rand, or as spare parts.

Fig. 4-17. Magazines manufactured by General Shaver, division of Remington Rand, were made of sheet steel and welded down the back. Inset enhanced for clarity. Craig Riesch collection.

216

Military and Commercial Pistols

The **Type 5E** magazine was manufactured by General Shaver Division of Remington Rand. These magazines were made of sheet steel spot welded down the back, refer to Figure 4-17. In early magazines, the base plate was *riveted* on. The magazines show grind marks on the sides and were blued.

The **Type 5F** magazine was also manufactured by General Shaver and made of sheet steel, spot welded into a tube along the back and ground flat along the sides. These later magazines had the base plate *welded* on. The welds were very distinctive as they form rectangular indentations on either side, see Figure 4-18A, arrows.

Fig. 4-18A. Rectangular spot weld marks (arrow) identify this Type 5 magazine as manufactured by the General Shaver Division of Remington Rand.

Two variations of follower were used by General Shaver and are briefly described here and near the end of this chapter. The back of the **1st Variation** follower was smooth with slightly rounded corners on early followers. The **2nd Variation** follower had a wide groove to eliminate friction against the weld on the inside of the magazine. All General Shaver magazines had slightly rounded edges at the bottom. The inside bottom of the follower had a chamfer facing the spring, see Figure 4-18B.

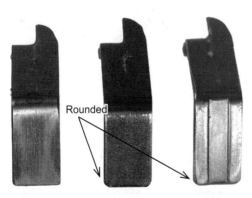

Rounded

Fig. 4-18B. Magazine followers compared, left to right: Colt Type 5A, General Shaver, Type 5, 1st Variation and Type 5, 2nd Variation.

NOTE: All Government Model 1911A1 magazines manufactured during World War II for military contracts were blued and

Model 1911, M1911A1

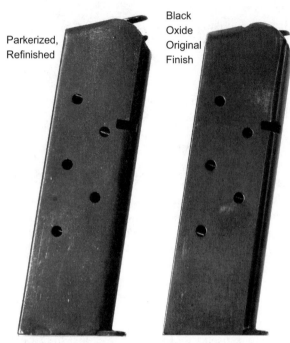

Parkerized, Refinished

Black Oxide Original Finish

have a shiny appearance. Parkerized magazines are the result of refinishing and have a dull finish caused by a light sandblasting before being dipped in the Parkerizing solution, see Figure 4-19. The bluing process used was referred to by the Ordnance Department as "Black Oxide" and commercially as the "Du-Lite," or "Penetrate" process. Both were proprietary, trademarked processes of the Du-Lite

Fig. 4-19. Parkerized .45 ACP magazines have been refinished and have a dull non-reflective appearance (left). Original .45 ACP magazines had a black oxide finish and have a shiny appearance (right).

Chemical Corporation and the Heatbath Corporation, respectively. The difference is hard to see in a black-and-white photo, but look for a very smooth, shiny finish on original magazines.

Table 4-4			
World War II Model 1911A1 Magazines			
(U.S. Military)			
Subcontractor	Destination	Type	Marking
Colt	Colt Factory	5A	Unmarked
M.S. Little Co.	U.S. Government	5B	L (base plate top lip)
M.S. Little Co.	Colt	5B	C-L (base plate bottom)
Risdon Mfg. Co.	U.S. Government	5C	R (base plate top lip)

Military and Commercial Pistols

Table 4-4, cont.			
World War II Model 1911A1 Magazines			
(U.S. Military)			
Subcontractor	Destination	Type	Marking
Risdon Mfg. Co.	Colt	5C	C-R (base plate bottom)
Scovill Mfg. Co.	U.S. Government	5D	S (base plate top lip)
Scovill Mfg. Co.	Colt	5D	C-S (base plate bottom)
General Shaver	Remington Rand	5E	G (base plate top lip)
General Shaver	Remington Rand	5F	G (base plate top lip)

Post-World War II Magazines

In spite of the millions of Government Model 1911/1911A1 magazines estimated to have been manufactured during World War II, the demand continued by the U.S. military and those governments who received the Model 1911A1 as Lend-Lease or military aid. The renewed commercial market also required new magazines as the Government Model underwent a resurgence of interest. In 1970 Colt reintroduced the Model 1911A1 as the Series 70 , followed by the Series 80. In late 1990, a look-alike copy of the Model 1911A1 was introduced as the Model 1991. It was a pretty good copy although it had blued finish, aluminum trigger, no lanyard loop, truncated diamond wood grips, and a flat mainspring housing.

More Colt Magazines

Colt continued to manufacture magazines after World War II while at the same time also subcontracting their manufacture to outside firms. Magazines manufactured by Colt, or for Colt, were marked as such in a variety of formats with the Colt name and/or logo. A large quantity remained in stock after military contracts for the Model 1911A1 were canceled, and these blued or black oxide-finished magazines can be distinguished from those manufactured by the M.S. Little-led cooperative only by the lack of an identifying initial(s) on the base plate.

The majority of postwar Model 1911A1 magazines were blued or finished in black oxide. Others matched pistols that were finished in chrome and nickel plate (both smooth and brushed). A much smaller number were made with an electroless nickel finish starting in the early 1980s.

Model 1911, M1911A1

Two types of Colt postwar magazines were manufactured. Until the late 1960s, Colt magazines were generally Type 5B magazines made of seamless steel tubing with welded base plates. The author has chosen to call them **Type 6** magazines.

Starting in the late 1960s, a Type 6 Colt commercial magazine was placed into production based on the Type 5F magazine developed by General Shaver. There were two variations of the Colt-manufactured magazines, or those subcontracted to Colt.

The **Type 6A** commercial magazine was made of sheet steel folded to shape and welded down the back. The base plates were surface welded to the magazine body, nicely polished to remove all machining marks, and blued. Base plates were usually given a matte finish. These were marked on the base plate "**COLT/45 AUTO**" and the contractor's initial, usually "**M,**" see Figure 4-20.

The **Type 6B** commercial magazine was also made of sheet steel formed into a tube and welded down the back. Final polishing was not quite as good as the Type 6A magazines and

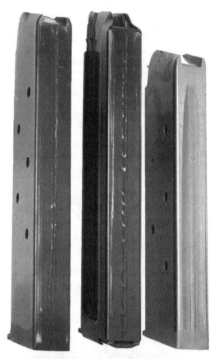

Fig. 4-20. These three post-World War II Colt magazines were welded down the back and the .45 ACPs were marked "M" on the bottom of the base plate. Left to right: magazine from a Lightweight Commander, 1950; Service ACE, 1985; Commercial Colt Officer's Model, 1988.

Military and Commercial Pistols

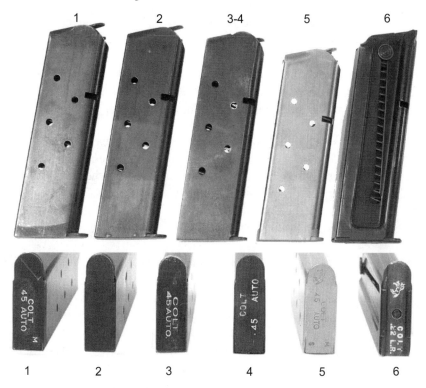

Fig. 4-21. Colt post-World War II production magazines: (l-r) 1) commercial, 2) unmarked military production circa 1946-47 supplied, in this case, with a Model 1911A1 National Match pistol, 3) Colt commercial, pre-WWII, 4) Colt commercial production, Series 70, 5) Colt Officer's Model commercial production, 1980s, and 6) Colt commercial ACE, .22-caliber magazine.

do show some grinding and polishing marks. The base plate was welded to the magazine. These were marked on the base plate with the Rampant Colt logotype followed by "**COLT/45 AUTO**" and the contractor's initial, usually "**M**."

The **Type 6C** commercial magazines (Figure 4-21, 4) were very similar to the Type 6A but carried the marking, "**COLT/.45 AUTO**, "with a decimal point but without the elongated type as the pre-World War II Type 4 commercial magazines. They have been observed in commercial Model 1911A1s manufactured in the immediate postwar period. Some

Model 1911, M1911A1

Type 6C magazines may have been left over from prewar commercial stocks which escaped use during the war.

Colt manufactured a **Type 7** magazine that holds eight rounds. The magazine body is the same length and width as the seven-round magazine but uses a flatter magazine follower and a thinner-diameter mainspring.

Post-World War II Military Contract Magazines

The buildup of U.S. forces for both the Korean and Vietnam Wars, plus the innumerable pacifying and police actions in which the United States military participated from 1945 through 1984 when the Beretta M9 replaced the Model 1911A1 as the sidearm of the U.S. military, created a constant demand for pistol magazines.

These post-World War II military magazines appear to be based on the Colt Type 5. They were made from seamless tubing or from welded sheet steel with welded base plates. They can usually be identified by the markings on their base plate which take the form of an eleven-digit Federal Stock number (1948 to 1974) or a 12+ digit National Stock Number from 1975 on, see Figure 4-22. For instance, stamped on the base of a Model 1911A1 magazine in the author's collection is the marking, "**19200-/ASSY 5508694/MFR. 19204.**" This identifies the item as a pistol magazine for the Colt Model 1911A1 as manufactured by Rock Island Arsenal after 1974. Another is marked "**19200-/ASSY 5508694/MFR. 1M291.**" This magazine was manufactured by Check-Mate Indus-

Fig. 4-22. Model 1911A1 post-World War II U.S. military contract magazine manufactured by Check-Mate Industries showing the Department of Defense procurement information.

tries, Inc., Wyandanch, New York, and since 1984, the sole supplier of M1911A1 magazines to the U.S. Government.

NOTE: The collector should be aware that rejected Model 1911A1 magazines from various manufacturers have been purchased as surplus

222

Military and Commercial Pistols

and repackaged by unscrupulous dealers in simulated contract wrapping. The base plates have been stamped with real or spurious national stock numbers. For one possible way to identify "real" contract magazines, go to http://www.bpn.gov/bines/choose.asp and select "Search." Type the manufacturer's code (the last five alphanumeric characters) in the "Cage" box. This will at least verify whether or not the manufacturer actually exists and did have a contract or contracts to furnish Model 1911A1 magazines.

Table 4-5
Post-World War II Period Magazines

Type/ Characteristics	6		Post-World War II
	A	B	
Magazine Body	Welded, seam down back		Steel Tube
Base Plate	Sides covered		
Base Plate Fastened	Welded, no spot weld marks		Spot weld marks
Indented Magazine Catch	Yes		
Lanyard Loop	No		
Top, Rear	Square Corners		Angled Corners
Base Plate Marking	COLT/M 45 AUTO	Logo COLT/M 45 AUTO	None or Federal or National Stock Number
Manufacturer	Colt	Colt or Subcontractors	Various
Finish	Black oxide		

Other Commercial Magazines

The number of magazines manufactured for the Government Model 1911 and Model 1911A1 by various manufacturers is well beyond the scope of this book. More than sixty years have passed since the end of World War II, and dozens of clones of the Model 1911 pistol have been manufactured in this country and abroad. Most of their manufacturers either produced their own magazines or bought them from suppliers. Magazines manufactured for clones of the Government Model 1911 or 1911A1 may

223

Model 1911, M1911A1

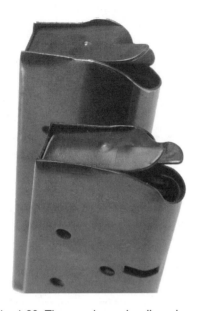

Fig. 4-23. The popular and well-made MEC-GAR magazines can always be identified by their rounded-top follower (front) rather than the dimple of the Colt design (rear).

not function well, or not at all, in any but the pistol for which they were manufactured.

Perhaps one of the largest manufacturers of commercial magazines has been MEC-GAR srl of Gardone, Italy. MEC-GAR has produced a wide range of magazines for various handguns. Some MEC-GAR .45 ACP magazines were marked on the left side with the company name and logo, while others were not. MEC-GAR magazines can usually be identified by their follower which has a rounded top rather than the Colt dimple, see Figure 4-23. In the author's experience, MEC-GAR magazines are top quality and have provided excellent service in any of the Model 1911s, Model 1911A1s, Series 70, Series 80 or the Model 1991 Series Colt pistols and clones he has tested. Other commercial magazines may or may not be marked with the name of their manufacturer, or distributor, and their quality will vary greatly.

FOREIGN MANUFACTURED MAGAZINES

Magazines for the Model 1911 and Model 1911A1 have been widely manufactured around the world. Most have been made by, or in, countries using licensed or foreign aid-supplied Model 1911 or Model 1911A1s in their military and/or police forces.

Argentinian Magazines

Magazines made by Colt for the Argentine contracts, and those manufactured in Argentina, are the Type 4, folded and welded sheet-steel pattern with the bottom plate attached with two rivets through both sides.

Military and Commercial Pistols

The serial number of the original pistol was stamped on the bottom of Argentine-made magazines used in government or police service, see Figure 4-24.

Original Argentine magazines show the characteristic two-tone coloration that resulted from heat-treating the magazine lips. Because of their long service in the Argentine military and police, many Argentine magazines have been refinished and reblued. These may show wire brush marks and/or an even blue coloration, depending on their condition.

Fig. 4-24. Argentine magazines for the Model 1927 are similar to the Type 4 magazine but have the original pistol's serial number stamped on the bottom.

The collector should note that many Colt pistols were sold commercially in Argentina, and the magazines supplied with those pistols will be the standard commercial magazines for their serial number range.

British Magazines
Colt magazines supplied for commercial Model 1911-type and Model 1911A1-type pistols sold in Great Britain were the same as those manufactured for military pistols during the same periods.

Before World War I, Model 1911s in both .45 ACP and .455 Webley chamberings were available on the commercial market. Magazines for those pistols chambered for the .455 Webley cartridge were usually marked ".455 ELEY" on the base plate with or without the decimal point before the "4." The Eley company was the largest manufacturer of the cartridge in Great Britain—designed originally for the .455 Webley semi-automatic pistol—and so it is commonly known as the .455 Eley.

NOTE: The .45 ACP cartridge is a rimless design with a case diameter of 0.470 inch and a rim diameter of 0.476 inch. The .455 Webley cartridge is semi-rimmed with a case diameter of 0.476 inch and the semi-rim has a diameter of 0.522 inch, maximum, refer to Figure 4-11.

Model 1911, M1911A1

Military Model 1911s prefixed "W" will (with the exception of a few locally manufactured magazines during World War II) show the marking "**CAL. .455/ELEY**" and the British broad arrow signifying government ownership, see Figure 4-25.

During World War I, the British military received a large number of Model 1911 pistols with the serial number prefix "W." Three types of magazines have been observed: British **Type 1** magazines were marked with the British broad arrow on the bottom of the base plate toe and "**CAL. 455/ELEY**" with and without a decimal point on either side of the lanyard loop. These

were provided with the "W"-prefixed pistols during World War I.

The British **Type 2** military contract for the .455 Eley cartridge magazine was marked in the same manner as the Type 1 but has the serial number of the pistol's receiver stamped on the under-

Fig. 4-25. Magazines for the British .455 Webley or Eley cartridge are wider than the .45 ACP magazine and are marked "455 ELEY" with and without a decimal point. Some may show the "Broad Arrow" on the bottom of the base plate.

side of the toe. These are generally attributed to Royal Air Force ownership. The collector should be careful here as these markings were not originally applied at the factory, but in the 1920s by RAF armorers; they were stamped by hand using individual stamps. In all RAF magazines so marked which have been observed, a serif type face was used.

The British **Type 3** magazine was manufactured in the United Kingdom by Beesley of St. James Street during and after World War I. These magazines were blued and do not show the temper mark. In place of the lanyard ring, a screw eye was welded to the bottom plate. These magazines are marked only "**.455**" on the bottom behind the screw eye and the view or counting holes are punched in the right side only. Both seven-round and twenty-round magazines were manufactured. They were sold in bridle leather double cases with straps and hooks intended to be attached to sword rings on the officer's belt. These magazines were pri-

Military and Commercial Pistols

vately purchased for the most part, although the Royal Naval Air Service did purchase a small quantity for testing.

Magazines provided with British Purchasing Commission (BPC) pistols or Lend-Lease pistols will be the Colt Type 4 or 5 in .45 ACP. No M1911A1 .455 Webley (Eley) caliber pistols were supplied through the auspices of the BPC or Lend-Lease.

Norwegian Magazines
Colt sold three hundred Model 1911 pistols to the Norwegian Ministry of Defense in 1913. The examples examined were equipped with the Type 3 lanyard loop. Magazines manufactured in Norway for the Model 1914 were based on the Colt Type 3 pattern, all with lanyard loops and pinned bases, see Figure 4-26.

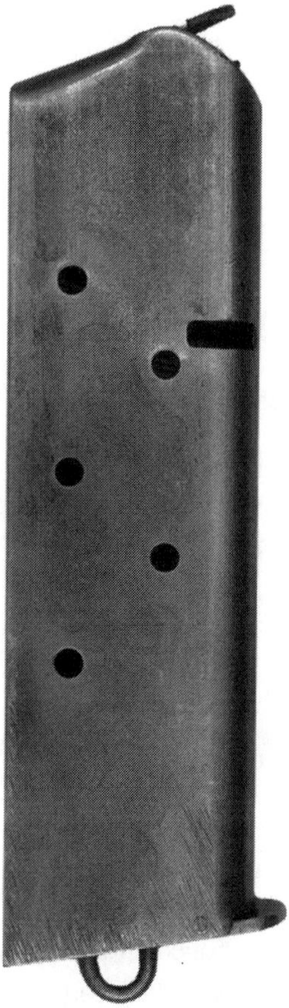

MAGAZINE SPRINGS
The magazine springs used in the Model 1911/Model 1911A1 magazine were formed in the shape of a repeating "Z." They were nominally 0.405 inch wide, by 7.4 inches long and formed from spring steel wire 0.050 inch in diameter, see Figure 4-27.

Fig. 4-26. Magazines made for the Norwegian Model 1914 had pinned bases and lanyard loops and resembled the Colt Type 3 magazine.

Two types were used. The **Type 1** magazine spring ended in a quarter turn at the front with a short right-angle bend that pressed against the bottom of the follower. It was used in all Type 1 through 4 magazines.

The **Type 2** magazine spring ended in a three-quarter turn at the rear and a loop. The change was made to apply more even pressure to the bottom of the follower. It was used in all Type 5 and subsequent magazines.

Model 1911, M1911A1

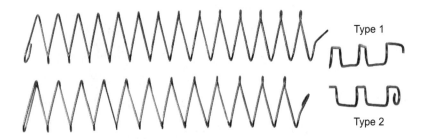

Fig. 4-27. Top, Type 1 magazine spring. Bottom, Type 2. The inset on the right indicates the difference in the end that pressed against the follower.

MAGAZINE FOLLOWERS

The magazine follower was a platform on which the cartridge(s) rested. It was pushed up from the bottom of the magazine by the magazine spring. The cartridge was held in the magazine against the pressure of the magazine spring by the flexible lips at the top of the magazine. The magazine follower was stamped from sheet steel 0.478 inch wide and 2.15 inches long. The rear 0.85-inch-long section was bent backward at a 120-degree angle and guided the follower up and down in the body. The front lip was split with the left half bent down 0.3 inch and forward to form a ledge which engaged the slide stop when the magazine was empty to hold the slide open. The forward parts of both split halves were rounded. A dimple was punched in the center of the top segment to provide added lift to the cartridge. The dimple supported the case and prevented the bullet from rotating down against the follower and possibly causing a misfeed.

Three types of followers were developed, see Figure 4-28.

The **Type 1** follower was manufactured by Colt, Springfield Armory, Singer, and all other contractors and subcontractors with one exception. The magazine follower was flat; the rear, bent-down section, which acted as a guide, was square at the corners.

The **Type 2** follower was manufactured by the General Shaver division of Remington Rand. Because the General Shaver magazines were welded down the back, the guide portion of the follower had to be modified to prevent snagging on the welded seam.

228

Military and Commercial Pistols

The **1st Variation** General Shaver follower had a smooth back and rounded bottom corners. The **2nd Variation** General Shaver magazine follower had a groove pressed into the guide which provided smoother operation by bridging the magazine tube weld.

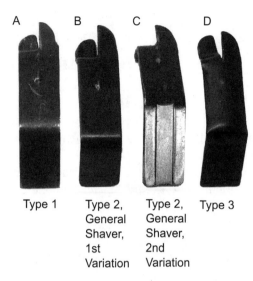

| Type 1 | Type 2, General Shaver, 1st Variation | Type 2, General Shaver, 2nd Variation | Type 3 |

The **Type 3** follower was used with the Series 70 National Match pistols. It differed from the standard magazine follower in that the follower was rounded to provide a more positive feed.

Fig. 4-28. Magazine followers: A) Type 1; B) Type 2, 1st Variation; C) Type 2, 2nd Variation; and D) Type 3, Series 70 National Match.

MAGAZINE FINISHES

The magazine was generally given the same type of finish as the pistol's receiver and slide. From the start of production to circa serial #735,000 in mid-1941, this was a heat bluing applied in a furnace. After mid-1941, all Colt magazines were given a black oxide treatment, either Du-Lite or Penetrate.

World War II magazines and all Colt commercial post-World War II magazines were finished using the Du-Lite black oxide process.

If a Colt Model 1911/1911A1 was finished in nickel, silver, chrome or other platings, the magazine was often plated in the same manner. But a customer could special order any magazine finish, and blued magazines were often ordered with nickel- or silver-plated pistols for the contrast.

Springfield Armory magazines were copper plated for approximately 0.630 inch below the magazine lips at the rear, then heat-treated. The bottom part of the magazine showed heat-color markings that appear to have been an artifact of the gas welding process.

CHAPTER 5
SERIAL NUMBERS

COLT SERIAL NUMBERS

Colt produced the Model 1911 at the urging of General William Crozier (U.S. Army Chief of Ordnance from 1901 to 1918). The initial production went to satisfy military contracts. Commercial production was interwoven with the government contract production and the first commercial model, serial number C1, was shipped from the Colt factory on April 13, 1912.

To keep the government and commercial lines of pistols separate, each was numbered within its own serial number range. U.S. Government contract pistols were serial numbered only with a variation of the "No." prefix. This range also included production by Springfield Armory, Singer, Remington Rand, Ithaca, and Union Switch & Signal; and the assigned blocks ran from serial numbers 1 through 2,660,318. Singer numbers were prefixed "№ S" and ran from S800,001-S800,500. Commercial models were manufactured by Colt and serial numbered in their own range with a "C" prefix until 1950 at C240,227 when the "C" became a suffix and continued to 336,169C.

"Other" calibers such as the .22 ACE and Service Model ACE, the various Super .38 and 9 mm Luger pistols were serial numbered in their own ranges. Consult the appropriate tables later in this chapter.

NOTE: U.S Military Model 1911A1 production by Colt ended at serial number 2,368,781. Colt duplicated numbers assigned to Ithaca, Remington Rand and Union Switch & Signal in 1943. See Tables 5-9, -10, and -11.

Remington Arms-UMC was assigned its own serial number ranges; Remington Arms-UMC numbers were prefixed "NO" without a period and ran from 1 to 21,676. Winchester, North American Arms Company, A.J. Savage, and National Cash Register Company during World War I did not reach production and so were not assigned serial number blocks. Harrington & Richardson never began production during World War II. They were assigned the serial number block H800,501-H801,000 but it was never used.

Military and Commercial Pistols

NOTE: While the factory and government serial number records of military contract pistols are as complete as can be expected over a forty-year, non-computerized period, there is a bit of controversy surrounding the more esoteric commercial models and caliber change kits. The serial number charts shown below have been compiled from direct observation and from the lists compiled by a number of authors. It is as accurate as observations and the source materials permit. If you have, or know of, a pistol that falls outside of any of the ranges listed, the author would be grateful to receive the information for later editions of this book.

COLT PREFIXES AND SUFFIXES

Commercial production of the Model 1911 and Model 1911A1 was prefixed with a "C" and ran from C1 through C240,227 at which point the "C" became a suffix and continued from 240,228C to 336,169C in 1969. The new Series 70 line of Model 1911A1 type pistols was introduced the next year and the serial numbering in this line began at G01002 with the prefix "70."

Certain other lines of Model 1911s and Model 1911A1s manufactured by Colt received an identifying prefix as well. Those manufactured for the British military under contract in caliber .455 Webley during World War I received a "W" prefix. But most others, such as those pistols manufactured for Canada (1914 contract), Norway, Russia and later for Argentina, were taken directly from commercial production and retained their "C" commercial prefix. Model 1911 pistols manufactured under license in Norway were numbered in their own serial number range.

Model and caliber variations manufactured by Colt, such as the Service Model ACE (but not the original ACE), received a distinguishing prefix, "SM." The .22 ACE did not have a prefix. The .22-.45 and .45-.22 caliber conversion kits were prefixed "U." Service Model ACE kits manufactured after World War II were not serial numbered.

Colt .38 Special conversion kits for the Super .38 pistol received the suffix "H." Kits to convert the .45 ACP pistol to the Colt .38 Special received the suffix "O." Both kits were also numbered in their own sequence, see Table 5-17.

National Match pistols manufactured before World War II were numbered in the commercial series with the prefix, "C." After World War II, they were given the "NM" suffix. The Super .38 National Match

Model 1911, M1911A1

Pistols received an "NMR" suffix; the Lightweight Commander suffix was "LW," the steel commander was "CLW" and Series 70 Combat Commander suffixes were "70BS" and "70SC." See Also Appendix H.

NOTE: Model 1911 and Model 1911A1 "X"-prefixed serial numbers will occasionally be noted. These were replacement serial numbers assigned by the Ordnance Department for pistols that had their serial numbers damaged during repairs or rebuilds. They were issued for use between 1924-1954 and 1950-1957 and later. They are described in Table 5-12, below.

Finally, afficionados of the Model 1911/1911A1 owe a great debt to those who have searched Colt and other manufacturers' production records and those of the U.S. government over the years—notably Donald B. Bady, R.L. Wilson, Charles W. Clawson, William H. D. Goddard, Karl Karash and Edward Scott Meadows—to compile the serial number ranges listed in the charts below.

NOTE: Serial number ranges in the following tables are listed by receiving authority (i.e., U.S. Army, U.S. Navy, etc.) and calendar year. Slight adjustments to some sequences have been made by the author based on direct observation. See Tables 5-1, 5-2 and Appendices B and F.

U.S. Army Model 1911/1911A1 Serial Numbers

Table 5-1 U.S. Army Model 1911/1911A1 Serial Numbers, Colt			
Calendar Year	Serial Number Range	Calendar Year	Serial Number Range
1912	1-500 1001-1500 2001-2500 3801-4500 5501-6500 7501-8500 9501-10500 11501-12500 13051-17250	1937	(4) 710001-711605 711606-712349
1913	17251-36400 37651-38000 44001-60400	1938	712350-713645

Military and Commercial Pistols

Table 5-1, cont.
U.S. Army Model 1911/1911A1 Serial Numbers,
Colt

Calendar Year	Serial Number Range	Calendar Year	Serial Number Range
1914	60401-72570 83856-83900 84401-96000 97538-102596	1939	
1915	107597-109500 110001-113496 120567-125566	1940	717282-721977
1916	(1) 133187-137400	1941	721978-756733 (2) 856,101-856,300
1917	137401-151186 151987-185800 186201-209586 (2) 210387-215386 216187-216586 216587-216986	1942	756734-797640-800000 (5) 801001-856100 (2) 856,301-856,404
1918	217387-223952 223991-232000 233601-580600	1943	856101-985100 1088726-1092896 1096405-1208673 (2) 1279674-1279698
1919 (3)	580601-629500 629501-717386	1944	1609529-1743846
1924	700001-710000	1945	(6) 2244804-2380013

1. Colt manufactured 3,569 Model 1911s in the Springfield Armory serial number range (128617-133186). Many shipped out of sequence this year–see Appendix F for explanation.
2. Replacement serial numbers issued to Rock Island and Augusta Arsenals.
3. The last Model 1911 manufactured for the U.S. was circa serial #629500. The remaining 87,885 or so pistols in the WAR ORDER 14670-R32 (Sept. 18, 1917) were canceled Jan. 23, 1919.
4. Only 769 in this range were for the U.S. Army. The balance of 836 were for the U.S. Navy.
5. 6,575 commercial model 1911A1s were transferred to military contracts (circa 860003-866675)
6. Last Model 1911A1 manufactured for the U.S. Army by Colt was 2368781 shipped September 18, 1945. This left some 11,232 serial numbers unused in this contract.

NOTE: Colt duplicated 60,000 serial numbers in the Ithaca (856,405-916,404); 41,696 in the Remington Rand (916,405-958,100), and 4,171

Model 1911, M1911A1

in the Union Switch & Signal (1,088,726-1,092,896) ranges. These serial numbers were assigned by the Ordnance Department in error.

U.S. Navy Model 1911/1911A1 Serial Numbers

The U.S. Navy Model 1911s were marked on the right side of the slide "**MODEL OF 1911. U.S. NAVY**" between 1912 and 1915. After 1915, all Navy models were marked "**MODEL OF 1911. U.S. ARMY**" or "**MODEL I9IIAI U.S. ARMY,**" see Table 5-2.

Table 5-2 U.S. Navy Model 1911/1911A1 Serial Numbers Colt			
Calendar Year	Serial Number Range	Calendar Year	Serial Number Range
1912	501-1000 1501-2000 2501-3500 4501-5500 6501-7500 8501-9500 10501-11500 12501-13500	1937	(2) 710001-711605 711606-712349
1913	38001-43800 43801-43900 43901-44000	1938	
1914	96001-97537	1939	713646-717281
1915	(1) 109501-110000	1940	
1916		1941	
1917		1942	793658-797639
1918 (3)	223953-223990 232001-233600	1943	
1919 (4)		1944	
1924		1945	

1. All Model 1911s in Navy contracts through circa serial #110,000 were marked "**MODEL OF 1911. U.S. NAVY**" on the right side of the slide. After, no Navy distinguishing legend was used.

2. Only 836 of this serial number sequence were shipped to the U.S. Navy. The rest (769) went to the U.S. Army.

3. Three more groups of non-consecutively numbered pistols were shipped to the USMC in 1918.

4. Two more groups of non-consecutively numbered pistols were shipped to the USMC in 1918.

Military and Commercial Pistols

U.S. Marine Corps Model 1911 Serial Numbers

The Marine Corps placed separate orders with the U.S. Army Ordnance Department for the Model 1911 between 1912 and 1918. After, all were processed through the U.S. Navy. None were marked specifically for the U.S. Marine Corps on the slide, see Table 5-3.

Calendar Year	Serial Number Range
Table 5-3 **U.S. Marine Corps Model 1911** **Serial Numbers** **Colt**	
1912 (1)	3501-3800
1913	36401-37650
1914	83901-84400
1915	
1916	151187-151986
1917 (2)	185801-186200 209587-210386 215387-216186 216587-216986
1918 (3)	216987-217386

1. All USMC Model 1911s carried the U.S. Army marking on the slide.
2. To equip the U.S. Marine Expeditionary Force moving to France, U.S. Army Model 1911s in the circa serial # range 185,801-186,200 and 216,187-216,586 were transferred from the Army and replaced with an equal number of pistols from the Army contract later in October 1917.
3. After 1918, all USMC purchases were processed through the U.S. Navy.

Springfield Armory Model 1911 Serial Numbers

The situation at Springfield Armory regarding serial numbers by year is confusing, to say the least. The Springfield Armory manufactured the Model 1911 pistol between 1914 and 1917. As noted in Chapter 1, Springfield's production was supplementary to rifle production and was

Model 1911, M1911A1

originally intended to cease if rifle production exceeded 500 per day due to the unavailability of equipment, space, and manpower. Also, the Model 1913 cavalry saber and parts for the Model 1909 machine gun were being manufactured on some of this same machinery and all interfered with rifle production which was the Armory's priority. A survey showed that Colt, and outside contractors, could produce enough Model 1911 pistols to meet the needs of the military as the country entered World War I. Based on the survey and the pressing need to manufacture more Model 1903 Springfield rifles, pistol production was ended at the Springfield Armory on April 17, 1917.

In fact the survey was wildly optimistic. By March 1918, the shortage of pistols was estimated to be on the order of 900,000.

The Springfield Armory had been assigned six blocks of serial numbers, the last of which was suspended in mid-production. Total serial number allocation, including the last block, encompassed a total of 36,095 pistols but as researchers, notably Clawson, have shown, only 25,767 pistols in all were actually manufactured at the Springfield Armory.

Springfield Armory sent surplus parts to Colt in May 1917. The exact disposition of these parts in unknown. The unused serial numbers were reassigned to Colt where they appear to have been used as "replacement serial numbers" over the next few years. All observed serial numbers in this range (128,617-133,186) appear to be Colt-made receivers. They also shipped thirty-nine of the surplus receivers to the Quartermaster, Hoboken Barracks, New Jersey, for use as spares. These receivers were serial numbered from 130,517-130,555.

A review of the Annual Reports of the Chief of Ordnance to the Secretary of War for the fiscal years 1914-1918 shows the following numbers of pistols manufactured at the Springfield Armory by fiscal year:

Fiscal Year 1914 (July 1, 1913-June 30, 1914)	3,030
Fiscal Year 1915 (July 1, 1914-June 30, 1915)	15,359
Fiscal Year 1916 (July 1, 1915-June 30, 1916)	4,966
Fiscal Year 1917 (July 1, 1916-June 30, 1917)	2,412
Total	25,767

Military and Commercial Pistols

Ordnance Department procurement records show that all Springfield Armory Model 1911s between serial numbers 72,571 and 120,566, were received by January 8, 1916. Production was shut down from February through June 1916 and Semi-Annual reports show that 1,564 pistols were assembled between July 1 and December 31, 1916, and an additional 848 in the first half of 1917 (FY 1917) in the serial number ranges 125,567-127,130 and 127,131-127,978, respectively, see Table 5-4.

Table 5-4 U.S. Army Model 1911 Serial Numbers Springfield Armory	
Calendar Year	**Serial Number Range**
1914	72571-81750
1915	81751-83855 102597-107596 113497-120566
1916	125567-127130
1917	127131-127978

Springfield Armory Model 1911A1
National Match Serial Numbers

Following the Korean War armistice in 1953, attention in the military once again turned to match shooting. The Army was prevailed upon to devote some small resources to both rifle and pistol marksmanship, and the Ordnance Department issued orders for the Springfield Armory to prepare "match quality" Model 1911A1 pistols. Their production is summarized in Table 5-5.

Table 5-5 Springfield Armory National Match Pistol Production, Quantity Produced (1)			
Calendar Year	**Number Rebuilt Per Year**	**Calendar Year**	**Number Rebuilt Per Year**
1955	800	1961	972

Model 1911, M1911A1

Table 5-5, cont. Springfield Armory National Match Pistol Production, Quantity Produced (1)			
Calendar Year	Number Rebuilt Per Year	Calendar Year	Number Rebuilt Per Year
1956	1,250	1962	3,025
1957	None	1963	2,418
1958	635	1964	800
1959	1,065	1965	1,773
1960	2,717		

(1) Serial numbers are in the Model 1911A1 range and are mixed. Pistols were usually drawn from surplus World War II production, any manufacturer. The pistols were rebuilt and accurized at the Springfield Armory and are marked "SA" on the right side of the frame. Pistols were sold to competitors at the National Matches. Unsold pistols were usually rebuilt for use the following year. These will usually show an additional "SA" mark.

Remington Arms-UMC Model 1911 Serial Numbers

Remington Arms–UMC Company received two contracts to produce 500,000 Model 1911 pistols. Production was delayed by inaccurate drawings until August 1918. The company's contracts were canceled shortly after the armistice was signed on November 11, 1918. Remington Arms-UMC delivered the last of its 21,677 pistols to the Ordnance Department in May 1919. The Remington Arms-UMC pistols were manufactured in their own separate serial number range as shown in Table 5-6.

Table 5-6 U.S. Army Model 1911 Serial Numbers, Remington Arms-UMC (1)	
Month/Year	Serial Number Range
August 1918	1-138
September 1918	139-510
October 1918	511-4657
November 1918	4658-8535
December 1918	8536-12573

Military and Commercial Pistols

Table 5-6, cont. U.S. Army Model 1911 Serial Numbers, Remington Arms-UMC (1)	
Month/Year	**Serial Number Range**
1919	12574-21677 (2)

1. Serial number data from Remington Arms-UMC report, "Serial Numbers of .45 Colt Automatic Pistols Manufactured Under Contract # P4537-3338Sa, Remington Arms-UMC to Major Lee O. Wright, Ord. Dept. U.S.A.," July 26, 1923.
2. Questions exist as to whether the total number manufactured is 21,676 or 21,677.

Singer Model 1911A1 Serial Numbers

Singer manufactured 500 Model 1911A1 pistols which were shipped to the U.S. Army Air Force after December 5, 1941 (S800,001 through S800,500). The company was granted an additional contract for 15,000 pistols but it was canceled so that Singer could concentrate their war effort on the M5 Artillery Fire Control Director, which was considered a critical program.

Table 5-7 U.S. Army Model 1911A1 Serial Numbers Singer Manufacturing Company	
Calendar Year	**Serial Number Range**
1941	S800001-S800500

General Note: Educational Order No. W-ORD-396. 500 only produced.

Harrington & Richardson Model 1911A1 Serial Numbers

Harrington & Richardson Arms received an Educational Contract to produce the Model 1911A1 pistol. Other wartime work had higher priority and so none were produced.

Table 5-8 U.S. Army Model 1911A1 Serial Numbers Harrington & Richardson	
Calendar Year	**Serial Number Range**
1941	H800501-H801000

General Note: Proposed Educational Order. None produced, serial number block not used.

Model 1911, M1911A1

Ithaca Model 1911A1 Serial Numbers

The Ithaca Gun Company was awarded wartime contract W–740-ORD-2263 in May 1942 to manufacture 60,000 Model 1911A1 pistols. The company did not move vigorously to procure manufacturing equipment, which was growing scarcer by the month. As a consequence, they were sent 6,200 surplus receivers that had been reclaimed by the Ordnance Salvage Board following World War I. These were a combination of unfinished Colt receivers and salvaged receivers. They were refurbished by Ithaca and were used in the serial number range circa 856,405 to 870,000. In addition, Colt provided over 7,000 newly manufactured but unmarked receivers that were used in approximately the same serial number range. The earlier Colt 1911 receivers can be identified by Frank Hosmer's inspection stamp, "H," near the disconnector hole. Colt also provided over 2,200 new, unmarked slides to Ithaca in late 1942 and early 1943. Some receivers have been observed with an "I" (which was subsequently dropped) between the "№" and the serial number similar to the "S" prefix on Singer. Ithaca received five contracts in all.

Table 5-9 U.S. Army Model 1911A1 Serial Numbers Ithaca Gun Company, Inc.	
Calendar Year	Serial Number Range
1943 (2)	856405-916404 (1) 1208674-1279673 1441431-1471430
1944 (2)	1816642-1890503
1945 (2) (3)	2075104-2134403 2619014-2693613

1. Colt duplicated 60,000 serial numbers in this first Ithaca serial number range.
2. Pistols were not shipped in numerical sequence and there is overlap year-to-year.
3. Ithaca production actually ended with serial number 2660318 leaving 33,294 serial numbers unused.

Remington Rand Model 1911A1 Serial Numbers

A contract was issued to the company by the Ordnance Department on May 22, 1942, to manufacture 125,000 Model 1911A1 pistols. By the

Military and Commercial Pistols

end of production in 1945, the company produced the majority of parts but depended on High Standard for barrels and Keyes Fibre for stock panels and other subcontractors for minor parts such as triggers, mainsprings, and stock screw bushings as well as other parts. Remington Rand also made extensive use of its other divisions to produce parts.

Calendar Year	Table 5-10 U.S. Army Model 1911A1 Serial Numbers Remington Rand, Inc. Approximate Serial Number Range (1)
1942 (3)	916405-921700 (2)
1943 (3)	921701-1041404 *119703* 1279699-1441430
1944 (3)	1471431-1609528 1743847-1816641 1890504-2075103
1945 (3) (4)	2134404-2244803 2380014-2619013

1. Serial number ranges are approximate since Remington Rand shipping records are lost.
2. Colt duplicated 41,696 serial numbers in this range.
3. Pistols not shipped in numerical order; overlap between years.
4. According to Remington Rand, production actually ended with serial number 2465139 leaving 153,874 serial numbers unused.

Union Switch & Signal Model 1911A1 Serial Numbers

The company was awarded Contract W-ORD-2211 by the Ordnance Department in May 1942 to manufacture the Model 1911A1 pistol. Production began in January 1943, but the company was notified a few days later that their contract would be canceled as the requirement for the Model 1911A1 had been reduced. The company participated in the production of receivers, operating slides and bolts for the M1 Carbine. On June 26, 1943, the Ordnance Department requested that US&S produce the M1911A1 after all, plus an additional 25,000. US&S delivered the total order of 55,000 Model 1911A1s by November 27, 1943.

241

Model 1911, M1911A1

Table 5-11 U.S. Army Model 1911A1 Serial Numbers Union Switch & Signal Company (1)	
Calendar Year	Serial Number Range
1943	1041405-1096404 (2)
1. Colt duplicated 4,171 Model 1911A1 serial numbers in the US&S Serial number range. 2. US&S manufactured exactly 55,000 Model 1911A1 pistols.	

Replacement Serial Numbers

Beginning in 1924, replacement serial numbers were issued as needed to U.S. military arsenals, commands and depots for use on salvaged, repaired, or refinished receivers where the serial number was no longer visible to avoid duplication of serial numbers which had already been used, see Table 5-12. A total of 5,313 replacement serial numbers were issued between 1924 and 1957. From 1924 to 1925, some 3,385 were issued to restore Model 1911s rebuilt after World War I. A few of these numbers were apparently in use as late as 1953. In 1941-1942, 329 more replacement serial numbers were issued and between 1949 and 1957, 1,599 more were issued. Most of these replacement serial numbers can be identified by an "X" prefix.

Prior to 1924, Colt appears to have used the Springfield Armory suspended serial number range 128,617-133,186 and to a lesser extent, the 1917 block (210,387-215,386) as replacement receivers when needed. However, since there was little rebuild activity during World War I, only a small number of replacement receivers were needed.

Rebuild activity at the Springfield Armory between the wars prompted the first "X" serial number series (X1,000-X1,178) to be assigned. Later, X1,179 and X1,180 were assigned to the Manila Arsenal. Finally, X1,181-X4,385 were also assigned to Springfield.

At the start of World War II, rebuild activity at the Rock Island and Augusta Arsenals was getting underway. The Ordnance Department decided to assign separate new, unused serial number ranges to these facilities for use as replacement numbers. Serial numbers 856,101-856,300 and 856,305-856,404 were assigned to Rock Island Arsenal. Serial numbers 856,301-856,304 were assigned to Augusta Arsenal. At a later date, Augusta Arsenal was also assigned the serial number range 1,279,674-

Military and Commercial Pistols

1,279,698. None of the numbers assigned to Rock Island Arsenal or Augusta Arsenal were used with the "X" prefix. Only two pistols from these non-"X"-prefixed replacement number serial ranges have been reported to the knowledge of the author and technical editors.

After World War II, additional serial numbers were assigned in small batches in the range X2,693,614-X2,695,212 on an "as needed" basis. This last serial number range did not duplicate any previously used serial numbers, but as the Ordnance Department was unsure of any possible future production, the "X" prefix was used to avoid the possibility of duplication.

Table 5-12 U.S. Army Ordnance Department Replacement Serial Numbers (X-Prefix only)		
Serial Number Sequence	Used By	Year Approved
X1000-X1178 (1)	Springfield Armory	1924
X1179-X1180	Manila Arsenal	1924
X1181-X4385	Springfield Armory and Augusta Arsenal	1925-1953
856101-856300 (2)	Rock Island Arsenal	1941
856301-856304 (3)	Augusta Arsenal	1942
856305-856404	Rock Island Arsenal	1942
1279674-1279698	Augusta Arsenal	1943 (?)
X2693614-X2693665	Raritan Arsenal	1949
X2693666-X2693785	Rock Island Arsenal	1949
X2693786-X2693885	Tokyo Ordnance Center	1950
X2693886	Unknown	1950
X2693887-X2693893	Mt. Rainier Ordnance Depot	1950
X2693894-X2693920 (4)	Ogden Arsenal	1951
X2693921-X2693922 (5)	Ogden Arsenal	1951
X2693923-X2693932 & X2693934 (4)	Ogden Arsenal	1951

Model 1911, M1911A1

Table 5-12, cont.

U.S. Army Ordnance Department Replacement Serial Numbers (X-Prefix only)

Serial Number Sequence	Used By	Year Approved
X2693933 & X2693935-X2693938 (5)	Ogden Arsenal	1951
X2693939-X2693943 (6)	Ogden Arsenal	1951
X2693944-X2693953	Raritan Arsenal	Unknown
X2693954-X2694039	U.S. Navy/Marine Corps	1951
X2694040	U.S. Caribbean Command	1952
X2269041	U.S. Marine Corps	1952
X2694042-X2694048	Rock Island Arsenal	1952
X2694049-X2694148	Unknown	1952
X2694149-X2694158	Unknown	1952
X2694159-X2694358	Rock Island Arsenal	1952
X2694359-X2694378	Raritan Arsenal	1952
X2694379	U.S. Marine Corps	1952
X2694380-X2694392 (4)	Raritan Arsenal	1952
X2694393-X2694394	Rock Island Arsenal	1952/53
X2694395	Rock Island Arsenal	1952/53
X2694396-X2694695	Augusta Arsenal	1952/53
X2694696-X2694995	Augusta Arsenal	1953
X2694996	Rock Island Arsenal	1953
X2694997	Rock Island Arsenal	1954
X2694998	Rock Island Arsenal	1955
X2694999-X2695198	229th Ordnance Depot, Yokohama	1955
X2695199-X2695201	Raritan Arsenal	1955
X2695202 (7)	U.S. Air Force	1955
X2695203	Rock Island Arsenal	1955

Military and Commercial Pistols

Serial Number Sequence	Used By	Year Approved
Table 5-12, cont. U.S. Army Ordnance Department Replacement Serial Numbers (X-Prefix only)		
X2695204-X2695205	Rock Island Arsenal	1955
X2695206	Red River Arsenal	1955
X2695207-X2695208 (4)	Rock Island Arsenal	1956
X2695209	Fort Sill, Oklahoma	1956
X2695210	Rock Island Arsenal	1956
X2695211-X2695212	Minnesota Military District	1957

1. Issued under the authority of the Springfield Armory, Springfield, Mass.
2. Under the authority of the Chief of Ordnance, Washington, D.C.
3. The Ordnance Department issued replacement serial numbers (856,101-856,404) but without the "X" prefix.
4. Model 1911 only.
5. Model 1911A1 only.
6. Not used.
7. X numbers issued from X2695202-X2695212 compiled by Lt. Col. R. C. Kuhn.

Colt Commercial Model 1911/1911A1 Serial Numbers

Colt commercial production of the Model 1911/1911A1 and its successors were assigned a separate serial number range to prevent confusion with the Ordnance Department-acquired Model 1911s and later, Model 1911A1s. Commercial serial numbers were given the prefix "C" until 1950 when the "C" became a suffix. In 1970 with the advent of the "Series 70" the serial numbering system was changed to include the year "70" and the letter "G" for Government Model.

Collectors should be aware that commercial pistols were not always shipped in the year of manufacture. Many were shipped months and even years out of serial number sequence. Only in 1946 is there a degree of certainty that a pistol was manufactured and shipped that same year, as Colt had zero commercial inventory and production was resumed at serial number C220,001.

Model 1911, M1911A1

	Table 5-13 Model 1911/1911A1 Colt Commercial Serial Numbers		
Calendar Year	Serial Number Range	Calendar Year	Serial Number Range
1912	C1-1899	1942	C208800-C215018
1913	C1900-C5399	1943	No Commercial Production
1914	C5400-C16659	1944	No Commercial Production
1915	C16660-C27699	1945	No Commercial Production
1916	C27700-C74999	1946	C220001-C222001
1917	C75000-C99000	1947	C222002-C233001
1918	C99001-C105999	1948	C230500-C238000
1919	C106000-C120999	1949	C238501-C240000
1920	C121000-C126999	1950 (7)	C240001-C240227 240228C
1921	C127000-C128999	1951	247701C-253179C
1922	C129000-C133999	1952	253180C-259549C
1923	C134000-C134999	1953	259550C-266349C
1924	C135000-C139999	1954	266350C-270549C
1925	C140000-C144999	1955	270550C-272549C
1926	C145000-C150999	1956	272550C-276699C
1927	C151000-C151999	1957	276700C-281999C
1928	C152000-C154999	1958	282000C-283799C
1929	C155000-C155999	1959	283800C-285799C
1930	C156000-C158999	1960	285800C-288799C
1931	C159000-C160999	1961	288000C-289849C
1932	C161000-C164799	1962	289850C-292299C
1933 (1)	C164800-C174599	1963	292300C-293799C
1934	C174600-C177999	1964	293800C-295999C
1935 (2)	C178000-C179799	1965	296000C-300299C
1936	C179800-C183199	1966	300300C-308499C

Military and Commercial Pistols

Calendar Year	Serial Number Range	Calendar Year	Serial Number Range
Table 5-13, cont. Model 1911/1911A1 Colt Commercial Serial Numbers			
1937 (3)	C183200-C188699	1967	308500C-315599C
1938 (4)	C188700-C189599	1968	315600C-324499C
1939	C189600-C198899	1969	324500C-336169C
1940 (5)	C198900-C199299		
1941 (6)	C199300-C208799		
Colt Series 70			
1970	70G01002-70G05550	1979	89185G70-89186G70 to 99999G70 01000B70
1971	70G05551- 70G18000	1980 (9)	Unknown
1972	70G18001-70G34400		
1973	70G34401-70G43000	1981 (10)	70B00000-72630B70- 99999B70 to 70S40479-70L25219
1974	70G43001-70G73000	1982	70B11247-70B47460
1975	70G73001-70G88900	1983	70B47461-70B56689 to FG1000-?
1976 (8)	70G88901-70G99999- 01001G70-?	1984	FG21625-FG44264
1977	13901G70-45199G70	1985	FG44265
1978	45200G70 -?		

1. National Match .45 automatic pistol "introduced." No specific serial number range.
2. Some receivers in this serial number range were not assembled until 1946 and later.
3. As confusing as it sounds, a large number of receivers between 190,000-192,000 were produced in 1937 and completed up to 1942.
4. A number of receivers between 193,000-199,000 were produced in 1938 and completed up to 1942.
5. A number of receivers between 199,000-203,000 were produced in 1940 and completed up to 1942.
6. Unknown quantity of serial numbered receivers were produced in 1941 and transferred to military contracts.
7. "C" prefix becomes suffix. Transition numbers are not consecutive.
8. Change in serial number format.
9. Change in serial number format started March 20, 1979.
10. Change in serial number format started Oct. 17, 1981.

Model 1911, M1911A1

Colt Series 70, Nickel-Plate, Super .38, and 9 mm Serial Numbers

Beginning in 1972, Colt applied different serial number ranges to nickel-plated .45-caliber pistols, and to Super .38 and 9 mm pistols.

Table 5-14 Colt Series 70, Miscellaneous Serial Numbers			
Calendar Year	Nickel-Plate Serial Number Range	Super .38 Serial Number Range	9 mm Serial Number Range
1972	X70N20801-X70N21020	70S03801-70S06500	70L02601-70L03400
1973		70S06501-70S07851	70L03401-70L04000
1974		70S07852-70S09050	70L04001-70L04400
1975		70S09051-70S01999	70L04401-70L06000
1976		70S20000-70S20200	70L06601-70L08319
1977		70S20201-70S25720	70L08320-70L11200
1978		70S25721-70S29813	70L11201-70L113981
1979		70S29814-70S35747	70L113982-
1980		70S35748-70S40478	Unknown
1981		70S40479-70S45629	70L25219-70L29084
1982		70S45630-70S51633	70L29085-70L33196
1983		70S51634-70S52124	70L33197-70L34232

Colt ACE, Service Model ACE, .22-.45 and .45-.22 Conversion Kit Serial Numbers

The ACE and Service Model ACE were numbered in their own serial number range before World War II, as were the conversion kits. Colt resumed production in 1978 of the Service Model ACE with the floating chamber." Production of the .22-.45 conversion kit was resumed in 1947 but without serial numbers, as no receiver was supplied with the kit. The last serial-numbered .22-.45 conversions were prewar or wartime production sold in 1946. No .45-.22 conversion kits were manufactured after World War II.

Military and Commercial Pistols

Table 5-15 .22 ACE and .22 Service Model ACE Colt (Serial number ranges listed are estimates)				
Calendar Year	ACE	Service Model ACE	.22-.45 Conversion	.45-.22 Conversion
1931	1-4000			
1932	4001-4400			
1933	4401-4972			
1934	4973-4950			
1935	4951-6150	SM1		
1936	6151-7150	SM2-SM10		
1937	7151-9000	SM11-SM50		
1938	9001-9550	SM51-SM491 (1)	U1	U1
1939	9551-10250	SM453-SM1119 (1)	U2-400	U1-U18
1940	10251-10500	SM901-SM952 SM1120	U401-U900	U19-U60
1941	10501-10790	SM1121-SM1550-Intermittent	U901-U1100	U61-U112+
1942		SM1551-SM2715	U1101-U1400	
1943		Intermittent	U1401-U1701 to U1750	
1944		Intermittent		
1945		SM2716-SM3725 to SM13803 Gaps in sequence Parco-Lubrite finish		

Model 1911, M1911A1

Calendar Year	ACE	Service Model ACE	.22-.45 Conversion	.45-.22 Conversion
Table 5-15, cont. .22 ACE and .22 Service Model ACE Colt (Serial number ranges listed are estimates)				
1946			U2001-U2670 (1)	
1947	10791-10918 10935 (2)		Serial numbers no longer applied	
1948-1977				
1978		SM14001- SM21140		
1979		SM21141- SM27105		
1980		SM27106- SM33487		
1981		SM33488- SM40221		
1982		SM43830		

1. Gaps in serial numbers seen in this year.
2. Serial numbers in 1947 are not always consecutive.

Colt Super .38 and Super Match .38 Serial Numbers

The Super .38 was numbered in its own serial number range and finished in either blue or nickel plate. From 1929 to the start of World War II, some 34,450 Super .38s were produced. After, they were assembled with a variety of prewar, wartime and some new commercial production through circa serial #37,834 in 1946. When postwar commercial production resumed, the Super .38 was arbitrarily jumped to serial number 40,001 and continued until 1968-69 at serial number 202,188. The serial numbering procedure was changed in 1969 and restarted at CS001,001. In 1971, the .45 ACP, 9 mm, and .Super .38 production lines were combined and all were designated as the Series 70, and later, the Series 80, by cartridge.

250

Military and Commercial Pistols

	Table 5-16 Super .38 Model and Super Match .38 Automatic Pistols Colt Commercial Production		
Calendar Year	Serial Number Range	Calendar Year	Serial Number Range
1929	1-5849	1950	73301-78900
1930	5850-9849	1951	78901-86400
1931	9850-13649	1952	86401-95501
1932	13650-13999	1953	95502-107300
1933	14000-15099	1954	107301-112950
1934	15100-17299	1955	112951-117800
1935 (1)	17300-19249	1956	117801-120000
1936	19250-24049	1957	120001-124500
1937	24050-32099	1958	124501-129600
1938	32100-33449	1959	129601-136900
1939	33450-34449	1960	136901-148800
1940 (2)	34450-?	1961	148801-155200
1941	Limited or no production	1962	155201-158850
1942	Limited or no production	1963	158851-163000
1943	Limited or no production	1964	163001-167800
1944	Limited or no production	1965	167801-172000
1945	Limited or no production	1966	172001-177600
1946 (3)	36551-37834	1967	177601-186200
1947	40001	1968-1969	186201-192200 to 202188 CS001001
1948	40002-56700	1970	CS001002- CS002800- CS005280 See Table 5-14 for continuation of the Super .38 in the Series 70
1949	56701-73300		

1. Super Match .38 Pistol introduced.
2. 1,200 Super Match .38 Pistols bought by the British Purchasing Commission.
3. Gap of approximately 2,100 serial numbers during WWII years. Pistols listed in 1946-47 were primarily assembled from prewar parts.

Model 1911, M1911A1

Colt .38 Special Kit ("H" and "O" Suffix) Serial Numbers

The (U.S.) Army Advanced Marksmanship Unit (AAMU) at Fort Benning, Georgia, modified the Model 1911A1 to fire a modified rimmed .38 Special cartridge. The cartridge that resulted was known as the .38 AMU. The Colt factory furnished modified parts—slide, barrel, bushing, firing pin, extractor, ejector, recoil spring, and magazine as a kit. The shooter furnished the rest of the pistol. Most kits were produced under contract to the U.S. government, but a limited number, estimated to be less than six hundred, were sold commercially from 1964 through 1970 to target pistol dealer Gil Hebard. A .45 ACP conversion kit was also offered in similar quantities during this period.

Table 5-17
The .38 Special Kit ("H" Suffix) for Super .38 ACP Pistols
The .38 Special Kit ("O" Suffix) for .45 ACP Pistols
Colt Serial Numbers

Calendar Year	Serial Number Range	Calendar Year	Serial Number Range
1964	00100H-00404H 00100O-00754O	1968	No H kits produced No O kits produced
1965	00405H-Unknown 00755O-00901O	1969	No H kits produced 00902O-01164O
1966	Unknown low number of H kits No O kits produced	1970	Unknown-00434H No O kits produced
1967	Unknown low number of H kits No O kits produced		

Colt Gold Cup and Super .38 National Match Serial Numbers

The National Match pistol was reintroduced by Colt in 1957 as the "Gold Cup National Match Automatic Pistol." Like its pre-World War II predecessor, it had a hand-fitted action, adjustable wide-grooved trigger, and adjustable sights as standard. Unlike the pre-World War II National Match Pistols, it had a flat mainspring housing. In 1960, the Super .38 National Match Automatic Pistol was put into production.

Military and Commercial Pistols

Table 5-18
Gold Cup National Match Automatic Pistol (NM)
Super .38 National Match Automatic Pistol (NMR)
Colt Commercial Production

Calendar Year	Serial Number Range	Calendar Year	Serial Number Range
1957	10NM and 26NM	1971	70N01002-70N02001
1958	27NM-1850M	1972	70N02002-70N06201
1959	1851-3600NM	1973	70N06202-70N08901
1960	3601NM-5550NM 100NMR-499NMR (1)	1974	70N08902-70N11301
1961	5551NM-7450NM 500NMR-3499NMR 101MS-855MS (2)	1975	70N11302-70N22301
1962	7451NM-8850NM 3500NMR-3699NMR	1976	70N22302-70N31600
1963	8851NM-10900NM 3700NMR-4,799NMR	1977	70N31601-70N40401
1964 (3)	10901NM-12500NM 4800NMR-4999NMR	1978	No Production
1965	12501NM-14700NM 5000NMR-5399NMR	1979	70N66934-70N80734
1966 (3)	14701NM-16600NM 5400NMR-?	1980	70N80735-70N92647- 70N99999 to 01000N70
1967 (3)	16601NM-19500NM NMR production unkown	1981	01001N70-11066N70
1968 (3)	19501NM-25450NM NMR production unkown	1982	11067N70-27050N70
1969 (3)	25451NM-35799NM 25451NM-32250NM NMR production unknown	1983	27051N70-28674N70 to FN01000

Model 1911, M1911A1

	Table 5-18, cont.		
	Gold Cup National Match Automatic Pistol (NM)		
	Super .38 National Match Automatic Pistol (NMR)		
	Colt Commercial Production		
Calendar Year	**Serial Number Range**	**Calendar Year**	**Serial Number Range**
1970	32251NM-35800NM to 37025NM Series 70 begins at 70 N01001 5950NMR-7000NMR	1984	FN01001-FN03652
		1985	FN03653-FN11680

1. Super .38 National Match Pistol introduced using NMR suffix.
2. Estimated 754 NM pistols have "MS" suffix.
3. Only a small number of NMR pistols produced in these years.

Colt Lightweight Commander and Commander Serial Numbers

The Government Model was one of the finest military pistols ever developed and rode comfortably in the holster that hung from the military cartridge belt. But it was heavy and long, and the military holster unsuited for concealed carry by licensed civilians. In the 1930s, Colt had received numerous requests for a lighter, smaller version but World War II intervened before anything concrete could be developed. In 1949, Colt introduced a new pistol with an aluminum frame, the "Lightweight Commander." Not only was it 13.5 ounces lighter than the standard Government Model but the receiver was 0.75 inch shorter and the slide was 6.6 inches long. In 1970, an all-steel receiver "Combat Commander" was introduced. Both were available in blued and nickel-plated finishes, including satin nickel, and in .45 ACP, 9 mm and Super .38 calibers.

	Table 5-19		
	Commander Model Automatic Pistol (LW and CLW)		
	Combat Commander Automatic Pistol (70BS and 70SC)		
	Officer's Model (FA)		
	Colt Commercial Production		
Calendar Year	**Serial Number Range**	**Calendar Year**	**Serial Number Range**
1949 (1)	001LW-0065LW	1968	49652LW-53401LW to 60277LW

Military and Commercial Pistols

Calendar Year	Serial Number Range	Calendar Year	Serial Number Range
	Table 5-19, cont. **Commander Model Automatic Pistol (LW and CLW)** **Combat Commander Automatic Pistol (70BS and 70SC)** **Officer's Model (FA)** **Colt Commercial Production**		
1950	66LW	1969	CLW001001-CLW005101
1951	6000LW-20300LW	1970 (2) (3)	CLW005102 70BS01001 70SC1000
1952	20301LW-30099LW	1971	CLW009751 70SC01401
1953	30100LW-32199LW	1972	CLW13051-CLW016900 70BS6501-70BS14849 70SC05401-70SC19000
1954	32200LW-34899LW	1973	CLW016901-CLW017549 70BS14850-70BS18900 70SC19001+ (4) 70SC56801- 70SC57398
1955	34900LW-37199LW	1974	CLW017550-CLW019200 70BS18901-70BS26000 70SC27201-70SC36549
1956	37200LW-38449LW	1975	CLW019201-CLW023999 70BS26001-70BS37900 70SC36550-70SC45200
1957	38450LW-39200LW	1976	CLW024000-CLW0249399 70BS37901-70BS52800 70SC45201-70SC50200
1958	38501LW-39200LW	1977	CLW029400-CLW032800 70BS52801-70BS6899 70SC450201-70SC57900
1959	39450LW-41499LW	1978	CLW032801-CLW032800 70BS6900-70BS85976 70SC57900-70SC66936
1960	41500LW-44150LW	1979	CLW032801 70BS85977-70BS97566- 70BS99999 70SC66937-70SC73404
1961	44151LW-42000LW	1980	CLW042849-CLW045253 80BS1001-80BS9008 70SC3405-70SC78617

255

Model 1911, M1911A1

<table>
<tr><td colspan="4">
Table 5-19, cont.
Commander Model Automatic Pistol (LW and CLW)
Combat Commander Automatic Pistol (70BS and 70SC)
Officer's Model (FA)
Colt Commercial Production
</td></tr>
<tr><td>Calendar Year</td><td>Serial Number Range</td><td>Calendar Year</td><td>Serial Number Range</td></tr>
<tr><td>1962</td><td>42001LW-42400LW</td><td>1981</td><td>CLW045254-CLW047043
80BS9009-80BS17664
70SC78618-70SC82625</td></tr>
<tr><td>1963</td><td>42401LW-43000LW</td><td>1982</td><td>CLW047044-CLW048973
80BS17665-80BS528089
70SC82626-70SC86450</td></tr>
<tr><td>1964</td><td>44151LW-45300LW</td><td>1983</td><td>CLW048974-CLW049714
80BS528090-80BS431218
70SC86451-70SC87350
to FC01001-FC049999 (5)
70SC86451-70SC87350</td></tr>
<tr><td>1965</td><td>45301LW-46950LW</td><td>1984</td><td>FC05000-FC10951
FC01000-FL02948 (6)
FA02001-FA09552 (7)</td></tr>
<tr><td>1966</td><td>46951LW-49650LW</td><td>1985</td><td>FC10952-
FL04911-
FA-09553-</td></tr>
<tr><td>1967</td><td>496951LW-?</td><td></td><td></td></tr>
</table>

1. Commander model with lightweight aluminum receiver production begins. Suffix to 1968 is "LW"; after 1968, prefix is "CLW."
2. Combat Commander, all-steel receiver, begins. Prefix is "70SC" for nickel finish or "70BS" for blued finish.
3. Changeover to Series 70 manufacture and serial numbering.
4. Produced out of sequence.
5. Commander becomes part of Series 80.
6. Combat Commander becomes part of Series 80.
7. Colt Officer's Model (not to be confused with "General Officer Model M15" which was manufactured exclusively for the U.S. military by Rock Island Arsenal).

General Officer M15 Serial Numbers

The issue of a special pistol to general officers of the U.S. Army seems to have begun in 1944. These first issues were the Colt Automatic Pocket Pistol, Caliber .380 Model M. From 1950 to 1972, the General Officer pistol was the Colt Automatic Pocket Pistol, Caliber .32 Model M. In the 1960s, work began at Rock Island Arsenal to produce a new General

Military and Commercial Pistols

Officer pistol when the supply of the .32-caliber pistols began to run low. Production of the .32-caliber ACP pistols had ended at Colt in 1947 and so Rock Island set out to design a smaller, lighter pistol than the G.I.-issue Model 1911A1 that would be more comfortable for generals to carry in combat zones. The new pistol, in .45 ACP, was designated the M15 and manufactured from existing stocks of M1911A1 pistols at Rock Island. They received a special serial number beginning with GO1. A total of 1,004 M15 Pistols were issued between 1972 and 1982, see Table 5-20.

Table 5-20 General Officer M15 Pistol Manufactured at Rock Island Arsenal		
Manufacturer	**Serial Number Range**	**Month/Calendar Year**
Rock Island Arsenal	GO1-GO150	October 1972
	GO151-GO250	September 1973
	GO251-GO350	October 1973
	GO351-GO450	November 1973
	GO451-GO550	December 1973
	GO551-GO650	January 1974
	GO651-GO750	February 1974
	GO751-GO850	March 1974
	GO851-GO950	April 1974
	GO951-GO1004	May 1974

General Note: Records account for 1,004 M15 pistols manufactured, 150 in October 1972 with the balance at the rate of 100 per month from September 1973 to May 1974 (*The Colt U.S. General Officer's" Pistol*, Greeley, IV). Note, that these are manufacture dates, not issue dates.

Colt Argentine Contract Model 1911/1927 Serial Numbers

In April 1914, the Marina Argentina (Argentine Navy) acquired Model 1911s in .45 ACP in the serial number range C6201-C6401. The following year, the Argentine government purchased 1,000 more which were designated the "Modelo 1916." A further 10,000 were ordered in 1919. These were all numbered in the Colt commercial series, and shown in Table 5-21.

Model 1911, M1911A1

In 1927, 10,000 more were ordered for the Argentine Army. These were uniquely serial numbered in their own series, 1-10,000. The serial number for each pistol was stamped on the top of the slide, under the mainspring housing on the receiver, and on the top of the barrel but not on the right side of the receiver. Following this contract, the Argentine government licensed the Model 1911A1 for production at Rosario, Argentina, in a government factory.

Manufacturer	Serial Number Range	Calendar Year
Colt 1911	C6201-C11621	1914
	C20001-C21000	1916
	C86790-C116000	1919
M1927 (Colt 1911A1)	1-10000 (*)	1927-28

Table 5-21
Argentine Models of 1911 and 1927

* This contract was serial numbered in its own sequence. Serial numbers were stamped on top of the slide, under the mainspring housing, and top of the barrel.

British World War I Contracts, 1915 and 1918 (W) Prefix—Colt

British World War I Colt Model 1911s are easy to identify as their serial numbers are prefixed "W" for "Cartridge, Pistol, Self Loading, .455 Inch Mark 1" or "Mark 1z" as developed by the firm of Webley & Scott and improved by George Kynoch, Ltd. The cartridge was adopted in 1912 by the Admiralty for the .455 Webley Self Loading Pistol and in 1916 by the Army as well. To further confuse the issue, the cartridge is often referred to as the .455 Eley, after the English company that manufactured the majority of .455 cartridges. Before World War I, Colt sold both .45 ACP and the .455 caliber pistols in England through their London Agency and then through the London Armoury Company. All .455 caliber Colt Model 1911s are believed to show the prefix "W" before the serial number.

Table 5-22 presents the estimated serial number ranges for all British government Model 1911 purchases (all prefixed "W") through 1919. All .455 Webley caliber pistols received the "W" instead of the "C" prefix as they were probably manufactured in separate batches be-

Military and Commercial Pistols

cause of the dimensional differences in receiver and slide from normal .45 ACP production. Serial numbers were compiled from British shipping and War Department records.

From	To	Number Purchased
Table 5-22		
Model 1911		
British World War I Contracts, 1915 and 1918 (W) Prefix		
Colt Serial Numbers		
(British Shipping and War Department Records)		
1915		
W19001	W190010 to W19700 (?)	200
1916		
ca. W29001	W76000	2,600
1917		
W70200	ca. W100000	500
1918		
W94100	W106800	5,000
1919		
W102600	W110695	5,000
Total	10,000	
General Note: Commercial pistols were not assembled and shipped in numerical order by Colt. Serial number ranges for all commercial and British military contract pistols will therefore overlap.		

Canadian Military Model 1911 and Model 1911A1 Contracts

According to Canada's National Statistical Agency, in 1914, the population, not including Newfoundland and Labrador, was 7,899,000, too small to support a large manufacturing sector, and especially a small-arms sector large enough to equip the Canadian forces sent to Europe. While the nation was able to equip most of its Army with the Canadian-designed-and-built Ross rifle, it did not prove satisfactory in combat and was withdrawn by 1917 at the latest. Handguns for officers and non-commissioned officers were provided by Great Britain and the United States, primarily from Colt and Smith & Wesson.

259

Model 1911, M1911A1

During World War II under the provisions of the Lend-Lease program, the Canadian military received the Model 1911A1 in the serial number range shown in Table 5-23.

Table 5-23
Canadian Military Model 1911 and 1911A1 Contracts

Manufacturer	Serial Number Range (Non-inclusive)	Totals	Calendar Year
Colt (M1911)	C5400-C16599	5,000	1914
Colt (M1911A1)	930000 to 936000	1,515	1943

Norwegian Models of 1912, 1914, and Pistole 657

The Norwegian government was the second foreign government to purchase the Model 1911 for its military forces. Norwegian Ordnance Officers had followed the U.S. automatic pistol trials closely and by 1914, an agreement had been reached with Colt and Fabrique Nationale to license the manufacture of the pistol in Norway. Under the Nazi occupation (1940-1945), production of the Model 1914, which had ended in 1933, was resumed as the Pistole 657(N) for issue to German forces in Norway. A final small batch was again manufactured after the war for the Norwegian military.

Table 5-24
Norwegian Models of 1912, 1914, and Pistole 657(N)

Manufacturer	Serial Number Range	Calendar Year
Kongsberg Vapenfabrik	1-500 (1)	1914
Colt Firearms	C18501-C18850 + 50 (2)	(April) 1915
Kongsberg Vapenfabrik	501-22,000	1917-1933
Kongsberg Vapenfabrik	22001-30500 (3)	1940-45
Kongsberg Vapenfabrik	30501-32874	1947-1987

1. Three Model 1911s purchased for trials.
2. Norwegian Army, manufactured by Colt.
3. German Occupation Force; will show Nazi proof marks.

Military and Commercial Pistols

Imperial Russian Military Model 1911s

Imperial Russia had a large, modern arms manufacturing capability at the start of World War I, but even so, could not manufacture all of the small arms needed by its 14-million-man army. So, like Great Britain and France, it turned to outside sources. The Mosin-Nagant Model of 1891 was manufactured in the United States by Remington Arms and New England Westinghouse to supplement Russian production. A total of 51,000 Model 1911s in the serial number range shown in Table 5-25 were also purchased by the Imperial Russian government through the Colt London Agency. Because of the time involved in shipping from the United States to England to Russia and further problems moving material along the single-track railway line between the Arctic ports and St. Petersburg, it is doubtful if many reached combat forces. All Colt Model 1911s shipped through the London Agency were marked in Cyrillic, АНГЛ. ЗАКАЗЪ (English Order).

Table 5-25 Imperial Russian Model 1911 Military Model Purchases		
Manufacturer	Serial Number Range	Calendar Year
Colt	C23000-C89000	1916-1918

CHAPTER 6
MARKINGS—RECEIVERS

COLT MARKINGS

Colt military and commercial markings differed. Commercial models were marked **GOVERNMENT MODEL** instead of **MODEL OF 1911.** (later **MI9IIAI) U.S. ARMY** and lacked the **UNITED STATES PROPERTY** and U.S. Army Ordnance Department inspection markings. Commercial serial numbers had a "C" prefix or suffix until 1970. Singer-built Model 1911A1s had a prefix, "№ S" and a very few early Ithaca receivers showed an "№ I" prefix. All other Ordnance Department–purchased Model 1911/1911Als used the abbreviation for "number" as the prefix.

U.S. MILITARY CONTRACT SERIAL NUMBER FORMAT

Special Army Model 1911 pistols serial numbers 1 through 15 were stamped by hand in a type face without serifs (sans serif) and without a prefix on the *left* side of the receiver. These pistols were part of the final test series that took place starting on March 15, 1911, and were not part of the original military contract for the Model 1911. Serial #2 was used to prepare the Ordnance Department manual on the new Model 1911 pistol. It was then sent to Rock Island for use in designing a new holster.

Prefix: From serial #s 1-4,500, the prefix was "No.", see Figures 6-1 and 6-3. From serial #s 4,501-EOP the prefix was changed to "№", see Figure 6-2. All prefixes were in sans serif type regardless of orientation, see Figure 6-4.

From serial #s 1-7,500, the prefix and serial number were stamped on the right side of the receiver ahead of the slide stop pin hole, refer to Figure 6-1. After, to the end of production, the prefix and serial number were moved *behind* the slide stop pin hole, refer to Figure 6-2.

Serifs: From serial #s 1-4,500, the serial numbers had ornamental serifs, refer to Figure 6-3. From serial #s 4,501-629,500, all serial numbers were stamped in a sans serif type face, refer to Figure 6-2. From serial #700,001 to circa serial #2,250,000, the serial numbers had serifs; after, the type face was again sans serif, except for the "1."

Military and Commercial Pistols

Fig. 6-1. Between serial #s 1-7,500, the serial number (arrow) on Colt Model 1911s was stamped on the right side of the receiver, forward of the slide stop hole. Karl Karash collection.

Fig. 6-2. Between serial #7,501 to the end of Colt production, the serial number was stamped behind the slide stop pin hole.

Fig. 6-3. Between serial #s 1 and 4,500, the Colt-applied serial numbers were stamped in a type face with ornamental type face was sans serif. Karl Karash collection.

Model 1911, M1911A1

From circa serial #s 1-4,500, the prefix "No." did not have serifs.

No. 256

After circa serial #4,501 to the end of production, the period following the prefix "No." was eliminated, and the "o" was raised and underlined. The underscore is even with the bottom line of the "N" lettering.

N⍛ 9863

All numbers and letters between serial #s 4,501-629,500 were stamped without serifs. After, two fonts were used, one in which only the "1" had a serif (see Figure 6-4) and the other with serifs (Figure 6-8).

Orientation: Circa serial #s 1-629,500, the serial number and prefix were vertical. Between circa serial #s 700,001-2,275,000, the prefix and serial number were slanted slightly to the right.

N⍛718553

Circa serial #2,275,001-EOP, the abbreviation for "number" and the serial number were again vertical.

Fig. 6-4. The two styles of prefix used on Colt Model 1911/1911A1 pistols: (above) to serial #4,500; (below) after. Karl Karash collection.

N⍛ 2280193

COLT COMMERCIAL MODEL SERIAL NUMBER FORMAT

Location: From serial #s C1-C2,250, the serial numbers on all *commercial* Model 1911s were stamped on the left side of the receiver in a type face with ornamental serifs. After, to the end of production, the serial number was stamped on the right side behind the slide stop pin hole. The prefix "No" was not used on commercial models.

C 1031

Orientation and Serifs: Circa serial #s C1-C130,000, the prefix and serial number were vertical and in a sans serif type face. The "C" had a small serif at the top of the stroke. It reappeared at circa serial number 170,001-220,001.

Circa serial #s C130,001-C198,000: prefix vertical, serial number ornamental and slanted right. The "1" had a definite serif, refer to Figure 6-5.

C *183076*

Military and Commercial Pistols

Fig. 6-5. Examples of prefixes and serial numbers. A) Prefix with serifs, serial number without, both vertical. B) Prefix without serifs and vertical, serial numbers with serifs and slanted to the right. C) Series 70/80 prefix and serial numbers are without serifs and vertical. The collector is cautioned that minor differences throughout production will appear but the majority of pistols will conform to the descriptions in the text.

In the serial number range C198,001-circa C240,227 serial number and prefix were slanted to the right. All post-World War II Government Model markings (with some overlap) between circa C235,001-336,169C are sans serif and vertical. Table 6-1 summarizes all of the Colt military and commercial serial number formats.

Model 1911, M1911A1

Table 6-1
Colt Military and Commercial Serial Number Format

S/N Range Military	Military Receiver	
	Prefix	Serifs/Type Face Orientation
1-4,500 (1)	No.	Prefix sans serif, s/n ornamental, both vertical
4,501-7,500 (1)	N℗	Prefix & s/n sans serif, both vertical
4,501-EOP	N℗	Prefix sans serif
4,501-629,500	N℗	Prefix and s/n sans serif, both vertical
7,501-629,500 (2)	N℗	Prefix & s/n sans serif
700,001-870,000	N℗	Prefix and s/n mixed serif, sans serif, slanted
870,001-2,275,000 (2)	N℗	S/n sans serif (except "1"), slanted
2,275,001-EOP (2)	N℗	Prefix & s/n sans serif, vertical
S/N Range Commercial	**Commercial Receiver**	
	Prefix	**Serifs**
C1-C2,250 (3)	C	Prefix & s/n ornamental serifs, vertical
C1-C130,000 (2)	C	S/n sans serifs, vertical. Prefix, small serif top of "C"
C130,001-C198,000 (2)	C	Prefix vertical. S/n slanted and ornamental. "1" had serif
C170,001-C220,001	C	Prefix, small serif top of "C"
C198,001-C235,000 (2)	C	Prefix & s/n serifs, slanted (4)
C235,001-336,169C (2)	C (4)	Suffix & s/n sans serif, vertical

1. Right side of receiver, forward of slide stop pin hole.
2. Right side of receiver, behind slide stop pin hole.
3. Marked on left side of receiver.
4. "C" changes to suffix at s/n 240,228C; some s/ns slanted, some vertical in range ca. C220,001-C240,227.

U.S. Property Marking

On the left side of the receiver ahead of the trigger guard were letters with serifs 0.10 inch high from serial #s 1-104, see Figure 6-6:

UNITED STATES PROPERTY

After serial #105, the letters in the marking were in sans serif type and reduced in size to 0.06 inch high to end of production and remained on the *left* side of the receiver to circa serial #510,000, see Figure 6-7.

Military and Commercial Pistols

At circa serial #510,001 to the end of military production in 1945, the marking was moved to the *right* side of the receiver just behind the slide stop pin hole. It was stamped with letters in a sans

Fig. 6-6. The "UNITED STATES PROPERTY" marking in letters with serifs was stamped on the left side of the receiver to circa serial #104. Karl Karash collection.

serif style 0.06 inch high, see Figure 6-8:

UNITED STATES PROPERTY

Model Marking—Military

Found on the right side of the slide to serial #712,349 (changed to receiver in the Model 1911A1). See Figure 6-9 and Chapter 7 for details.

NOTE: In 1924, the Ordnance Department ordered 10,000 pistols and required a number of improvements that would result in the change in designation to "Model 1911A1." Collectors refer to these 10,000 pistols as the "Transitions" partly because, as the drawings had not been updated, they were still marked **MODEL OF 1911.** The designation Model 1911A1 was officially adopted by the U.S. Army and in 1938, starting with serial #712,350, the

Fig. 6-7. From circa serial #s 105-510,000, the marking was reduced to 0.06 inch high. Karl Karash collection.

model marking was changed to read **M1911A1 U.S. ARMY** and moved from the slide to the right side of the receiver.

Model 1911, M1911A1

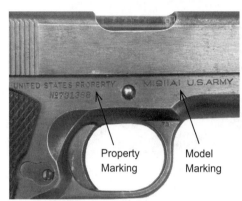

Fig. 6-8. From circa serial #510,000- EOP, the "UNITED STATES PROPERTY" marking was on the right side of the receiver above the serial number. Bud Davey collection.

Property Marking

Model Marking

From circa serial #712,350 to the end of production, the model marking was stamped in sans serif type on the right side of the receiver (refer to Figure 6-8), above the serial number and forward of the slide stop pin hole:

MI9IIAI U.S. ARMY

Model Marking— Commercial

The model marking on the commercial Model 1911 and 1911A1 was stamped on the right side of the receiver: from serial #s C1 to circa C5,000 ahead of the slide stop pin hole in serif type; after, behind until the advent of the Series 70, see Figure 6-10:

GOVERNMENT MODEL

Starting with the Series 70 and continuing through the Series 80, the address was stamped on the right side of the frame above the serial number in sans serif type, see Figure 6-11:

COLT'S PT. F.A. MFG. CO. HARTFORD, CONN. U.S.A.

and the model marking was placed on the right side of the slide, see Chapter 7.

Ordnance Department Inspector's Marking

At the Colt factory, the Ordnance Department inspection marking was stamped by the Ordnance Department military officer or civilian employee, usually stationed at the factory but subordinate to the

Fig. 6-9. The "MODEL OF 1911. U.S. ARMY" marking was on the right side of the slide from the start of production to circa serial #712,349. Karl Karash collection.

268

Military and Commercial Pistols

Fig. 6-10. Model marking on commercial Model 1911/1911A1s (right) was stamped on the right side of the receiver until the start of the Model 70 series.

Fig. 6-11. In the Series 70 (below), the Model marking was stamped on the right side of the slide. The Colt name and address was stamped on the receiver behind the slide stop pin hole.

Model Marking

Address

commander of the Springfield Ordnance District. He was responsible for seeing that all pistols met specifications for materials, quality, and workmanship. If accepted, his initials or symbol were stamped on the pistol, usually on the left side behind the trigger guard. Ordnance inspectors and their marks are summarized in Table 6-2 and Figure 6-12.

Table 6-2 U.S. Ordnance Department Final Inspection Marks All Colt-Manufactured Model 1911 and Model 1911A1 Pistols, Caliber .45				
Ordnance Department Inspector	Initials	Period of Service	Comment	Marking (see figure)
Walter G. Penfield, Major, USA	WGP	1911-1914	Circa #s 1-101,500. Intertwined initials inside a circle	

269

Model 1911, M1911A1

Ordnance Department Inspector	Initials	Period of Service	Comment	Marking (see figure)
Gilbert H. Stewart, Major, USA	GHS	1915-1918	Circa #s 101,500-230,000. Intertwined initials inside a circle	
John M. Gilbert, Lt. Colonel, NA	JMG	1917-1918	Circa #s 230,000-302,000. Intertwined initials with "G" forming the enclosing circle	
Ordnance Department Eagle, Type 1	Eagle Head, various numbers or letters	1918-1919 (Colt only)	Colt: circa #s 300,000-629,000. Eagle head often above the sans serif initial "S" followed by a number or number and letter.	S4
Ordnance Department Eagle, Type 2	Eagle Head E1 or E28	1918-1919	Remington Arms-UMC: circa #s 1-500 eagle head above the sans serif initial "E" and numeral "1"; circa 501-EOP, sans serif initial "E" and numeral "28."	E28

Military and Commercial Pistols

Table 6-2, cont. U.S. Ordnance Department Final Inspection Marks All Colt-Manufactured Model 1911 and Model 1911A1 Pistols, Caliber .45				
Ordnance Department Inspector	Initials	Period of Service	Comment	Marking (see figure)
Walter T. Gorton, Captain, USA	WTG	Dec. 5, 1921 to March 3, 1926	Circa #s 700,001-710,000. Left side of receiver, behind trigger, intertwined initials. Two cartouches were used; the earliest without a surrounding circle, the later with a surrounding circle	
Frederick W. Hauf, Chief Ordnance Inspector, Colt Firearms	H	1936 to 1940	"H" final acceptance mark circa #s 712,350-717,281. Single initial H (with or without serifs) on left of receiver, below magazine catch	H
Charles S. Reed, Major, USA	CSR	1938 to 1940	Left side of receiver, below slide stop, sans serif initials, no box, circa #s 717,280-723,000	CSR
John K. Clement, Colonel, USA	JKC	1939-1942	Model 1911A1 pistols, July 1, 1939 to June 30, 1942. Also, all Singer Model 1911A1 pistols, circa #s S800,001-S800,500	JKC
Robert Sears, Colonel, USA	R.S.	1937-1941	Left side of receiver, below slide stop, sans serif initials in rectangular box, circa #s 723,001-750,500. Colt Model 1911A1	R.S.

Model 1911, M1911A1

Table 6-2, cont. **U.S. Ordnance Department Final Inspection Marks** **All Colt-Manufactured Model 1911 and Model 1911A1 Pistols, Caliber .45**				
Ordnance Department Inspector	**Initials**	**Period of Service**	**Comment**	**Marking (see figure)**
Waldemar S. Broberg	W.B.	June-November 1941 to June 3, 1942	W.B. in rectangle. Colt Model 1911A1, circa #s 750,501-861,000	**W.B.**
Guy H. Drewry, Brig. General, USA	G.H.D.	June 1942 to July 1945	G.H.D. No enclosing rectangle. Colt Model 1911A1, circa #s 845,001-2,360,600	**G.H.D.**
John S. Begley (civilian) Chief, Springfield (MA) Ordnance District	J.S.B.	July 1945 to December 1945	J.S.B. No enclosing rectangle. Colt Model 1911A1, circa #s 2,360,601 to End of Production	**J.S.B.**

The period 1936-1942 can be somewhat confusing when trying to figure out which inspector markings should appear in what serial number ranges. In 1936, Frederick W. Hauf, a civilian employee of the Ordnance Department, was promoted to Chief Inspector of Ordnance at Colt. He maintained a permanent office at the Colt plant in Hartford. For unknown reasons, his full initials were not stamped on U.S. military contract pistols for three years even though required by regulations. Instead, a single initial, H or **H** (usually without serifs, but during 1938, sometimes with) was stamped on the left side of the receiver below the magazine catch between circa serial #s 712,350-717,281, see Figure 6-13, arrow.

NOTE: Between circa serial numbers 710,001-710,999, no Ordnance Inspection marking of any kind will be found on U.S. military contract pistols. The "P" proof mark was added to the left side of the receiver at circa serial #711,000.

Military and Commercial Pistols

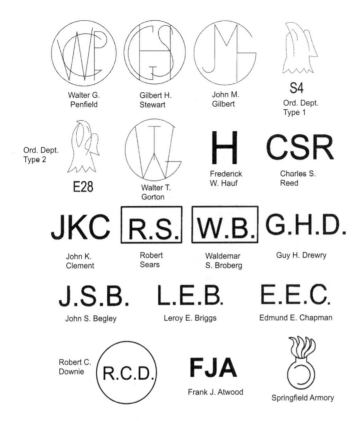

Walter G. Penfield

Gilbert H. Stewart

John M. Gilbert

S4
Ord. Dept. Type 1

Ord. Dept. Type 2

E28

Walter T. Gorton

H
Frederick W. Hauf

CSR
Charles S. Reed

JKC
John K. Clement

R.S.
Robert Sears

W.B.
Waldemar S. Broberg

G.H.D.
Guy H. Drewry

J.S.B.
John S. Begley

L.E.B.
Leroy E. Briggs

E.E.C.
Edmund E. Chapman

Robert C. Downie
R.C.D.

FJA
Frank J. Atwood

Springfield Armory

Fig. 6-12. U.S. Ordnance Department, all final inspector's marks summarized.

Fig. 6-13. Frederick W. Hauf, a civilian employee of the Ordnance Department, stamped only his initial "H" on receivers between serial #s 712,350-717,281. Karl Karash collection.

Model 1911, M1911A1

Circa serial #712,300, a provisional inspector's acceptance marking will be found stamped on the top of the receiver near the disconnector hole. For the year 1938, it will be one or several single initials within an oval. In 1939, the mark was an **R** in an oval for Charles S. Reed who replaced Hauf at the Colt factory as Chief Inspector of Ordnance, see Figure 6-14, arrow.

Starting in 1940 at circa serial #717,280, the mark was changed to **CSR**. As before, it was stamped both on top of the receiver near the disconnector hole and on the left side of the receiver below the magazine catch.

Fig. 6-14. At circa serial #712,300, the provisional inspector's acceptance marking (arrow) was stamped on the top of the receiver. Karl Karash collection. (Image enhanced.)

Finally, in October 1942, (circa serial #830,000) the provisional inspection marking was terminated; the Crossed Cannon symbol of the Ordnance Department (Figure 6-15) was adopted as the final inspection marking and stamped on the right rear of the receiver behind the right grip panel.

Verified Proof Mark—Colt

Colt's verified proof mark, **VP**, was stamped on Colt-made U.S. Government contract pistols starting at circa serial #710,001. The initials were contained within a triangle and stamped on the upper left

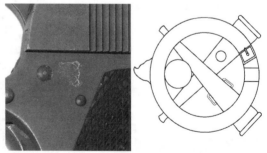

Fig. 6-15. The U.S. Ordnance Department's crossed cannon symbol was used as the final acceptance marking starting in October 1942. Some were tipped to the 9 o'clock position.

274

Military and Commercial Pistols

side of the trigger guard bow, see Figure 6-16. The verified proof mark on U.S. Government production pistols was nominally 0.07 inch high.

Fig. 6-16. The Colt "verified proof" mark was used on all commercial production and from circa serial #710,001 on Colt military production.

The Colt verified proof mark appeared on all **commercial pistols** from the start of production. At least three sizes of the mark were used. From the start of production to circa C20,000, the "VP" mark was nominally 0.08 inch high. From circa serial #s C20,001-C130,000, the "VP" was reduced in size to a nominal 0.07 inch high. From circa serial #C130,001 to the end of production, the "VP" mark was a nominal 0.05 inch high. The exact size of the marking will vary as new dies replaced old ones. The "VP" mark was stamped through the finish.

NOTE: The 0.07- and 0.05-inch-high verified proof marks were used concurrently to about 1941, circa serial number C199,500 on commercial pistols.

Proof Mark

The "**P**" proof mark was not stamped on any Ordnance Department–ordered Model 1911 receiver or slide. Model 1911 barrels received a "**P**" proof mark after circa serial #24,500.

The "**P**" proof mark is only found on the Model 1911A1 receiver from circa serial #s 711,000 to the end of production. It was stamped on the left side of the receiver behind the trigger guard. The size of the "**P**" mark varied with the different inspectors, as did its exact location (some were above the magazine catch button, others behind or below). All were in a sans serif type face, see Figure 6-17, arrow. Both "P" marks on slide and receiver should be identical.

The "**P**" proof mark was stamped before the finish was applied on Colt-manufactured Model 1911A1 receivers.

275

Model 1911, M1911A1

Fig. 6-17. The "P" proof mark (arrow) was stamped on the left side on military contract pistol receivers from serial #711,000 to the end of production.

The contract for the second order of the Model 1911A1 pistols, placed on April 13, 1937, required a prick punch mark "approximately 1/4 inch above the magazine catch and on top of the slide 1/2 inch forward of the rear sight." This requirement was never implemented for new pistols but may have been used on some refurbished and repaired pistols.

SPRINGFIELD ARMORY MARKINGS
Serial Number Format

The abbreviation for "number" and the serial number were marked on all Springfield production of the Model 1911 pistol on the right side of the receiver in sans serif type in the following form:

№ 83651

The underscore below the "o" is even with the bottom line of the "N." Figure 6-18 shows the only marking on the right side of the receiver.

U.S. Property Marking

The property marking of the Springfield Armory Model 1911 was stamped on the left side of the receiver ahead of the slide stop pin hole in sans serif letters 0.10 inch high throughout production:

Fig. 6-18. Only the serial number was marked on the right side of Springfield Armory receivers.

276

Military and Commercial Pistols

UNITED STATES PROPERTY

Figure 6-19 shows the marking on the left side of the receiver.

Model Marking

It was applied to the right side of the M1911 slide. See Chapter 7.

Ordnance Department Inspector's Mark

All Springfield Armory–manufactured Model 1911 pistols were marked with the Ordnance Department symbol, the flaming bomb, on the left side of the receiver behind the trigger as the final inspection and acceptance mark, see Figure 6-20, arrow.

Fig. 6-19. The "UNITED STATES PROPERTY" marking was stamped on the left side of Springfield Armory receivers.

This mark was also originally intended to delineate Springfield Armory Model 1911 pistols from Colt-manufactured Model 1911 pistols

Fig. 6-20. The Ordnance Department flaming bomb mark was stamped on all Springfield Armory receivers.

by replacing the rampant colt logotype. A flaming bomb symbol also appeared on slides manufactured by A.J. Savage Munitions Company. It was a company logotype and not the Ordnance Department marking.

Proof Mark

The "**P**" proof mark was stamped on the left lug of the Springfield Armory-made barrels starting at circa serial #102,600 and not on the receiver or slide. Barrel markings are described in Chapter 8.

Model 1911, M1911A1

Other Springfield Armory Markings

Other receiver parts, or parts associated with the receiver, on Springfield Armory–marked Model 1911s were *usually* marked "**S**" in a sans serif type face and included among other parts, the grip safety, hammer, mainspring housing, magazine catch, safety lock, sear, and trigger. Figure 6-21 shows a sample Springfield part marked "**S**" and Table 6-3 lists all parts usually so marked.

Fig. 6-21. Certain parts of Springfield Armory Model 1911s, like this slide stop, carry an "S" identification stamp.

Table 6-3
Springfield Armory Model 1911 Parts Marked "S"

Part	Location
Barrel	Barrel lug (right and left)
Barrel Bushing *	Reverse face, bottom, left
Extractor	Middle
Firing Pin Retainer Plate *	Inside, back
Sear	Left side
Hammer *	Hammer strut slot
Magazine Catch *	Between thumb piece and catch, in the curve
Slide Stop *	Reverse face
Safety Catch	Reverse face
Trigger *	Bottom
Grip Safety *	Left side
Mainspring Housing	Reverse face

* Springfield Armory parts observed with the "S" sometimes omitted.

278

Military and Commercial Pistols

REMINGTON ARMS-UMC MARKINGS
Serial Number Format
The abbreviation for "number" and the serial number were stamped on all Remington Arms-UMC Model 1911 pistols before the finish and in sans serif

Fig. 6-22. The serial number was marked on the right side of the Remington Arms-UMC receiver (arrow 1); an inspector's number was marked on the upper right trigger guard (arrow 2). Mike Strietbeck collection.

type (except the numeral "1") without a period after the abbreviation, and in the following form. Remington Arms-UMC receiver markings on the right side are shown in Figure 6-22. Letters and numbers were 0.10 inch high:

NO 14561

U.S. Property Marking
The property marking on the Remington Arms-UMC–manufactured Model 1911 was stamped on the left side of the receiver ahead of the slide stop pin hole in sans serif letters 0.10 inch high from start to finish of production, see Figure 6-23, arrow A:

UNITED STATES PROPERTY

279

Model 1911, M1911A1

Fig. 6-23. Property (A), Army Inspector of Ordnance (B), and final inspection (C) markings on Remington Arms-UMC Model 1911s were stamped on the left side of the receiver. Mike Strietbeck collection.

Model Marking

Most Remington Arms-UMC Model 1911 pistols were marked in two lines on the right side of the slide. Note the spacing:

MODEL OF 1911

U.S.ARMY CALIBER .45

Some very late pistols had a single line marking. See Chapter 7, Slide Markings, for details.

Army Inspector of Ordnance Marking

Two Army inspectors were assigned to Remington Arms-UMC to inspect Model 1911 production. The first was Captain Leroy E. Briggs (March-August 1918). The second was Major Edmund E. Chapman, who served in this role from August 1918 to the end of production.

As production did not begin until August 1918 it is unlikely that Captain Briggs inspected any Remington Arms-UMC Model 1911s as he was also charged with inspecting all Colt Model 1892, 1894, 1896 and 1901 and 1903 double-action revolvers being repaired and refurbished by the Bridgeport plant at that time. His inspection marking, **L.E.B.,** as seen on

Military and Commercial Pistols

Fig. 6-24. The initials of Captain Leroy E. Briggs stamped on a U.S. Army Model 1903 refurbished revolver. He probably did not accept any Remington Arms-UMC Model 1911s.

refurbished double-action .38-caliber revolvers, is shown in Figure 6-24.

Major Chapman's inspection marking was stamped on the left side of the receiver, behind the trigger in sans serif letters 0.09 inch high, see Figure 6-25:

E.E.C.

NOTE: After serial #3,500 or so, it appears as if the final period in "E.E.C." has been dropped. In fact, it was worn down on the die but is usually visible with a magnifying glass.

This inspection marking was stamped after the pistol was completed, through the blued finish. On pistols in good condition with finish remaining in this area, the letters will be surrounded by slight ridges of displaced metal that are lighter in color than the surrounding metal. If this discoloration is not present around the

Fig. 6-25. Major Edmund E. Chapman inspected Remington Arms-UMC Model 1911 pistols for the Ordnance Department. Mike Strietbeck collection.

initials, look for evidence that the pistol has been refinished. Ordnance inspector's markings found on Remington Arms-UMC Model 1911s are summarized in Table 6-4.

Model 1911, M1911A1

Table 6-4 U.S. Ordnance Department Final Inspection Marks, Remington Arms-UMC Model 1911 Pistol, Caliber .45				
Army Inspector of Ordnance	Ordnance Inspector Initials	Period of Service	Comment	Marking
Edmund E. Chapman, Major, USA	E.E.C. above Eagle	1918-1919	Remington Arms-UMC Model 1911s. Left side of receiver, behind trigger, sans serif letters, stamped after finish was applied	**E.E.C.**
Ordnance Department Eagle, Type 2	E.E.C. above Eagle	1918-1919	Ca. serial #1-500, Eagle head raised vertically, often above the sans serif initial E1. Ca. 501-EOP, E28. Stamped on left side of receiver, behind the trigger, above the magazine catch and on left front trigger guard and above the firing pin stop.	**E1** OR **E28** Fig. 6-26

Inspection Markings

The final inspection marking found on Remington Arms-UMC pistols was the "eagle's head" over an alphanumeric identification stamped below the Ordnance Department inspector's cartouche as follows: from serial #s 1-500, the **Type 2** "eagle head" over "E1"; circa serial #s 501-EOP, the **Type 2** "eagle head" over "E28"; see Figure 6-26 in Table 6-4.

NOTE: The "eagle head" marking was first used to mark the U.S. Model of 1917 Enfield Rifle for acceptance. The Model of 1917 Rifle was manufactured by Remington Arms-UMC at their Ilion, NY, and Eddystone, PA, plants, and by Winchester Repeating Arms Company.

Military and Commercial Pistols

The upper left side of the trigger guard, the flat above the firing pin stop plate, and the bottom of the mainspring housing were marked **E,** the provisional inspection marking of Walter H. Evans in sans serif type from serial numbers 1 to circa 13,281-15,000 (see Figures 6-27 and 6-28).

From circa serial #15,001 to the end of production, the **E** inspection marking on the mainspring housing *may* have been eliminated but serial #s 18,449 and 21,512 do show the "**E.**"

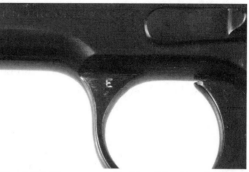

Fig. 6-27. The upper left side of the Remington-Arms UMC trigger guard was marked E to circa serial #15,000. Mike Strietbeck collection.

Proof Mark
Remington Arms-UMC receivers were not proof marked. Barrels were usually marked "P" which was visible through the ejection port.

Other Remington Arms-UMC Markings
A mark consisting of an **X** within a circle stamped on any Remington Arms-UMC Model 1911 part indicates that the part was rejected and condemned. Some of these parts *may* have been used by employees to assemble "lunch box" pistols or they may have been used to assemble pistols after the Remington Arms-UMC contract was canceled. Such pistol parts may have an **E** provisional inspection marking but no final inspection markings (eagle head/number), acceptance markings (**E.E.C.**), or serial number. If one of these receivers does have a serial number it was either applied by the individual making the

Fig. 6-28. An "E" was also stamped on the bottom of the mainspring housing. Mike Strietbeck collection.

Model 1911, M1911A1

pistol or the receiver was taken from an authorized and accepted U.S. military pistol.

SINGER MARKINGS
Serial Number Format
The Singer Manufacturing Company of Elizabeth, New Jersey, was one of two companies (the other was Ithaca—for a short while) to include a three-letter prefix (**№ S**) before the serial number (S800,001-S800,500) on a U.S. military contract pistol. Figure 6-29 shows the markings on the right side of the Singer receiver. The abbreviation for "number" and the serial number itself were in a sans serif type face and were 0.10 inch high:

№ S800244

The underscore is even with the bottom of the "N."

U.S. Property Marking
All Singer-manufactured Model 1911A1 pistols were marked on the right side, behind the slide stop pin hole and above the serial number in sans serif type 0.10 inch high, refer to Figure 6-29:

Fig. 6-29. Markings on the Singer Manufacturing Company Model 1911A1 receiver. Karl Karash collection.

UNITED STATES PROPERTY

Model Marking
This marking was stamped on the right side of all Model 1911A1 receivers manufactured by Singer in sans serif letters 0.10 inch high forward of the slide stop pin hole, refer to Figure 6-29:

M 1911 A1 U.S. ARMY

Military and Commercial Pistols

Fig. 6-30. Markings on the left side of the Singer Manufacturing Company Model 1911A1. Karl Karash collection.

Note the spacing between the "**M**" and "**I**," and "**I**" and "**AI**" lettering.

Proof Mark
The Ordnance Department proof mark was a **P** stamped on the left side of the receiver behind the trigger guard, just above the magazine release, see Figure 6-30.

Ordnance Department Inspector's Marking
The Singer Manufacturing Company was in the New York Ordnance District. Colonel John K. Clement was Army Inspector of Ordnance from July 1, 1939, to June 30, 1942. His initials without periods were stamped on the left side of the receiver behind the trigger guard in sans serif letters 0.09 inch high and without periods, refer to Figures 6-12 and 6-30:

JKC

Model 1911, M1911A1

Ordnance inspector's markings found on Singer Manufacturing Company Model 1911s are summarized in Table 6-5.

Table 6-5 U.S. Ordnance Department Final Inspection Marks, Singer Model 1911A1 Pistol, Caliber .45				
Army Inspector of Ordnance	Initials	Period of Service	Comment	Marking
John K. Clement, Colonel, USA	JKC	1939-1942	New York Ordnance District. All Singer Model 1911A1 pistols, serial #s S800,001-S800,500	**JKC**

HARRINGTON & RICHARDSON

Harrington & Richardson was assigned a block of serial numbers (800,501-801,000) as part of an Educational Contract. They were instructed to use the prefix "H" before the serial number, but the contract was dropped before the factory produced even a single Model 1911A1 that was accepted by the Ordnance Department.

ITHACA MARKINGS
Serial Number Format

The abbreviation for number and the serial number marked on all Ithaca Gun Company production of the Model 1911A1 pistol was in sans serif type (except the numeral "1"s) in the following form. Letters and numbers were 0.10 inch high.

№ 1226943

The underscore was aligned with the bottom of the "N." Figure 6-31 shows the markings on the right side of the Ithaca receiver.

NOTE: A very few early-production Ithaca receivers will show an "I" for "Ithaca" immediately preceding the serial number.

Military and Commercial Pistols

From circa serial #1,208,674, the start of the second Ordnance Department Ithaca contract to the end of production, serial numbers were stamped on completed, finished receivers as the last production operation.

The other receiver markings, **UNITED STATES PROPERTY** and **M 1911 A1 U.S. ARMY** and **Nº**, unlike the serial number, were stamped *before* the polishing and finishing process.

Fig. 6-31. Markings on the right side of the Ithaca Gun Company Model 1911A1. Note the space between the **Nº** and the serial number.

There is a distinct space between **Nº** and the serial number. These post-1,208,674 serial numbers will usually appear sharper and crisper than the other receiver markings, and the metal in the recesses of the numbers will appear different in texture and color than the prefix, **Nº**.

U.S. Property Marking

As shown above in Figure 6-31, all Ithaca-manufactured Model 1911A1 pistols were marked on the right side, behind the slide stop pin hole and above the serial number in sans serif type 0.09 inch high:

UNITED STATES PROPERTY

Model Marking

The model marking on Ithaca-manufactured Model 1911A1 pistols was stamped on the right side of the receiver in sans serif letters 0.10 inch high forward of the slide stop pin hole:

M 1911 A1 U.S. ARMY

Collectors should note that between circa serial #s 906,000-916,400 and 1,208,674-1,208,700, the model marking may appear on the right side of the slide instead of on the receiver.

287

Model 1911, M1911A1

Note the spacing between the "**M**" and "**I**," and "**I**" and "**AI**," refer to Figure 6-31.

Ordnance Department Inspector's Marking

The Ordnance Department inspector assigned to the Ithaca Gun Company, Inc., was Colonel Frank J. Atwood of the Rochester, New York Ordnance District. His initials, without periods, were stamped on the left side of the receiver behind the trigger guard and just below the slide stop lever in sans serif letters 0.09 inch high. Figure 6-32 shows all markings on the left side of the Ithaca receiver:

FJA

Fig. 6-32. Markings on the left side of the Ithaca Model 1911A1. Karl Karash collection.

Table 6-6 U.S. Ordnance Department Final Inspection Marks, Ithaca Model 1911A1 Pistol, Caliber .45				
Army Inspector of Ordnance	**Initials**	**Period of Service**	**Comment**	**Marking**
Frank J. Atwood, Colonel, USA	FJA	June 1942 to March 1946	FJA No enclosing rectangle. All Remington Rand and Ithaca Model 1911A1s	**FJA**

288

Military and Commercial Pistols

Proof Mark

The Ordnance Department proof mark **P** was 0.12 inch high. It was stamped on the left side of the receiver near the magazine release, and in front of the rear sight (0.12 inch high) on the slide, refer to Figure 6-32.

Ordnance Department Final Inspection Mark

The Ordnance Department's final inspection marking, the Crossed Cannons, was stamped on all Ithaca Model 1911A1 receivers at the right rear between the hammer and disconnector pin holes, see Figure 6-33. The mark was stamped after the receiver was Parkerized and may show bright bare metal through the finish.

Fig. 6-33. The crossed cannons final inspection marking was stamped on all Ithaca receivers at the right rear. Many are partial strikes.

Other Markings

From the start of Ithaca production at serial #856,405 to circa serial #1,279,673 at the end of the second contract, a small ordnance bomb symbol 0.12 inch high (smaller than the Colt marking) was stamped inside the recoil spring shroud as well as under the firing pin stop plate in the slide.

Starting at circa serial #900,000, Ithaca began stamping factory inspection markings consisting of various symbols on the left front trigger guard. They appear intermittently at first. Symbols observed by the author include two connected triangles, arrowhead, Swiss cross, and a crescent on a base, see Figure 6-34.

NOTE: Early receivers used by Ithaca were received from Ordnance Department inventory. These were mostly manufactured by Colt during the World War I period and were either unused or salvaged from damaged pistols. Those of Colt origin can be identified by the markings characteristic of Colt production at the time: Francis (Frank) Hosmer's "H" indicating a U.S. Government contract order, or the short mainspring

Model 1911, M1911A1

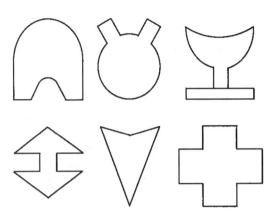

Fig. 6-34. These symbols were used as factory inspection markings on Ithaca Model 1911A1 receivers after circa serial #900,000.

shroud. The receiver may or may not show an assembler's initial depending on whether or not it was a new or salvaged receiver.

REMINGTON RAND MARKINGS
Serial Number Format

Two forms of the abbreviation for "number" and the serial number were marked on the Remington Rand production of the Model 1911A1 pistol. From the start of production at serial #916,405 to circa serial #s 955,000-1,015,499, the abbreviation for the word "number" and the serial number itself was stamped in a sans serif type face (except the numeral "1"s). Letters and numbers were 0.10 inch high:

№ 917300

The underline under "o" was even with the bottom of the "N," see Figure 6-35.

From circa serial #s 955,001-1,015,499 to the end of production, the abbreviation for the word "number" consisted of uppercase letters without an underline. The change was made at the same time as new management personnel were in-

Fig. 6-35. Early Remington Rand Model 1911A1 receivers were stamped with the abbreviation for "number" as shown. Ty Moore collection.

Military and Commercial Pistols

stalled and was intended to delineate pistols made under the two systems, see Figure 6-36. The abbreviation for number was followed by a period (although it is difficult to see). It and the serial number were stamped in a sans serif type face:

NO. 1291547

There was a small space between the abbreviation for number and the serial number itself on all Remington Rand pistols. All receiver markings, **UNITED STATES PROPERTY, M 19II AI U.S. ARMY**, and **Nº**, were stamped before the polishing and finishing process. But after the change to the **NO.** prefix the *serial number* itself was stamped *after* the receivers were finished, through the Parkerized finish. This makes the serial number appear sharper and crisper than other receiver markings, depending on condition. The finish in the recesses of the numbers should appear flattened and nonporous, or lighter in color, than the surrounding finish.

Fig. 6-36. Starting at circa serial #s 955,001-1,015,499, the prefix was changed to "NO."

Clean the area with a light solvent or a mild solution of detergent to wash away any dirt and grime. After the change to **NO.** (circa serial #s 955,001-1,015,499) the space between **U.S.** and **ARMY** was wider.

Preproduction, experimental, and presentation Remington Rand pistols do not follow the Ordnance Department serial numbering procedure. Presentation pistols and preproduction show only the serial number (one to three digits) in a type face with partial serifs but without the prefix "NO." The numbers were stamped by hand. A Remington preproduction and presentation Model 1911A1 in the author's collection is serial numbered "72" and the number was slanted slightly to the right, see Figure 6-37. Other examples observed show the numbers vertical but in the same type face.

Model 1911, M1911A1

ERRS-marked Remington Rand pistols have been called "Experimental Remington Rand" pistols but there is no evidence that this means "experimental." Since all show late manufacturing characteristics, it is unlikely that they had anything to do with experimentation. Other prefixes noted will show the abbrevia-

Fig. 6-37. Are these preproduction or presentation Remington Rand Model 1911A1s? It is not known for certain but the serial number on this example, "72," was stamped by hand and did not have a prefix, MODEL or U.S. PROPERTY marking. North Cape Publications collection.

tion for number plus the prefix, **E**, **ER**, **ERRS** followed by a serial number (one to three digits) all in sans serif type:

NO. ERRS 27

Fig. 6-38. Markings on the right side of the Remington Rand Model 1911A1 receiver.

U.S. Property Marking

All Remington Rand–manufactured Model 1911A1 pistols were marked on the right side, behind the slide stop pin hole and above the serial number with this marking in sans serif type 0.10 inch high in one line:

UNITED STATES PROPERTY

Figure 6-38 shows the markings on the right side of the Remington Rand receiver.

Military and Commercial Pistols

Model Marking

The model marking on Remington Rand–manufactured Model 1911A1 pistols was stamped on the right side of the receiver in sans serif letters 0.10 inch high forward of the slide stop pin hole (Figures 6-35 and 6-38):

M 1911 A1 U.S. ARMY

Note that the spacing between "**U.S.**" and "**ARMY**" was wider after circa serial #s 955,001-1,015,499.

Ordnance Department Inspection Mark

The Army Inspector of Ordnance assigned to the Rochester Ordnance District which included Remington Rand, Inc., at Syracuse, New York, was Colonel Frank J. Atwood. His initials, without periods, were stamped on the left side of the receiver behind the trigger guard and just below the slide stop lever in sans serif letters 0.09 inch high and without periods:

FJA

Fig. 6-39. Ordnance Department Inspection marking on Remington Rand Model 1911A1s.

The size of his initials in the stamp seems to vary slightly throughout the production run, suggesting that one or more new stamps may have been used, see Figure 6-39.

Table 6-7				
U.S. Ordnance Department Final Inspection Marks, Remington Rand Model 1911A1 Pistol, Caliber .45				
Army Inspector of Ordnance	Initials	Period of Service	Comment	Marking
Frank J. Atwood, Colonel, USA	FJA	June 1942 to March 1946	FJA No enclosing rectangle. All Remington Rand 1911A1s	**FJA**

293

Model 1911, M1911A1

Proof Mark

The Ordnance Department proof mark **P** was 0.09 inch high and stamped on the left side of the receiver near the magazine release (refer to Figure 6-39) and on top of the slide, see Figure 7-20.

Final Ordnance Inspection Mark

The Ordnance Department's final inspection marking, crossed cannons, was stamped on all Remington Rand Model 1911A1 receivers at the right rear between the hammer and disconnector pin holes, refer to Figure 6-33. The mark was stamped after the receiver was Parkerized and bright bare metal may show through.

Other Markings

At circa serial #1,300,000, Remington Rand factory inspectors began adding their own final inspection markings in the form of letters and numbers to both sides of the trigger guard, see Figure 6-40. The practice continued to the end of production.

UNION SWITCH & SIGNAL COMPANY MARKINGS

Serial Number Format

The abbreviation for "number" and the serial number on all US&S production of the Model 1911A1 pistols were marked as follows throughout production—the abbreviation for "number" was in sans serif type and the serial number was

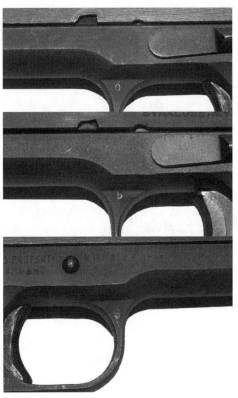

Fig. 6-40. Remington Rand inspectors stamped their assigned numbers or initials onto both sides of the trigger guard from circa serial #1,300,000 to the end of production.

294

Fig. 6-41. Markings on the right side of the Union Switch & Signal receiver. Karl Karash collection.

marked in a sans serif type face (except the numeral "1"s). Letters and numbers were 0.10 inch high:

№ 1075403

The underscore below the "o" was on the same level as the bottom of the "N." Figure 6-41 shows all markings on the right side of the US&S receiver.

U.S. Property Marking

The U.S. property marking (refer to Figure 6-41) was stamped on the right side of the receiver through the finish, behind the slide stop pin hole and above the serial number in a sans serif type face 0.10 inch high:

UNITED STATES PROPERTY

Model Marking

The Model marking (refer to Figure 6-41) was stamped on the right side of the receiver just ahead of the slide stop pin hole in a sans serif type face 0.10 inch high:

M 19II AI U.S. ARMY

Note the spacing between the "**M**" and "**I9II**," "**19II**" and "**AI**."

Model 1911, M1911A1

Final Ordnance Inspection Marking

US&S Model 1911A1s *were never* stamped with the Ordnance Department crossed cannon insignia during their entire production run.

Ordnance Department Inspector's Marking

The Union Switch & Signal Company was located at Swissvale, Pennsylvania, in the Pittsburgh Ordnance District. Robert C. Downie, a civilian, was Army Inspector of Ordnance from July 2, 1942–October 15,

Fig. 6-42. Markings on the left side of the Union Switch & Signal receiver. John Domoslai collection.

1945 (commissioned a Lt. Colonel, U.S. Army, in March 1943). His cartouche was R.C.D. within a circle and was stamped on the left side of the receiver just below the slide stop throughout production, see Figure 6-42.

Army Inspector of Ordnance	Initials	Period of Service	Comment	Marking
Table 6-8 **U.S. Ordnance Department Final Inspection Marks,** **Union Switch & Signal Model 1911A1 Pistol, Caliber .45**				
Robert C. Downie, Lt. Colonel, USA	R.C.D.	July 1942 to October 1945	R.C.D. enclosed within a circle. Union Switch & Signal Model 1911A1. Served as both final inspection and acceptance stamp, circa #s 1,041,405-1,096,404	R.C.D.

296

Military and Commercial Pistols

Proof Mark

The "P" proof mark *was not* stamped on the US&S receiver or slide from the start of production at serial #1,041,405 to circa serial #1,060,000.

From circa serial #1,060,001 to the end of US&S production, the **P** proof mark without serifs (0.09 inch high) was stamped on the left side of the receiver behind and either above or below the magazine release button, refer to Figure 6-42. See Chapters 7 and 8 for US&S slide and barrel markings.

U.S. ARMY ORDNANCE FINAL INSPECTION MARKINGS— A SUMMARY

The Ordnance Department final inspection marking consisted of the initials of Army Inspector of Ordnance assigned to a specific ordnance district, and, in the case of Colt Firearms, to a specific factory. The initials were stamped on the left side of the receiver above the magazine catch to signify that every part had been inspected and gauged, and that the assembled pistol had been tested to make certain that it operated according to the standards and specifications set forth by the Ordnance Department. The final inspection marking was stamped on the pistol prior to acceptance by the Ordnance Department. Of course, the inspections were carried out by officers or civilian employees subordinate to the Army Inspector of Ordnance who were delegated to use his initials.

NOTE: One civilian inspector, Frederick W. Hauf, Chief Ordnance Inspector, Colt Firearms, used only the initial of his last name, **H** or **H**, from 1936 to 1940 (**H** with serifs in 1938 only).

U.S. Army Ordnance Markings

Ordnance District Commanders

U.S. Army Inspector of Ordnance initials (final inspection markings) which served as the indication that the pistol met all specifications established by the Ordnance Department are summarized for the reader's convenience in Table 6-9 by name, period of service and serial number range or the manufacturer to which they were assigned. Also, refer to Figure 6-12 for a summary of all final inspector's markings.

Model 1911, M1911A1

Army Inspector of Ordnance	Initials	Period of Service	Comment	Marking
Walter G. Penfield, Major, USA	WGP	1911-1914	Circa #s 1-101,500. Intertwined initials inside a circle	
Gilbert H. Stewart, Major, USA	GHS	1915-1918	Circa #s 101,500-230,000. Intertwined initials inside a circle	
John M. Gilbert, Lt. Colonel, NA	JMG	1917-1918	Circa #s 230,000-302,000. Intertwined initials with "G" forming the enclosing circle	
Ordnance Department Eagle, 1st Type		1918-1919	Used by Colt: circa #s 300,000-629,000. Eagle head often above the sans serif initial "S" followed by a number or by number and letter	S4
Ordnance Department Eagle, Type 2		1918-1919	Used on all Remington Arms-UMC M1911s Eagle head above initial "E" followed by a numeral "1," serial #s 1-500; serial #s 501-EOP, E28	E28

Military and Commercial Pistols

Table 6-9 cont. Summary All U.S. Ordnance Department Final Inspection Marks, All Model 1911 and Model 1911A1 Pistols, Caliber .45				
Army Inspector of Ordnance	Initials	Period of Service	Comment	Marking
Ordnance Department Inspectors		1914-1918	1914-1917 Springfield Armory 1918 Colt	
Leroy E. Briggs, Captain, USAR	L.E.B.	1918	Probably never inspected and marked Remington Arms-UMC pistols. Included only for completeness	**L.E.B.**
Edmund E. Chapman, Major, USA	E.E.C.	August 1918-June 1919	Remington Arms-UMC: Model 1911s, all production. Left side of receiver, behind trigger, sans serif letters, stamped after finish was applied.	**E.E.C.**
Walter T. Gorton, Captain, USA	WTG	Dec. 5, 1921 to March 3, 1926	Colt: ca. #s 700,001-710,000. Two cartouches were used; the earliest without a surrounding circle, the later with a surrounding circle	
Frederick W. Hauf, Chief Ordnance Inspector, Colt Firearms	H	1936 to 1940	Colt: ca. 712,350-717,281. Single initial H without serifs. In 1938, serifs were sometimes seen.	**H**

Model 1911, M1911A1

	Table 6-9, cont. Summary All U.S. Ordnance Department Final Inspection Marks, All Model 1911 and Model 1911A1 Pistols, Caliber .45			
Army Inspector of Ordnance	**Initials**	**Period of Service**	**Comment**	**Marking**
John K. Clement, Colonel, USA	JKC	July 1939-June 1942	Singer: New York Ordnance District, #S800,001-S800,500	**JKC**
Charles S. Reed, Major, USA	CSR	August 1938-December 1940	Colt: ca. #s 717,280-723,000 Left side of receiver, below slide stop, sans serif initials, no box	**CSR**
Robert Sears, Colonel, USA	R.S.	August 1937-June 1941	Colt: ca. #s 723,001-750,500 Hartford Ordnance District. Left side of receiver, below slide stop, sans serif initials in rectangular box	**R.S.**
Waldemar S. Broberg	W.B.	June-Nov. 1941 to June 3, 1942	Colt: ca. #s 750,501-861,000. W.B. in rectangle.	**W.B.**
Guy H. Drewry, Brig. General, USA	G.H.D.	June 1942 to July 1945	Colt: ca. #s 845,001-2,360,600 Springfield Ordnance District. "G.H.D." No enclosing rectangle	**G.H.D.**
John S. Begley, Chief, Springfield (MA) Ordnance District	J.S.B.	July 1945 to Dec. 1945	Colt: Serial #s 2,360,601 to End of Production. "J.S.B." No enclosing rectangle.	**J.S.B.**

Military and Commercial Pistols

Army Inspector of Ordnance	Initials	Period of Service	Comment	Marking
			Table 6-9, cont. **Summary** **All U.S. Ordnance Department Final Inspection Marks,** **All Model 1911 and Model 1911A1 Pistols, Caliber .45**		
Robert C. Downie, Lt. Colonel, USA	R.C.D.	July 1942 to October 1945	Union Switch & Signal: ca. #s 1,041,405-1,096,404. R.C.D. enclosed within a circle. All Union Switch & Signal Model 1911A1s. Served as both final inspection and acceptance stamp	R.C.D.
Frank J. Atwood, Colonel, USA	FJA	June 1942 to March 1946	FJA No enclosing rectangle. All Remington Rand and Ithaca Model 1911A1s	**FJA**

Ordnance Provisional Acceptance Markings

The Ordnance Department provisional acceptance mark was applied by an

Ordnance inspector to indicate that it had met and passed a preliminary inspection of the finished receiver. The mark usually consisted of the initial of the inspector's last name, applied to the top of the receiver near the disconnector hole, see Figure 6-43 for an example. Provisional acceptance markings are shown in Table 6-10.

Fig. 6-43. Ordnance Department provisional inspector marks (arrow) were stamped on top of the receiver near the disconnector hole from ca. serial #s 101-830,000 at Colt until replaced by Crossed Cannon mark. "H" is Frank Hosmer.

Model 1911, M1911A1

	Table 6-10 Provisional Acceptance Marks Colt Model 1911 and Model 1911A1 Pistols, Caliber .45	
Marking	**Significance**	**Comment**
G	Government Production Order	Not a provisional inspection marking but a Colt factory abbreviation for "Government Contract." Included here for clarity. Stamped below or to the side of the disconnector hole on U.S. military Model 1911/1911A1s throughout production.
H	Frank Hosmer	Top of receiver, above disconnector hole ca. s/n 101-10,000 with serifs; ca. s/n 10,001-133,186 without serifs. Ca. 137,401-710,000 without serifs.
S	W. E. Strong	Used circa s/n 133,187-137,400 in place of Hosmer's "H." Sans serif letter. Do not confuse with "S" on Colt pistols signifying commercial sale.
H	Frederick Hauff	Top of receiver, right of disconnector hole. "H" provisional inspection initial. Seen with and without serifs. ca. s/n 711,606-712,349.
H.O.L.	Possibly Major Henry O'Leary, USA	Various inspector's initials stamped on top of receiver to right of disconnector hole. ca. s/n 712,350-713,645.
R	Charles S. Reed, Major, USA	Top of receiver, right of disconnector hole ca. 713,646-717,281.
CSR	Charles S. Reed, Major, USA	Top of receiver, right of disconnector hole ca. 717,282-723,000.
RS	Robert Sears, Colonel, USA	Top of receiver, right of disconnector hole ca. 723,001-760,000.
H	unknown	Top of receiver, right of disconnector hole. Seen primarily on converted commercial production pistols, 1941-42.

Military and Commercial Pistols

	Table 6-10, cont. Provisional Acceptance Marks Colt Model 1911 and Model 1911A1 Pistols, Caliber .45	
Marking	Significance	Comment
Ordnance Department Flaming Bomb Symbol	February 1942 to October 1942 at Colt; Mid-1943 to End of Production at Ithaca	Flaming Bomb replaced inspector's initials ca. s/n 760,000-830,000. Stamped on top of the receiver, right of the disconnector hole. (Used intermittently with large sans serif "H" mark in this period). Used to mid-1943 (circa #s 1,245,000-1,279,673) on many Ithaca Model 1911A1s only. Stamped on rear of slide under firing pin stop and in the receiver barrel channel until end of production. The Ithaca mark was smaller than that used by Colt. Final inspection mark, all Springfield Armory pistol production.
Ordnance Department Inspection Mark	October 1942 to end of U.S. government contract production	Crossed cannon emblem of the U.S. Army Ordnance Corps, first use on Colt, Remington Rand and Ithaca Model 1911A1s starting October 1942 at circa #830,000 at Colt and all Ithaca and Remington Rand production. It was never stamped on Union Switch & Signal Model 1911A1s.

REPAIR AND OVERHAUL FACILITIES MARKINGS

Commercial or military pistols repaired or overhauled at Colt were *usually* marked "K" on the right side of the trigger guard. As an aside, a "K" mark is also seen on some new military and commercial barrels as an inspection mark ahead of the barrel lug between circa serial #s 700,001-710,000 and should not be confused with the repair "K" mark.

Model 1911, M1911A1

Model 1911s and Model 1911A1s returned through military channels to the Springfield Armory or other Ordnance arsenals for repair or refurbishment were not generally marked as such until about 1937. In general, the initials of the facility doing the work were stamped on the right side of the receiver. If the work was done at the Springfield Armory, the initials "SA" were usually stamped on the right side of the receiver, see Figure 6-44, arrow A. If the repair or refurbishment was done at an Army, Navy, Marine Corps, or Air Corps/Air Force maintenance facility, the pistol was almost never marked as such. National Match pistols rebuilt and reissued for a

Fig. 6-44. Arrow A indicates that this M1911A1 was refurbished at the Springfield Arsenal ("SA" for Springfield Armory). "T" shown by Arrow B indicates that it was fired for targeting.

second season were proof-fired but not remarked. The "T" marking on some may indicate that the sights have been aligned properly (arrow B).

Augusta Arsenal (AA) and Rock Island Arsenal (RIA) repair markings have also been observed.

Table 6-11 lists the U.S. Army arsenals known to have repaired and refurbished pistols.

Table 6-11 Model 1911/1911A1 U.S. Army Ordnance Department Repair Facilities		
Augusta Arsenal	AA (usually on left)	
Benicia Arsenal	BA	
Raritan Arsenal	RA	
Rock Island Arsenal	RIA (followed in mid-1950s by the initials...)	EB (Ernest Blind)
		FK (Frank Krack)

304

Military and Commercial Pistols

Table 6-11, cont. Model 1911/1911A1 U.S. Army Ordnance Department Repair Facilities	
Springfield Armory	SA
San Antonio Arsenal	SAA

Additional Military Model Markings—Prefixes and Suffixes

The standard prefix applied to Model 1911 and 1911A1 serial numbers was the abbreviation for "number" as described above in the paragraphs relating to serial number formats for the various manufacturers.

An additional prefix, as noted, was the "S" or "I" applied to Singer-manufactured Model 1911A1s or some very early Ithaca Model 1911A1s (very few so marked) immediately after the prefix.

The last prefix used was "X." It was applied to serial numbers issued either by the Springfield Armory to 1941, or the Chief of Ordnance, after, see Figure 6-45. These serial numbers were issued to Ordnance facilities to renumber receivers with damaged or obliterated serial numbers. These pistols are easy to counterfeit; the price paid for an example should take into account its documentation or lack thereof. Table 5-12 in Chapter 5 provides a listing of all known X-numbers.

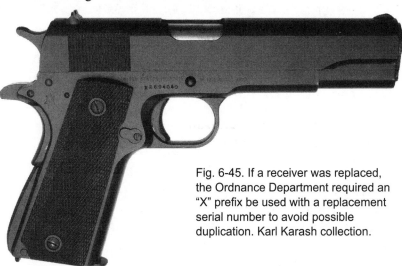

Fig. 6-45. If a receiver was replaced, the Ordnance Department required an "X" prefix be used with a replacement serial number to avoid possible duplication. Karl Karash collection.

Model 1911, M1911A1

Colt is known to have provided replacement receivers using the serial number of the original receiver with "R" stamped after the serial number (suffix). The commercial "C" on Colt pistols became a suffix after serial #C240,227. After the Ordnance Department inadvertently assigned serial numbers to Colt in 1943 that duplicated some in the Ithaca, Remington Rand, and US&S ranges, it became standard practice for the U.S. Army to stamp an "A," "B," etc. suffix to pistols with duplicate serial numbers when they found them.

COMMERCIAL PRODUCTION—COLT RECEIVER MARKINGS
Serial Number Format

Colt commercial serial number styles mentioned above are discussed in greater detail here with other commercial markings.

Colt Model 1911 commercial production began on March 9, 1912, after 500 Model 1911s had been produced for the U.S. military. The first commercial serial number was "C1." Colt commercial production used the prefix "C" and did not include the abbreviation for number. From circa serial #s C1-C2,250, the prefix "C" and serial number was stamped on the left side of the receiver in a type face with ornamental serifs.

At circa serial #C2,251 the serial number was moved to the right side of the receiver behind the slide stop pin hole, refer to Figure 6-5A and Table 6-1. The "C" prefix had a serif at the top of the stroke to circa #C130,000 did not. A space was inserted between the "C" and the serial number.

From circa serial #s C1-C130,000, the serial number was vertical. Between circa serial #s C130,001-C240,227, the serial number was slanted slightly to the right in a serif type face, refer to Figure 6-5B. The serif at the top of the prefix "C" stroke was dropped but reappears between circa serial #s C170,001-C220,001 only, refer to Table 6-1. This format continued to the end of the Model 1911A1 production in 1970.

Commercial serial #s circa 240,228C-336,169C are vertical and sans serif. The suffix lacks serifs. Since the start of the Series 70 the practice has been to locate the serial number in a vertical, sans serif type style on the right side of the receiver, behind the slide stop pin hole, refer to Figure 6-5C.

Military and Commercial Pistols

Model Marks

All commercial Model 1911s and Model 1911A1s carried the model marking on the right side of the receiver. From the start of commercial production to circa serial number C5,000, the model marking was stamped ahead of the slide stop pin hole. After, it was stamped behind the slide stop pin hole and above the serial number, see Figure 6-46. This format remained in use to the end of commercial Model 1911A1 production in 1970.

Fig. 6-46. To circa serial #5,000, the commercial model marking was stamped ahead of the slide stop pin. After, it was stamped behind the slide stop pin hole to the end of production.

NOTE: After World War II, the model marking appears on the slide on some commercial models but was omitted completely on the first circa 500 postwar pistols, circa serial #s C220,001-C220,500.

GOVERNMENT MODEL

Production Marks

It was the practice of the Colt factory to mark each pistol according to its order type on top of the receiver near the disconnector hole, see Figure 6-47.

Pistols manufactured under U.S. Government contract were marked **G.** Those made for commercial sale were marked **S.** Those manufactured for sale in Argentina were marked **O.**

Model 1911, M1911A1

Fig. 6-47. Colt production markings (clockwise): S = commercial sale; E= .445 Webley (Eley) cartridge; O = Argentine contract; G = U.S. Government contract.

Those intended for sale in Great Britain, or for the .455 Eley cartridge, were marked "**E**" for Eley (or possibly England). Many of these were British government World War I contracts.

NOTE: Model 1911 and Model 1911A1 pistols with **G** marked slides and **S** marked receivers have been observed, or vice versa. These are usually pistols that were assembled or repaired using a rejected "military" part or leftover commercial part from the 1941-1945 period.

Colt Factory Verified Proof Mark

All commercial Model 1911 pistols were stamped with Colt's "verified proof," a stylized V and P within an inverted triangle, on the left side front of the trigger bow throughout production, see Figure 6-48.

The VP proof mark was not stamped on military production pistols until circa serial #710,001.

NOTE: The "VP" proof mark may be seen on pistols sent to Colt for commercial repair or refurbishment by GIs who brought them home. It is believed that the "VP" mark would only be applied to pistols whose barrel was replaced and subsequently proof-fired.

Fig. 6-48. Colt's "VP" proof mark was stamped on all commercial receivers and all U.S. government production from circa serial #710,001 to the end of production.

Military and Commercial Pistols

Colt Factory Commercial Inspection Markings

From the start of commercial production to circa serial #C189,600 commercial inspector's markings were usually found stamped *on the top of the receiver* at the one to three o'clock position relative to the disconnector hole and the *lower left side of the trigger guard*, see Figure 6-49, arrow A. They should not be confused with the production markings, "G," "S," "E," or "O," arrow B.

Also beginning at circa serial #C130,000, an inspection mark was stamped on the *upper left side front* of the trigger guard, above the Colt "VP" proof mark. Marks observed to date include "1" and "W," see Figure 6-50. Near the same time, an assembler's mark was stamped on the *upper right* trigger guard bow.

At the start of Series 70 production in 1970, inspection markings in the form of numbers were again stamped near the disconnector hole and on the *front left side* of the trigger guard bow, see Figure 6-51.

Series 70, 80 and the current Model 1991 series inspection marks were stamped on the *upper left and right side* of the trigger guard bow as letters in sans serif type. Observed letters include "E" in the post-World War II period and "G" in the Series 70, see Figure 6-52.

Table 6-12 summarizes all Colt commercial markings stamped on the receiver with the exception of assembler's markings. These are listed in Table 6-13, below.

Table 6-12 Summary Colt Commercial Receiver Markings				
Serial Number	**Model Marking**	**Production Marking**	**Verified Proof**	**Inspection Markings**
Circa #s C1-C2,250, left side, prefix, s/n have ornamental serifs	Circa #s C1-C5,000, right, forward of slide stop pin hole	"S" commercial production "G" Government overrun, intermittent	"V" and "P" intertwined in inverted triangle, all commercial production	C1-ca. C189,600, 1-3 o'clock at disconnector hole

Model 1911, M1911A1

Fig. 6-49. (Left) Assemblers' and production letters or numbers (arrow A).

"S" is the commercial marking (arrow B).

Fig. 6-50. (Right) At circa serial #C130,000, an inspection mark (arrow) was stamped on the upper left front trigger guard bow. An assembler's mark was stamped on the right trigger guard bow.

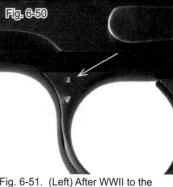

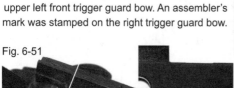

Fig. 6-51. (Left) After WWII to the Series 70, inspector's numbers were again stamped near the disconnector hole and on front left side of the trigger guard bow (arrows).

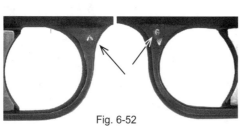

Fig. 6-52. (Left) From the start of the Series 70 (1970) to the present, factory inspector's marks are stamped on the right and left upper sides of the trigger guard.

Fig. 6-53. (Below) Numbers or letters were used by assemblers until mid-1918 (arrows).

Fig. 6-52

Military and Commercial Pistols

Table 6-12, cont. Summary Colt Commercial Receiver Markings				
Serial Number	**Model Marking**	**Production Marking**	**Verified Proof**	**Inspection Markings**
Circa #s C2,251-C130,000, right, C, small serifs, s/n sans serif		Commercial production, "S" marked intermittently		C1-C189,600, stamped top of receiver near disconnector hole
Circa #s C1-C130,000, C & serial numbers are vertical "C" with serif	Circa #s C5,001-EOP, right, behind slide stop pin hole	Commercial production under Argentine military/police contract, marked "O"		Inspection marking— upper left and assembler's marking, upper right trigger guard bow
Circa #s C130,001-C170,000, C vertical, sans serif, s/n slanted forward		British military or commercial .455 caliber sale, "W" s/n prefix, "E" top of receiver to 1920	"V" and "P" intertwined in inverted triangle, all commercial production	
Circa #s C170,001-C220,00, C with serif & s/n sans serif slanted forward	Some post-WWII, left side of slide			Post-World War II production, 5 o'clock at disconnector hole and on left front of trigger guard bow.
C220,001-336,169C &, Series 70/80 serial #s vertical, sans serif				Left and right front trigger guard bow

Model 1911, M1911A1

Colt Assembly Marks

Letters and numbers used to identify the workmen who assembled the Model 1911/1911A1, both commercial and military, were stamped on the slide and receiver.

From the start of production to circa serial #460,000, assemblers were assigned *letters or numbers*. The marks were usually stamped on the receiver near the disconnector hole and on the *bottom rear* of the trigger guard bow to about 1918, circa serial #510,000 (C100,000). Refer to Figure 6-53.

From circa serial #s 460,001 to 710,000, *numbers* were used exclusively and were usually stamped on the receiver near the disconnector hole and on the *bottom left* of the trigger guard.

From circa serial #710,001 to the end of production, an assembler's marking in the form of a number only was stamped on the upper right side of the trigger guard bow, see Figure 6-54.

Fig. 6-54. From 1919 to the end of production, assemblers were identified by number only.

Known Colt factory assembler's marks are shown in Table 6-13.

Some Colt factory assembler's marks that can be identified to specific individuals are shown in Table 6-13.

Table 6-13 Known Colt Factory Assembler's Marks		
1	J.F. Kinnarney Circa 1-40,000	Disconnector hole*
2	Axel Liljegren Circa 40,001-89,000	Disconnector hole*
4	Axel Liljegren Circa 101-40,201	Disconnector hole*
4	F.J. Kapmeyer Circa 60,401-580,600	Disconnector hole*

Military and Commercial Pistols

	Table 6-13, cont. Known Colt Factory Assembler's Marks	
5	J. Malloy Circa 101-89,000	Disconnector hole*
7	L.F. Robinson 1-60,400	Disconnector hole*
8	W. Kay Circa 60,401-580,600	Disconnector hole*
A	J. McIntyre Circa 1-40,000	Disconnector hole*
A	J. Malloy Circa 101,301-123,400	Disconnector hole*
b	J. Malloy Circa 89,000-101,300	Disconnector hole*
e	W.P. Valentine circa 91,201-141,200	Disconnector hole*
G	J. McIntyre 60,401-580,600	Disconnector hole*
O	Unknown circa 135,000	Disconnector hole*
Q	P.M. Quinlan Circa 101-30,300	Disconnector hole*
R	Gabriel Rice Circa 101-30,300	Disconnector hole*
R	Unknown 166,000	Disconnector hole*
S	Unknown Circa 17,000-18,000	Disconnector hole*
t	J.F. Kinnarney Circa 60,401-580,600	Disconnector hole*
T	J.B. Thurton Circa 101-50,100	Disconnector hole*
V	W.P. Valentine Circa 101-40,200	Disconnector hole*
y	? Ackert Circa 15,000-580,600	Disconnector hole and left, bottom rear of trigger guard*
Z	L.F. Robinson Circa 60,401-580,600	Disconnector hole*
* Stamped through finish		

Model 1911, M1911A1

BRITISH COMMERCIAL AND MILITARY MARKINGS ON COLT MODEL 1911 AND 1911A1 RECEIVERS

The subject of British markings on firearms is a complicated issue and is discussed at length in Appendix G.

One additional marking unique to British Model 1911 pistols is the marking "JJ" found on both commercial and early British government contract Model 1911s sent to Great Britain between 1914 and 1919. It may be the mark of an employee of the London Armoury Company, Colt's British sales agent, or a British inspector at the London or Birmingham proof houses as the marks predate the 1925 Proof Laws and are found on *both* commercial and military contract Model 1911s but not Model 1911A1s, see Figure 6-55.

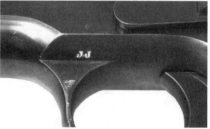

Fig. 6-55. The ornamental italic "*JJ*" mark found on Model 1911s sent to Great Britain may be the initials of a British proof house inspector.

National Rifle Association Marked Model 1911s

Between 1915–1917 and 1920–1922, the Ordnance Department allowed the sales of Model 1911 pistols to life members of the National Rifle Association or members of affiliated rifle clubs so that they could compete in the National Matches on an even level with service members. At least ninety-five Springfield Armory and forty-seven Colt Model 1911s were sold.

Fig. 6-56. "N.R.A."- marked U.S. Model 1911 released by the Springfield Armory in 1916. William Fairbairn collection.

Model 1911s sold by the Ordnance Department through the National Rifle Association were marked "N.R.A.," with periods, in sans serif type below the serial number or in front of the slide stop pin, see Figure 6-56.

CHAPTER 7
SLIDE MARKINGS

Slide markings on Colt Model 1911 and 1911A1 pistol, and those made by other contractors, is a complicated subject. Changes in marking generally fall into fixed serial number ranges, as defined below. Some changes were required by additions to patent markings or model changes. Others were made when dies wore out and were replaced. The collector should keep in mind that minor changes in appearance of lettering or logotypes were usually due to wear on dies. It should be noted that periods (".") were used to separate months, days, and years in the patent dates and "Hartford" from "CT" circa serial #s 1-132,500. After, commas (",") were used.

A review of the Colt logotype, the rampant colt, has been placed at the end of this chapter because of its complexity. The author has identified at least ten different styles of the Colt logotype to use as one more aid to identify the period in which a slide was manufactured. Readers are invited, and encouraged, to add to this list of Colt logotypes. Actual photos of slide markings will be found in Appendix I.

SLIDE MARKINGS BY SERIAL NUMBER—U.S. MILITARY
Colt, Left Side, Patent and Address
The markings stamped on the left side of the Model 1911 slide were agreed to by Colt and the Ordnance Department in May 1911. The markings were:

From circa serial #s 1 to 83,855 (C1-C6,500) on the left side of the slide:

PATENTED APR.20.1897	COLT'S PT.F.A.MFG.CO.
SEPT.9.1902. DEC.19.1905. FEB.14.1911	HARTFORD,CT. U.S.A.

See Figure 7-1, A. A few exceptions in the range will use commas.

From serial #1 through circa serial #84, the lettering in the patent block was 0.06 inch high while the letters in the Colt address were 0.08 inch high.

Model 1911, M1911A1

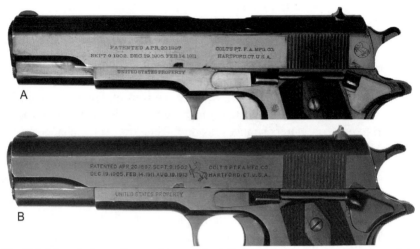

Fig. 7-1. View A shows the marking on the left side of U.S. Model 1911s to serial #83,855 and the circled Colt logo (to ca. serial #20,000). View B shows the sans serif marking used from circa serial #247,291 to the end of production with the logo between the patent and address blocks after ca. serial #20,001.

Between circa serial #s 85-247,290 the letters and numbers in *both* the patent and address block were reduced to 0.06 inch in height. A serif type face was used.

At serial #83,856, the 1913 patent date was added to the patent block on the left side.

Starting at circa serial #247,291 and continuing through the end of production, the patent and address blocks on the left side of the slide were roll-marked in a sans serif type face. The height of the letters and numbers remained 0.06 inch, see Figure 7-1, B.

From the start of production through circa serial #20,000, the rampant colt logotype in two variations was stamped in a circle at the rear of the slide, behind the grasping grooves.

From circa serial #s 20,001-275,000 to 285,000, the rampant colt logotype was stamped *without* the circle at the rear of the slide, behind the grasping grooves.

Military and Commercial Pistols

Starting at circa serial #s 275,001 to 285,000 through the end of military production, the rampant colt only was stamped on the left side of the slide between the patent and address blocks. It was moved from the left and stamped on the slide's right side after C130,000 to the start of the Series 70 with special order exceptions.

Fig. 7-2. The right-side slide marking on U.S. Government contract production slides A) circa serial #s 1-180,000; B) from circa serial #s180,001-629,500 and 700,001-712,349, both in slightly varying type styles and sizes.

NOTE: For a detailed description of the style and location of the Colt logotype, and its use, see "Rampant Colt Logotypes" and Table 7-1 at the end of this chapter.

Colt (Military), Right Side, Model Marking
The right side of the slide was marked:

MODEL OF 1911. U.S. ARMY

It was stamped in a type style with *serifs* that was 0.09 inch high from the start of production to circa serial #180,000, see Figure 7-2.

The same style is also seen in the serial number ranges 209,587-210,386 and 215,387-215,786 which were delivered to the U.S. Marine Corps.

Between circa serial #s 180,001-260,000, a *sans serif* type face was used. The letters and numbers were 0.09 inch high, refer to Figure 7-2.

MODEL OF 1911. U.S.ARMY

Between circa serial #s 260,001-629,500 and 700,001-712,349 (late 1918 through 1937) the same marking was stamped in *sans serif* type using letters 0.11 inch high.

317

Model 1911, M1911A1

Fig. 7-3. From circa serial #712,350 to the end of production, Model 1911A1 slides were blank on the right side (with the exception of two batches of Ithaca M1911A1s, see text). Photo courtesy of Bud Davey from his collection.

From serial #712,350 to the end of military contract production, the marking was not applied to the slide but was stamped on the right side of the receiver, forward of the slide stop, see Figure 7-3, arrow.

NOTE: Replacement slides manufactured from August 1938 to October 1943 were marked on the right side:

U.S. MODEL I9II AI. U.S. ARMY

These replacement slides were manufactured by Colt, Ithaca, Remington Rand and Union Switch & Signal as their contracts came into the force. All replacement slide production by all manufacturers ended in October 1943. The marking was believed necessary as pistols manufactured before serial #712,350 did not carry the model marking on the receiver. The type style was sans serif and the letters were wider than in previous slide markings. Lettering was 0.12 inch high.

Colt (Military) Slide, Proof Mark

Receivers, slides, and barrels of the Model 1911 were not proof marked prior to circa serial #24,500 as a suitable proof cartridge was not available. From circa serial #24,501 to the end of production, proof-firing was carried out and a "**P**" proof mark was applied to the top of proof-tested barrels, see Chapter 8.

Military and Commercial Pistols

Circa serial #711,000 to the end of production, a "**P**" proof mark was stamped on the top of all Colt Model 1911A1 slides and on the left side of the receiver, behind the trigger. The marking was in sans serif type 0.09 inch high and located 0.8 inch ahead of the rear sight, see Figure 7-4. The receiver marking may appear larger due to being struck deeper.

Fig. 7-4. A "P" proof mark was stamped on all U.S. military contract slides ahead of the rear sight, serial #711,000-EOP.

Colt (Military and Civilian), Slide Serial Numbers

The receiver serial number was stamped in the slide's hammer recess, under the firing pin stop from circa serial #s 710,001-1,208,673 (C128,001-C221,000), see Figure 7-5.

Colt-Provisional Inspector's Slide Markings

The provisional inspector's mark (**H** with serifs) was stamped horizontally below the firing pin hole on military slides from circa serial #199-399. From circa serial #400-6,500 to 7,500, the **H** with serifs was stamped sideways above the firing pin hole. From circa serial #6,500-7,500 to 710,000, the **H** without serifs was stamped vertically above the firing pin hole. Between circa serial #s 133,187-135,00, the provisional inspection mark was **S** stamped vertically above the firing pin hole.

Fig. 7-5. The receiver serial number was stamped in the hammer recess, circa serial #s 710,001-1,208,673.

Colt—Miscellaneous Slide Markings

At circa serial #710,001 (C135,000) to the end of military and commercial production, the left, rear of the slide (held upside down) was marked "N" to indicate the change from Class "C" steel to SAE 1035 steel, see Figure 7-6.

All Model 1911 slides only will show two or more inspection letters, numbers, or symbols stamped on the bottom.

Model 1911, M1911A1

Fig. 7-6. The letter "N" (arrow) was stamped on the bottom of the slide to indicate that the slide was made from SAE 1035 steel rather than the old Class "C" steel.

Navy Model 1911 Slide Markings

All U.S. Navy marked slides manufactured by Colt carried the standard address and rampant colt markings on the left side.

Model 1911s delivered to the United States Navy in the serial ranges 501-1,000, 1,501-2,000, 2,501-3,500, 4,501-5,500, 6,501-7,500, 8,501-9,500, 10,501-11,500, 12,501-13,500, 38,001-44,000, 96,001-97,537, and 109,501-110,000 were marked:

MODEL OF 1911. U.S. NAVY

in a type face with serifs and letters 0.09 inch high on the right side in one line, see Figure 7-7.

Marine Corps Model 1911 Slide Markings

All Model 1911 slides manufactured by Colt and intended for the U.S. Marine Corps carried the standard address and rampant colt markings on the left side.

Fig. 7-7. U.S. Navy Model 1911s slide marking to serial #110,000. Karl Karash collection.

Model 1911s delivered to the U.S. Marine Corps were all marked on the right side in one line in the type style of the manufacturing period:

MODEL OF 1911. U.S. ARMY

SLIDE MARKINGS, COLT COMMERCIAL

Commercial slide markings differed from military slide markings at different periods. See Appendix I for photographs of slide markings.

320

Military and Commercial Pistols

Colt (Commercial), Right Side

From serial #s C1-circa C130,000 (1922) the legend on the right side was in serif type. The spelling "calibre" was used until 1949:

COLT AUTOMATIC
CALIBRE .45

From serial #s C130,001-C221,000, the legend read in sans serif type:

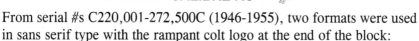

From serial #s C220,001-272,500C (1946-1955), two formats were used in sans serif type with the rampant colt logo at the end of the block:

COLT AUTOMATIC
CALIBRE .45

or

GOVERNMENT COLT AUTOMATIC
MODEL CALIBRE .45

From serial #s 272,501C to 336,169C (1956 to mid-1970s), the marking was in one line in sans serif type:

COLT'S PT. MFG. CO. HARTFORD, CONN. U.S.A.

From mid-1970s and all Series 80 .45-caliber non-National Match pistols were marked on the right side of the slide in sans serif type:

COLT'S GOVERNMENT MODEL

Other current model markings can be examined at the Colt's Manufacturing Company LLC Web site at www.coltsmfg.com.

Colt (Commercial), Left Side

From circa serial #s C1-C6,500 (1911-1913), the patent information and address blocks were in a type style with serifs and the same as the military:

PATENTED APR.20.1897   **COLT'S PT.F.A.MFG.CO.**
SEPT.9.1902. DEC.19.1905. FEB.14.1911   **HARTFORD,CT. U.S.A.**

At circa serial #s C6,501 the "August 19, 1913" patent date was added and the two block style continued to C130,000 (1922). The rampant colt logo without the circle remained at the rear of the slide serrations. The type face had serifs:

321

Model 1911, M1911A1

PATENTED APR.20.1897.SEPT.9.1902.   COLT'S PT.F.A.MFG.CO.
DEC.19.1905. FEB.14.1911.AUG.19.1913   HARTFORD,CT. U.S.A.

From circa serial #s C130,001 to C215,018 (1922 to 1942) the patent and address markings were integrated into one block, in sans serif type, in two lines with commas replacing periods after 1916:

COLT'S PT. F. A. MFG. CO. HARTFORD, CT. U.S.A.
PAT'D APR. 20,1897. SEPT.9,1902. DEC.19,1905. FEB.14,1911.AUG.19,1913.

Between C220,001-circa C221,500 surplus military slides were used. At circa #s C220,001 in 1946 when commercial production resumed, the patent information was dropped. The new style was in use through circa serial #C231,999 (1947). The type style was sans serif:

COLT GOVERNMENT MODEL AUTOMATIC PISTOL CAL. 45

Between circa serial #s C232,000-270,999C (1948-1955), the style was changed as follows. The type style was sans serif:

COLTS MFG. CO. HARTFORD CT U.S.A.

From circa serial #s 270,500C to 336,169C, the format was again changed. The rampant colt logo appeared at the right of the block. The type style was sans serif ("*COLT*" may also appear in italic letters):

GOVERNMENT ★ MODEL ★ COLT AUTOMATIC CALIBER .45

NOTE: Address and Model markings were sometimes transposed on early post-World War II production.

The Series 70 and some Series 80 slides were marked in two lines, the top line in an outline type style with serifs and the bottom line in a sans serif type face:

COLT'S MK IV/SERIES '70
.45 AUTOMATIC CALIBER

Military and Commercial Pistols

The 1991 Series pistols are marked on the *left* side in three lines. The top line is in italic with serifs; the bottom two lines are in sans serif type:

─────── *COLT* ───────
GOVERNMENT MODEL
.45 AUTOMATIC CALIBER

The left side of the Series 80 slides are marked:
COLT MK IV
⎯ Series 80 ⎯

NOTE: Other current model markings are shown on the Colt's Manufacturing Company Web site, www.coltsmfg.com.

Colt National Match Slide Markings

The original pre-World War II Colt National Match pistols are marked on the left side exactly like the commercial .45 pistols of the period with the address and patent information in two lines:

COLT'S PT. F. A. MFG. CO. HARTFORD, CT. U.S.A.
PAT'D APR.20,1897. SEPT.9,1902. DEC.19,1905. FEB.14,1911.AUG.19,1913.

On the right side, the model designation is roll marked in a sans serif type face. The rampant colt logo appears at the end of the block. "Automatic Calibre .45" is in two lines:

NATIONAL MATCH COLT AUTOMATIC CALIBRE.45

Series 70/80 National Match slides are marked on the right side in sans serif type, with the outline of a trophy cup at the end of the block:

GOLD CUP ▽
NATIONAL MATCH

The left side of the slide is marked and "caliber" is re-spelled and the first line is an outline style of type.

COLT'S MK IV/SERIES '70
GOLD CUP NATIONAL MATCH
.45 AUTOMATIC CALIBER

Model 1911, M1911A1

Colt Super .38 Model Automatic Pistol

The pre-World War II Colt Super .38 was marked on the *right* side in sans serif type. Super .38s manufactured before World War II continued to be sold through 1946 (serial #s 1-37,834). The rampant colt logo was marked at the end of the block:

COLT SUPER .38
AUTOMATIC

And the left side was marked, also in sans serif type:

COLT'S PT. F.A. MFG. CO. HARTFORD, CONN. U.S.A.
PAT'D APR.20,1897. SEPT.9,1902. DEC.19,1905. FEB.14,1911. AUG.19,1913.

From circa serial #40,001-#124,500 (1947 through 1957 with the restart in the serial numbering sequence), the *right* side of the slide was marked in sans serif letters:

COLT'S MFG. CO. HARTFORD CT. U.S.A.

And the left side of the slide was marked as in the pre-World War II period above in sans serif letters followed by the rampant colt logotype.

Colt Super Match .38 Automatic Pistol

The Colt Super Match .38 Pistol was produced and sold between 1935 and 1941-42. It was marked on the left side of the slide in sans serif type followed by the rampant colt logotype:

SUPER MATCH **COLT** AUTOMATIC
CALIBER .38

Colt ACE Slide Markings

The pre-World War II ACE was marked on the right side in sans serif type. The word "ACE" was contained within a diamond:

COLT ◁ACE▷ **.22** LONG
RIFLE

The left side was marked in sans serif type. The rampant colt logo was stamped at the end of the block:

Military and Commercial Pistols

COLT'S PT. F.A. MFG. CO. HARTFORD, CONN. U.S.A.
PAT'D APR.20,1897. SEPT.9,1902. DEC.19,1905. FEB.14,1911. AUG.19,1913.

Colt Service Model ACE Markings

The prewar Service Model ACE with the floating chamber was marked in sans serif type on the *right* side as shown immediately below.

The *left*-side patent information included the Colt address, Williams' patents, and Colt logotype:

PATENT NUMBERS □ 2,090,656 □ 2,090,657

The post-World War II Service Model ACE was remarked "ACE" on the *right* side in sans serif letters in a diamond with the single word, but was still designated as the Service Model ACE on the left:

The *left* side carried the same marking as the pre-World War II Service Model ACE. Both the pre-World War II and the post-World War II Service Model ACE models were marked on the right side of the receiver with the Colt address.

Colt .22-.45 Conversion Unit

The Service Model ACE conversion unit was marked on the *left* side from the start of production to the end in 1940 in a sans serif type face. Post-World War II conversion units sold between 1946 and as late as 1949 were actually produced before and during World War II. The rampant colt logotype was marked at the end of the block. Marking arrangements varied:

.22-.45 CONVERSION UNIT

After 1946 the Service ACE Conversion Unit was not serial numbered. The marking, in sans serif type, was changed from the pre-World War II marking. The name "Service Model ACE" was not used:

325

COLT <small>CONVERSION
UNIT</small> .22 <small>LONG
RIFLE</small>

From 1955 through the Series 70 and 80, the *left* side was marked as follows with the rampant colt logotype marked at the end of the block:

<small>CONVERSION
UNIT</small> **COLT** <small>AUTOMATIC
CAL. 22 LR</small>

Colt .45-.22 Conversion Kit

The .45-.22 Conversion kit was used to change the .22 Service ACE to .45 ACP. They were manufactured and sold before World War II only. They were marked in three lines on the *left* side in sans serif type:

COLT <small>AUTOMATIC
C A L . 4 5</small>
<small>.45-.22 CONVERSION UNIT</small>

Commander Slide Markings

Both the Colt Lightweight Commander (circa serial #s 001LW-39,199LW) and all Combat Commander models were stamped on the *right* side of the slide in sans serif type from the start of production:

COLT'S MFG. CO. HARTFORD, CT. U.S.A.

From circa serial #39,200LW to start of Series 70 production:

COLT'S PT. F.A. MFG. CO. HARTFORD CT. (or CONN.) U.S.A.

The *left* side of the Combat Commander was marked "**GOVERNMENT MODEL**" in sans serif letters for a short period and then as follows:

<small>COMMANDER
MODEL</small> **COLT** <small>AUTOMATIC
CALIBER .45</small>

Those Commander models in 9 mm or Super .38 had the "**9 mm LUGER**" or "**SUPER .38**" substituted after the word "**CALIBER.**"

NOTE: Commander models manufactured after 1970 will show one of the following marking on the *right* side of the slide:

COLT'S COMBAT COMMANDER ★ MODEL ★

and this on the *left*:

<small>COMBAT
COMMANDER</small> **COLT** <small>AUTOMATIC
CALIBER .45</small>

Military and Commercial Pistols

SPRINGFIELD ARMORY SLIDE MARKINGS

Springfield Armory stamped both the Eagle and the Model marking on the *right* side of the slide:

 MODEL OF 1911. U.S. ARMY.

The letters and numbers were in *sans serif* type 0.10 inch high. The eagle measured 0.390 inch wide from wingtip to wingtip and 0.310 inch high from right wingtip to base, see Figure 7-8.

Fig. 7-8. Springfield Armory right-side slide markings.

The patent dates and address were stamped on the *left* side of the slide as shown in Figure 7-9. The patent dates were stamped in sans serif type 0.09 inch high. The middle line of the patent date on the author's sample was 2.06 inches long. There are some peculiarities in the spacing of the

Fig. 7-9. Springfield Armory left-side slide markings.

patent dates which are shown in the photograph above: i.e., no space between the "." and "20" in the first line; the space between the "T." and "9" at the start of the second line, and the space after the "9" and between the "1" in "1905" in the middle of the second line, and so on.

REMINGTON ARMS-UMC COMPANY SLIDE MARKINGS

The Remington Arms-UMC slide markings follow the Ordnance Department guidelines. The Colt patent dates are on the *left* side of the slide, separated by the Remington Arms-UMC logo and the company address:

Model 1911, M1911A1

PATENTED DEC. 19. 1905   MANUFACTURED BY
FEB.14.1911.AUG.19.1913.   REMINGTON ARMS UMC CO. INC.
COLT'S PT.F.A. MFG.CO.   BRIDGEPORT. CONN. U.S.A.

The letters were in sans serif type 0.12 inch high. Note the spacing between letters and numbers, see Figure 7-10.

Fig. 7-10. Remington Arms-UMC left-side slide markings. Mike Strietbeck collection.

The model and caliber designation was marked on the *right* side of the slide in sans serif letters 0.1 inch high, see Figure 7-11. The model marking was in line with the front edge of the ejection port; the caliber designation was centered below the model. Again, note the spacing between words:

MODEL OF 1911
U.S.ARMY CALIBER .45

Fig. 7-11. Remington Arms-UMC right-side slide marking. Mike Strietbeck collection.

At circa serial #20,000 to the end of production at serial #21,676, some slides were marked on the *right* side:

MODEL OF 1911. U.S. ARMY

The slide was marked "E" in the hammer recess, above the firing pin stop plate from serial #s 1 to circa 15,000, see Figure 7-12, arrow. With the provisional inspection mark, "E" for Walter H. Evans. The provisional inspection marks are also found on the upper left side of the trigger guard

328

Military and Commercial Pistols

and the bottom of the mainspring housing in the same serial number range.

From circa serial #15,001 to the end of production, the **E** provisional inspection marking above the firing pin stop, trigger guard were phased out or replaced with the Type 2 eagle mark. But the **E** remained on the mainspring housing (as noted on serial #s 18,449 and 21,512).

Fig. 7-12. Provisional inspector marking in the hammer recess of the Remington Arms-UMC slide. Mike Strietbeck collection.

With the expectation that a final Allied massive offensive would take place on the Western front in the spring of 1919, the Ordnance Department sought for ways to increase the number of pistols that would be needed by the mass troop deployments to France planned for the autumn and winter months. Contracts were let in the summer of 1918 to three additional companies judged capable of manufacturing the Model 1911 pistol.

NORTH AMERICAN ARMS CO., LTD., SLIDE MARKINGS

North American Arms Company, Ltd., using facilities and equipment leased from the Ross Rifle Plant, was awarded a contract to manufacture the Model 1911 on July 1, 1918. As the war ended only four months later, production had not yet begun and there are no records of North American Arms pistols being received by the U.S. Ordnance Department. Apparently, an unknown number of pistols were finished and sold commercially, as several legitimate North American Arms Model 1911 pistols are known to exist. They were marked on the left side of the slide only (see Figure 7-13) with the address of the company in sans serif letters 0.10 inch high, centered above the slide lever release notch:

**MANUFACTURED BY
NORTH AMERICAN ARMS CO.LIMITED
QUEBEC,CANADA.**

Note the spacing between words. North American Arms Co., Ltd., Model 1911s do not have U.S. property or inspector's acceptance markings.

Model 1911, M1911A1

National Cash Register Company, Slide Markings

A contract was let in July 1918 to the National Cash Register Company of Dayton, Ohio, for the manufacture of 100,000 pistols, subsequently increased to 500,000. The war ended before any were produced.

A.J. Savage Munitions Company, Slide Markings

The A.J. Savage Company of San Diego, California, was awarded a contract in July 1918 to manufacture 100,000 Model 1911 pistols. The contract was suspended in December of that year and Savage delivered only parts, primarily springs, and apparently an unknown number of slides, some of which were used as replacements. When used as replacement slides, they were refinished, along with the receiver and other parts, to a black or Parkerized finish. The Ordnance Department sold surplus Savage slides in the late 1920s or early 1930s. These slides were blued. Blued slides are not considered "military contract" slides by collectors.

The Savage slides were marked on the left side with the Colt patent dates and the company logotype, a flaming bomb with an "S," marked within, above the slide release notch in sans serif letters 0.12 inch high. Collectors should note that this is not the U.S. Army Ordnance Department's final inspection mark, see Figure 7-14:

PATENTED DEC.19.1905
FEB.14.1911.AUG.19.1913.
COLT'S PT. F.A.MFG.CO.

Note the spacing between letters and numbers. The company name marking was not authorized before the contract was canceled.

The right side of the A.J. Savage-manufactured slides may have been marked **Model of 1911.U.S.Army** when used as replacement slides on the Model 1911 pistol. The marking was in a sans serif type face 0.10 inch high.

NOTE: Ordnance Department records showing the acceptance of A.J. Savage slides have not been found as of this date. View all purported "military" pistols equipped with an A.J. Savage slide with a skeptical eye and consider them to be reworks at best.

Military and Commercial Pistols

Fig. 7-13. North American Arms Model 1911 slide markings. Courtesy of Little John's Antique Arms, Inc.

Fig. 7-14. A.J. Savage left-side slide markings. Karl Karash collection.

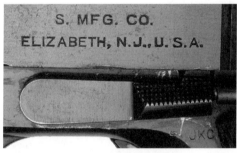

Fig. 7-15. Singer Manufacturing Company left-side slide markings. Karl Karash collection.

Fig. 7-16. Ithaca Gun Company left-side slide markings.

Fig. 7-17. Ithaca right-side slide markings, seen largely between serial #s 906,000-916,400.

Model 1911, M1911A1

SINGER MANUFACTURING COMPANY, SLIDE MARKINGS

The Singer Manufacturing Company manufactured five hundred model 1911A1 pistols in 1941 under an Educational Contract designed to prepare companies for wartime production.

Singer slides were marked on the left side (Figure 7-15) in sans serif type 0.10 inch high:

S. MFG. CO.

ELIZABETH, N.J., U.S.A.

The marking was centered above the slide release lever. Note the spacing between the "N.J.," and "U." in "U.S.A." The right side of the slide was unmarked. The last comma is above the line.

The "**P**" proof mark was stamped on the top of the slide forward of the rear sight. The "**P**" is reversed and the base points to the muzzle.

ITHACA GUN COMPANY, SLIDE MARKINGS

Ithaca slides were always marked on the left side with the company name and address and on the right side, only intermittently with the model marking.

The left side (Figure 7-16) was marked in sans serif letters 0.10 inch high forward of the grasping groove and centered above the slide stop:

ITHACA GUN CO., INC.

ITHACA, N.Y.

The right side of the slide carried the model marking on some between circa serial #s 906,000-916,400, see Figure 7-17. Some slides are found marked with the model marking into the second contract to circa serial #1,208,674-1,208,700:

M I9II AI U.S. ARMY

After circa serial # 1,208,674-1,208,701, Ithaca slides were not marked on the right side. See also Chapter 6, Markings–Receivers.

The "**P**" proof mark was stamped on top of the slide, ahead of the rear sight and parallel to the bore. The marking was in an extended sans serif type, 0.12 inch high.

Military and Commercial Pistols

The slide was also marked with the Ordnance Department's flaming bomb symbol rotated onto its left side from the start of production starting at circa serial #856,405 to circa serial #1,279,673 near the end of the second contract, see Figure 7-18. The marking was stamped in the slide's hammer recess above the firing pin hole behind the firing pin stop. The flaming bomb was also stamped in the barrel recoil lug channel as well. It is sometimes seen on later serial numbers, but rarely.

Fig. 7-18. Ithaca slides between serial #s 856,405-1,279,673 were marked with the Ordnance flaming bomb symbol (arrow). Occasionally seen after.

REMINGTON RAND, INC., SLIDE MARKINGS

Three variations have been observed in Remington Rand slide markings and are probably due to the remanufacture of the dies used to stamp the marking, since all carry the same information but in a slightly different size and format, see Figures 7-19 A, B, and C.

The address marking only was stamped on the left side of the side. The right side was always blank.

The **Type 1** slide marking used letters 0.10 inch high in an "extended" sans serif type face. The marking was in two lines and both were justified to the same length, 1.35 inches, refer to Figure 7-19A. It was in use from the start of the Remington Rand contract at serial #s 916,405 to circa 930,000 in 1943:

REMINGTON RAND INC.
SYRACUSE, NEW YORK

The **Type 2** slide marking was similar to the Type 1 except New York was changed to N.Y. and "U.S.A." was added. The type was the same extended sans serif face and the length was 1.35 inches, see Figure 7-

333

Model 1911, M1911A1

Fig. 7-19A. Remington Rand left-side marking, Type 1.

Fig. 7-19B. Remington Rand left-side marking, Type 2.

19B. It was in use starting at circa serial #s 930,001 through 1,020,000 with overlap at both ends.

REMINGTON RAND INC.
SYRACUSE, N.Y. U.S.A.

Fig. 7-19C. Remington Rand left-side marking, Type 3.

The **Type 3** slide marking used a condensed sans serif type face to provide a line length of 1.20 inches, see Figure 7-19C. It overlapped with use of the Type 2 marking from circa serial #1,000,000 to the end of production. After circa 1,020,000, the Type 3 slide marking was used exclusively:

REMINGTON RAND INC.
SYRACUSE, N.Y. U.S.A.

The "**P**" proof mark was stamped on top of the slide, ahead of the rear sight. It was usually parallel to the bore or tilted slightly to the right. The marking was in an extended sans serif type, 0.09 inch high, see Figure 7-20.

Fig. 7-20. The "P" proof mark was stamped on all Remington Rand slides forward of the rear sight throughout production.

An inspector's initial, usually "**G**," will be found in the slide's hammer recess, beneath the firing pin tunnel,

Military and Commercial Pistols

and covered by the firing pin retainer plate, see Figure 7-21.

UNION SWITCH & SIGNAL, SLIDE MARKINGS

Like the Remington Arms-UMC M1911, the Union Switch & Signal M1911A1 slides also carried the manufacturer's logotype. The left side of the slide (Figure 7-22) was marked in sans serif letters 0.10 inch high:

Fig. 7-21. An inspector's initial will be found in the hammer recess of Remington Rand slides.

 U.S. & S. CO.
SWISSVALE, PA. U.S.A.

US&S slides (and receivers) did not show the "**P**" proof mark until circa serial #1,060,000. An authentic and correct US&S pistol will *either* show no "**P**" proof marks on slide and receiver, or it will show the "**P**" proof mark on both parts.

RAMPANT COLT LOGOTYPE

The rearing colt clutching two thrown spears or lances was the Colt company's logotype. It was stamped

Fig. 7-22. Union Switch and Signal logotype. Karl Karash collection.

on the slide of all commercial and military Model 1911s and 1911A1s in all calibers and models, see Figure 7-23. Needless to say, it was only marked on Colt products and not subcontracted M1911s and M1911As manufactured by other companies.

Some care is required when determining which logo appears on a particular slide. As dies wore out, lines within the logo became broken or disappeared altogether, changing the logo's appearance. Examine any

Model 1911, M1911A1

Fig. 7-23. Rampant Colt logotype.

questionable logo with a good magnifying glass and compare to the descriptions and photos shown below.

Rampant Colt Logotype Placement

From the start of military production for the U.S. Ordnance Department to circa serial #285,000 the logotype was stamped on the left rear of the slide, behind the serrations, see Figure 7-24A.

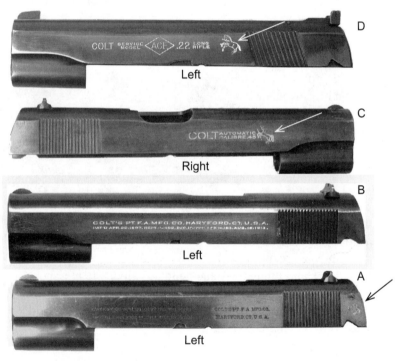

Fig. 7-24. Some Rampant Colt logotype variations: A) circa #s 1-285,000 and C1-C130,000; B) #C130,001-C216,000 and C220,001-240,288C; C) logotype on right side circa 130,001-216,000 and C220,501-2410,288C; D) From 240,289C to the end of production, including all Series 70/80 models.

Military and Commercial Pistols

From #285,000 to the end of military production, the logotype was stamped in the center of the left side of the slide between the patent and address blocks, refer to Figure 7-23.

From the start of commercial production to circa serial #C130,000, the rampant colt was stamped behind the slide serrations on the left side of the slide, refer to Figure 7-24A.

From circa serial #'s C130,001-C216,000 and C221,501-240,288C, the rampant colt was stamped on the right side of the slide, after the model marking, refer to Figure 7-24C. Between circa serial #'s C220,001-C221,500, surplus military slides were used with the rampant colt on both sides.

From circa serial #240,289C to the end of commercial production, the rampant colt logo was stamped on the left side of the slide after the model marking including the Series 70, 80 and 90 Models and variations—Super .38, Super Match .38, Service ACE, National Match, and both Lightweight Commander and Commander models, refer to Figure 7-24D.

The current exception to the rule is the Colt Gunsite and XSE series where the Colt logo is again at the rear of the slide behind the grasping serrations.

Rampant Colt Logotype Styles
Ten types of the rampant Colt logo have been observed. A total of 108 commercial and military models of the Model 1911 and Model 1911A1 were examined to produce the following *suggested* descriptions and chronology. The author asks the reader to please recognize that this is not a definitive list as the number of pistols examined is by no means a statistically valid sample. It serves only as a starting point for determining whether or not a slide matches a receiver.

NOTE: The Colt logotype was stamped on the left side of all Model 1911 and Model 1911A1 military slides. Until circa serial #C130,000, the Colt logotype was stamped on the left side of commercial slides. After circa serial #C130,001, the Colt logotype was stamped on the right side of the slide. After World War II to the start of the Series 70, the logotype continued to be stamped on the right side of all commercial slides. Start-

Model 1911, M1911A1

ing with the Series 70, the logotype was returned to the left side of the slide. The exception is the Colt Lightweight Commander, which had the logotype on the left side throughout its production.

The **Type 1** logo shows the rampant colt standing on an arc and enclosed within a circle at the rear of the slide. Eight lines were used to define the rippling mane and the tail ending above the rear hooves.

Two variations were used during this period. The **1st Variation** logo shows the colt in proper proportion and was used during the earliest production in 1912 circa serial #s 1-4,500 (military) and C1-C600 (commercial), see Figure 7-25, A.

The **2nd Variation** logo is similar in that the colt stands on an arc and is enclosed by a circle, but the figure of the colt is slightly elongated and has what can only be described as a dopey expression on its face. It was used from circa serial #s 4,501-20,000 in the military range and not at all in the commercial range, see Figure 7-25, B.

The **Type 2** logo was used from circa serial #s 20,001-128,500 (military) and C601-C23,000 (commercial) in the period 1913 to 1915 and shows the rampant colt only without the arc and surrounding circle at the rear of the slide. Four lines were used to define the rippling mane. The tail ended above the rear hooves and the front hooves were too large in proportion to the rest of the animal, see Figure 7-26.

The **Type 3** logo was used in the period 1915-1918, from circa serial #s 128,501 to 275,000-280,000 (military) and C23,001-C90,000 (commercial). Two variations appear to have been used interchangeably throughout the period. Both variations were stamped on the left side of the slide.

In the **1st Variation**, the colt's neck is arched and the mane is defined by what appear to be eleven dimples. The tail ends below the rear hooves, see Figure 7-27, A.

The **2nd Variation** logo shows a more crudely rendered Colt without the arched neck. The tail also ends below the rear hooves, refer to Figure 7-27, B.

338

Military and Commercial Pistols

Fig. 7-25. Colt logotype, Type 1, 1st and 2nd Variations

Fig. 7-26. Colt logotype, Type 2

Fig. 7-27. Colt logotype, Type 3, 1st and 2nd Variations

Fig. 7-28. Colt logotype, Type 4

Figs. 7-29, 30 and 31, Colt logotypes: Types 5, 6, and 7

Figs. 7-32, 33, and 34, Colt logotypes: Types 8, 9, and 10

Model 1911, M1911A1

The **Type 4** was in use from circa serial #s 275,001 to 300,000 (military, 1918) between the patent and address blocks and C90,001-C130,000 (commercial, 1919-1924) at the end of the slide. The use of the Type 4 logo appears to overlap with the Type 5. The figure of the colt is well rendered with the head perhaps a bit too small for the body. The neck is vertical with the head curved forward. Six lines define the rippling mane. The tail again ends above the rear hooves, see Figure 7-28.

The **Type 5** logo was used for a very short time in 1940 and overlapped with the Type 4. It appears to have been in use from circa serial #s 300,001-720,000. The colt's neck is curved and the head thrust forward. The mane is defined by five lines. The colt's back is straight whereas all others are curved, see Figure 7-29. It was roll-marked between the patent and address blocks.

The **Type 6** logo was used in 1942 on military pistols only, from circa serial #s 720,001-850,000. Six lines that some have described as looking like elm leaves define the flowing mane. The neck is curved and the head forward. Front and rear legs below the knees are defined by a single line. The most distinctive aspect of this logo is the last third of the tail which is formed by a separate "diamond," see Figure 7-30. It was roll-marked between the patent and address blocks.

The **Type 7** logo was used on commercial pistols in the C130,001-C221,000 serial number range but only in 1943 from circa serial #s 850,001-1,125,000 on U.S. military pistols. It overlaps in usage with the Type 8. The Type 7 is very similar to the Type 6 but the tail is more defined. The neck is more curved with the head thrust forward. The throat is also more concave than the Type 6, see Figure 7-31. It was roll-marked on the left side between the patent and address blocks.

The **Type 8** logo appears to be somewhat of an anomaly. It was nicely rendered with a full, arched neck and what can easily be described as a "flame" tail. Most significantly, the spear passing through the legs is actually above the left knee. This is the first Colt logotype with the spear above either knee. It appears on 1943 production Colt slides in the circa

Military and Commercial Pistols

serial number range 865,000-934,000, roll-marked on the left side between the patent and address blocks.

It is also seen on pre-World War II slides in the circa serial number range C162,001-C207,000 as well as post-World War II commercial slides, overlapping somewhat with the Type 4 logo, see Figure 7-32.

The **Type 9** logo was used from 1943 to the end of U.S. *military* production in 1945, in the range circa serial #1,125,001-EOP. The Type 9 logo is quite amateurish in rendition and as the die wore, became little more than a stick figure. It is also seen on commercial Model 1911A1s manufactured in the first few years after the war as surplus military slides were refinished and used up in *commercial* production, see Figure 7-33. It was roll-marked on the left side between the patent and address blocks.

The **Type 10** logo is seen on post-World War II commercial production through Series 70 production marked on the right side of the slide. The line along the colt's neck that defined the bottom of the mane was eliminated and five curved lines were used to delineate the ripples. Again, the spear passing through the legs is above the left knee. The animal is thicker bodied; no longer a colt but an older horse, see Figure 7-34.

NOTE: The same logotype "type" or design was used on all Colt 1911 and 1911A1 production no matter the caliber or model in the same time period. To determine if a logotype on a slide in correct on a Super .38, .22 ACE, Lightweight Commander, etc. check the serial number against the serial number charts in Chapter 5 and compare to the photographs and the time line in the text above and in Table 7-1.

Type	Variation	Serial Number Range		Year(s)	Figure
		Military	Commercial		
1	1	1-4,500	C1-C600	1912	7-25A
	2	4,501-20,000	N/A	1912	7-25B

Table 7-1
Colt Logotype by Type and Serial Number Range

Model 1911, M1911A1

Table 7-1, cont. Colt Logotype by Type and Serial Number Range					
Type	Variation	Serial Number Range		Year(s)	Figure
		Military	Commercial		
2		20,001-128,500	C601-C23,000	1913-1915	7-26
3	1 & 2	128,501 to 275,000-280,000	C23,001-C90,000	1915-1918	7-27A 7-27B
4		275,001 to 300,000	C90,001-C130,000	1918 (M) 1919-1924 (C)	7-28
5		300,001-720,000	?	1939-1940	7-29
6		720,001-850,000	N/A	1942	7-30
7		850,001-1,125,000	C130,001-C221,000	1924-1942 (C) 1943 (M)	7-31
8		865,000-934,000	C162,001-C207,000 (1)	1943 (M) 1939-40 & 1946-1948 (C)	7-32
9		1,125,001-EOP	N/A (2)	1943-1945 (M)	7-33
10		N/A	Post-World War II		7-34

1. May appear on 1943 production military slides and on pre- and post-WWII slides as late as 1948.
2. May appear on some immediate post-WWII slides as surplus military parts were used up.
(M) = military production.
(C) = commercial production.

CHAPTER 8
BARREL MARKINGS

MODEL 1911/1911A1 BARRELS

Barrels for the Model 1911 and Model 1911A1 pistol manufactured under U.S. Army Ordnance Department contract as well as commercial barrels were marked by each manufacturer, and by certain subcontractors, starting at circa serial #430. Marks included an inspector's mark, a proof mark, and on some barrels, the manufacturer's code or mark.

Colt Barrel Marks

Colt barrel markings are a complicated subject and the issue has been addressed by numerous authors and researchers in the past. Offered below is a simplified description. Basically, a Colt .45 ACP barrel manufactured for the Ordnance Department was proofed and marked with the letter "P," a provisional inspector's initial from circa serial #430 and the legend **COLT 45 AUTO**. Commercial barrels were marked similarly during any period but without the Ordnance Department inspector's initials or number and the "P" proof mark.

Table 8-1 provides a compilation of all known Colt barrel markings as observed by other authors and researchers—and by this author—by serial number range.

NOTE: Colt barrels were not marked with the proof mark "P" from the start of production to circa serial #24,500.

Table 8-1 Barrel Marks, Colt Firearms		
Marking	**Serial Number Range, Circa**	**Location**
H (serifs)	430-6,500 (1)	Francis L. (Frank) Hosmer's provisional inspection on the barrel hood, turned horizontal to line of bore. U.S. military contract only. Figure 8-1A.

Model 1911, M1911A1

Table 8-1, cont.

Barrel Marks, Colt Firearms

Marking	Serial Number Range, Circa	Location
H (sans serif)	6,501-24,500 (1)	Barrel hood, vertical. U.S. military contract only. Figure 8-1B.
H, P or P, H (sans serif)	25,001-110,000 (1), (2)	Top of barrel, horizontal to line of bore. U.S. military contract only. Figure 8-1C.
H, P (sans serif)	110,001-133,187 137,401-425,000 (1), (2)	Top of the barrel, in line with the bore. U.S. military contract only. Figure 8-1D.
S (sans serif, early) H (sans serif, late) P (sans serif)	133,187-137,400 (1)	W.E. Strong, provisional inspection mark, top of barrel in line with bore. U.S. military contract only. Figure 8-1E. P sometimes marked on right rear recoil lug.
& H P (sans serif, early) HP intertwined (sans serif, late)	Within the range circa 210,387-580,600 (1)	Front of barrel lug, bottom side on barrels manufactured for Colt by A. H. Fox from mid-1917-1918. Figure 8-1F.
HP intertwined (sans serif)	425,001-710,000 (1)	Top of barrel, across the bore. U.S. military contract only. Figure 8-1G.
K (sans serif) HP intertwined (sans serif)	700,001-710,000 (1)	U.S. military contract only. K on bottom of barrel, HP top of chamber.
COLT 45 AUTO, P (sans serif)	710,001- 2,368,781	Left side of barrel, above lug. "P" stamped on left side of lug. U.S. military contract and commercial barrels. Various inspector initials. Some 1945 production show the boxed "C." Figure 8-1H.
COLT 45 AUTO, P (without box) C in box (sans serif)	2,075,000- 2,368,781	"COLT 45 AUTO" on left side of barrel, above lug. "P" on left side of lug. "C" in a box with rounded corners on right side of lug. U.S. military contract and commercial barrels. Figure 8-1I.
COLT 45 AUTO MATCH	C178,000- C221,000	Left side above barrel lug. National Match pistols only

Military and Commercial Pistols

	Table 8-1, cont.	
	Barrel Marks, Colt Firearms	
Marking	**Serial Number Range, Circa**	**Location**
COLT 45 AUTO, P, C in box (sans serif) P, C in box (sans serif) Also, no P or C in box	Post-World War II to MK IV/Series 70 production, any .45-caliber model	"COLT 45 AUTO" top of barrel, visible in ejection port. May or may not have "P" on left side of lug and "C" in a box with rounded corners on right side of lug. U.S. military replacement contract and commercial barrels. Figure 8-1J.
COLT 9 MM AUTO	1950 to 1969	"COLT 9 MM AUTO" top of barrel, visible in ejection port. May or may not have "P" on left side of lug and "C" in a box with rounded corners on right side of lug. Figure 8-1K.
COLT .45 AUTO MK. IV / SERIES '70 P; C in box (sans serif) Also, no P or C in box	Series 70 Production, any .45-caliber model	"COLT .45 AUTO MK. IV/SERIES '70" top of barrel, visible in ejection port. Commercial barrels only. Figure 8-1L.
COLT 9 MM AUTO MK. IV / SERIES '70 P; C in box, no serifs	Series 70 Production, all 9 mm models	"COLT 9 MM AUTO MK. IV/SERIES '70," top of barrel, visible in ejection port. Commercial barrels. Figure 8-1M.
COLT SUPER .38 AUTO	40,001 to EOP	"COLT SUPER .38 AUTO" top of barrel, visible in ejection port. Commercial barrels. Figure 8-1N.
COLT .38 SPEC. NM (3) ★★MK. III ★★	3,700 to EOP	"COLT .38 SPEC. NM" top of barrel, visible in ejection port. Commercial barrels. Figure 8-1O.
COLT .45 AUTO N.M.	10NM to 35,800NM	"COLT .45 AUTO N.M." top of barrel, visible in ejection port. Commercial barrels. Figure 8-1P.

Model 1911, M1911A1

Table 8-1, cont.		
Barrel Marks, Colt Firearms		
Marking	**Serial Number Range, Circa**	**Location**
COLT .45 AUTO N.M. MK. IV/SERIES '70	70N01001 to EOP	"COLT .45 AUTO N.M. MK. IV/SERIES '70" top of barrel, visible in ejection port. Commercial barrels. Figure 8-1Q.
.45 AUTO NM 7790513 (Serial Number added to barrel) "C" in box	1956-1968 Springfield Armory National Match M1911A1	Two o'clock position, over chamber. Figure 8-1R. Can be any 1911A1 serial number or manufacturer.
B	Inspection marking, between circa serial #2,340,000-EOP	Colt barrel, forward of lug. Use was intermittent.
D	Inspection marking, between circa serial #2,340,000-EOP	Colt barrel, forward of lug. Use was intermittent.
F	Inspection marking between circa serial #900,000-EOP	Colt barrel, forward of lug, Use was intermittent.
G (small, early; large, late)	Inspection marking, circa serial #711,200-933,000	Colt barrel, forward of lug.
K	Inspection marking combined with "P," between circa serial #700,001-710,000	Colt barrel, forward of lug. Figure 8-1S.
M	Post-World War II, military replacement and commercial barrels	Magnaflux test mark for magnetic testing for barrel cracks and voids. Figure 8-1T.
N	Inspection marking all combined with "P" between circa serial #900,000-1,740,000	Colt barrel, forward of lug, Use was intermittent.

Military and Commercial Pistols

Table 8-1, cont. Barrel Marks, Colt Firearms		
Marking	**Serial Number Range, Circa**	**Location**
7	Inspection marking between circa serial #900,000-EOP. May also show "P"	Colt barrel, forward of lug, Use was intermittent.
7791193	Federal catalog number	Post-World War II, Top of barrel.

1. Not on commercial barrels.
2. May appear as "H P" or "P H" marking.
3. Of five examples examined, three had Colt inspector's markings, two did not.
General Note: Military barrels usually have an inspector's number or initial on bottom of barrel, in front of the lug.

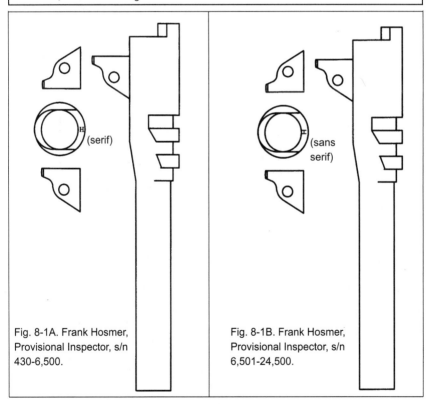

Fig. 8-1A. Frank Hosmer, Provisional Inspector, s/n 430-6,500.

Fig. 8-1B. Frank Hosmer, Provisional Inspector, s/n 6,501-24,500.

Model 1911, M1911A1

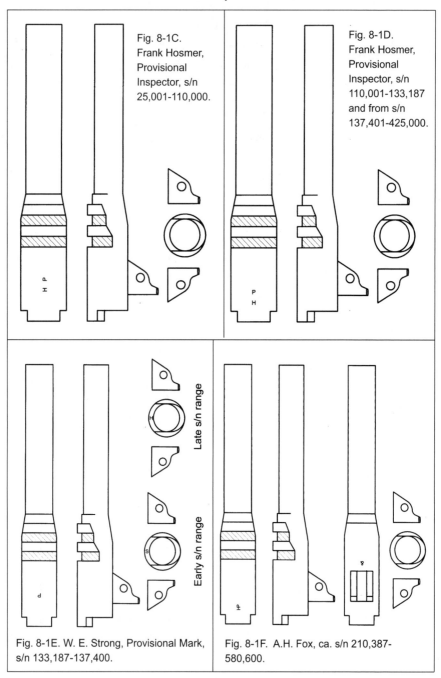

Fig. 8-1C. Frank Hosmer, Provisional Inspector, s/n 25,001-110,000.

Fig. 8-1D. Frank Hosmer, Provisional Inspector, s/n 110,001-133,187 and from s/n 137,401-425,000.

Fig. 8-1E. W. E. Strong, Provisional Mark, s/n 133,187-137,400.

Fig. 8-1F. A.H. Fox, ca. s/n 210,387-580,600.

Military and Commercial Pistols

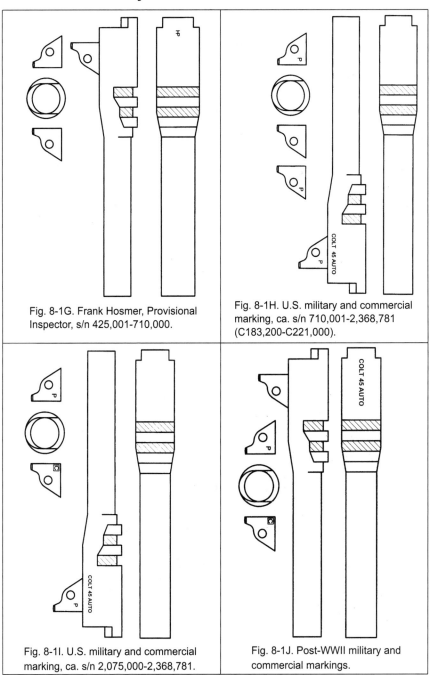

Fig. 8-1G. Frank Hosmer, Provisional Inspector, s/n 425,001-710,000.

Fig. 8-1H. U.S. military and commercial marking, ca. s/n 710,001-2,368,781 (C183,200-C221,000).

Fig. 8-1I. U.S. military and commercial marking, ca. s/n 2,075,000-2,368,781.

Fig. 8-1J. Post-WWII military and commercial markings.

349

Model 1911, M1911A1

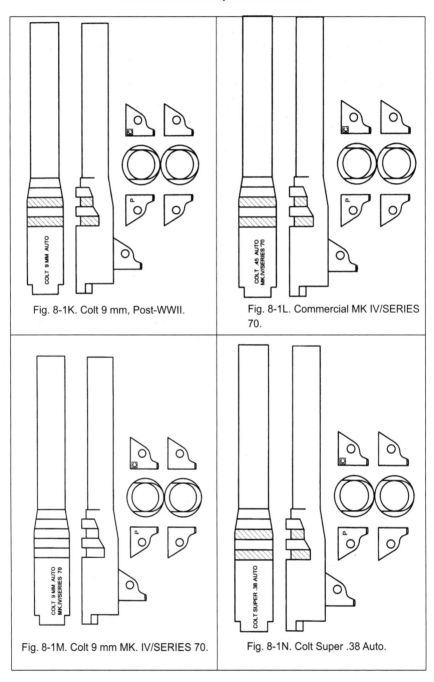

Fig. 8-1K. Colt 9 mm, Post-WWII.

Fig. 8-1L. Commercial MK IV/SERIES 70.

Fig. 8-1M. Colt 9 mm MK. IV/SERIES 70.

Fig. 8-1N. Colt Super .38 Auto.

Military and Commercial Pistols

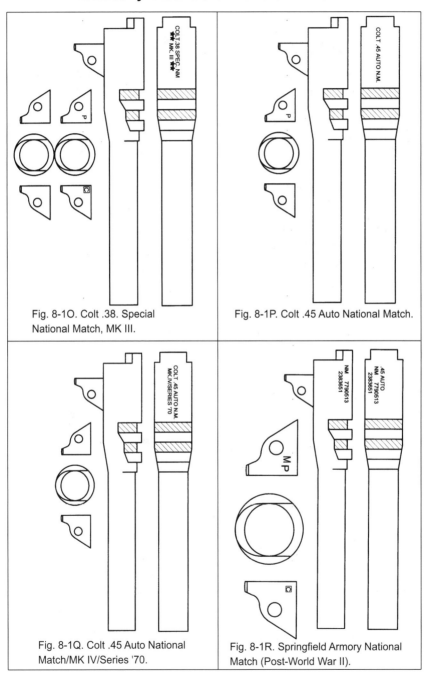

Fig. 8-1O. Colt .38. Special National Match, MK III.

Fig. 8-1P. Colt .45 Auto National Match.

Fig. 8-1Q. Colt .45 Auto National Match/MK IV/Series '70.

Fig. 8-1R. Springfield Armory National Match (Post-World War II).

351

Model 1911, M1911A1

Fig. 8-1S. Inspection marking combined with the "Proof" mark.

Fig. 8-1T. Magnaflux test mark(arrow) for magnetic testing for cracks and voids, post-WWII, military replacement and new commercial barrels.

SPRINGFIELD ARMORY BARREL MARKS (see Figures 8-2A-G)

Marking	Serial Number Range, Circa	Location
S (sans serif)	72,571-77,000	Right lug, horizontal. Figure 8-2A.
S, M or MD (sans serif)	77,001-83,855	"S" on right lug, vertical. "M" or "MD" on barrel hood. Figure 8-2B.
S, P, J (sans serif)	102,597-107,596	"S" on right lug, horizontal. "P" on left lug, horizontal. "J" on barrel hood. Figure 8-2C.
S, S, P (sans serif)	113,497-120,566 125,567-133,186	"S" on right lug, horizontal. "S" on barrel hood, vertical. "P" on left lug, horizontal. Figure 8-2D.
S, P (sans serif)	Replacement barrels, 1919-1937	"S" on left lug, top, horizonal. "P" on left lug, bottom, horizontal. Figure 2-8E.
S, P (sans serif)	Replacement barrels, 1938-1941	"S" and "P" on left lug, vertical. Figure 8-2F.

Table 8-2
Barrel Marks, Springfield Armory

Military and Commercial Pistols

	Table 8-2	
	Barrel Marks, Springfield Armory, cont.	
Marking	Serial Number Range, Circa	Location
S, P, Heat Lot Number* (sans serif)	1941-1943 replacement barrels	"S" on left lug, front, vertical. "P" on left lug rear, vertical. Heat lot number consisted of three characters and a number on left side of barrel, above lug. Figure 8-2G, above.
S, P (sans serif) Crossed Cannon symbol	Replacement barrels circa 1943 to End of Production in the same year.	"S" on left lug, front, vertical. "P" on left lug rear, vertical. Crossed cannon ordnance symbol on front or rear top of right lug. Figure 8-2G, below.
7791193 (sans serif)	Federal Catalog Number	Post-World War II, top of barrel.

* Heat lot numbers observed are: AG1, AG-1, BF1, BH1, PX-1, PX-8, REP 1, REP 2, REP 3.

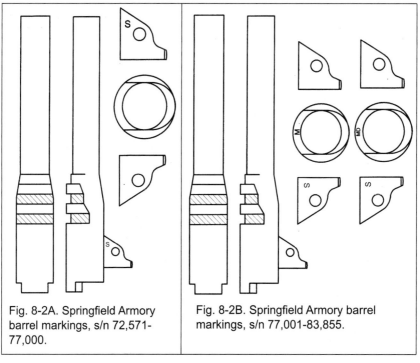

Fig. 8-2A. Springfield Armory barrel markings, s/n 72,571-77,000.

Fig. 8-2B. Springfield Armory barrel markings, s/n 77,001-83,855.

Model 1911, M1911A1

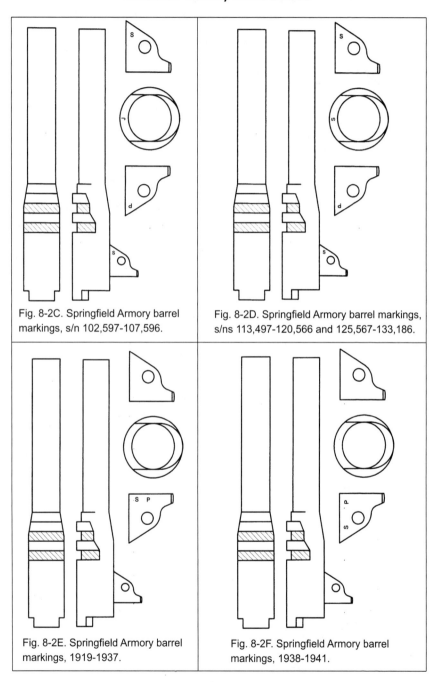

Fig. 8-2C. Springfield Armory barrel markings, s/n 102,597-107,596.

Fig. 8-2D. Springfield Armory barrel markings, s/ns 113,497-120,566 and 125,567-133,186.

Fig. 8-2E. Springfield Armory barrel markings, 1919-1937.

Fig. 8-2F. Springfield Armory barrel markings, 1938-1941.

Military and Commercial Pistols

Remington Arms-UMC Barrel Marks

Barrels made for Remington Arms-UMC Model 1911s were often marked "P" for proof on the right side of the lug from circa serial #s 1 to 1,000; after, the "P" proof mark was moved to the top of the barrel along the centerline to the end of production. See Figure 8-3.

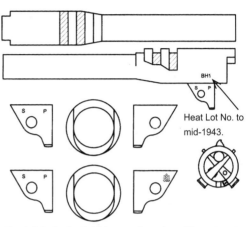

A.H. Fox Company Barrel Marks

The A.H. Fox Company served as a subcontractor to Colt Firearms during late 1917 and into 1918 to produce barrels, slide stops, grip safeties, safety locks,

Fig. 8-2G. Springfield Armory barrel markings: top, to mid-1943, bottom, after mid-1943 to EOP.

and plunger tubes. Colt barrels marked with an ampersand ("&") ahead of the barrel lug may have been manufactured by A.H. Fox as they appear in 1918 only, refer to Figure 8-1F.

Singer Manufacturing Company Barrel Marks

Singer manufactured the barrels for the 500 Model 1911A1s built under an educational contract. No manufacturer's mark was stamped on the barrel. The lug carried the "P" proof mark stamped on the left lug, behind and above the link pin hole.

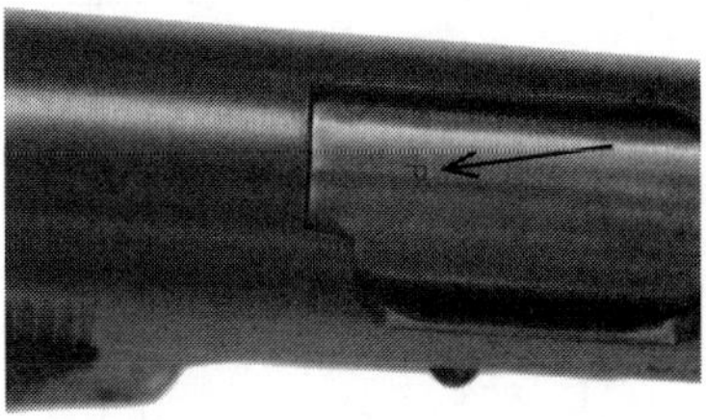

Fig. 8-3. Remington Arms-UMC "P" proof mark on barrel. Only the first 1,000 or so had the proof mark on the right side of the lug.

Remington Rand Barrel Marks

At the start of Remington Rand production, Colt supplied approximately 5,000 finished barrels, and more later. These were marked in accordance with Colt procedures of the period:

COLT 45 AUTO

355

above the left barrel lug and "**P**" on the right barrel lug. Sans serif. Refer to Figure 8-1H.

Standard production barrels for Remington Rand Model 1911A1s after the first 10,000 pistols were manufactured by High Standard. They were marked "**P**" for proof on the left barrel lug and "**HS**" on the right barrel lug, see Figure 8-4.

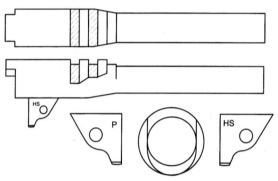

Fig. 8-4. High Standard–manufactured barrels were installed in most Remington Rand, the majority of Ithaca, and all US&S Model 1911A1s. They were proof-marked "P" on the left barrel lug and stamped "HS" on the right barrel lug.

An unknown number of .45 ACP caliber barrels were obtained by Remington Rand from the Flannery Bolt Co. to be used as original and replacement barrels from mid-1944 to early 1945. Flannery barrels were marked "**F**" on the right barrel lug, usually above the link pin hole, and "**P**" on the left barrel lug, usually above and behind the link pin hole, see Figure 8-5.

Ithaca Barrel Marks

At the start of production, Ithaca may have used some Colt-manufactured barrels in the early stages of the first contract, serial #856,405-circa serial #865,000. They carried the Colt markings

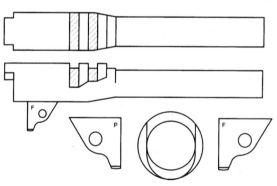

Fig. 8-5. Flannery Bolt Company manufactured .45-caliber automatic barrels from mid-1944 to early 1945. They were marked "F" on the right barrel lug and "P" on the left barrel lug.

of that period and would have been used in the very first Ithaca pistols:

above the left barrel lug and "**P**" on the right barrel lug. Sans serif, refer to Figure 8-1H.

The vast majority of barrels used in original Ithaca production Model 1911A1s were manufactured under contract by High Standard. These were marked "**HS**" on the right barrel lug, usually above and behind the link pin hole. The "**P**" proof mark was stamped on the left lug, usually above and behind the link pin hole, refer to Figure 8-4.

An unknown quantity of barrels were obtained from Flannery Bolt Co. as original equipment or replacements in 1944 and 1945. Flannery barrels were marked "**F**" on the right barrel lug and the "**P**" proof mark was stamped on the left barrel lug, both initials above the link pin hole, refer to Figure 8-5.

NOTE: Ithaca, Remington Rand, and Union Switch & Signal furnished High Standard and Flannery barrels packaged as replacement parts.

Union Switch & Signal Barrel Marks
All original barrels in US&S Model 1911A1s were manufactured by High Standard. They were marked "**HS**" on the right barrel lug above the link pin hole. The left side was marked with the "**P**" proof mark, refer to Figure 8-4.

SUBCONTRACTOR MANUFACTURED BARRELS
High Standard
The High Standard Manufacturing Company produced Model 1911A1 barrels that were used both as original equipment for Remington Rand, Ithaca, and Union Switch & Signal. They were also used as replacement barrels (field and depot) in all Model 1911A1 pistols, regardless of the manufacturer.

High Standard barrels were marked with the "**P**" proof without serifs on the left side of the lug and "**HS**" without serifs on the right side, refer to Figure 8-4. Early production barrels to late 1942 show a "**P**" that was 0.12 inch high. After, the "**P**" mark was 0.080 inch high. Note that ac-

Model 1911, M1911A1

tual measurements may vary slightly depending on the force with which the die was struck.

Flannery Bolt Company

The Flannery Bolt Company was subcontracted to manufacture barrels for the Model 1911A1 from mid-1943 (an estimated total of 313,700). Most were used as replacement barrels but many were sent to both Remington Rand and Ithaca to use as original and replacement equipment between mid-1944 and into 1945. The barrels were manufactured on equipment on loan from the Springfield Armory.

Flannery Bolt Company barrels are marked with the "**P**" proof mark without serifs on the left lug and with an "**F**" without serifs on the right lug, refer to Figure 8-5.

Post-World War II Commercial Barrel Marks

Barrels for commercial use manufactured from 1947 to the end of (commercial) Model 1911A1 production in 1969 were marked on the top of the barrel, visible through the ejection port:

COLT 45 AUTO

They were also marked "**P**" on the left lug and with a "**C**" in a box on the right lug, no serifs.

Barrels made for the 9 mm, Super .38 and National Match models were marked as shown in Figures 8-1, K; 8-1, M; 8-1, N; and 8-1, O.

Barrels made for Model 1911A1 and National Match M1911A1 after World War II—but not the Series 70 National Match—pistols were also marked "**M**" without serifs. The "**M**" indicated that the barrel had passed a magnetic particle test for cracks or other defects, refer to Figure 8-1T.

Post-World War II National Match Pistols—U.S. Military

In the late 1950s and through the 1960s, Model 1911A1 pistols rebuilt for use in the National Matches by U.S. military personnel at Springfield Armory appear to have barrels purchased new from Colt which were taken from commercial National Match inventories. They were marked at the 1 to 2 o' clock position over the chamber:

Military and Commercial Pistols

.45 AUTO
NM   7790513

The left side of the lug was stamped "P" and "M," the latter indicating that it had been magnafluxed. The right lug was stamped with the boxed "C" Colt logotype. These markings were stamped on the barrel after polishing and prior to finishing, refer to Figures 8-1R and 8-1T.

After the pistol was assembled at Springfield, the barrel was then stamped with the receiver's serial number below the "**NM**" and part number. Slight ridges of displaced metal can be easily seen surrounding the numbers.

MISCELLANEOUS BARREL MARKINGS
Argentina Barrel Markings
Barrels manufactured in Argentina are quite recognizable as they have the full or partial receiver serial number stamped on top of the barrel over the chamber and visible through the ejection port. No other markings have been observed, see Figure 8-6.

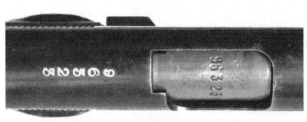

Fig. 8-6. Argentine-made barrels will show the receiver serial number on top of the barrel, visible in the ejection port.

British Barrel Markings
Barrels for the Model 1911, purchased by the British military from the period of World War I through the end of World War II, were marked with 1) the government property mark, the broad arrow; 2) with the proof mark, crossed pennants; 3) and with an inspector's mark, usually a crown with the initial(s) of the reigning monarch over the initial or number of the War Department inspector, see Figure 8-7.

NOTE: Firearms acquired by the British military before World War I will often show the broad arrow over "**WD**" for War Department.

Model 1911, M1911A1

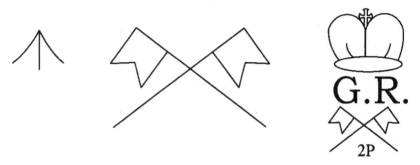

Fig. 8-7. Markings signifying British military ownership, left to right: Broad Arrow; Crossed Pennants proof mark, and reigning monarch's crown and initials over crossed pennants above the inspector's identification.

The Model 1911/1911A1 was declared obsolete and surplus to military needs in 1947 and released for commercial sale. These will show proof marks on the barrel relating to the proof law of 1904, 1925, or 1955. See Appendix G for a complete explanation.

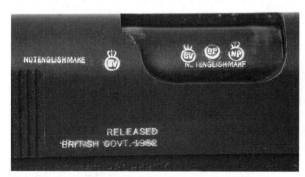

Fig. 8-8. Lend-Lease Model 1911A1s released from British military service after 1947 will show the legend, "RELEASED BRITISH GOVT." and the year.

Lend-Lease Model 1911A1s and other M1911/M1911A1 pistols that were used in and released from British military service after 1947 will also show the legend **RELEASED BRITISH GOVT.** and the year as shown in Figure 8-8.

British Commercial Markings

British commercial proof laws and markings date from 1631. The proof laws that concern the Model 1911/1911A1 pistols, and in particular, the barrel, are those of 1904, 1925, and 1955. The proof marks were applied under government supervision and are summarized in Table 8-3 below. See Appendix G for a more thorough discussion.

Military and Commercial Pistols

Table 8-3	
British Commercial Markings Found on Model 1911/Model 1911A1 Pistols	
Proof Rules of 1904 (1904-1925)	
London	**Birmingham**
Proof Mark	
Crown over intertwined GP—barrel	Crown over BP—barrel
View Mark	
Crown over V on barrel, receiver, and slide	Crown over BV—barrel, receiver, and slide
Proof Rules of 1925 (1926-1954)	
Proof Mark	
Crown over intertwined GP within a circle—barrel	Crown over BP within a circle—barrel
View Mark	
Crown over V in circle—barrel, receiver, and slide	Crown over BV within a circle—barrel, receiver, and slide
Nitro Proof	
Arm upraised with Sword over NP within a circle—barrel	Crown over NP within circle—barrel
Viewer's Proof	
Not applicable	Crossed scepters with initials and/or numbers on right left and bottom
NOT ENGLISH MAKE stamped on all firearms not manufactured in Great Britain — 1925-1955 only	
Proof Rules of 1955 (1955 to Present)	
Proof Mark	
Crown over intertwined GP—receiver and slide	Crown over BNP—receiver and slide
Nitro Proof	
Arm upraised with Sword over NP within a circle—barrel .45" (or .455") .900" 7 TONSPER □"	Crown over BNP .45" (or .455") .900" 7 TONSPER □"

CHAPTER 9
FINISHES AND ENGRAVING

Although it may appear that the question of finishes applied to the Model 1911 or Model 1911A1 is complicated, in fact it is not. As noted in Chapter 2, only seven types of finish were routinely applied to any Model 1911 or Model 1911A1 by any manufacturer to the end of World War II. They included 1) heat or fire bluing, 2) chemical bluing—also called browning, 3) Du-Lite (a black oxide finish), 4) Penetrate (another black oxide finish), 5) Parkerizing, as well as 6) Parco-Lubrite (both mixtures of phosphoric acid and powdered iron, zinc or manganese), and 7) nickel plate at various times for commercial models. Other finishes such as gold or silver plate, chrome, etc. were available on special order.

NOTE: From the start of production to circa serial #2,400 (military) and C4,000 (commercial), all small parts were heat-blued to a bright, iridescent or fire blue color. These parts included the grip panel screws, triggers, slide stops, thumb safeties, and ejectors. After aging and wear, the fire blue finish becomes less pronounced.

Understanding finishes is a bit easier if you know how they were applied by Colt. To start, Colt "heat-blued" commercial models from the start of production in 1911 to 1941 when commercial production ended during World War II. Military models were heat-blued until the advent of Parkerizing between circa serial #s 734,001-735,001. The following description of heat-bluing is condensed from "A Trip Through the Present Plant of Colt's Manufacturing Company," *A Century of Progress*, published in 1937. While it refers to the commercial heat-bluing process, the procedure was the same for the military contract pistols, differing only in the amount and type of polishing the parts received.

In the period before World War II, the Model 1911 and Model 1911A1 receiver and slide were forged from steel blanks. Barrels were cut from steel rod stock. Smaller parts were forged and machined to shape or machined from steel sheet stock. For instance, a slide was sawed from a steel blank and forged to shape in a drop forge. It was trimmed in a punch press to remove excess metal,

Military and Commercial Pistols

and shot blasted to remove scale. It was then heat treated—normalized—to relieve stress. In fact, after every succeeding machine tool operation, the slide was normalized again.

By the time the slide was finished, more than half the weight in steel from the original blank had been removed. By the time the receiver was finished, it had been reduced in weight from 43.5 ounces to 13.0 ounces. The slide and receiver were hand-filed to assure the proper fit and both were serial numbered [not all slides at all times—ed.]. A total of 1,200 operations were performed to manufacture one Colt .45 pistol. Polishing of parts was done by hand by skilled workmen to bring the metal surfaces to a very high polish. The smoother the polish, the deeper the "blue."

Heat-bluing was conducted in a bank of rotary furnaces in the Colt plant. The parts were degreased in heated gasoline and rubbed with a mixture of whiting and alcohol as a final polish and to remove any last trace of polishing compound, metal chips or dust and skin oils. The parts were placed on special rack with slide and receiver together and inserted into the rotary furnace heated to 500 degrees Fahrenheit. Air was excluded from the furnace by inserting a mixture of petroleum oil and animal bone charcoal which excluded oxygen that would discolor the part. Over the next five hours, the temperature is increased to 650 degrees, bringing the carbon in the steel to the surface and imparting a deep blue-black color.

In addition to heat-bluing before World War II, nickel-plating was available for commercial pistols, although not especially popular. Gold-, silver-, and chrome-plating could also be special ordered. Almost always, the type of finish other than blue was noted in the shipping record. A Colt letter of authenticity can usually establish a factory finish.

Only one U.S. military Model 1911A1 with a nickel finish is known. It is serial number 1,113,489 as reported by E. Scott Meadows. Another, serial number 1,113,488, was chrome-plated and sent to Major F.M. Volberg, Office of the Chief of Ordnance, Small Arms Branch at the Pentagon on August 31, 1943. While there may have been other nickel- or even chrome-plated U.S. military Model 1911 or Model 1911A1 pistols, verified examples are unknown to the author.

Model 1911, M1911A1

In an effort to speed up production of the Model 1911 during World War I, the Ordnance Department asked Colt to decrease the amount of time and effort spent polishing and finishing the pistol. This resulted in the so-called "Black Finish" Model 1911s, described in greater detail below.

Du-Lite and Penetrate were proprietary black oxide processes and are described below. The black oxide process was used to finish all Singer and Union Switch & Signal pistols, and early Ithaca and Remington Rand pistols to mid-1943. Some parts such as barrels and magazines manufactured during World War II had the black oxide finish.

Parkerizing is a process that lays down a phosphate coating on the surface of the steel. It is described below.

Parco-Lubrite was a form of Parkerizing that provided a smoother, less grainy finish to the steel by requiring less preliminary sandblasting.

All blued and Parkerized receivers after circa serial #710,000 to (Colt) ca. serial #s 1,700,000-1,710,000 had their bullet ramps ground smooth after finishing and will present a brighter appearance. After circa serial number 1.7 million, Colt switched to the Parco-Lubrite finish which produced a smooth enough finish that the bullet ramp did not need to be smoothed and so it will match the color of the rest of the receiver.

All finishes are described in the paragraphs below and summarized in Table 9-1.

MILITARY FINISHES
Oil Finish

The first military Model 1911s received the same finish which produced a bright blue finish—termed an "oil finish" — as did the Colt commercial pistols. Commercial pistols from C1-C10,000 received the oil finish. Military pistols manufactured from serial #1 to circa 2,400 are thought to have received the same oil finish but interestingly enough, Karl Karash has reported that observed military pistols in the serial number range 501-1,000 appear to have a "dull" finish but with finer polishing than post-serial #2,400 military pistols. Also, a trial lot of pistols circa serial number 1,275 received the later dull finish.

To obtain the almost mirror-like finish to the metal which imparted the glossy blue-black color, the parts were subjected to a series of polishings using ever finer grades of abrasive. Much of this finish was

Military and Commercial Pistols

done by hand against wheels especially shaped for the part. The polishing process was divided into three stages: rough, fine, and oil finish in which oil was applied to the wheel for the final polish. The parts were then cleaned in hot gasoline, dried and loaded into special racks and placed in furnaces stoked with charcoal. After a few minutes, the parts were withdrawn and rubbed with oakum and whiting. The process was repeated up to six times until the workman was satisfied that the proper blue coloring had been obtained. Small parts—ejector, hammer, magazine catch, rear sight, safety, slide stop, grip screws and trigger—were placed in cast-iron vessels containing the charcoal and bone mix and heated to obtain what was termed "fire blue" because of its blue iridescent color.

The heat of the burning charcoal at between 600 and 650 degrees Fahrenheit colored the metal but it was not a rugged finish and was easily scratched and worn away. Heat-bluing combined with the final oil polishing produced a mirror finish deeper than could be obtained with a chemical bluing process.

Dull Finish

The Army objected that the bright oil finish reflected light and scratched easily and in January 1912, asked that the finish be made as dull as possible to eliminate the gleam in the sunlight. Colt eliminated the oil polishing stage, ending the process with the fine polish stage which the Army then referred to as a "dull finish." The dull finish was used on all military contract pistols from circa serial #s 2,401 to 170,000. It was also applied to all commercial pistols until production ended during World War II (C10,001-C215,018). It was also applied to post-WWII commercial pistols through the Series 70/80. This finish is also referred to as a "matte" finish by some collectors.

Brushed Finish

During 1917, in an effort to speed wartime production, the Army requested that the amount of polishing be reduced even further. Colt changed the type of abrasives used and produced a "matte blue" effect. Collectors often refer to this as a "brushed" finish. It was applied to U.S. military pistols in the circa serial # range 170,001-312,000 and again from circa serial #s 580,001-734,000 to 735,000.

Model 1911, M1911A1

Remington Arms-UMC also used a form of the brush finish on all their production.

Black Finish

In 1918, Colt installed gas-fired rotary ovens (referred to above in the excerpt from "A Trip Through the Present Plant of Colt's Manufacturing Company," *A Century of Progress*) which allowed better control of temperatures. In mid-year, the Army again asked Colt to speed up production and suggested that the finishing process be reduced even further. Colt responded by eliminating the fine polishing stage altogether. As a result, the first-stage "rough" polishing left whorls in the metal and the surface was so dull that a dark black finish resulted. This process was applied to all U.S. military pistols in the circa serial #s 312,001-580,000 range.

Springfield Armory Finish

Springfield Armory finished their pistols with a chemical process called "browning." This was a process that used multiple applications of a chemical solution to compound with the metal. Between applications, the surface of the metal was "carded" or brushed. The process was repeated until the proper depth of finish was obtained. "Browning" is similar to the rust bluing process and had been used by the Armory since the introduction of the Model 1873 .45-70 Springfield rifle and carbine.

Du-Lite®

Du-Lite® is a black oxide processes similar to bluing developed and patented by the Du-Lite Company of Middletown, Connecticut. Black oxide is a conversion coating which forms when parts are immersed in the alkaline aqueous salt solution at approximately 285 degrees F. The reaction between the iron of the ferrous alloy and the hot oxide bath produces a layer of magnetite (Fe_3O_4) on the actual surface of the part. The company claimed that the process causes the finish to "penetrate" the top layers of the metal, and so it was considered more durable than bluing. Penetrate® is a similar solution also used by Colt.

All Singer Model 1911A1 pistols were finished using the Du-Lite process. Because Singer polished the metal parts to a high degree, Singer Model 1911A1s, when new, exhibited a satin black finish.

Ithaca and Remington Rand both used the Du-Lite process for a short time at the start of their production runs (circa serial #s 856,405-

Military and Commercial Pistols

916,404 and circa serial #s 916,405-995,000 to 1,015,499 respectively). After the serial number ranges listed, both Remington Rand and Ithaca Parkerized their remaining production. Union Switch & Signal pistols received the Du-Lite finish over a light sandblasting throughout production. Because the metal on all but the Singer pistols was lightly sandblasted, they will exhibit a dull, non-reflective blackish finish. All Model 1911A1 barrels manufactured during World War II were finished using the Du-Lite black oxide process. Parkerized barrels have been refinished.

Parkerizing

Parkerizing is a patented process by which a rust-resistant, non-glare matte finish is applied to the surface of steel. A solution consisting of powdered iron, zinc, or manganese, and dilute phosphoric acid is applied to the steel part. The surface metal is dissolved by the acid and replaced by insoluble phosphates. The result is a non-reflective, slightly etched finish which is quite, but not completely, rustproof. When Parkerizing was applied to firearms, the steel surfaces were usually lightly sandblasted to increase the surface area and obtain better adhesion.

The color of military Parkerizing ranges from light gray through gray-green to almost black, depending on the dyes added to the solution and to later storage. For instance, Colt's Parkerizing tended toward a dark gray. But when the pistols were oiled and/or packed in Cosmoline, the Parkerized finish often turned a gray-green color. The addition of manganese to the Parkerizing solution produced a dark, almost black color.

The Colt factory, after a series of tests, began Parkerizing the Model 1911A1 between circa serial #s 734,001-735,001. Pistols in this range will be either blued or Parkerized. But slides and receivers will have the same finish. If slides and receivers have a mixed finish, they have probably been changed at some point. The exception to this rule are Model 1911A1s between circa serial #s 1,700,001-1,710,001 when slides and receivers may be mismatched in smoothness and color. During this period, Colt changed their finishing process from Parkerizing to Parco-Lubrite. Parts finished with the Parco-Lubrite process did not have to be sandblasted to the extent that Parkerized parts did. A number of pistols with Parco-Lubrite slides and Parkerized receivers have been observed in this serial number range.

Model 1911, M1911A1

Remington Rand initially finished the Model 1911A1 pistol with a black oxide finish using the Du-Lite process. But between circa serial #s 995,000-1,015,499, Remington Rand phased in the Parkerizing process and continued its use to the end of their production run. Pistols made during this period will have either the Du-Lite or Parkerized finish. The color of the finish on slides and receivers must match on each pistol; otherwise, parts have been changed.

Ithaca also used the Du-Lite process from the start of its production at serial #856,405 to circa serial #916,404. From circa serial #1,208,674 to the end of production, all Ithaca pistols were Parkerized.

Union Switch & Signal installed the equipment for Parkerizing in August 1943, but continued to use the Du-Lite process to the end of their M1911A1 production..

Parco-Lubrite

Parco-Lubrite is a proprietary finish developed in the early 1940s. It was a trade name originally used by the Parker Chemical Company, now Henkel Technologies. The process refers to a family of manganese phosphate chemical conversion coating processes for steel or iron in which some of the metal is removed from the surface during the pickling reaction and becomes incorporated into the new coating that's developed. The manganese phosphate conversion coating has a higher thermal stability than other conversion coatings like zinc phosphate (Parkerizing) and produces a finer crystal size. In the case of the M1911A1, a much lighter sandblasting was required which resulted in a smoother finish.

Colt applied the Parco-Lubrite finish to pistols in the circa serial #1,090,000 range but the process was stopped when the Ordnance Department's Pistol Integration Committee objected that it did not meet the requirements listed for protective finishes. Testing was conducted and it was approved again in December 1944. The Parco-Lubrite finish is thought to have been used on Colt military pistols from serial #s 1,700,001-1,710,001 to the end of military production. Original pistols finished with the Parco-Lubrite finish can often be identified by their unground bullet ramps.

Commercial Finishes

The high-gloss "oil finish" bluing was applied to all commercial production from the start of production to circa serial #C6,000 and intermittently to serial #C10,000. After, the Dull finish was applied until commercial

Military and Commercial Pistols

production ended during World War II (circa C215,018). It should be noted that after about circa serial #C130,000, the degree of polishing was reduced slightly on commercial pistols in the interest of economy, but the difference is hardly noticeable. When commercial production resumed after World War II, all commercial Model 1911A1s received the so-called "dull" finish which was applied until circa serial #C235,000 in 1948. From circa serial #s C235,001-336,169C and the end of commercial M1911A1 production, commercial pistols received the Du-Lite black oxide finish. At about this time, Colt stopped polishing the rounded parts of slide and receiver and began bead blasting them instead to produce a matte finish. Flat parts continued to be polished, although since hand polishing had been mostly eliminated, the parts were polished by machine. All Series 70 and 80 production received a black oxide finish as standard.

NOTE: The "Dull" finish was anything but. It was dull only in comparison to the high gloss "oil" finish.

A bright nickel-plate finish was offered in the 1935 Colt catalog. The first known standard catalog nickel-plated pistol was circa serial #C179,800. Also offered at the same time were full gold or silver plating and combinations of gold and silver slides with blued receivers. An electroless nickel finish was offered in the Series 70 and 80 pistols. Stainless steel pistols were also offered in both the 70 and 80 series.

Colt offered a black Parkerized finish on their commercial Model 1991A1 version of the Model 1911A1. A variety of other finishes are currently available on special order. See Table 9-1 for Model 1911/1911A1 finishes.

Markings vs. Finishes

All markings except those shown in Table 9-2 were stamped on the Model 1911/1911A1 before final polishing and finishing.

A die when stamped will cause metal to be displaced; some of it compacts below and some is pushed to the sides of the die strike, and some will be forced to the surface alongside the die strike. This displaced steel, unless polished away, will be denser than the surrounding metal, and absorb the final finish differently. In short, a letter or number stamped into steel after polishing or after the finish is applied will be surrounded by a "halo" of, usually, lighter finish.

369

Model 1911, M1911A1

Table 9-1 Type of Finish, Model 1911/1911A1 Military and Commercial		
Manufacturer	**Serial Number Range**	**Type Finish**
Colt Military	1-2,400	Military Oil finish (blue)
	2,401-170,000	Military Dull finish (blue)
	170,001-312,000	Military Brush finish (blue)
	312,001-580,000	Military Black finish (blue)
	580,001-734,000 to 735,000	Military Brush finish (blue)
	734,001-735,001-1,700,000 to 1,710,000	Military Parkerized
	1,700,001-1,710,001-EOP	Military Parco-Lubrite
Colt Commercial (1)	C1-C10,000	Oil finish (blue)
	C10,001-C215,018	Commercial Dull finish (blue)
	C179,800	Commercial Nickel plating introduced, used as ordered
	C220,001-C235,000	Commercial Dull finish (blue)
	C235,001-336,169C (EOP)	Commercial Du-Lite
Springfield Armory	All	Browning
Remington Arms-UMC	All	Brush finish (blue)

Military and Commercial Pistols

Manufacturer	Serial Number Range	Type Finish
	Table 9-1, cont. **Type of Finish, Model 1911/1911A1** **Military and Commercial**	
Singer	All	Du-Lite (satin-like polish, no sandblasting)
Remington-Rand (2)	916,405-995,000 to 1,015,499	Du-Lite over sandblast
	1,015,500-2,465,139 (EOP)	Parkerized
Ithaca (2)	856,405-circa 916,404	Du-Lite over sandblast
	Circa 1,208,674-2,660,318 (EOP)	Parkerized
Union Switch & Signal	All	Du-Lite over sandblast

1. Commercial Colt pistols after C10,000 received a higher degree of polishing than military pistols after s/n 2,400.

2. Du-Lite finish phased out and Parkerizing phased in during serial number overlap.

It was the practice at Colt, and most gun manufacturers, to stamp most markings before polishing and finishing and so this ridge of denser metal surrounding the marking was usually removed. Markings stamped after polishing and finishing will often show both a bright shine of steel and the halo effect, depending on the condition of the firearm. On military arms which show use, the bright shine of the steel may have dulled and darkened as the result of corrosion. But in many cases, this provides one more clue as to whether or not the firearm has been refinished.

This does not seem to hold true on those Ithaca and Remington Rand Model 1911A1s (serial #s 1,208,674-EOP and 955,000 to 1,015,499-EOP, respectively) which had the serial number applied with a punch press after finishing. A close examination of the serial numbers

Model 1911, M1911A1

of twelve pistols considered to be in original condition shows Parkerized finish in the depths of the numbers made by the die stamp and not bright, bare metal. The difference is most striking if you compare the serial number itself to the prefix, **NO.** and the **UNITED STATES PROPERTY**, marking both of which were struck before the pistols were Parkerized, see Figure 9-1.

Examination under a microscope showed the finish to be flattened and smoothed, as if the die had compacted rather than cut through the finish. The serial numbers were then compared to the Ordnance Department final inspection marking, the crossed cannon on the right side of the receiver, all of which showed at least some bare metal in the die strike.

Fig. 9-1. Above, Remington Rand serial numbers stamped *through* the original Parkerized finish. Compare their sharp edges to the eroded edges of the prefix and property marking which were sandblasted and stamped *before* finishing. Below, refinished National Match receiver. Note how the serial numbers have been eroded by the additional sandblasting. The prefix has almost disappeared.

Table 9-2
Markings Stamped Through Finish

Marking	Part
Factory inspection markings	Trigger guard, top of receiver, bottom of slide
Ordnance Acceptance — Inspector's Initials or cartouche	Receiver, left
Ordnance Crossed Cannon	Receiver, right

Military and Commercial Pistols

Table 9-2, cont.	
Markings Stamped Through Finish	
Marking	**Part**
Proof (P)	Slide, receiver (Ithaca, Remington Rand, US&S)
Repair marks	Receiver
Serial Numbers	Remington Arms-UMC (all production)
	Ithaca (1,208,674-EOP)
	Remington Rand (955,001 to 1,015,499-EOP)
Verified Proof	Trigger guard, left front (Colt)

ENGRAVED GOVERNMENT MODELS

A detailed examination of engraved Government Models from the Colt factory is beyond the scope of this text. Likewise, it would be impossible to adequately cover non-factory engraved Government Models as there were literally hundreds of gunsmiths and others who engraved a Government Model during its nearly one hundred years of production. A brief discussion of factory engraved Government Models will have to suffice.

In the latter part of the 19th century, the demand for engraved Colt firearms was so high that the factory kept an inventory of engraved shotguns and revolvers on hand. By the start of the 20th century, the demand had begun to fall off. In 1885, 202 handguns were engraved; by 1925, the total had fallen to 48, not counting the common .22-caliber revolvers and .41-caliber derringers.

Over the production life of the Government Model and its successors, the type and amount of engraving coverage has varied. In the first few decades, it was designated as Type 1, 2, and 3 with Type 2, for some reason, providing the most extensive coverage. The factory price for engraving in 1913 ranged from $3.50 to $12.50 added to the price of the weapon ($67 to $239.00 in 2006 dollars). In 1955, the Colt catalog was advertising "standard engraving" at $120.00 and De Luxe Engraving at $200.00 ($824.45 and $1,374.08 in 2006 dollars).

With the establishment of the Custom Repair Department in the early 1970s and its expansion into the Custom Gun Shop in 1976, the styles of engraving were redefined. Grade A provided coverage over one-quarter of all metal surfaces; Grade B over one-half, Grade C over

Model 1911, M1911A1

three-quarters, and Grade D provided full coverage on all metal surfaces including screw heads. Each engraving job was priced individually.

Current Colt Custom Shop coverage can be seen on their Website, http://www.coltsmfg.com/cmci/custom.asp. Three types of engraving are offered, American, English, and Nimschke in three levels, Standard, Expert, and Master.

Colt Factory Engravers of the Past

When the Government Model was first introduced to the commercial market in 1912, the Colt factory engraver was Cuno Helfricht, a Colt employee. While many of the Colt firearms engraved in the period 1870 through 1900 were actually done by other employees working under Helfricht's supervision, from 1910 on, he appears to have done most of the engraving himself with the aid of one or two employees. Colt records as compiled by R.L. Wilson in his excellent *The Book of Colt Engraving* show that Helfricht engraved at least 140 Government Model pistols—seven of which had gold inlays—and inscribed or monogrammed 160 more.

Fig. 9-2. A Colt Model 1911A1 commercial pistol engraved by master engraver Rudolph J. Kornbrath.

Helfricht was succeeded in 1921 by master engraver Rudolph J. Kornbrath who worked with Colt on a subcontract basis until 1937. Kornbrath signed most of his work so it is easy to determine which Government Models of the period were engraved by him. Figure 9-2 provides an example of a Kornbrath-engraved Government Model, C160986.

Wilbur A. Glahn was employed by Colt as an engraver from 1919 to 1923. After leaving Colt, he set up a separate shop with E. R. Houghton, a jewelry engraver, and engraved for Colt on a contract basis. His first shop, known as Houghton & Glahn, was reestablished in 1926 as the Aetna Stamp and Engraving Company of Hartford. Before he retired in 1950, Glahn is known to have engraved twenty-five National

Military and Commercial Pistols

Match .45 pistols, twenty-two ACE .22-caliber pistols, eight Service Model ACE pistols, four .22-.45 conversion kits, three .45-.22 conversion kits, thirty-two Super .38 pistols pre-1942 and six postwar, 36 Super Match .38s and an unknown number of Government Model .45s.

William H. Gough operated an independent engraving business in Utica, New York. Much of his firearms engraving was done on a free-lance basis for Colt, but also for Remington Arms and other gun manufacturers. Before World War II, he employed as many as twenty craftsmen; as they left to enter military service, Gough replaced them with women employees. No estimate of the number of Government Models his shop engraved is available.

Alvin F. Herbert was employed by both Smith & Wesson and Colt for fifteen years as a Master Engraver; during this time he operated his own engraving shop as well. Herbert is probably the best known of all the 20th-century Colt factory engravers because of his distinctive engraving styles. He is known to have engraved twenty-five Government Models, some half-dozen Super .38s, fifteen or fewer National Match pistols, and fifteen or so Commander Models. Herbert left Colt in 1968 due to poor health.

In 1961, Colt established a contractual relationship with the new firm of A. A. White Engravers headed by Herb Glass, Sr., and master engraver Alvin A. White. The Custom Engraved Gun Department at Colt was supervised by Herb Glass, and Al White worked under contract to him. Most firearms engraved by the firm are marked "**AA WHITE/ENG**" or "**A.A. White ENG**," this last found mostly on engraved Colts.

In the early 1970s, Colt expanded its in-house engraving department as part of the Custom Repair Department under the management of Al DeJohn. A new class of coverage, "D," was introduced which covered the entire firearm, including screw heads, with engraving. Among the several master engravers employed by the "Custom Shop" have been Robert B. Burt, Daniel Goodwin, and Leonard Francolini.

As of this writing, all engraving orders are handled through the Colt Custom Gun Shop which can be contacted through Colt's Manufacturing Company LLC Customer Service Department at P.O. Box 1868, Hartford, CT 06144-1868, U.S.A. or by phoning 800-962-COLT.

CHAPTER 10
ACCESSORIES

CLEANING KIT

In June 1911, the Springfield Armory was ordered to manufacture 400 cleaning kits for the U.S. Model 1911 pistol, see Figure 10-1. The design had been approved as the Model 1912 Pistol Cleaning Kit in February 1912. It was made of blued steel and included A) 10 screwdrivers, B) 10 brass cleaning rods threaded for a bristle brush for cleaning the bore and pierced for a cleaning cloth, C) 10 bristle brushes, D) 1 oil can, and E) 1 grease pot for Cosmic (lubricant). All were contained in a blued steel box with a removable wooden tray and a rack for the cleaning rods that lay across the top of the box. Reports of the Chief of Ordnance to the Secretary of War show that Springfield Armory manufactured 74,220 cleaning kits and components for the Model 1911 in 1919.

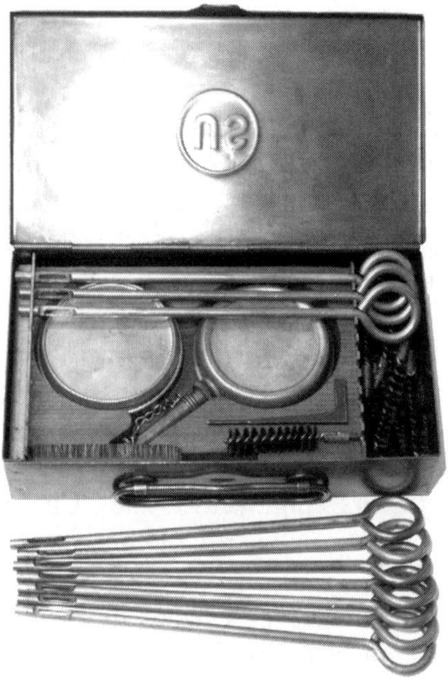

A similar cleaning kit was manufactured and issued during World War II. The box was Parkerized but instead of a separate rack and tray for the grease pot and cleaning rods, metal dividers were welded inside of the box, see Figure 10-2. World War II and later cleaning rods were made of Parkerized steel.

Screwdriver

Six variations on the screwdriver for the Model 1911 and 1911A1 were manufactured, five for the U.S. Army Ordnance Department and one for commercial purposes, see Figure 10-3.

Fig. 10-1. Model 1912 Pistol Cleaning Kit. Craig Riesch collection.

Military and Commercial Pistols

The original **Type 1** screwdriver was manufactured by Colt and was the same as issued with the Model 1903 and Model 1909 service revolvers. A total of 31,344 screwdrivers were included in the original order for the Model 1911 pistol. The Ordnance Department objected to the design and refused to accept them. The screwdrivers were L-shaped with a wide blade (7/32 inch) on the short leg and a narrow blade, (3/32 inch) on the long leg. The

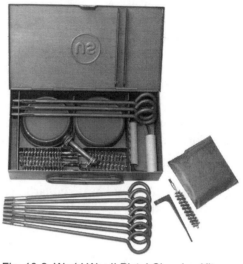

Fig. 10-2. World War II Pistol Cleaning Kit. Craig Riesch collection.

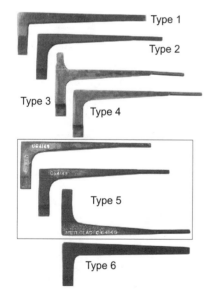

Fig. 10-3. Model 1911/1911A1 Screwdrivers as ordered by the Ordnance Department.

Ordnance Department required that the blade on the short end be 1/4 inch wide and that the long leg end in a drift punch. Colt, which had manufactured some 9,000 screwdrivers to that point, agreed and annealed the long end and machined it into a drift punch. The blade remained 7/32 inch wide. The remainder of the order were manufactured with the drift punch and the 1/4 inch blade. Colt screwdrivers were highly polished and blued.

The screwdrivers (Figure 10-3) for the M1911/1911A1 pistols were manufactured by the Stanley Rule & Level Company (today, known as Stanley Works) and others between 1916 and 1945 in six types.

377

Model 1911, M1911A1

The **Type 2** screwdriver was very similar to the later Colt screwdrivers but shows a definite ring on the long end where the drift punch begins. It was polished and blued.

The **Type 3** screwdriver was modified according to Ordnance Department specifications which required a small screwdriver head opposite the large screwdriver head to permit the magazine catch lock to be removed. This gave it the appearance of a "tomahawk." The Type 3 screwdriver was color case-hardened so that the smaller screwdriver blade did not bend or break. It was manufactured from November 1918 to 1920.

The **Type 4** screwdriver was similar to the Type 2 screwdriver but with only one screwdriver head and was color case-hardened. It was manufactured in small quantities at the same time as the Type 3.

The **Type 5** screwdriver was manufactured during World War II. It was hardened and Parkerized. It can be identified by the part number "C64149" on the long shank. They were manufactured by Stanley Works, National Needle Company, and Metlglas.

The **Type 6** screwdriver was manufactured by Colt, and other companies, for commercial purposes. They are usually unmarked and vary in dimensions.

Cleaning Rod

Five types of cleaning rods were made for the Model 1911/1911A1. The five were alike in design but can be differentiated by material and marking. The cleaning rod was later designated the M4 Cleaning Rod and assigned the part number 5564102, see Figure 10-4.

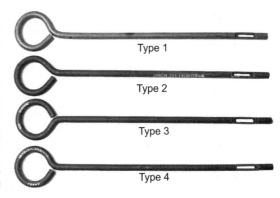

Fig. 10-4. Cleaning rods for the Model 1911/1911A1.

Military and Commercial Pistols

The original **Type 1** cleaning rod was similar to that issued for the revolver. It was made of brass and had a ring-type handle and a slot for a cleaning cloth. The rod was 8.55 inches long and 0.218 inch in diameter. The ring handle was 1.348 inches in diameter. The slot for the cleaning cloth was nominally 0.090 inch wide and 0.615 inch long. The end was drilled and tapped for a bristle cleaning brush.

The Type 1 cleaning rod was made of brass and manufactured from August 1912 to circa 1940.

The **Type 2** cleaning rod, designated the "M4 Cleaning Rod," was made of steel and manufactured from August 1942 to 1945. It was marked with the part number "C64102-4." The USCB Company marked their initials on the handle. Other companies which manufactured the Type 2 cleaning rod were O'Hare Manufacturing Company ("O'Hare MFG. CO." on loop) and U.H. CO (marked on loop).

The **Type 3** cleaning rod was manufactured after World War II and continues in use today. It was made of steel and was marked with the part number "5564102." The Type 3 cleaning rod was manufactured by Springfield Armory (and marked "SA"). Other manufacturers and their markings noted were "D.A.D.," "E.T. CO.," "J.A.M.," "K, " "M.F.I.," "NHA," and "O'HARE MFG CO.," "S.W.T.," "Y.H.M." The markings are found on the handle followed by the part number.

During the 1950s, the U.S. military adopted a federal stock number program as computerization of federal inventories spread. The **Type 4** cleaning rod was identical to the Type 3, and the later Type 5 but for the federal stock number stamped into the rod, "1005-00-556-4102." In many instances, the federal stock number simply adopted the old part number system.

The **Type 5** cleaning rod was marked with the NATO stock number "2X867 1005-00-556-4102," but otherwise was just like the Type 4. Unmarked steel cleaning rods are probably reproductions or aftermarket products.

Model 1911, M1911A1

Oiler

The oiler was a round, flat can with a spout that contained standard U.S. military oil lubricant of the time. Two types were manufactured of brass or steel. They were both 2.175 inches in diameter, and 0.594 inch thick. The can had a spout 1.520 inches long. The spout screwed to the pot so that it could be removed for refilling. A rubber gasket sealed the opening. A chain connected to the cap and spout to prevent loss, see Figure 10-5.

Fig. 10-5. Types 1 and 2 oilers. Craig Riesch collection.

The **Type 1** oiler was brass.

The **Type 2** oiler was similar in size and shape to the Type 1 but was galvanized steel and painted olive drab.

Grease Pot

The grease pot had the same dimensions as the oiler but without the spout. The top of the pot could be removed. It contained a lubricating grease called "Cosmic" instead of oil, see Figure 10-6. Starting around 1938, the grease pot was emptied of grease and used as a spare parts container.

Fig. 10-6. Types 1 and 2 grease pots. Craig Riesch collection.

The **Type 1** grease pot was made of brass.

The **Type 2** grease pot/ spare parts container was the same size and shape as the Type 1 but was steel painted olive drab and manufactured and used throughout World War II and into the Vietnam War.

Military and Commercial Pistols

Cleaning Brushes

Cleaning brushes were used to remove powder fouling from the bore. They were threaded on the end to be attached to the cleaning rod. The cleaning brush was designated the M5 Bore cleaning brush and assigned the part number 5504036, see Figure 10-7.

The **Type 1** cleaning brush was made with boar bristles inserted into twisted brass wire.

The **Type 2** cleaning brush was manufactured and used during and after World War II. They were made with brass bristles inserted into twisted steel wire.

Type 1

Type 2

Fig. 10-7. Types 1 and 2 cleaning brushes.

Lanyard

The Ordnance Department required all military revolvers and pistols manufactured after 1901 to be equipped with a lanyard loop. The decision was based on unit returns that showed a significant number of handguns lost by cavalry troopers while on horseback. The lanyard which was subsequently developed was made of braided linen thread formed into a loop and secured by a leather chape to which was attached a spring-loaded snap. A slide of leather was sewn onto the lanyard loop that allowed the soldier to shorten the loop around his neck and shoulder.

During World War II, air crew discovered that no matter how well a pistol was fastened into a holster, either hip or shoulder, if they had to bail out, chances were very good that they would lose the pistol, unless it was attached with a lanyard. The lanyards manufactured for the revolvers had a snap that was too thick to fit through the lanyard loop on the Model 1911. Accordingly, a new lanyard with a smaller chape and snap was designed, see Figure 10-8.

Model 1911, M1911A1

The **Model 1901** lanyard manufactured for the revolver had a snap hook that was too thick to fit through the lanyard loop on the Model 1911. Accordingly, a new lanyard with a smaller chape and snap was designed, see Figure 10-8.

The **Type 1** lanyard had a chape made of steel and a snap with a thinner body. The slide

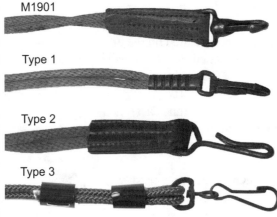

M1901

Type 1

Type 2

Type 3

Fig. 10-8. Top to bottom: 1901 revolver lanyard, Type 1, Type 2, and Type 3 lanyards.

was changed to brass. These were in use to the start of World War II.

The **Type 2** lanyard was made of braided cotton thread. The chape was changed to leather and was sewn to the ends of the lanyard. The snap was changed to an elongated hook. The example is marked "HICKOCK 1943."

The **Type 3** lanyard was currently issued for use with all military revolvers and pistols, including the Model M9 and Model 1911A1, and its clones, now in service. It was made of braided nylon dyed in two shades of olive drab. The slide was made of plastic. The chape had been replaced with two plastic tubes. The lanyard cord was doubled back on and sewn to itself. Two plastic tubes cover each end. The bottom tube was allowed to slide back and forth but the top tube was stapled to the cord. A snap hook was attached through the bight.

HOLSTERS

U.S. military holsters ordered by the Ordnance Department fall into seven models: 1) Holster, Pistol, Caliber .45, Model of 1912 (mounted), 2) Holster, Pistol, Caliber .45, Model of 1912 (dismounted), 3) Holster, Pistol, Caliber .45, Model of 1916, 4) Holster, Pistol, Caliber .45, M3 Shoulder, 5) Holster, Pistol, Caliber .45, Holster, M7, Shoulder, 6) Hol-

Military and Commercial Pistols

ster, Pistol, Black, .45 Caliber, General Officer Type II, and 7) the M-12 holster.

All U.S. military holsters for the Model 1911 or Model 1911A1 were made of russet harness leather until 1956 when the change was made to black leather.

NOTE: When new the leather used to make the Model 1912 and later Model 1916 holsters was a pinkish color. The application of leather dressings, dirt and perspiration gradually turned the leather to the reddish chocolate brown that is so familiar today.

Model 1912 Mounted Holster

Special Army Model serial number 2 (a test pistol and not military contract serial number 2) was sent to Rock Island Arsenal on August 17, 1911, to be used for designing the holster. As an aside, test pistol serial number 2 was used to illustrate the manual, *Description of the Automatic Pistol, Caliber .45, Model of 1911.*

The Model 1912 holster was manufactured with a double slot at the rear for a leg belt or strap that secured the holster to the thigh. A swivel assembly was mounted on the extension which allowed the holster to rotate forward with the position of the leg when the wearer was on horseback or in a vehicle. A double hook attachment secured the holster to the Model 1910, 2nd Variation mounted waist belt, the Model 1910 Dismounted belt or any of its successors. To prevent the magazine release from being accidentally depressed by being forced against the side of the holster, a leather-covered block was sewn to the back of the holster to push the side of the pistol away from the leather. The block had a cutout opposite the magazine catch. A separate reinforcing piece of leather was sewn at the rear junction of the front and back pieces of the holster. The flap that covered the pistol was marked in an oval, "**US**" or "**USMC.**"

Two types of the Model 1912 Mounted Holster were manufactured.

The **Type 1** Model 1912 Mounted Holster was manufactured from 1911 to 1914, see Figure 10-9A. It was made in two variations. All had in common the long extension that was attached with four copper rivets, two on each side, to the holster body. The extension was also sewn to

Model 1911, M1911A1

the body with a vertical double line of stitching between the rivets. The extension was cut straight across at the bottom. A double hook passed through the bight of the extension. The block, or rest, was sewn to the back of the holster and its stitched outline can clearly be seen. The block was made of wood from poplar or maple.

In the **1st Variation** of the Type 1 the steel double hook passed through a brass tube contained in the bight of the extension, see Figure 10-9B, arrow. Also, the outside and

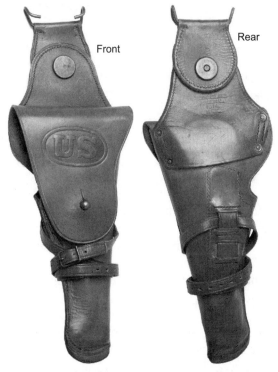

Front

Rear

Fig. 10-9A. Model 1912 Mounted Holster, Type 1. Craig Riesch collection.

bottom edges of the rest, but not the top edge, were covered with leather. This variation was only manufactured for a few months in 1911 and 1912, see Figure 10-10.

In the **2nd Variation**, the entire block was covered with leather, refer to Figure 10-10. Also, the brass tube was removed and the double hook was made of brass.

Fig. 10-9B. Brass tube used to protect the leather. Jack Ricketts collection.

The **Type 2** Model 1912 Mounted Holster was manufactured in 1915 only. When the Type 2 rear sight was introduced at circa serial #62,000, it was found that the wider rear sight caught on the edge of the lower

384

Military and Commercial Pistols

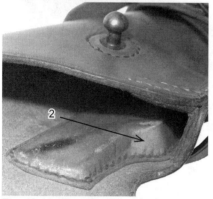

extension rivet. The solution was to extend the bottom edge of the extension and move the rivet down 0.75 inch on the right, see Figure 10-11, arrow. The extension was again fastened to the body with four copper rivets and a vertical double line of stitching between the rivets.

NOTE: In 1917, replacement extensions with swivel assemblies were made to repair Model 1912 holsters. Apparently, far more were made than were ever used because quite a few in new condition were sold in the late 1960s through the 1970s as surplus items. A number of unscrupulous dealers and individuals used them to modify Model 1916 holsters and pass them off as original Model 1912 holsters. They can easily be identified by the fact that a holster so modified is dated 1917 on the extension—no Model 1912 mounted holsters were made after 1915—and they lack the dou-

Fig. 10-10. The top of the block rest was not leather-covered (arrow 1) in the Type 1, 1st Variation M1912 holster, but was (arrow 2) in the 2nd Variation.

ble slot at the mid rear for the leg strap, see Figure 10-12.

Model 1912 Dismounted Holster

The dismounted holster was developed first for the U.S. Marines Corps and other users who did not need the swivel attachment. The Signal Corps specifically requested this type of holster.

The body of the holster was attached to a long extension that depended from the belt. The top of the extension was turned over and secured with two brass rivets. A double hook attachment was inserted into the bight of the extension and was secured by a sheet metal bracket held in the bight of the extension by the two rivets. Immediately below and centered be-

Model 1911, M1911A1

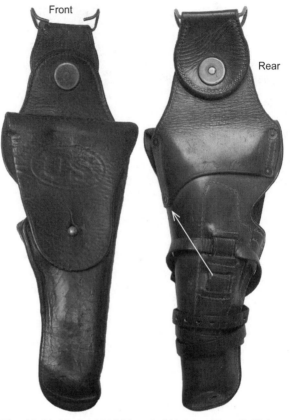

tween the two rivets was a stud. The holster flap was made oversize and could be turned back and secured by pushing the closing slit past the stud. The intent was to have the pistol uncovered ready for instant use while still carrying it in the holster. The holster was marked with "**US**" for the Army issue and "**USMC**" for the Marine Corps issue. Some Model 1916 holsters were modified to the dismounted pattern with the U.S.M.C.-type double hook but all were marked "**US**."

Fig. 10-11. Model 1912 Mounted Holster, Type 2. Note that the bottom of the extension and rivet are lower at the left rear (arrow). Craig Riesch collection.

Two types of the Model 1912 Dismounted Holster were made.

The body of the holster and the extension in the **Type 1** were one piece. The holster, minus the flap, and bottom piece were cut from a single piece of saddle leather, folded over and stitched down the rear side. The bottom piece was sewn into the bottom seam of the holster. The back of the holster was extended upward to form the extension. The top part of the extension was doubled over; a sheet metal bracket which held the double hook belt attachment was secured in the bight with two brass rivets with heads 0.423 inch in diameter. The holster flap was a separate piece sewn to the holster in such a manner that it also secured the front part of

Military and Commercial Pistols

Fig. 10-12. Swivel attachment extensions were manufactured during World War I to repair Model 1912 Holsters. A large number were found and sold on the surplus market in the 1960-70s and sewn to Model 1916 Holsters by unscrupulous individuals.

the extension. The block, or rest, was sewn to the rear of the holster. The small "reinforce" at the upper junction where the front and back halves were sewn together was actually a small, half-inch-wide strip of leather stitched to the front and back, see Figure 10-13A.

The **Type 2** Model 1912 Dismounted holsters were made from Model 1916 holsters during and after World War I. A separate extension without the swivel was manufactured from a double fold of leather. It contained the iron bracket and double hook attachment riveted in the bight. These holsters can be identified by the separate extension with a rounded lower edge and original stitching remaining in the holster body. It was riveted to the back of the holster but not stitched, see Figure 10-13B. All modified Type 2 Dismounted Holsters were marked "US" only. None were marked "USMC."

NOTE: Leg straps supplied with the Model 1912 Mounted Holster were made of russet collar leather, according to specifications. They were 0.5 inch wide and 18.5 inches long. Early leg straps made from 1911 to mid-1912 had brass buckles; after, the buckles were iron, see Figure 10-14.

Model 1916 Holster
The Model 1916 holster was basically the Model 1912 mounted holster without the long extension and swivel attachment. The swivel did not always function properly and many soldiers found the long extension a nuisance and uncomfortable, preferring a holster that rode closer to the waist. The extension was redesigned to eliminate the long drop and

Model 1911, M1911A1

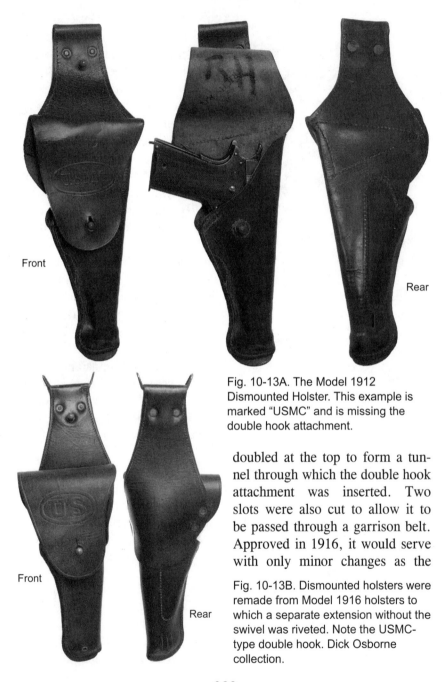

Front

Rear

Front

Rear

Fig. 10-13A. The Model 1912 Dismounted Holster. This example is marked "USMC" and is missing the double hook attachment.

doubled at the top to form a tunnel through which the double hook attachment was inserted. Two slots were also cut to allow it to be passed through a garrison belt. Approved in 1916, it would serve with only minor changes as the

Fig. 10-13B. Dismounted holsters were remade from Model 1916 holsters to which a separate extension without the swivel was riveted. Note the USMC-type double hook. Dick Osborne collection.

Military and Commercial Pistols

Brass   Iron

Fig. 10-14. Leg straps for the Model 1912 Mounted Holster had brass buckles from 1911 to mid-1912, but iron buckles afterward.

issue holster for the Model 1911 and Model 1911A1 service pistols until replaced in 1984 by the M-12 holster for the new Beretta M9 service pistol. The M-12, it should be noted, was also used with the Model 1911A1 pistol.

The Model 1916 holster was made of the same russet harness leather as the Model 1912 holsters, see Figure 10-15. The extension was attached to the rear of the holster with four brass rivets and was also sewn to the back along its circumference. U.S. Army Ordnance Department Specifications called for the holster to be manufactured with all brass furniture. The button, or stud, was to be made of brass but electroplated with a bronze finish. The stitching was to be done by machine using a waxed white thread with a lock stitch The leg tie or thong was to be made of elk skin leather. The block, or rest, was to be made of seasoned, dried poplar or maple and covered with leather.

After 1956, the leather was dyed black and the double hook attachment was usually made of steel. The part number, "7791466," was also stamped on the holster.

Three Types of Model 1916 Holster were manufactured.

The **Type 1** Model 1916 Holster was manufactured between 1916 and 1918. It had a brass double hook and rivets and a small, 0.12-inch internal diameter rivet in the drain hole, refer to Figure 10-15. Belt slits were 1.9 inches long.

The **Type 2** Model 1916 Holster was manufactured 1941-1945 with a brass or steel double hook attachment and rivets, and a large 0.18-inch internal diameter drain hole, see Figure 10-16. Belt slits were 2.3 inches long.

389

Model 1911, M1911A1

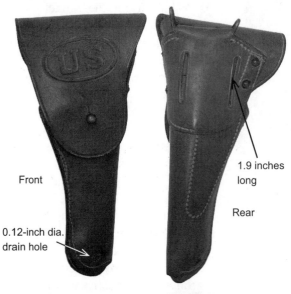

Front

0.12-inch dia.
drain hole

1.9 inches
long

Rear

Fig. 10-15. Type 1 Model 1916 Holsters were manufactured from 1916 to mid-1918 with brass metal parts, small belt slits, and a small drain hole.

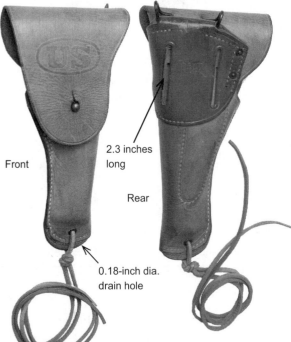

Front

2.3 inches
long

Rear

0.18-inch dia.
drain hole

Fig. 10-16. Type 2 Model 1916 Holsters were manufactured from mid-1941 to 1945 with brass or steel parts, large belt slits, and large drain hole. Craig Riesch collection.

Military and Commercial Pistols

Type 1   Type 2

Fig. 10-17. A comparison of Type 1 and Type 2 drain holes and belt slits on the Model 1916 holster.

Figure 10-17 shows a comparison of the belt slits and drain holes on the Type 1 and Type 2 Model 1916 holsters.

The **Type 3** Model 1916 Holster was made from 1956 through 1985. The brass or steel rivets were replaced by steel brads. The double hook attachment appears to be made of stainless steel. The leather was thinner than formerly and was dyed black, see Figure 10-18.

NOTE: Many World War I and World War II Model 1916 holsters were dyed black after 1955 to conform to the new regulations.

Suspensions

Leather hangers, or suspensions, were manufactured and used to suspend the Model 1916 Holster from a garrison or dress belt. The suspensions were made from russet harness leather, doubled and

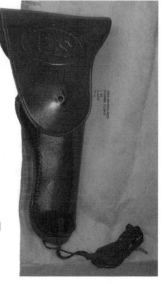

Fig. 10-18. Model 1916 Holster, Type 3 with steel brads and dyed black. This holster was manufactured by Cathay Enterprises, was shipped in August 1987, and is shown with its original packaging.

Model 1911, M1911A1

sewn along the sides. Two eyelets were inserted along the bottom for the double hook attachment. The suspensions were made in two types, see Figure 10-19.

Fig. 10-19. Left to right, Type 1 and Type 2 belt suspensions for the Model 1916 holster.

The **Type 1** suspension was rectangular in shape and had small eyelets. It was made from 1912-13 to 1923.

The **Type 2** suspension was in the shape of a trapezoid with curving sides. It had larger eyelets and was made from 1923 through the early 1980s. The suspensions were also used with the bayonet scabbard.

M-12 Holster

The M-12 holster (see Figure 10-20) was designed for both the M9 Beretta and the M1911A1 pistols. It was designed and manufactured by Bianchi Interna-

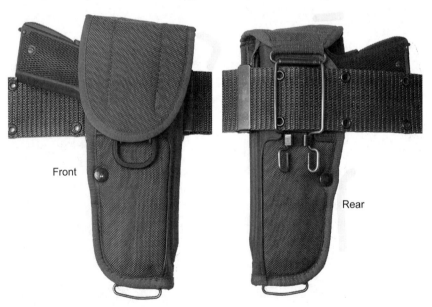

Front

Rear

Fig. 10-20. M-12 Holster designed by Bianchi International.

Military and Commercial Pistols

tional of Temecula, California, and adopted in 1984 by the Department of Defense. The holster is a major departure from previous U.S. military holsters. It is made from ballistic nylon and polyethylene foam sandwiched together to form a protective sheath. The holster is attached to a new web pistol belt adopted at the same time with a new type of "Quick-Lock" fastener which consisted of two spring-wire arms which overlap the belt and are secured in two clips below the belt. The flap is secured over the pistol by a pull-down hook that slips into a plastic reinforcing shell which encircles the holster. Slots in the shell also enable the holster to be threaded directly onto the belt with the Quick-Lock fastener removed. A plastic cleaning rod is carried in a pocket molded into the reinforcing shell. A flattened ring is attached to the bottom of the holster for a tie-down cord.

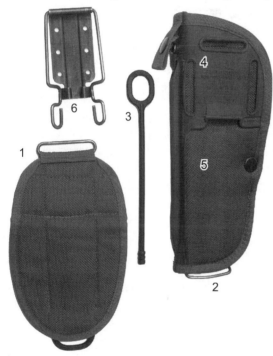

The M-12 holster is ambidextrous; by rearranging the flap and Quick-Lock fastener, the holster can be worn on the right or left side, butt to the rear or forward, as the wearer requires. It can also be quickly disassembled into its component parts for cleaning, see Figure 10-21.

Fig. 10-21. M-12 components: 1) flap, 2) tie-down ring, 3) cleaning rod, 4) reinforcing shell, 5) holster body, and 6) Quick-Lock fastener.

Holster markings are on the plastic reinforcing shell: (front) US and (back) **M-12/PART #9388057/NSN 1095-01-194-3343/BIANCHI INTERNATIONAL/19200** and on the inside of the Quick-Lock belt fastener, **BIANCHI/INTERNATIONAL/UNIVERSAL MILITARY HOL-**

Model 1911, M1911A1

STER/U.S. AND FOREIGN PATENTS PENDING. Reproductions of the M-12 holster will not have these markings.

Holster, Pistol, Black, .45 Caliber, General Officer Type II

This holster was manufactured for the M15 pistol for issue to general officers between 1972 and 1982. The holster was made of black leather and was based on a commercial design called the "Deputy," sized to fit the smaller M15 .45-caliber pistol. Instead of a flap, a single strap with two press fasteners secured the pistol. The holster was cut from a single piece of leather, folded and sewn together. An extension with a belt loop was sewn to the back of the holster at an angle so that the pistol rode comfortably on the hip. A leather metal reinforcing plate was sewn onto the back of the holster. The leather covering was extended upward to form the back of the extension. The front part of the extension was folded over and two snaps were riveted in place which fastened to the back of the extension. This allowed the holster to be removed from the belt. The holster and magazine pocket were manufactured by Bucheimer of Valencia, California. They were marked on the back **DEPUTY/BU-CHEIMER/VALENCIA/CALIF./CLARK/B16-74/PAT.3.200.022**.

NOTE: The Bucheimer Deputy model holster was a standard commercial entry in their holster line in the 1960s and 1970s. Nothing distinguishes the commercial holster from those issued with the M15 pistol except unimpeachable documentation. See Plate 8, color portfolio.

Parade/Ceremonial Holsters

Model 1916 holsters were manufactured of white or black patent leather starting in 1956. These holsters were issued to certain ceremonial units, honor guards, and military police. Most appeared to have been made by the Service Arms Company of Yonkers, New York, and by Cathay Enterprises. The stud was replaced by a Lift-the-Dot fastener in many of these holsters, and iron or steel brads replaced the rivets.

Commercial Hip Holsters

Commercial hip holsters for the Model 1911 appeared first in 1913 in an Abercrombie & Fitch catalog, and probably others as well. The Model

Military and Commercial Pistols

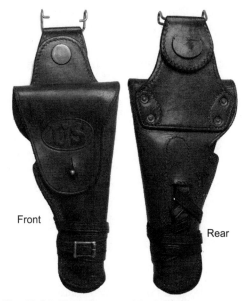

Front

Rear

Fig. 10-22. This Abercrombie & Fitch commercial Model 1912 holster was made of Russian leather for sale to officers.

1912 Mounted Holster was marketed primarily to military officers who were required to purchase their own uniforms and accoutrements. While officers could purchase their equipment from Quartermaster stores, many officers, with private means, preferred to buy better-quality commercial products. An example of a commercial Model 1912 Mounted Holster made of Russian leather is shown in Figure 10-22. It was sold by Abercrombie & Fitch. The leather is a finer, more supple grade than the harness leather preferred by the Ordnance Department because of its better wearing qualities. Notice that the swivel plate on the back of the extension is covered with a flap of leather. This prevented the brass swivel plate from abrading the officer's uniform. Model 1916 holsters were also offered commercially as were other patterns, notably those by Audley during World War I.

HOLSTER MARKINGS

The Model 1912 and 1916 holsters were embossed on the front flap, "US" within an oval. The maker's name and year of manufacture were embossed on the back of the holster, usually on the extension. It should be noted that not all holsters ordered by the U.S. Army Ordnance Department are so marked.

Those Model 1912 or Model 1916 holsters marked "**USMC**" or with the Marine Corps eagle, globe and fouled anchor were probably commercial products sold to Marine officers and enlisted men. The "**USMC**" marked Model 1912 *dismounted* holster was not manufactured at Rock Island

Arsenal but by a private contractor as it shows none of the usual Rock Island markings. Some 1,300 Model 1912 *mounted* holsters are thought to have been manufactured for the Marine Corps by Rock Island Arsenal in 1912-1913 but no examples are known to the author. The Type 2 Model 1912 dismounted holsters were marked "**US**" only as they were modified from Model 1916 holsters. The collector will note unit markings on some holsters; these were applied after issue.

U.S. military holsters were manufactured at Rock Island Arsenal before and during World War I. After, a number of private companies also manufactured holsters under contract to the Ordnance Department. Table 10-1 contains a list of manufacturers observed by the author.

SHOULDER HOLSTERS
M3 Holster (Shoulder)
The actual genesis of the shoulder holster for the Model 1911/1911A1 is obscure. Several styles had been developed commercially before World War II. At least two experimental models for the military were developed and tested in the late 1930s at the request of mounted troops, vehicle drivers, and air crewmen for whom the hip holster was uncomfortable and in the way, see Figure 10-23.

The M3 shoulder holster was authorized in 1942 for air crew. The holster was cut from a single piece of russet harness leather, folded over and stitched along the right edge. The outline of the pistol was also stitched in place. A securing strap was passed through a slot near the top of the holster and stitched to the back. A single D-ring for the suspension strap was sewn to the side of the holster. A belt loop was stitched to the bottom of the holster and closed with a snap fastener. A single leather strap with a buckle was sewn to the top of the holster. The wearer looped the suspension strap over his neck so that the holster rested under the left armpit. The length of the suspension strap was adjusted to suit the wearer by looping it through the D-ring and pulling it through the buckle. To prevent the holster from swinging freely under the arm, the wearer's waist belt was threaded through the belt loop on the bottom of the holster. The M3 was manufactured by several companies during World War II, as shown in Table 10-1.

Military and Commercial Pistols

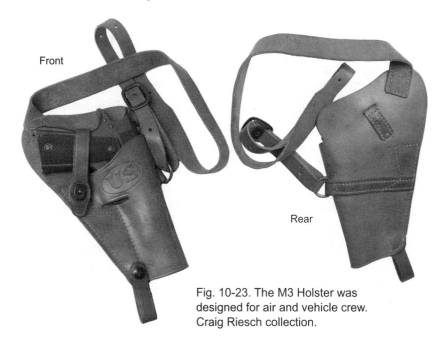

Front

Rear

Fig. 10-23. The M3 Holster was designed for air and vehicle crew. Craig Riesch collection.

M7 Holster (Shoulder)

The M7 was a modification of the M3 shoulder holster that corrected some of the problems experienced with the M3, see Figure 10-24. It was approved for use in 1944. By the end of World War II, it had replaced the M3 in use. Manufacturers are listed in Table 10-1.

The M7 was quite similar to the M3 but a second strap was added to encircle the chest. To make the M7 more comfortable to wear, a pad was added to the neck strap. The right end (when worn) of the shoulder strap was attached to the holster by a D-ring on a tab sewn to the holster body. The shoulder strap had three sets of holes (right, left and middle) that allowed it to be adjusted to fit. The left end of the shoulder strap was attached to a D-ring on a tab sewn to the holster body and secured with a leather lace. A Conroy-type buckle allowed further adjustment. The chest strap was folded over the shoulder strap and secured with a leather lace. The other end was folded and passed through a snap hook and swivel. The free end of the chest strap was passed through a Conroy-type buckle. A series of holes along the middle of the chest strap allowed it to be adjusted to the size of the wearer.

Model 1911, M1911A1

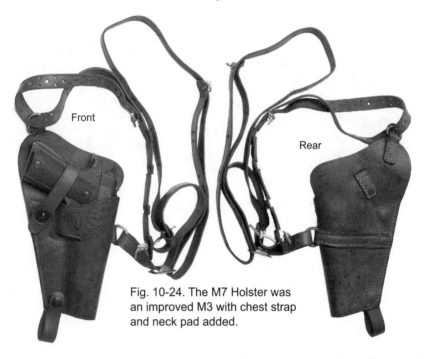

Front

Rear

Fig. 10-24. The M7 Holster was an improved M3 with chest strap and neck pad added.

M3/M7 Markings

The U.S. Ordnance Department required that both the M3 and M7 holsters be stamped with the manufacturer's name or trademark in letters 1/4 inch high and the initials "MRT" (Mildew Resistant Treatment) for those so treated, and the date of treatment in letters 1/4 inch high, see Figure 10-25. In practice most, but not all, M3s and M7s, like the Model 1916 holster, were "stamped" with the letters "US," the manufacturer's name and date of manufacture.

Fig. 10-25. Markings on the back of the M3 and M7 holsters.

Military and Commercial Pistols

		Table 10-1		
		Holsters for Model 1911/1911A1 Pistols		
Manufacturer	**Model**	**Date or Part Number (1)**	**Marks (2)**	**Color**
Hip Holsters				
Pre-World War I				
Rock Island Arsenal	1912 Mounted U.S. Army U.S.M.C.	1912-1915	US (in oval) H.E.K. USMC (in oval)	Russet
Unknown	1912 Mounted U.S.M.C.	Undated	USMC (in oval)	Russet
Unknown	1912 Dismounted U.S.M.C.	Undated	USMC (in oval)	Russet
Modified from Model 1916	1912 Dismounted U.S.M.C., Signal Corps	Undated or Hoyt 1918	US (in oval)	Russet
Abercrombie & Fitch (3)	1912 Mounted U.S. Army	None	US (in oval)	Russet
World War I				
A-K-C	1916	1918	US (in oval)	Russet
A.L.P. CO	1916	1918	US (in oval)	Russet
Anton	1916	1918	US (in oval) F.W.T.	Russet
Boyt	1916	None	U.S. (in oval) E.T.C.	Russet
Brauer Bros	1916	1917, 1918	US (in oval)	Russet
Brown	1916	?	US (in oval)	Russet
Clinton	1916	1917, 1918	US (in oval) F.W.T.	Russet
Crump	1916	None	US (in oval)	Russet
F.I.E.	1916	1917	US (in oval)	Russett
Graton and Knight (G&K)	1916	1917, 1918	US (in oval) J.A.O. A.G.	Russet

Model 1911, M1911A1

Table 10-1, cont. Holsters for Model 1911/1911A1 Pistols				
Manufacturer	**Model**	**Date or Part Number (1)**	**Marks (2)**	**Color**
Hoyt	1916	1917 (rear), 1918 (front)	U.S. (In oval) J.J.M.	Russet
Ladrew	1916	None	US (in oval)	Russet
Rock Island Arsenal	1916	1916, 1917	US (in oval)	Russet
S&R Co (Sears & Roebuck)	1916	1917, 1918	US (in oval) J.T., J.P.C. L.N.O.	Russet
Warren	1916	1917, 1918	US (in oval) J.A.O.	Russet
Unknown	1916	(None)	US (in oval) G.E.B.	Russet
Pre-World War I Patent Holsters, Private Purchase				
Audley Patent, mounted and hip	None	1914-? None	AUDLEY/ PATENT/ OCT. 13. 1914	Russet
Mills, dismounted, web (U.S.M.C. model)	None	1914 MILLS (logo)	MILLS PATENT	Khaki (web)
Mills, mounted, web, (U.S. Army Model)	None	1914 MILLS (logo)	MILLS PATENT, Date (bottom)	Khaki (Web)
World War II				
Boyt	1916	1941, 1942 1943, 1944, 1945	US (in oval) Year	Russet
Brauer Bros	1916	1943, 1944	US (in oval)	Russet
Craighead	1916	1944	US (in oval)	Russet

Military and Commercial Pistols

Manufacturer	Model	Date or Part Number (1)	Marks (2)	Color
Table 10-1 , cont. Holsters for Model 1911/1911A1 Pistols				
Crump	1916	1942	US (in oval)	Russet
ENGER-KRESS	1916	1942	US (in oval) with or without year	Russet
Graton & Knight	1916	1940, 1943	US (in oval) Year	Russet
Harphan Brothers	1916		US (in oval)	Russet
H.R.C. (Canada)	Web (tan)	1942	H.R.C.	Khaki
Hunter	1916	1945	US (in oval)	Russet
Keyston Brothers	1916		US (in oval) K.B./H.A.B.	Russet
Milwaukee Saddlery Co.	1916	1942, 1943, 1944	US (in oval)	Russet
Mosser	1916		US (in oval)	Russet
ROLEN LCA	1916	1944	US (in oval)	Russet
Sears	1916	1942, 1943, 1944, 1945	US (in oval)	Russet
S.B. Co.	1916	None	US (in oval)	Russet
Textan	1916		US (in oval)	Russet
Walsh	1916	1944	US (in oval)	Russet
Warren Leather Goods	1916	None	US (in oval)	Russet
Western Mfg.	1916		US (in oval) H.A.G.	Russet
Post-World War II				
Boyt	1916	7791466	US (in oval) Part Number	Black
Bolen Leather Products	1916	7791466	US (in oval) Prod./7791466	Black
Bucheimer	1916	7791466	US (in oval)	Black
Cathay Enterprises	1916	7791466	US (in oval)	Black

Model 1911, M1911A1

Table 10-1 , cont.				
Holsters for Model 1911/1911A1 Pistols				
Manufacturer	**Model**	**Date or Part Number (1)**	**Marks (2)**	**Color**
Hunter Leather Company	1916	7791466	US (in oval)	Black
Nordic Manufacturing	1916	7791466	US (in oval)	Black
Warren	1916		US (in oval)	Black
Bianchi	M-12	See text	See text	Green
Shoulder Holsters				
World War II				
Boyt U.S.	M3/M7	1943, 1944, 1945	US (in oval) US or USN year or none	Russet
Boyt (U.S.M.C.)	M3/M7	1943,1944, 1945	USMC (in oval) U.S.M.C./ year or none	Russet
ENGER-KRESS	M3	1943-1945	US (in oval) U.S.	Russet
Sears	M3	1942, 1943, 1944, 1945	US (in oval) SEARS SADDLERY/1943-1944	Russet
Post-World War II				
Bloomberg	1916	None	M.R.T./month/year	Black
Boyt	M7	1944 – 1970s	US (in oval) U.S./ no year	Russet/ Black
Bucheimer	M3	7791527	US (in oval)	Black
Bucheimer	M7	7791527	US (in oval)	Black
ENGER-KRESS	M7	7791527	US (in oval) U.S.	Black
Hunter		7791527	US (in oval)	Black
INTER-ORDNANCE (?)	M7	7791527	US (in oval)	Russet
KPM		7791527	US (in oval)	Black

Military and Commercial Pistols

Manufacturer	Model	Date or Part Number (1)	Marks (2)	Color
Table 10-1 , cont. Holsters for Model 1911/1911A1 Pistols				
General Officer Holsters				
Bucheimer	Commercial—Deputy		DEPUTY/ BUCHEIMER/ VALENCIA/CALIF./ CLARK/B16-74/ PAT.3.200.022	Black

1. Other dates may be noted as well as those listed.
2. All holsters purchased by the U.S. Army Ordnance Department were required to have the maker's name and year of manufacture stamped on the back. Not all contractors included the year.
3. Probably a commercial holster sold to officers.
GENERAL Note: "MRT" for Mildew Resistant Treatment marked on some WWII holsters after 1943. Some also dated.

NONREGULATION HOLSTERS FOR THE MODEL 1911/1911A1

Within months of the adoption of the Model 1911 pistol, independent manufacturers began turning out holsters for both the commercial market and as improvements on the military's designs. Chief among them were the Mills Woven Cartridge Belt Company of Worcester, Massachusetts, see Figure 10-26. They designed a holster using their patented weaving process. It was field-tested and found not to be as serviceable as the leather Model 1912 holster. The chief complaints were that the woven canvas shrunk when wet, made it very difficult to draw the pistol when the holster was wet, and also accelerated rusting when wet. Also if the brass cap on the bottom of the holster was dented or torn off, the holster became unserviceable. After a third test with much the same results, the Ordnance Department informed the Mills company that

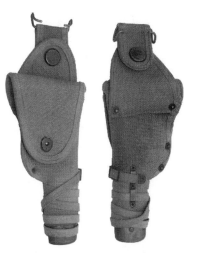

Fig. 10-26. Mills Woven Cartridge Belt Company Army web holster. Although never officially adopted, it was sold commercially. Mark Esslinger collection.

403

Model 1911, M1911A1

the holster would not be purchased. But from the number of them available, it appears that many officers and even some enlisted men preferred the woven canvas holster and purchased them privately. Sears & Roebuck offered this holster in their catalog in the 1920s.

Between 1914 and 1918, the Mills company manufactured a web holster which they referred to as the "U.S.M.C. Woven Automatic Pistol Holster for the Model 1911 Pistol," see Figure 10-27. The holster had been submitted to the Marine Corps which had expressed some interest in it, but it was never adopted. The British and Canadian military purchased an unknown quantity of them during World War I. They were advertised in the Mills, Bannerman, Sears Roebuck catalogs for a number of years after World War I.

In 1932, the Rock Island Arsenal experimented with a woven canvas holster. The holster, a fair duplicate of the Model 1916 holster in canvas, was approved as a substitute standard but was not produced.

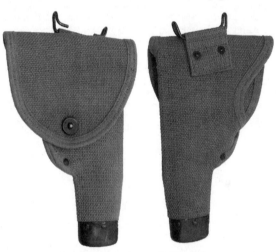

Fig. 10-27. Mills Woven Cartridge Belt Company called this fabric holster the "U.S.M.C. Automatic Pistol Holster," but it was never adopted by the Marine Corps. Mark Esslinger collection.

During World War II, the Canadian Army purchased woven canvas holsters for issue with the Colt Model 1911 and the Inglis-Browning P35 pistols (these holsters are described below), as was done by the British military.

Other designs were submitted over the years to the Ordnance Department using various materials including rubberized fabric and plastic. None of these holsters were ever adopted or issued, except for trials, to the soldier. The reader is referred to Edward Scott Meadows' excellent book, *U.S. Military Holsters and Pistol Cartridge Boxes,* for a more detailed discussion.

Military and Commercial Pistols

HOLSTERS FOR SOME OTHER MILITARY SERVICES

A wide range of commercial holsters for the Model 1911/1911A1 have been produced over the past century, but only a very few types for the U.S. and Allied or friendly military services. Selected examples are described below.

Argentine Holsters

The Argentine military developed a flap holster with a magazine pocket for the Model 1927 Sistema Colt in that year. It was very well made of fine harness leather and dyed brown, see Figure 10-28. The holster was also used for the Sistema Ballester-Rigaud and Sistema Ballester-Molina pistols which were variations on the Model 1927. In the 1950s, the holsters issued to the Army were

Fig. 10-28. Argentine Model 1927 leather holster.

dyed green. Naval and Air Force holsters continued to be dyed brown. In the late 1940s and early 1950s a woven canvas holster was also issued that carried the three .45 ACP caliber pistols and the 9 mm Browning High Power, see Figure 10-29.

British Commonwealth Holsters

During World War I, British officers and others who carried the Model 1911 pistol generally did so in a commercially purchased holster, as the standard issue holster for the .455 Mk VI revolver would not fit the Model 1911. In a photograph taken on December 29, 1915, Winston Churchill, who was then

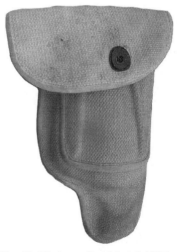

Fig. 10-29. Argentine Model 1927 fabric holster.

Model 1911, M1911A1

Fig. 10-30. The Royal Air Force Model 1927 Mills Holster was issued to aircrew for the .45 pistol, and later for the Inglis-Browning 9 mm pistol. Left, WW II issue; right, post-WW II issue in darker blue.

commanding a battalion of the Royal Scots Fusiliers in France, appears to be carrying his privately purchased Model 1911 in his left jacket pocket.

By 1927, the majority of Model 1911s in British military service were in the Royal Air Force. The Mills Company designed a holster for the RAF that was made of blue woven fabric, see Figure 10-30. This holster continued to be issued to 1947 when the Model 1911A1 was declared obsolete and withdrawn from service.

The holster resembles that issued for the .38/200 Enfield No. 2 Mk I Revolver during World War II but can be distinguished by the wooden plug in the bottom.

A similar, but more elaborate holster was issued by the Canadian military but can usually be distinguished by its tan color and fabric plug. Most were marked "H.R.C." and the year of manufacture, see Figure 10-31. These holsters were also used by other Commonwealth forces during and immediately after World War II

Fig. 10-31. Canadian Army web fabric holster for the Model 1911A1 and Inglis-Browning P35 pistols. This example is marked "H.R.C. 1942."

Military and Commercial Pistols

for both the Model 1911A1 and the Ballester-Molinas. They continued in use when the British Commonwealth changed to the Inglis-Browning.

South Vietnamese Holsters

During the war in Vietnam, the South Vietnamese government issued contracts to companies in both South Vietnam and Taiwan to produce military uniforms and equipment. A copy of the Model 1916 holster was manufactured in country and issued to those officers, noncommissioned officers, and special operations forces which were armed with the Model 1911A1, see Figure 10-32.

Fig. 10-32. South Vietnamese Army holster for the Model 1911A1. Ed Cote collection.

U.S. Constabulary Holsters

One of the more interesting, and lesser-known, military units of the U.S Armed Forces was established in 1946 in the American sectors of West Germany and Austria. Designated the U.S. Constabulary, it was a paramilitary police unit composed of volunteers from the 1st and 4th Armored Divisions and commanded by Major General Ernest N. Harmon. It was organized along the lines of a mechanized cavalry unit; its function was to serve as an augmented military police unit to maintain both military and civil security and to patrol the borders of the American sector. The Constabulary force wore a uniform slightly different than that of the regular army at the time. The military police component was issued a holster for the Model 1911A1 pistol that was identical to the Model 1916 holster but nominally, without the "US" marking. Because of the difficulty

407

Model 1911, M1911A1

the Constabulary had in obtaining equipment, these unmarked holsters may have been privately purchased or obtained by the Constabulary outside of normal Army supply services. It was worn on the belt with a

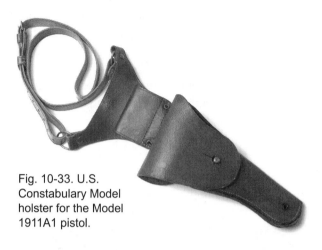

Fig. 10-33. U.S. Constabulary Model holster for the Model 1911A1 pistol.

Type 1 or Type 2 Suspension and Shoulder Strap that went over the left shoulder, see Figure 10-33. The Constabulary worked closely with West German federal and local police and was disbanded in 1952.

Survival Vests

At least three variations of a survival vest were issued for air crew during World War II and after. The intent was to provide the crewman with everything he would need to survive if shot down behind enemy lines. Figure 10-34 shows the survival vest issued to U.S. Army Air Force air crewmen during World War II. It was made of medium-weight canvas dyed olive green. It had pockets for

Fig. 10-34. U.S.A.A.F. Survival Vest issued to air crew during WWII. Ed Cote collection.

Military and Commercial Pistols

rations, ammunition (the .45 ACP M15 Shot Cartridge), maps, water purification tablets, first- aid kit, combat/survival knife, and other items. When loaded with equipment, ammunition, knife and pistol, the vest was bulky and restrictive and more popular with bomber crew than fighter pilots who had less room to move around.

Other designs were also tested by the Army Air Force, Navy and Marines for use by aircrew but not adopted.

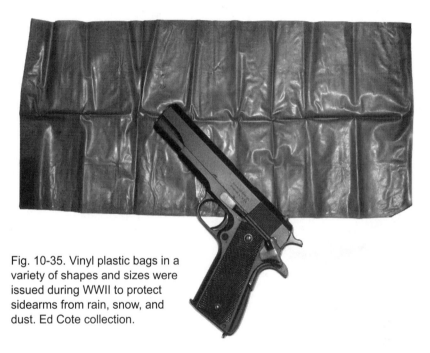

Fig. 10-35. Vinyl plastic bags in a variety of shapes and sizes were issued during WWII to protect sidearms from rain, snow, and dust. Ed Cote collection.

Pistol Protector

During World War II, a variety of vinyl plastic pockets and bags were issued to soldiers armed with pistols and revolvers. The soldier was intended to put the sidearm in the bag, some of which were shaped like holsters, and close it so that it was protected from rain, snow, or dust. The sidearm was then carried in the regular holster. Figure 10-35 shows one such vinyl protector that was issued to the U.S. Army Air Force air crew. It was a simple rectangular bag. The pistol was inserted butt first and the bottom rolled or folded up to make a waterproof or dust proof enclosure.

Model 1911, M1911A1

FABRIC MAGAZINE POCKETS

Both leather and woven canvas magazine pockets (the correct Ordnance Department designation was "pocket") were manufactured for the Model 1911/1911A1 pistol under contract to the U.S. Army Ordnance Department. The woven magazine pockets are by far more numerous than the leather magazine pockets.

Fabric Magazine Pocket Types

Seven types of magazine pockets were manufactured during the U.S. military service use of the pistol. All had two pockets woven or sewn to a canvas back. A flap was sewn to the back of the magazine pocket at the base and at the top of the pocket. The sides were left unsewn so that the magazine pocket could be slipped over a pistol or mounted rifle belt. The flap was folded over the top of the magazine pockets. The end of the flap was cut into a triangular shape and two snaps closed over, one for each magazine pocket. A snap closure was riveted to the outside of the flap passing over the ammunition belt so that it could be secured to a stud on the belt to hold it in place. The woven magazine pocket (Types 1-4) were manufactured by the Mills Woven Cartridge Belt Company from their first contract in February 1912 through 1919 for the U.S. Army, Marine Corps, U.S. Navy and Coast Guard. The fourth type was also manufactured by another company, Russell.

Fig. 10-36. The Mills Woven Cartridge Belt Company inserted this warning into every magazine pocket they manufactured.

An early complaint against the fabric magazine pockets was that they were not as waterproof as the leather pockets and promoted rusting. The Mills company packed a slip of paper in each magazine pocket they manufactured, warning the soldier about rusting and suggesting that they keep magazines well oiled. They continued to insert the slip of paper in each magazine pocket until their production ended after World War I, see Figure 10-36.

Military and Commercial Pistols

The **Type 1** magazine pocket can be identified as follows: 1) Rimless eagle snaps were used to close the flap, 2) the flap was double layered, 3) no snap for securing pouch to the web belt was used, and 4) the snaps on the flap were not reinforced. These pouches were made in 1912-1914 for two contracts, see Figure 10-37.

Type 2 magazine pocket: 1) Rimmed eagle snaps, 2) double layered flap, 3) no snap for securing the pocket to the web belt, 4) unreinforced snaps on the flap, 5) the bottom of each magazine pocket was gathered or puckered to ease the fit of the magazine. The majority of the Type 2 magazine pockets were manufactured in 1914 through 1916, see Figure 10-38. The male

Fig. 10-37. Magazine Pocket, Type 1. Rimless eagle snaps. The pocket was green in color. Craig Riesch collection.

portion of the snap was reinforced with a washer starting in 1915.

Type 3 magazine pocket: 1) Rimmed eagle snaps, 2) single layered flap, 3) a snap for securing the pocket to the pistol web belt was installed, 4) flap folded over to reinforce the snaps, 5) puckered pocket bottom, 6) bottom reinforced with a double row of stitching. The majority were manufactured in 1916-1917, see Figure 10-39. U.S.M.C Type 3 magazine pouches were made with an Eagle/Globe/Anchor snap.

Type 4 magazine pocket: 1) Lift-the-Dot type fastener replaced the snap fasteners over each pocket, 2) single layered flap, 3) snap for securing the pocket to the web belt installed, 4) flap folded over to reinforce the snaps, 5) puckered pocket bottom, 6) bottom not reinforced with a double row of stitching. This is the most common World War I magazine pocket and was manufactured from 1917 into 1919 by Mills and by Russell, see Figure 10-40.

Model 1911, M1911A1

NOTE: The Type 1 through 4 magazine pockets were of interwoven construction, i.e., the backing and pocket were woven together, not sewn together. The Type 2 magazine pocket was also made with the Eagle-Globe-Anchor for the U.S. Marine Corps.

Type 5 magazine pocket: Similar to the Mills Type 4 but manufactured by various contractors to the Ordnance Department during World War I. They are mostly distinguished by a lighter weight of canvas flap than the rest of the body, by the manufacturer's marking, usually a name or logotype, the month and year of manufacture, and the fact that the pockets were stitched to the backing, see Figure 10-41.

The **Type 6** magazine pocket was properly designated the "Pocket Magazine, Double Web, M1923." It was similar to the Mills Type 4 except that the bottoms of each pocket were no longer gathered or puckered. Instead of the back and pockets being woven in one piece like the Mills products, the separate pockets were sewn to the backing. The body was formed of one piece of canvas, folded back on itself to form the backing. The edge of the flap was again folded on itself to reinforce the single Lift-the-Dot fastener. The snap was retained on the inside of the backing to attach the pocket to the web belt. The Type 6 was manufactured by various manufacturers during World War II in khaki color only, see Figure 10-42.

The **Type 7** was similar to the Type 6 but was newly designated the "Pocket Magazine, Double Web, Enlisted, Model-1923." The pocket flap was folded back on itself and sewn for reinforcement. The back was doubled to allow it to slide over a belt, and the fabric was dyed Army OD green. This magazine pocket was manufactured during the Korean War period, see Figure 10-43.

The **Type 8** magazine pocket was similar to the Type 6 except the separate backing which formed the belt loop was removed. In its place, a rectangle of fabric was sewn to hold two ALICE clips. This permitted the magazine pocket to be removed without the soldier having to remove the web belt. Manufactured after 1956 as the "Pocket, Ammunition, Magazine, M-1956."

Military and Commercial Pistols

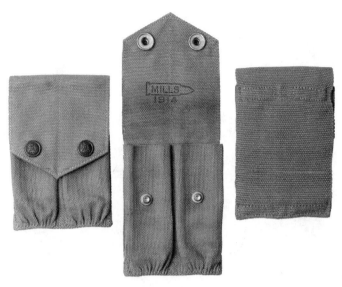

Fig. 10-38. Magazine Pocket, Type 2. Rimmed eagle snaps, bottom of pockets gathered, but the flap was not reinforced. Green in color. Craig Riesch collection.

Fig. 10-39. Magazine Pocket, Type 3. Rimmed eagle snaps, snap for securing pocket to belt, and reinforced flap. Bottom of pockets reinforced with double row of stitching. Male portion of snap reinforced (arrow). Green in color. Craig Riesch collection.

Model 1911, M1911A1

Fig. 10-40. Magazine Pocket, Type 4 of interwoven construction. Lift-the-Dot fastener. Khaki in color. Craig Riesch collection.

Fig. 10-41. Magazine Pocket, Type 5. Manufactured by various subcontractors during World War I. The flap was sewn as a separate piece. Notice the difference in texture between the flap and the body. Khaki in color. Craig Riesch collection.

Fig. 10-42. "Pocket Magazine, Double Web, M1923." Manufactured in small quantities before and in great quantity during World War II. Khaki in color. Type 6. Craig Riesch collection.

Fig. 10-43. "Pocket Magazine, Double Web, M-1923." Manufactured during and after the Korean War to 1956. Dark OD Green in color. Type 7. Craig Riesch collection.

Military and Commercial Pistols

The Type 8 magazine pocket was manufactured in two variations. The **1st Variation** was made of canvas (Figure 10-44), while the **2nd Variation** was made of nylon, see Figure 10-45.

Type 9 magazine pockets were also manufactured after World War II for other branches of the service—Navy, Air Force, and the Coast Guard. These were marked on the back like the Type 6 or 7 magazine pouches as described below but were usually not marked "U.S." on the flap.

U.S.M.C. Magazine Pouch

The U.S. Marine Corps designed and used a magazine pouch during World War II and the Korean War that would hold either two M1 Carbine magazines or two .45 ACP magazines. USMC usage was "pouch" and not "pocket." To hold the narrower .45 ACP magazines in place, the bottom of each magazine holder was stitched at the bottom. The pouches were khaki and marked "**U.S.M.C.**"

Fig. 10-44. "Pocket, Ammo, Magazine, M-1956." Made of canvas fabric with ALICE clips and Army OD green in color. Type 8, 1st Variation. Craig Riesch collection.

with the manufacturer's name and date on the back, see Figure 10-46.

Markings—Fabric Magazine Pockets

Fabric magazine pockets for the Model 1911 were manufactured by Mills Woven Cartridge Belt Company and marked with indelible ink on the inside flap with "**MILLS**" inside the outline of a rifle cartridge. Specifications

Fig. 10-45. "Pocket, Ammo, Magazine, M-1956." Made of nylon, Army green in color. Type 8, 2nd Variation. Craig Riesch collection.

also called for the year of manufacture to be marked as well; the month

415

Model 1911, M1911A1

was added in 1916. Starting with the **Type 4**, the Mills company added patent information below the logotype: **PAT. JAN 28, '01-JUL 16, '07** before September 1918 and **PAT. JULY. 16, '07-OCT. 22, '13** after.

Russell products had the company name inked on the back, and later, on the inside of the flap, inside an oval plus the month and year of manufacture.

Fig. 10-46. This magazine pouch (not pocket) was made for the U.S. Marine Corps and was designed to hold two 15-round M1 Carbine magazines or two .45 ACP magazines. All were marked "U.S.M.C." Craig Riesch collection.

Manufacturing names observed on magazine pockets to the end of World War I include: "Mills" "Russell," "R.H. Long," "P.B. & Co.," "L.C.C. & Co.," and "F.S.F."

Manufacturing names observed on M1923 pockets include: "Avery," "Boyle," "E.O. Inc.," "Ero Mfg. Co.," "Hoff Mfg.," and "S. Froehlich, Co. Inc."

Starting with the **Type 6**, Model of 1923, the initials **U.S.** were stenciled on the flap above the fastener. The maker's name and date of manufacture was marked on the back.

The **Type 7** magazine pocket was stenciled on the back: **POCKET, MAGAZINE/DOUBLE WEB, ENLISTED** (or **E.M.**), **M-1923**/DSA part number/stock number. The initials **U.S.** (with and without periods) were stenciled on the flap. The initials "E.M." stood for "enlisted men."

The **Type 8, 1st Variation** magazine pocket was marked **U.S.** on the flap. The back was marked: **POCKET, AMMO MAGAZINE**/DSA number/lot number and NSN (National Stock Number).

Military and Commercial Pistols

The **Type 8, 2nd Variation** magazine pockets exhibit a variety of markings including **POCKET, AMMO MAGAZINE/OD7 .45 CAL/ DSA 100-M57 (or date of manufacture)/865 782 239.**

LEATHER MAGAZINE POCKETS

Leather magazine pockets were made concurrently with fabric magazine pockets. They were at first intended to be worn for parade or dress by all soldiers issued the Model 1911 pistol on the leather garrison belt.

Four types of leather magazine pockets were issued.

The **Type 1** leather magazine pocket was made of russet harness leather and was similar in appearance to the fabric magazine pouch. The back, flap, and pockets were cut from separate pieces of leather. The pockets were folded into shape and sewn to the back. The flap was riveted with four brass rivets at the corners and also sewn around the

Fig. 10-47. Leather Magazine Pocket. Early rimless snap on the left (1913-1914) and rimmed eagle snap on the right (1914-1915). Craig Riesch collection.

edge for reinforcement. The flap was fastened by a fastener placed between the two pockets.

Two variations were manufactured. The **1st Variation** had a rimless eagle button fastener, see Figure 10-47, left. The **2nd Variation** had a rimmed eagle button fastener, see Figure 10-47, right.

Both variations were manufactured at Rock Island Arsenal, the 1st Variation in 1913-1914 and the 2nd Variation in 1914-1915.

417

Model 1911, M1911A1

The **Type 2** leather magazine pocket was also made of russet harness leather and was quite similar to the Type 1, 1st and 2nd Variations, but the eagle button fastener was replaced with a single Lift-the-Dot fastener. The rear of the flap was lengthened to within one inch of the bottom of the pocket. The Type 2 leather magazine pocket was manufactured at the Jeffersonville Quartermaster Depot from 1922 to the end of World War II. The Type 2 leather magazine pocket was also made by a small number of contractors during World War II. Figure 10-48 shows an example manufactured by St. Paul Saddlery Company in 1942.

The **Type 3** leather magazine pocket was manufactured after World War II by a variety of subcontractors including Milwaukee Saddlery and L-F Company. They were similar to the Type 2 leather magazine pocket but made of black-dyed leather from 1956 through 1985 when production of the .45 ACP magazine pocket ended.

Fig. 10-48. Leather Magazine Pocket with the Lift-the-Dot fastener. This example was made in 1942.

All were marked with the marker's name and date. Rock Island Arsenal Type 1 and Jeffersonville Type 2 magazine pockets will also show an inspector's initials. Post-World War II Type 3 magazine pockets will show the manufacturer's name, military part number and government contract number.

The **Type 4** leather magazine pocket was made of black leather and was similar to the Type 3. It was intended for use with the General Officer Pistol M15. All were made by Bucheimer of Valencia, California, in 1971-1972, refer to Plate 8, color portfolio.

Military and Commercial Pistols

BELTS

The double hook fastener on the Model 1912 holster was designed to be used on a wide variety of ammunition belts worn by American military personnel of all branches. Brass eyelets were inletted into the top and bottom edges of all ammunition belts from 1903 into which the double hook fastener could be inserted. The same double hook attachment was used on canteens, first-aid pouches, etc. All pistol and cartridge belts from 1903 through 1981 were made with a wire hook and "T" fastener in place of a belt buckle. Variations in the "T" usually are the manufacturing artifacts by various makers.

Color and pocket fastener variations can help to identify periods of use. Rimless eagle snaps were in use from 1903 to mid-1914; rimmed eagle snaps were used from mid-1914 to March 1917. After, the "Lift-the-Dot" fastener was used to 1981. Belt and pocket colors were: khaki, 1903-1909; dark green 1909-1914; pea green from 1914-1916; khaki from late 1916-1943; OD green from 1943-1956; dark green from 1956-1984.

Pistol Belts

The original **Model 1910 Pistol Belt, 1st Variation** was manufactured with four pockets for carrying ammunition for the Model 1909 .45 (Long Colt) caliber revolver. It had rimless eagle snaps and was green in color. The belt had a T-closure in place of a belt buckle. All metal parts were darkened brass. It was manufactured circa 1910 to 1912, see Figure 10-49.

Fig. 10-49. Model 1910 Pistol Belt, 1st Variation, with four pockets for .45 revolver ammunition. Craig Riesch collection.

Model 1911, M1911A1

NOTE: All webbed pistol belts for the Model 1911 and 1911A1 used the T-closure as a buckle through the advent of the M1981 LC1 and LC2 belts.

The **Model 1910 Pistol Belt, 2nd Variation** was made without the four revolver ammunition pockets. The Magazine Pocket was slipped over the belt. Note the lack of eyelets through the center of the left hand side of the belt that were used on later types. Only one keeper was used. This belt was manufactured circa 1912-1913, see Figure 10-50.

Fig. 10-50. Model 1910 Pistol Belt, 2nd Variation, without the four revolver ammunition pockets and no center row of eyelets on the left. Craig Riesch collection.

The **Model 1910 Pistol Belt, 3rd Variation**. Similar to the 2nd Variation but with the center row of eyelets added on the left side. Only one keeper was used. Made circa 1913-1915, see Figure 10-51.

The **Model 1910 Pistol Belt, 4th Variation** was similar to the 3rd but a rimmed eagle snap was added to the belt to secure the magazine pocket. Made 1916-1917. Only one keeper was used. U.S.M.C pistol belts were made with an Eagle/Globe/Anchor snap, see Figure 10-52.

The **Model 1910 Pistol Belt, 5th Variation** was similar to the 4th Varia-

Military and Commercial Pistols

Fig. 10-51. Model 1910 Pistol Belt, 3rd Variation, made without the four revolver ammunition pockets but with the complete center row of eyelets. Craig Riesch collection.

Fig. 10-52. Model 1910 Pistol Belt, 4th Variation. Eagle snap added to secure magazine pocket. Craig Riesch collection.

Fig. 10-53. Model 1910 Pistol Belt, 5th Variation. Plain snap substituted for the eagle snap; second keeper added.

Model 1911, M1911A1

tion except a plain snap was substituted for the eagle snap to secure the magazine pocket. A second keeper was added by 1918 to all subsequent pistol belts. Manufactured circa 1917-1936. see Figure 10-53.

NOTE: Some Model 1910 pistol belts were also manufactured with a saber chape for mounted troops and officers, see Figure 10-54. Those belts without the saber chape were issued to dismounted troops.

The **Model 1910 Pistol Belt, 6th Variation** (aka Model 1936) was manufactured from circa 1936 to 1957. It had two keepers and was marked **U.S.** on the left side, see Figure 10-55.

Fig. 10-54. A saber chape was added to those Model 1910 pistol belts issued for mounted troops. Craig Riesch collection.

From 1936 to early 1943, the belt was Army tan; from 1943 to 1956, the belt was Army OD Green. The belt had two flat keepers that were

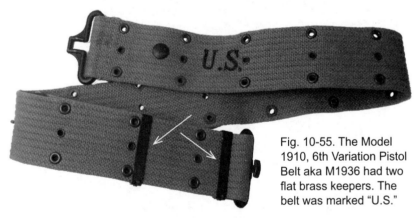

Fig. 10-55. The Model 1910, 6th Variation Pistol Belt aka M1936 had two flat brass keepers. The belt was marked "U.S."

stamped from sheet brass and later, steel. The late-war-period keeper was folded and the top and bottom were connected by a tab that was crimped in place, see Figure 10-56.

422

Military and Commercial Pistols

The **Model 1956 Pistol Belt** was dyed Army OD green. It had two "crimped tab" brass keepers that were "stepped" to allow them to pass over the belt eyelets more easily than the flat brass keepers made previously. The Model 1956 was manufactured circa 1956 to 1981, see Figure 10-57.

Fig. 10-56. Close-up of keepers used on the Model 1936 pistol belt.

Model 1972 Individual Equipment Belt
This belt was similar to the Model 1956 Individual Equipment Belt except it was made of nylon rather than woven cotton. Metal parts were made of brass.

Model 1981 LC1 and LC2 Individual Equipment Belt
This belt was first issued by the U.S. military before the adoption of the M9 Beretta. The belt was made of nylon without the center row of small eyelets for the adjusting hooks on the ends of the belt. The LC1 belt used the standard hook and tab closure but the LC2 used a new plastic belt plate made of gray plastic. The keeper had a raised tongue that slid into a slot on the buckle. The belt size could be adjusted from both ends using a folding toothed clamp, see Figure 10-58.

Cartridge Belts
Cartridge belts were issued to enlisted troops, mounted or dismounted. Broadly speaking, all mounted troops of the Cavalry and mounted artillery branches were issued the Model 1911 or Model 1911A1. All non-commissioned officers of the infantry and other branches were issued the Model 1911 or Model 1911A1.

The **Model 1903 Cavalry Belt, 1st Variation** had nine pockets for the Caliber .30, M1903, later Caliber .30, M1906 rifle cartridge. The magazine pocket was slipped over the left side of the belt. Rimless snaps were used on this belt. A leather chape with a wire attaching point for the saber was used with this belt, see Figure 10-59.

Model 1911, M1911A1

Fig. 10-57. The Model 1956 Pistol Belt had stepped keepers to allow them to pass over the eyelets more easily.

Fig. 10-58. The Model 1981 LC2 pistol belt.

Fig. 10-59. The Model 1903 Cavalry Belt, 1st Variation, with nine rifle ammunition pockets. The magazine pocket for the Model 1911 was worn on the left side. Craig Riesch collection.

Military and Commercial Pistols

Fig. 10-60. The Model 1903 Infantry Belt, 2nd Variation, with nine rifle ammunition pockets and the magazine pocket for the Model 1911 slipped over the left side. Craig Riesch collection.

Fig. 10-61. The revolver ammunition pockets on the left side of the Model 1909 Cavalry Belt were removed to make room for the .45 ACP magazine pocket (arrow). Craig Riesch collection.

A

B

Fig. 10-62. The Model 1910 Mounted Belt, 1st Variation, two revolver ammunition pockets (A) on either side. 2nd Variation (below) made without revolver cartridge pockets, allowing space for a .45 ACP magazine pocket (B). Craig Riesch collection.

Model 1911, M1911A1

The **Model 1903 Infantry Belt**, **2nd Variation** also had nine pockets for rifle cartridges. While neither of the Model 1903 belts were designed to be worn with the Model 1911, many belts were still in service when the new pistol was issued and so they would have been worn both by regulars and National Guardsmen. This variation did or did not have the saber chape, depending on whether issued to cavalry or infantry, and was made with rimless eagle buttons, see Figure 10-60.

The **Model 1909 Cavalry Belt** had four horizontal pockets, two on the left side and two on the right side to carry .45 (long Colt) cartridges for the Model 1909 Revolver. The pockets on the left side were cut off and the magazine pocket was slipped over the belt in their place, see Figure 10-61.

The **Model 1910 Mounted Belt** also had four horizontal pockets, two on the left side and two on the right side for .45 revolver cartridges which were removed from the left side when the belt was issued for use with the Model 1911 pistol. The Model 1910 was adjustable for waist size at the back. Four variations of this belt were made.

The **1st Variation** was made with the four revolver ammunition pockets, two on each end. Both the revolver and rifle ammunition pockets were interwoven, circa 1910-1913, see Figure 10-62, above. The belt was dyed green and had rimless eagle snaps. The **2nd Variation** was made without the revolver pocket but with space for the magazine pocket on the left side. The right side had rifle ammunition pockets. The rifle ammunition pockets were interwoven with the belt, circa 1914-1918, refer to Figure 10-62, below. The **3rd Variation** was the 1st Variation with the revolver pockets cut off the left side to make space for the magazine pocket.

The **4th Variation** of the Model 1910 Mounted Belt was manufactured by various contractors in 1918. The magazine pockets for the .45 ACP and .30-06 cartridges were made of lighter-weight canvas and sewn to the belt, see Figure 10-63. All were khaki-colored and had Lift-the-Dot fasteners.

The **Model 1912 Mounted Belt** was the first ammunition belt to be specifically designed for carrying the M1911 pistol. The space on the left

Military and Commercial Pistols

Fig. 10-63. The Model 1910 Mounted Belt, 4th Variation, was manufactured by contractors, and the pockets for ammunition were sewn to the belt. The magazine pocket slipped onto the left side. Craig Riesch collection.

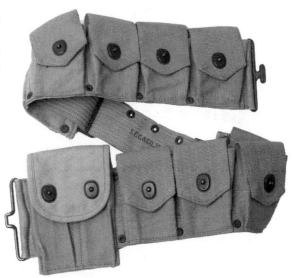

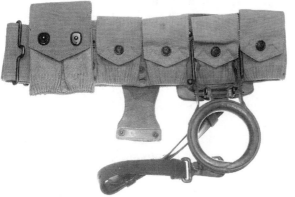

Fig. 10-64. The Model 1912 Mounted Belt was the first to be designed to carry the Model 1911 pistol in the Model 1912 holster. Craig Riesch collection.

Fig. 10-65. The Model 1918 Chauchat Rifleman's belt was manufactured with two magazine pockets for two magazines each of .45 ACP ammunition and a sheet metal cup riveted to the right side of the belt to hold the buttstock of the automatic rifle. Craig Riesch collection.

Model 1911, M1911A1

side of the belt between the hook fastener and the nine ammunition pockets which on the Model 1909 and Model 1910 Cavalry and Mounted belts had held the two-pocket revolver cartridge pouch, was now used for the Magazine Pocket. The Model 1912 Mounted Holster was attached to the right side of the belt, see Figure 10-64. This belt can easily be identified by its leather-covered rifle ring and rimmed eagle snaps. Later variations were made with Lift-the-Dot fasteners.

The **Model 1918 Chauchat** Rifleman's belt was manufactured by contractors and shipped to troops with the American Expeditionary Force in France in late 1917 and throughout 1918. The belt was designed to be used with the Chauchat machine gun, also called the Chauchat Automatic Rifle by the AEF, which fired the French 8 mm Lebel cartridge, and later, the American .30-06. Automatic riflemen were also issued the Model 1911 pistol and holster which was attached in the conventional manner. The two magazine pockets on the belt each held two .45 ACP magazines, and the Model 1916 holster could be attached to the belt. This belt was the first to have the sheet metal cup attached to the right side. In theory, the gunner mounted the Chauchat's buttstock in the cup for better control while firing from the hip as he advanced on an enemy position. The technique was somewhat suicidal and that, plus the Chauchat's inaccuracy and tendency to jam when it got hot, greatly limited the practice, see Figure 10-65.

The **Model 1918 Browning Automatic Rifle** belt was based on the earlier design for the Chauchat. It had the double magazine pocket for two .45 ACP magazines and four pockets to hold two twenty-round BAR magazines each. The sheet metal cup was made larger for the BAR's stock and the Model 1916 holster could be attached to the belt, see Figure 10-66.

The **Model 1923 Mounted Belt** was designed after World War I as an improvement on the older Model 1910 belt. It was similar to the Model 1910, 4th Variation belt but was better reinforced with larger round rivets rather than the previous oval rivets, see Figure 10-67. The middle row of eyelets was eliminated. The snaps were replaced with Lift-the-Dot fasteners and the pockets were no longer gathered at the base. The pockets had a gusset in the sides to allow room for two 5-round clips of .30-06

Military and Commercial Pistols

Fig. 10-66. The Model 1918 Browning Automatic Rifle belt was based on the Model 1918 Chauchat belt. One pocket held two .45 ACP magazines plus four pockets for BAR magazines. Craig Riesch collection.

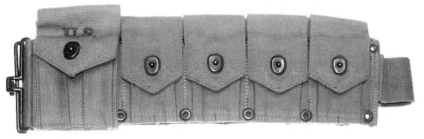

Fig. 10-67. The Model 1923 Mounted Belt was the last of the belts designed for mounted troops. This example was manufactured by Burlington Mills in 1941. Craig Riesch collection.

Fig. 10-68. The Model 1912 Cavalry Bandolier was issued to mounted troops. Twenty-one rounds of .45 ACP ammunition could be carried in the horizontal three pockets. Craig Riesch collection.

ammunition and they were sewn to the belt. Space was available on the left side of the belt for the .45 ACP magazine pocket, and the Model 1916 holster could be attached to the belt. The belt retained the T-closure and the adjusting strap at the rear, but without the grommets. The design was approved in 1923 but most were manufactured in 1940-1941.

BANDOLIERS

Bandoliers were issued to mounted troops only. They were designed before World War I and were worn crosswise over the neck and shoulder. Bandoliers had twelve vertical pockets that held one clip of .30-06 rifle ammunition and three horizontal pockets that held seven rounds of .45 ACP ammunition for the Model 1911 pistol, refer to Figure 10-68.

Designated the **Model 1912 Cavalry Bandolier**, it was made in two variations. The **1st Variation** had flat bottom pockets, eagle snap fasteners, and was contoured to the body. The **2nd Variation** was similar but was not contoured to the body and had Lift-the-Dot fasteners on the pockets, see Figure 10-69.

Fig. 10-69. Model 1912 Cavalry Bandoliers: Variation 1 eagle snap (top), and Variation 2 Lift-the-dot (bottom). Craig Riesch collection.

CHAPTER 11
AMMUNITION FOR THE MODEL 1911
AND 1911A1

A wide range of ammunition, both military and commercial, has been developed since the first experimental cartridges in 1906. A short history of various U.S. military issue cartridges is presented below. Non-military issue cartridges, and commercial loadings, and Super .38, 9 mm, and .22 rimfire, of which there are probably hundreds, are well beyond the scope of this text. The reader is referred to *History of Modern U.S. Military Small Arms Ammunition,* by Hackley, et al. for a complete discussion.

CALIBER .45 AUTOMATIC PISTOL BALL CARTRIDGE, MODEL OF 1911

The development of the .45 Automatic Pistol Cartridge began as early as 1904 when the Ordnance Department asked the Winchester Repeating Firearms Company to develop the new cartridge. Winchester produced a 200-grain round-nose-jacketed bullet in a tinned brass cartridge case.

Based on Winchester's work, the Frankford Arsenal developed two cartridges, one rimmed and the other rimless. Before much testing was accomplished and production could begin, the Ordnance Department decided on the rimless case. Unofficially designated the "Model 1906 Caliber .45 Automatic Pistol Ball Cartridge," some 10,000 were manufactured in 1906. The headstamp on the cases was "F A 4 06." The cartridge held a round-nose, jacketed, 230-grain bullet. The cartridge case was cannelured to prevent the bullet from seating itself deeper under recoil.

The following year, the Union Metallic Cartridge Company received a contract to manufacture 100,000 rounds of a similar cartridge, but with a slightly shorter case. The Ordnance Department requested that UMC use the Winchester-length case but the Frankford 230-grain bullet. No cannelure was required. The headstamp on these cases was "U.M.C. .45 A.C.P."

Again, the following year, a slight change was made to the width of the extractor groove, and UMC and Winchester were both given new production contracts for 100,000 and 350,000 cartridges respectively.

Model 1911, M1911A1

The Ordnance Department designated this cartridge the ".45 Automatic Colt Government."

In that same year, 1908, Frankford Arsenal was asked to produce 120,000 rounds for tests in the "Ely [sic] Colt Automatic Pistol." The cartridge was similar to the one manufactured by Frankford in 1906, but without the cannelure. The headstamp was "F A 11 08."

Union Metallic Cartridge Company was issued a third contract in 1909 to manufacture their 1908 bullet but with a case and bullet cannelure. This design, with two minor changes, became the "Caliber .45 Automatic Pistol Ball cartridge, Model of 1911." The changes related to a smaller primer pocket and the deletion of the bullet cannelure. The original UMC primer pocket was the same size as the primer pocket on the Caliber .30 rifle cartridge. The change was made to prevent rifle primers being used in pistol cartridges, and vice-versa.

First Production Contracts

The first production of the new .45 ACP cartridge specifically for the new Model 1911 pistol occurred in August 1911 and were headstamped "F A 8 11." It should be noted, though, that the manufacturing of the .45 ACP cartridge for testing purposes had been going on at Frankford Arsenal since 1906. The Ordnance Department ordered 600,000 cartridges in September 1911 with the headstamp "F A 9 11." All 1911 bullets had cupro-nickel jackets which gave a dull, tinned color, see Figure 11-1.

Fig. 11-1. Early Model 1911 with first-year production cartridges: the headstamps read "F A 9 11," "F A 10 11," "F A 11 11," and "F A 12 11."

The following year, the Ordnance Department approved the use of a tinned, gilding-metal-jacketed bullet. In addition to the Frankford production, Winchester and the new Remington Arms-Union Metallic Cartridge Company received contracts in 1912. Figure 11-2 shows a drawing, dated May 23,1912, of the .45 ACP cartridge case produced at the U.M.C.

432

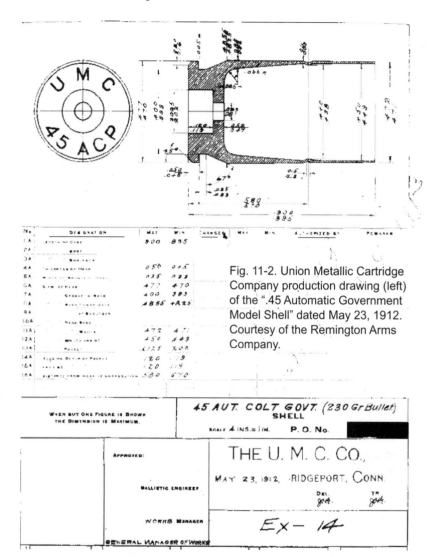

Fig. 11-2. Union Metallic Cartridge Company production drawing (left) of the ".45 Automatic Government Model Shell" dated May 23, 1912. Courtesy of the Remington Arms Company.

plant. The following year, Peters Cartridge Company and United States Cartridge Company also received production contracts.

World War I Ammunition Production
During World War I, Maxim Munitions Corporation, Pan American Munition Corporation, Peters Cartridge Company, Remington Arms-UMC,

Model 1911, M1911A1

United States Cartridge Company, and Winchester Repeating Arms Company all manufactured .45 ACP ammunition under Ordnance Department contracts. Pan American Munition only produced a few hundred rounds of the 75 million ordered; U.S. Cartridge Company ammunition had primer troubles and shipments were halted in June 1918.

In June 1917, the Ordnance Department directed that the month be dropped from the headstamp but cases as late as "10 17" have been observed. In the same year, the cartridge mouth was crimped with three circular or stab crimps to prevent the bullet in adjacent chambers from setting forward under recoil in the Model 1917 revolver. The stab crimp was used only during World War I and then only by contractors.

In April 1918, all production was directed to use shellac as a waterproofing material. Frankford and Winchester had been using shellac right along, but the other contractors had been using Japan wax which melted when stored at temperatures over 100 degrees Fahrenheit. In 1926, tinning of the bullet jacket was suspended.

Interwar Ammunition Production

During the interwar years, most ammunition for military purposes was produced at the Frankford Arsenal but contracts were also let to Winchester and Peters. The gilding-metal-jacketed bullet and the cannelured cartridge case continued in use. One problem encountered, particularly with Frankford-produced ammunition, was the double charging of cases. Bulls Eye No. 2 and Pistol Powder No. 3, both used as the propellant, were fine-grained powders that filled less than half the case. Double charging and sometimes triple charging occurred. Double charging usually provided the shooter with a surprise, but triple charging could be deadly. Frankford developed a production reloader in 1935 that could detect overcharging and it was in regular use by the following year.

In 1940, the standard issue .45 ACP ball ammunition used a 234-grain gilding-metal-jacketed, round-nose bullet in a brass cartridge case containing 5.6 grains of DuPont Pistol Powder, No. 5. The case neck was waterproofed before the bullet was inserted and a slight crimp was used to hold the bullet, if needed. The cartridge produced 820 ± 25 ft/sec and a mean radius of 2 inches at 50 yards.

In 1941, DuPont's 4768 powder was substituted. It was a bulkier powder and eliminated the threat of double or triple charging the case. It

Military and Commercial Pistols

continued in use to the end of the war. In September 1944, Western Ball Powder was also approved as a substitute.

In 1941, the cannelure in the cartridge case was eliminated but the three-point crimp continued to be used for those lots that failed the bullet pull test. The problem with bullet set back was considered very important now that large quantities of .45 ACP ammunition were also being used in the Thompson and M3 submachine guns.

CALIBER .45 AUTOMATIC PISTOL BALL CARTRIDGE, MODEL OF 1911 WORLD WAR II AMMUNITION PRODUCTION

The first contract for wartime production was actually released on October 16, 1941, to Western Cartridge Company for 50 million rounds of .45 ACP. Two more contracts quickly followed, the second to Remington Arms and the third to Winchester. All three were designated "educational contracts."

In 1942, with production on a wartime footing, three additional contracts were let to Peters Cartridge Company and Chrysler Corporation. Peters manufactured ammunition at their Kings Mills Ordnance Plant in Kings Mills, Ohio, with the first lots accepted in June 1942. But production only lasted for one month. Chrysler opened a new plant at Evansville, Indiana, and completed their first lot of ammunition in July 1942. Chrysler-Evansville could not produce enough .45 ACP ammunition, so a second plant near Evansville was opened, the Sunbeam plant. Cartridges made by the two plants can be distinguished by their headstamps—"EC" for the original Evansville plant, and "ECS" for the Evansville, Sunbeam plant.

Perhaps the most interesting development in .45 ACP ammunition during World War II was the use of steel cartridge cases and bullet jackets, see Figure 11-3. Experiments had been conducted with steel cases in 1918 and aluminum cases in the late 1920s; also aluminum and steel jacketed bullets in 1918.

In July 1942, Frankford Arsenal produced 26,000 steel cases for .45 ACP Ball ammunition for testing. A period of intensive testing followed with steel cartridge cases submitted by several manufacturers. The cases were coated with zinc to protect against rust and corrosion, but the zinc plating tended to oxidize and form a rough surface which caused feeding malfunctions in the chambers of the Model 1911A1 and

Model 1911, M1911A1

the Thompson Submachine Gun. A number of different coatings and treatments were tested and one called "Cronak" proved to resist rust and corrosion but was smooth enough to feed without causing malfunctions. Cronak, also called "iridite," is a process of applying chromium salts to plated metal surfaces. Cronak-treated steel cases were also used in the manufacture of steel M1 carbine cartridge cases, although these appear to have been used mostly for testing. The Cronak treatment was developed at the Frankford Arsenal and continued in use through the end of World War II.

The first production lot (FA 1364) of steel-jacketed bullets was

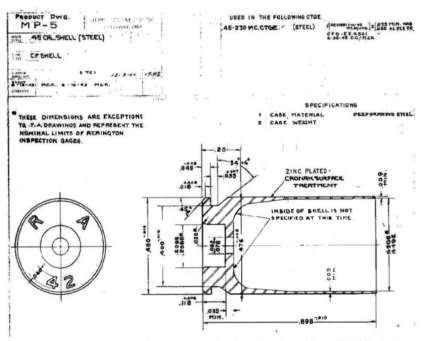

Fig. 11-3. Remington Arms Company production drawing of the .45 ACP steel cartridge case dated December 3, 1942. Courtesy of Remington Arms Company.

accepted for use on September 11, 1942. They were plated with a 0.0008-inch-thick plate of copper. The headstamp on the brass cartridge cases was "F A 4 2." In July of 1943, Frankford Arsenal changed the bullet jacket material to gilding metal (90-95% copper and 5-10% zinc). The first complete lot of gilding-metal-jacketed bullets was FA 1849 released

Military and Commercial Pistols

on August 10, 1943. Gilding metal jackets were used exclusively at Frankford Arsenal to May 1944, when copper-plated and gilding-metal-jacketed bullets were used interchangeably.

Cartridge lots containing steel cases received the prefix "S," or later, the suffix "X." If the lot contained both steel cases and steel-jacketed bullets, the suffix was "XC." Evansville manufactured the bulk of steel-cased ammunition during World War II.

Refer to Figure 11-3 for a Remington product drawing of a steel case with the headstamp, "R A 42." The steel cases were plated with zinc as a rust preventive.

The production of .45 ACP ammunition was cut back drastically in 1944 when surveys showed that the amount of ammunition required had been overestimated. Not even the additional use of the Thompson Submachine Gun or the new M3 Submachine Gun could justify the previous production schedules.

Figure 11-4 shows a comparison of cartridge types and finishes from World War I through match ammunition made in the mid-1960s.

Caliber .45 Automatic Pistol, Dummy Cartridge

The first dummy .45 ACP cartridges are thought to have been manufactured at the Frankford Arsenal in 1906. The case did not have a primer hole and the headstamp was "F A 4 06," indicating manufacture in April 1906.

Fig. 11-4. Sample .45 ACP cartridges, L-r: 1) brass case headstamped F A 5 17; 2) tinned brass case headstamped F A 31; 3) zinc-plated, Cronak-treated steel case and copper-clad steel bullet headstamped E C 42; 4) zinc-plated case, gilding-metal-clad steel bullet headstamped T W 45; 5) zinc-plated, Cronak-treated National Match Wadcutter headstamped W-W 45 AUTO.

Model 1911, M1911A1

Dummy cartridges were also made by, or for, the Hollifield Dotter training device manufactured by the Hollifield Practice Rod Company starting in 1912. The device was effective in rifle practice and was adopted by the U.S. Army for that purpose. The device trained shooters to pull the trigger evenly without jerking. A pointed rod was inserted into the barrel and rested against the dummy cartridge which had a spring-loaded stud extending through the case. When the firing pin struck the stud in the cartridge, it transmitted its force to the pointed rod which jumped forward to strike the target. The device proved far less effective in pistol practice and so was not adopted by the U.S. Army.

In early 1918, the first dummy cartridge was officially accepted for use in both the .45-caliber pistol and revolver. A standard service bullet was crimped into a tinned or untinned brass case. An inert primer was inserted and three holes were drilled near the base to indicate that it was a non-functioning cartridge. In addition to those made at Frankford Arsenal, dummy rounds were also manufactured by Remington Arms-UMC, U.S. Cartridge Company, Winchester, and Evansville (during WWII only).

During the 1920s, dummy rounds were in short supply for training and the *Cavalry School Manual on Pistol Marksmanship, 1920* provided information on preparing dummy cartridges from live ammunition.

The dummy cartridge was used primarily in live-fire training—a dummy round was mixed with live ammunition and loaded into a magazine by the instructor. The purpose was to detect "flinching" when firing. If the shooter jerked the pistol when the dummy round was "struck" simulating firing, the instructor could easily detect the problem and work with the shooter to correct it. To be most effective, the dummy round had to resemble the live rounds closely. In 1920, the Frankford Arsenal developed a dummy cartridge that used all service components. The case had one small hole at the base and a heavy stab crimp to hold the bullet. The case head was blackened for identification purposes. The following year, the Ordnance Department revised the specifications of the dummy cartridge so that it could be used for inspection, function, and training—proper loading and unloading techniques—and live-fire training. The cartridge, designated "Cal. .45 Dummy Cartridge, Model 1921," had a tinned case (later cases were not tinned) with three holes near the base, crimping cannelure, and three stab crimps spaced at 120 degrees around the case mouth to hold the service bullet. This cartridge, with minor variations in hole placement, crimp, and case finish,

Military and Commercial Pistols

continued in official use until the .45 pistol was withdrawn from service, see Figure 11-5.

During World War II, new, as well as fired cases with expended primers, were used to manufacture dummy .45 ACP cartridges. The cases were made of zinc-plated brass or steel and had two or three holes. Starting in August 1943, steel cases without primers were also used.

Fig. 11-5. Left, Cal. .45 Dummy Cartridge, M1921; right, a dummy cartridge (F A 18) made from a live round in the 1920s.

Caliber .45 Automatic Pistol Cartridge, Blank Cartridges

Work on a blank .45 ACP cartridge began as early as 1906 at the Frankford Arsenal. The first developed especially for the Model 1911 pistol was the Seagraves cartridge, after its inventor, Captain D. C. Seagrave, USA. It was a necked cartridge with a rimless case and a cup crimped over the mouth. It was used with a special nozzle which attached to the barrel. Work on developing a blank cartridge for training cavalry mounts was ended in late May 1924 after numerous designs produced at Frankford in small batches were developed and tested. None could ever be made to function with the Model 1911 reliably. Since there were sufficient .45-caliber revolvers available, the blank cartridges were used to train cavalry horses instead.

Starting in 1943, a successful blank cartridge for the Model 1911A1 was developed. Designated the M9, it was loaded with 10 grains of SR4990 powder and intended primarily for training K9 dogs. It was standardized as "Cartridge, Blank, Cal. .45 M9" on November 11, 1943, see Figure 11-6, right. The cartridge was manufactured using a steel case 1.108 inches long overall. At 0.881 inch from the base, the case was tapered a 19.5-degree angle to the mouth. A paper wad was inserted over 6 grains of powder and sealed with red lacquer a third of the way below the

Model 1911, M1911A1

case mouth. In 1944, Frankford Arsenal made additional M9 cartridges using copper-plated steel cases.

Complaints were quickly received about primer blow-back when the M9 blank cartridges were used in M1917 revolvers, although none when used in M1911A1 pistols. To solve the problem a crimp described as a "clover-leaf" was used to secure the primer. In actuality, the crimp looked more like a equilateral triangle with rounded corners. This cartridge modification was designated M9 (T1-E2). Some blank cartridges were also made up without primers and powder charges to serve for display.

A number of other .45 ACP blank cartridges were developed for such purposes as cutting cables on British and American barrage balloons, and for various series of tests.

.45 ACP Shot Cartridges

Beginning in 1943, the U.S. Army Air Force issued a .45 ACP cartridge filled with number 7 1/2 shot. The cartridges were intended to be used by aircrew shot down in hostile or remote areas to enable them to hunt small birds and animals to survive. Two different cartridges were issued, the M12 with a thin, round-nose brass shell and the M15 with the case elongated into a slightly rebated neck and closed with a lacquered cardboard wad, refer to Figure 11-6, left. Neither cartridge was particularly successful as the rifling tended to disperse the shot too widely.

The M12 shot cartridge was reclassified as a Substitute Standard on December 30, 1943, at the same time as the M15 cartridge was standardized. Originally, the wad used to close the case mouth was

Fig. 11-6. Blank and shot cartridges for the .45 ACP pistol: left, shot cartridge manufactured by Remington; right, blank cartridge made by Evansville and standardized as the M9 in 1943.

painted yellow, but on July 3, 1944, the color was changed to vermillion

Military and Commercial Pistols

to ease inspection and identification. Both the M12 and the M15 were manufactured by Remington Arms at their Bridgeport, Connecticut, facility and were packed in the Air Force's B-2 and B-4 emergency kits. Cartons contained a slip of paper with instructions on how to manually load and fire the cartridge in the Model 1911/1911A1 pistol. Until October 1943, the cartons were printed with the warning in English, German and Japanese that the shot cartridge was not to be used against "enemy troops." Use of shot cartridges against the enemy would have violated the Geneva Agreements. After, the warning was changed to: "For use in hunting small game effective range 25 feet."

Caliber .45 Signal and Tracer Cartridge

Prior to the start of World War I, the U.S. Army Signal Corps had requested that the Ordnance Department develop and supply a signal cartridge for the Model 1911 pistol. In an era before portable two-way radios were available, signaling by Verey pistol or mirror between separate units was the only way to coordinate actions.

The first signal cartridge used a service case with two grains of powder, probably Bulls Eye No. 2. It had a gilding-metal or lead-tin-jacketed bullet. The pyrotechnic charge was poured into a hole drilled into the bullet's base. The gilding-metal cap was fitted over the base and its sides extended along the bullet as far as the case mouth. Red, green and while smoke clouds were produced by varying the composition of the pyrotechnic. The smoke cloud produced lasted for up to five seconds and was said to be visible for up to two miles—under ideal conditions, obviously. This cartridge was never produced in quantity because the two grains of powder was not sufficient to function the Model 1911 pistol.

Work on a signal cartridge continued through World War I and after without success. In 1924, Frankford Arsenal produced five hundred rounds of a new cartridge with an improved powder capacity and tracer composition. But again the cartridge was not adopted. The following year, a concerted effort was made to develop a proper signal cartridge at Frankford Arsenal under the direction of L. D. Lewis, an Ordnance Engineer. A series of cartridges were designed and tested and each was assigned a "T" number. Between 1925 and 1931, some fifteen cartridge types were tested. But again the project was canceled although Frankford was allowed to continue development as service needs required.

441

Model 1911, M1911A1

In 1936, the Cavalry Board requested 2,500 signal cartridges for cavalry maneuvers and a further 2,500 in 1938. This bullet had been developed by L. D. Lewis in 1931 as TI-E-14. The bullet weight was 195 grains loaded into a plain brass case without a cannelure, and the color of the trace was painted on the nose. The cartridge was used by the Coast Guard and the Army Air Corps and was found to function properly and provide an acceptable trace. The cartridge was adopted in January 1938 as "Cartridge, Caliber .45, Tracer, M1." It was manufactured during World War II at the Evansville Ordnance Plant.

During World War II an extensive development program was undertaken at the Frankford Arsenal to produce a better tracer cartridge with a greater range and extended trace time. More than sixteen different combinations of bullet, tracing compound, primer, and cartridge case were tested and resulted in the T73 tracer cartridge. When this was also rejected, a contract was given to the National Fireworks Company, Inc., of West Hanover, MA, who developed the Cal. .45 Signal Cartridge, T92, which was finally accepted just before the start of the Korean War.

The T92 had a round-nose bullet made of clear cellulose acetate filled with thirteen grains of tracer compound that produced a bright red trace to an average height of 400 feet for an average of six seconds.

High-Pressure Test Cartridge

The first high-pressure cartridge for testing was developed at the Frankford Arsenal in 1906. They were headstamped "F A 4 06" and only a small quantity was manufactured. Proof testing of the Model 1911 barrel began at Colt in early 1913. Starting at serial #s 24,000-25,000, barrels that passed were marked "P" on the hood. As an example, early records indicate that 17,560 high-pressure test cartridges manufactured at Frankford Arsenal and delivered to Colt in 1915 were loaded with Bulls Eye Powder #2 to provide a pressure of 20,000 lbs. per sq. inch, 4,000 pounds over that generated by the service cartridge. These appear to have been headstamped "F A 4 15." Some 3,000,000 cartridges were manufactured at Frankford Arsenal during World War I.

In the early 1930s, the "Cal. 45. High-Pressure Test Cartridge, M1" was adopted. It provided a test pressure of between 21,000 and 23,000 lbs. per sq. inch. This cartridge continues in use today.

Military and Commercial Pistols

CALIBER .45 PISTOL NATIONAL MATCH AMMUNITION

In 1915, Frankford Arsenal was directed to prepare special ammunition for use in military matches that year. Special lots were again prepared the following year, and again in 1919 after the war when the National Matches resumed. Between 1920 and 1931, service lots of ammunition known to be accurate were used and repackaged as match ammunition. In 1930, the Western Cartridge Company accepted a bid to provide match ammunition. They shipped their Lot 607 to Frankford Arsenal to be tested against the Arsenal's lot 374. The WCC ammunition proved to be more accurate and they were awarded the contract for that year.

In 1932, Frankford Arsenal again began manufacturing match ammunition and by 1939, had delivered some 2,750,460 rounds. In 1939, an additional 40,000 rounds were also acquired from an unknown commercial source.

Only one lot of National Match Ammunition was manufactured in 1940. Lot 688 was made up at the Frankford Arsenal and headstamped "F A. 40" for use in the National Matches at Camp Perry, Ohio. At the 1941 National Matches, held at Camp Perry the following August 31-September 7, current issue ball ammunition was used.

When the National Matches resumed after World War II, all match ammunition was again drawn from selected stocks of service ammunition until 1960, except for a single lot made up in 1953 at Frankford Arsenal using a 210-grain bullet.

In 1960, based on research conducted at the Aberdeen Proving Grounds, a new case was designed with a new extraction rim slope of 26 degrees to eliminate extraction difficulties. The bullet was a 230-grain, lead core round nose with a gilding-metal jacket. The head was stamped "MATCH 60 RA" for the manufacturer, Remington Arms.

The following year, Remington produced an even more accurate lot with a new primer. The ammunition was manufactured in lots of 25,000 cartridges at a time in a continuous stream to provide the greatest possible consistency. The quality control was extensive and far surpassed that applied to any service lot. The finished ammunition had a 1960 head-stamp but was packaged in standard brown cartridge boxes with special red, white, and blue labels glued on to distinguish it from the 1960 production. The label showed an eagle in blue clutching the U.S. shield and was marked "MATCH" and "ORDBA Label 105, 23 Mar 61." Later

Model 1911, M1911A1

that same year, Remington produced additional match ammunition with a headstamp of "61." Production in succeeding years had that headstamp.

Match ammunition was also procured from the Federal Cartridge Company in 1961. Packed in standard 50-round brown boxes, it was labeled "BALL-MATCH" and the cartridge case headstamp was "FC 61 MATCH." Winchester also supplied .45 ACP semiwadcutter ammunition in at least one lot, WCC-40-6006. This was apparently their Super-Match X, 185-grain semi-wadcutter cartridge repackaged in brown cardboard boxes and labeled "50 CARTRIDGES/ CALIBER .45/MATCH WAD-CUTTER/LOT WCC-40-6006/ OLIN CORPORATION," see Figure 11-7.

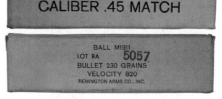

Fig. 11-7. "1965 Match cartridges manufactured by Remington Arms. Top, front and rear views of carton. Karl Karash collection.

Through the 1980s while the Model 1911A1 was still in use as the Match Pistol, ammunition for the National Matches were made by various contractors.

As of April 1994, there were seven different cartridges for the Model 1911A1 series of pistols in U.S. Army inventory (TM 43-0001-27), two more than in 1944 when five different cartridges were in inventory and the pistol was in general issue. Two of the additional cartridges reflect the Model 1911A1's use as a "target" pistol. During World War II, five cartridges were in general issue and during World War I, only ball ammunition and a dummy cartridge was available as general issue. See Table 11-1.

Table 11-1
Standardized .45 ACP Cartridges for U.S. Military General Issue

1994
1) Cartridge, Caliber .45, Ball, M1911
2) Cartridge, Caliber .45, Ball, Match 1911

Military and Commercial Pistols

3) Cartridge, Dummy, Caliber .45, M1921
4) Cartridge, Caliber .45, Match Wadcutter
5) Cartridge, Caliber .45, Ball, High Pressure Test, M1
6) Cartridge, Caliber .45, Tracer, M26
7) Cartridge, Caliber .45, Blank, M9

1944
1) Cartridge, Caliber .45, Ball, M1911
2) Cartridge, Dummy, Caliber .45, M1921
3) Cartridge, Caliber .45, Ball, High Pressure Test, M1
4) Cartridge, Caliber .45, Tracer, M1
5) Shot Cartridge .45, M15

1917
1) Cartridge, Caliber .45, Ball, M1911
2) Cartridge, Dummy, Caliber .45, M1918
3) Cartridge, High-Pressure Test, Caliber .45

Table 11-2 Specifications, Cartridge, Caliber .45, Ball, M1911 1912 Period	
Bullet length	0.657-0.667 inch
Bullet diameter	0.451 inch*
Bullet weight	230 grains (gilding metal jacket)
Case length	0.892-0.898 inch (brass case)
Case diameter	mouth: 0.4672-0473 inch
Cartridge length	1.262 to 1.275 inches
Velocity	830 fps
Cartridge weight	0.046 lb
Cartridge weight, 2,000 in 20-round boxes in zinc cases, in wooden crate	110 lbs
Adopted	1911

* Early U.S. military manuals show the M1911 bullet as 0.4505 inch in diameter.

HEADSTAMPS—.45 ACP

Table 11-3 lists all manufacturers of U.S. small-arms ammunition contracted by the U.S. Army Ordnance Department from 1911 to 1965. Those shown in boldface manufactured .45 ACP ammunition under contract to the U.S. Government.

Model 1911, M1911A1

Table 11-3 .45 ACP Cartridge Case Headstamps	
Abbreviation	**Manufacturer**
AO	Allegheny Ordnance Plant
DEN	Denver Ordnance Plant
DM	Des Moines Ordnance Plant
DOMINION	**Dominion, Canadian Industries, Ltd.**
EC	**Evansville Ordnance Plant**
ECS	**Evansville-Chrysler-Sunbeam Ordnance Plant**
EW	Eau Claire Ordnance Plant
FA	**Frankford Arsenal**
FC	**Federal Cartridge Company**
FCC	**Federal Cartridge Company**
KS	Allegheny Ordnance Plant (Kelly-Springfield)
LC	Lake City Ordnance Plant
LM	Lowell Ordnance Plant
M	Milwaukee Ordnance Plant
MAXIM	**Maxim Munitions Corporation**
PC	**Peters Cartridge Company**
P.C.CO	**Peters Cartridge Company**
RA	**Remington Arms Company**
REM	**Remington Arms Company**
REM-UMC	**Remington Arms-Union Metallic Cartridge Company**
SL	Saint Louis Ordnance Plant
TW	**Twin Cities Ordnance Plant**
U	Utah Ordnance Plant
U.S.C.CO	**United States Cartridge Company**
UT	Utah Ordnance Plant
W	Western Cartridge Company
WC	**Western Cartridge Company**

Military and Commercial Pistols

Table 11-3, cont.	
.45 ACP Cartridge Case Headstamps	
Abbreviation	Manufacturer
WCC	Western Cartridge Company
W.R.A.	Winchester Repeating Arms Company
WRA	Winchester Repeating Arms Company
W-W	Winchester-Western, Olin Corporation

PACKING BOXES

Ammunition for the Model 1911 was packed twenty rounds to a narrow, cardboard box with a cloth tear strip glued under the cover. The boxes were a natural tan color with a purple paper label that typically read:

1st Style (Frankford Arsenal) marked in either serif or sans serif type:

**20
CARTRIDGES, PISTOL BALL
CALIBER .45 M1911
POWDER, BULLS EYE, NO. 2 ARMY LOT ___
FRANKFORD ARSENAL
DWG B 503   AMMUNITION LOT __**

2nd Style (Frankford Arsenal) marked in either serif or sans serif type:

**20 PISTOL BALL CARTRIDGES, CAL. .45
For AUTOMATIC PISTOL, Model of 1911.
Smokeless Powder Muzzle velocity 800 ± 24 feet per second/
Dupont's Bulls Eye Powder, H, Lot No. __ of 19__
Manufactured at Frankford Arsenal,
Class 47, Division 1, Drawing 5.**

3rd Style (Contractor) marked in either serif or sans serif type, See Figures 11-8 and 11-9:

447

Model 1911, M1911A1

Fig. 11-8. Typical examples of Frankford twenty-round .45 ACP boxes of ammunition: top, WWI-era; bottom, WWII-era.

Fig. 11-9. WWI-era twenty-round boxes: top, United States Cartridge Company; bottom, Remington Arms-UMC.

Fig. 11-10. WWII-and-later-era fifty-round boxes. At left, Evansville and Remington Arms. Western Cartridge Company and Winchester Repeating Arms (right) were divisions of Olin Mathieson.

20 PISTOL BALL CARTRIDGES, CAL. .45
For AUTOMATIC PISTOL, Model of 1911.
Smokeless Powder Muzzle velocity 800 ± 24 feet per second/
Dupont's Bulls Eye Powder, H, Lot No. __ of 19__
Manufactured at the Winchester Repeating Arms Co.,
Class 47, Division 1, Drawing 5.

United States Cartridge, Co. apparently mispelled "muzzle" as "muzzel." Cartridge boxes loaded at Frankford Arsenal read "Disposal of emptied cartridge must be made as prescribed by A.R. 775-10" on the back paper label.

During World War II and after, .45 ACP ammunition was packed in fifty-round cardboard boxes that were marked in sans serif type:

50 CARTRIDGES
PISTOL BALL
CALIBER .45 M1911
AMMUNITION LOT ___
MANUFACTURERS' NAME

Figure 11-10 shows examples of various military 50-round cartridge boxes. No attempt has been made to describe commercial .45 ACP ammunition and cartridge boxes. Thousands of variations have probably been produced since 1912 and would require a book this size to quantify.

PACKING CASES

Ammunition for the Model 1911 was shipped in wooden crates holding two thousand rounds throughout the service use of the pistol, see

Fig. 11-11. World War I-era ammunition 2,000-round shipping crate. Craig Riesch collection.

Model 1911, M1911A1

Figure 11-11. Most crates were lined with waterproof sheet iron, which was soldered closed, see Figure 11-12. A wire or key allowed the sheet iron containers to be opened quickly. The cover for the crate was held in place by wing nuts on six j-bolts. During World War II, the sheet iron liner was sometimes replaced by a paraffin-coated cardboard liner.

Between 1911 and 1943, crates were typically marked:

2000 CARTRIDGES
PISTOL, BALL, CALIBER .45 1911
FOR AUTO-PISTOL M1911
PACKED IN CARTONS
CARTRIDGE LOT No. XXX
(Manufacturer) ____

The information was repeated on the top and partially on one end. A red color band for ball ammunition was painted on the crate. Other color bands were: blue (blank), green (dummy), yellow (high-pressure test), and tracer (green on yellow).

Later in the war, .45 ACP ammunition was packed six hundred rounds to a sealed metal can. Two metal cans were then placed in each wooden crate for a total of 1,200 rounds, see Figure 11-13. Between 1943 and 1950, crates were typically marked:

1200 CARTRIDGES CAL .45
IN CARTONS
T2AAF
BALL M1911   LOT EC-2486

During the Korean War period, caliber .45 M1911 cartridges were packed one thousand rounds in a metal ammunition can, and two cans were placed in a wooden shipping crate. The cans had reclosable lids and resembled the ubiquitous .50-caliber ammunition can.

These metal ammunition cans were used to the end of production and marked, see Figure 11-14:

1000 CAL. .45 CARTRIDGES
BALL M1911
CARTONS

450

Military and Commercial Pistols

Fig. 11-12. World War I-era shipping crate opened showing the tin liner. Craig Riesch collection.

Fig. 11-13. World War II-era 1,200-round shipping crate showing one of the metal cans holding 600 rounds.

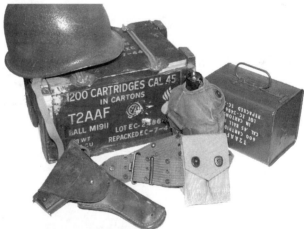

Fig. 11-14. Vietnam-era and later 1,000-round ammunition metal can.

Appendix A
Model 1911/1911A1 Exploded View

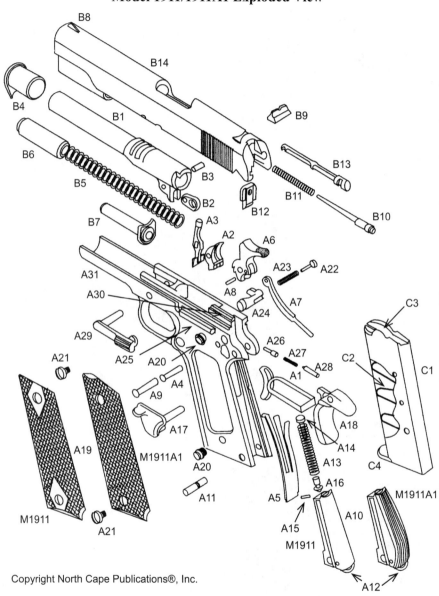

Model 1911/1911A1/Government Model
Nomenclature

A1. Trigger
A2. Sear
A3. Disconnector
A4. Trigger pin
A5. Sear, trigger, safety spring
A6. Hammer
A7. Hammer strut
A8. Hammer strut pin
A9. Hammer pin
A10. Mainspring housing
A11. Mainspring housing pin
A12. Lanyard loop
A13. Mainspring
A14. Mainspring cap
A15. Mainspring cap pin
A16. Mainspring housing pin retainer
A17. Safety lock
A18. Grip safety
A19. Stock panels (2)
A20. Stock screw bushings (4)
A21. Stock screws (4)
A22. Magazine catch spring guide
A23. Magazine catch spring
A24. Magazine catch housing
A25. Plunger tube

A26. Slide stop plunger
A27. Plunger spring
A28. Safety catch plunger
A29. Slide stop
A30. Ejector
A31. Receiver or frame
B1. Barrel
B2. Link
B3. Link pin
B4. Barrel bushing
B5. Recoil spring
B6. Recoil spring plug
B7. Recoil spring guide
B8. Front sight
B9. Rear sight
B10. Firing pin
B11. Firing pin spring
B12. Firing pin retainer plate
B13. Extractor
B14. Slide
C1. Magazine body
C2. Magazine spring
C3. Magazine follower
C4. Base plate, with or without
    lanyard loop

Appendix B
Colt Model 1911/1911A1
Military and Commercial Production

Serial Number Ranges Compared by Year		
Year	Military Serial Number Range	Commercial Serial Number Range (1)
1912	1-17250	C1-C1899
1913	17251-60400	C1900-C5399
1914	60401-102596	C5400-C16659
1915	107597-125566	C16660-C27699
1916	133187-137400 151187-151986 (2)	C27700-C74999
1917	137401-151186 151987-216986	C75000-C99000
1918	216987-551000 (1)	C99001-C105999
1919	551001-629500 (1)	C106000-C120999
1920	No military production	C121000-C126999
1921	No military production	C127000-C128999
1922	No military production	C129000-C133999
1923	No military production	C134000-C134999
1924	700001-710000	C135000-C139999
1925	No military production	C140000-C144999
1926	No military production	C145000-C150999
1927	No military production	C151000-C151999
1928	No military production	C152000-C154999
1929	No military production	C155000-C155999
1930	No military production	C156000-C158999
1931	No military production	C159000-C160999
1932	No military production	C161000-C164799
1933	No military production	C164800-C174599

Military and Commercial Pistols

Serial Number Ranges Compared by Year		
Year	Military Serial Number Range	Commercial Serial Number Range (1)
1934	No military production	C174600-C177999
1935	No military production	C178000-C179799
1936	No military production	C179800-C183199
1937	710001-712349	C183200-C188699
1938	712350-713645	C188700-C189599
1939	713646-717281	C189600-C198899
1940	717282-721977	C198900-C199299
1941	721978-756733	C199300-C208799
1942	756734-856100	C208800-C215018 (3)
1943	856101-958100 1088726-1092896 1096405-1,208,673	No commercial production
1944	1609529-1743846	No commercial production
1945	2244804-2368781 (4)	No commercial production (5)

General Note: Above serial number ranges are assigned or production ranges and not shipping dates.

1. Approximate serial range. Pistols were not necessarily shipped in numerical order and commercial pistols were sometimes shipped years out of sequence.

2. USMC pistols made out of sequence and shipped in 1916.

3. Last pre-World War II commercial pistol was s/n C215018. According to R.L. Wilson, most commercial 1942 production was used for military production.

4. Last military contract M1911A1 produced by Colt was s/n #2,368,781

5. Commercial production resumed in 1946 at C220,001

Appendix C
The Colt Company, 1945 to the Present

During the latter half of the 19th century and the first forty years of the 20th, Colt Patent Firearms was generally a well-founded, well-run company in a strong financial position. Its list of products on the eve of World War II was impressive and included other products as well as firearms— machinery, printing presses, ticket punches, plastics, and commercial dishwashing machines. In spite of the Great Depression that had roiled the 1930s, the company's position was substantial and it continued to pay dividends on its stock.

World War II brought both great benefits and problems to Colt. The company grew rapidly with the influx of war contracts, but management suffered badly as there was little time to find and train new supervisory personnel. Much of its equipment dated from the World War I-era, supplemented with new equipment acquired in the early 1940s but which had been hard-used during the war. When World War II ended in August 1945, Colt had more than 15,000 employees manufacturing a wide range of military equipment and weapons, including the Model 1911A1 pistol. Wartime production had exacerbated management and production flow problems in the company. When government contracts ended in 1945, costs accelerated. A short-sighted attempt to reduce those costs led to the layoff and firing of many highly paid mid-level production and management personnel who took with them a deep working knowledge of the techniques and procedures that made the company run. As a result, the company was not able to resume commercial production until late 1946.

Starting in 1949, Colt introduced a shortened version of the Model 1911A1, the Lightweight Commander, and its successor, the steel-framed Commander. Intended to make the pistol easier to carry for police detectives, undercover officers and licensed-to-carry-concealed individuals, the shortened slide and alloy framed pistol became a popular and profitable line. A new revolver, the Python, and an improved Trooper, the Mk III, were also commercially successful, see Figure C-1. But Colt's refusal to seriously develop a double-action semiautomatic pistol ultimately cost them the police market which they had dominated in the pre-World War II years.

Military and Commercial Pistols

Fig. C-1. Left to right: the Python .357 Magnum revolver, the Lightweight Commander in .45 ACP, and a 2nd Generation Single Action revolver in .45 Long Colt. Author's collection.

In 1955 and losing money monthly, Colt was acquired by Penn-Texas Corporation. Penn-Texas was an early conglomerate that included the Pratt & Whitney Company—the famous machinery maker, and not the aircraft engine producer. In 1959, a group of investors, fed up with Penn-Texas's business practices, took over the company and fired the president, Leopold D. Silberstein. Penn-Texas was reorganized as the Fairbanks Whitney Company of which Colt remained a part, and began to prosper once more.

In 1960, Colt was approached by ArmaLite, a small company in Costa Mesa, California. They had developed the prototype of a promising small-caliber, automatic rifle. Colt purchased the manufacturing rights and over the next few years, convinced the U.S. government to replace its heavy M14 select-fire infantry rifle with the new, lightweight, plastic-stocked M16 rifle, see Figure C-2.

Model 1911, M1911A1

Fig. C-2. Above, Colt AR15A1; below, the AR15A2 rifle, both civilian versions in the M16 series.

In 1964, Fairbanks (Whitney) Morse reorganized as Colt Industries. The firearms division became Colt's Inc. Firearms Division. Colt revived its commercial line of rifles with the introduction of the Sharps and Sauer models, and began manufacturing a series of black powder reproductions of its early percussion revolvers. The Custom Shop was established in-house in 1976 with staff engravers. The Custom Shop and engraving is discussed in Chapter 9 as it pertains to the Model 1911/1911A1.

The M16 rifle and its civilian counterpart, the AR15, proved a mainstay for the company which operated successfully enough until 1986, when the United Auto Workers called a strike which would continue for the next four years. Union employees were replaced and the company struggled on. In 1988, Colt lost the M16A2 contract to its Belgian rival, Fabrique Nationale, which had built a plant in the United States. The Colt Firearms Division was sold to C.F. Holdings, Inc., the following year. In 1990, the company was sold again, this time to a group of private investors and the State of Connecticut, which was desperate to retain the company jobs. The company was renamed again as the "Colt's Manufacturing Company."

Colt entered Chapter 11 Bankruptcy in 1992 and reorganized. In 1994, the main plant, which had stood for a century and a half along the Connecticut River, closed and new facilities in West Hartford were

Military and Commercial Pistols

opened. Starting in 2001, litigation brought by a coalition of politicians and antigun-groups proved very costly to the entire small-arms industry in the United States, even though more than ninety percent of the cases were thrown out by the courts before Congress acted to shield firearms manufacturers.

In November 2002, the company was split into separate military and commercial firms. Today, Colt Defense, Inc., manufactures and sells military and law enforcement products. The mainstay of Colt Defense is the M16 rifle which contract returned to Colt in 1998, plus extensive contracts for the M4 Carbine and M4 Commando and their variations and accessories. Colt Defense also acquired SACO which manufactured automatic weapons for the military, and Héroux-Devtek Inc. with its Logistics & Defense Division, Diemaco of Kitchener, Ontario, Canada. Diemaco manufactures the C-7 rifle and C-8 carbine, the Canadian Defense Forces versions of the M16 rifle and M4 carbine.

The commercial firm is today known as the Colt's Manufacturing Company. The commercial product line is somewhat reduced but far more in tune with today's market. Successors to the Model 1911 and Model 1911A1 have continued to be produced as the Series 70, Series 80 and as the Model 1991 and such other specialty lines as the Colt Gold Cup Trophy, Colt Special Combat Government, Colt .38 Super, Colt XSE, and Colt Defender. The last of the famed Model 1972 Peacemakers was built in 1995. Today's Peacemaker, called the Colt Cowboy, is manufactured in Italy but sold under the Colt name. In addition, the Colt Python revolver and the Colt National Match pistol are available through the Custom Shop.

Appendix D
The National Match Pistol

Beginning in 1920, the Springfield Armory was ordered to make available a specific number of Model 1911s (and later 1911A1s) every year for use in the National Matches. These pistols were fitted with wider front sights and matching rear sights, carefully selected barrels matched to bushings, tightened slides and trigger pulls set to between 6 and 7.5 pounds.

Henry "Fitz" FitzGerald, Colt's chief arms tester and company spokesman, and an amazing shot in his own right, attended virtually every National Match at either Caldwell, New Jersey, or Camp Perry, Ohio, in the 1920s and 1930s and operated an accurizing service for one and all. The service proved so popular that Colt *shipped* its first "match" pistol, #C130,711, on October 31, 1921. It was equipped with a "match" barrel that was marked M.B. in a circle on the rear top of the left barrel lug. During the 1930 National Matches Fitz showed Colt's newest product, a "National Match" pistol, that would soon be for commercial sale. The pistol was marked **NATIONAL MATCH** on the left side of the slide, and was equipped with the standard "Patridge"-type front and rear sight.

On December 31, 1930, the U.S. Coast Guard sent Colt a purchase order for five "match conditioned" pistols. They cost $27.50 apiece ($304.75 in today's dollars). The pistols had star-gauged barrels and knurled triggers but were not marked or classified as National Match pistols..

Author and researcher Timothy J. Mullin (*American Beauty: The Prewar Colt National Match Government Model Pistol*) has done extensive research in the Colt records to establish the chronology of the National Match pistol, as has Charles Clawson (*Colt .45 Service Pistols, Models of 1911 and 1911A1*). Between them, they have established the existence of at least seventeen pistols described in the Colt records as "National Match" pistols, sixteen of which were shipped in 1932, a year before the date commonly accepted as the starting date for the prewar National Match pistol. Seven of these pistols were shipped to the U.S. Coast Guard in January 1932.

Military and Commercial Pistols

The National Match pistol appears to have always been denoted as such in the factory records. The action was described as "hand honed." This meant that the trigger, sear, disconnector flat, strut, firing pin retainer, and the bottom of the slide were carefully polished by an expert workman. The pistols were fitted with the arched mainspring housing and the short Model 1911A1-style trigger adjusted to eliminate creep. The trigger pull could be specified by the customer and was set at the factory. Various options for checkering of parts were available for both National Match and Government Model pistols. The pistols were given a deep polish and blued. The top of the slide was sandblasted at the buyer's request. The grip panels were fully checkered walnut.

The National Match slide was marked on the right side:

NATIONAL MATCH COLT AUTOMATIC CALIBRE.45

The receiver serial number was stamped underneath the firing pin retainer plate, as was standard during the period. Receivers were not marked in any way to indicate that they were being used on a National Match pistol. Barrels were marked "M.B." inside a circle, but from 1935 on (circa serial #C177,000), they were marked on the left side above the barrel lug:

COLT 45 AUTO MATCH

The National Match pistol sold for $40.00 (the equivalent of $486.04 in today's dollars), almost twice the price of the standard commercial Government model which sold for $22.00 ($267.32).

In 1935, the Stevens Adjustable Rear Sight and barrels for the National Match pistol were now stamped:

COLT 45 AUTO MATCH

Nickel plating was made available for the first time as well. Factory engraving was also available as an extra-cost-option but R.L. Wilson (*The Book of Colt Firearms*) has estimated that only about twenty-five National Match pistols were engraved, most by Wilbur A. Glahn, who was the factory engraver at that time. In addition to walnut grip panels, ivory and mother-of-pearl grips were also available. Pearl grips were an additional $15.00 and ivory grips cost $8.75 plain and $17.50 carved ($120.79, $207.07, and $258.84 respectively in 2006 dollars).

Model 1911, M1911A1

Production of the "National Match" pistol, like all other of Colt's commercial firearms manufacture, ended in 1941. Production of accurized pistols for target matches was not resumed again until 1957 when the "Colt Gold Cup National Match" pistol was introduced. The new pistol had a deeply grooved, flat mainspring housing and a vertically serrated front face on the grip, a grooved, adjustable trigger, and was finished in what the factory termed "Royal Blue." The top of the slide was sandblasted to eliminate glare. In 1958, the Gold Cup National Match was priced at $125.00 ($819.99 in today's dollars). In 1970, the slide marking was changed left side to:

COLT'S MK IV/SERIES '70
GOLD CUP NATIONAL MATCH
.45 AUTOMATIC CALIBER

and on the right side, to:

GOLD CUP
NATIONAL MATCH

The pistol, known as the "Gold Cup Trophy," is currently available as part of the Colt's Manufacturing Company product line in both stainless or blued steel.

For a comprehensive study of Military match pistols, see the excellent *U.S. Military and Marksmanship Automatic Pistol*s by Bill Jenkins.

Appendix E
The Ballester-Molina Pistol

In 1927, the Argentine government ordered additional Government Model pistols in .45 ACP from Colt. The resultant "Modelo 1927a" featured the 1911A1 modifications recently adopted by the United States Army. After Colt delivered 10,000, the Argentine government built 74,866 more at its Domingo Mathcu factory in Rosario.

During the production run of the Modelo 1927, Argentine engineers suggested a few changes to simplify manufacturing. One of the engineers was Dr. Arturo Ballester of the Hispano Argentina Fabrica de Automoviles, SA (HAFDASA) of Buenos Aires, a firm created in 1929 by Ballester and Eugenio Molina to build cars, buses, trucks and diesel engines.

At the same time, the Bonifacio Echeverria factory in Spain was building a series of Model 1911 clones known as the "Star" pistols. Though based on Colt's design, the Star lacked some of its refinements, making it easier to produce. The .45-caliber Star Model P influenced the Ballester-Molina pistol's design.

In 1937, with war clouds gathering ominously over Europe and Asia, the Argentine military gave HAFDASA a contract to produce the new design. The resultant pistol is known variously as the Ballester-Rigaud, Ballester-Molina, or HAFDASA.

FOREIGN YET FAMILIAR

The Ballester-Molina is virtually the same size and shape as the U.S. Model 1911A1—8.5 inches long, with a 5-inch barrel and a 36-oz. unloaded weight, see Figure E-1. The Ballester-Molina uses the same seven-shot magazine as the M1911A1, and all operating controls are in the same locations.

The Ballester-Molina differs from the Model 1911A1 in that it lacks a grip safety and employs a pivoting trigger rather than the Government Model's sliding trigger, Figure E-2. The slide's grasping grooves provide an immediate way to distinguish between the two pistols. Instead of the M1911A1's eighteen evenly spaced vertical serrations, the Ball-

Model 1911, M1911A1

Fig. E-1. The Model 1911A1 and Ballester-Molina are similar in design. The Ballester-Molina lacks the grip safety and has a pivoting trigger.

Fig. E-2. The Model 1911A1 and Ballester-Molina receivers compared. Note that the Argentine pistol has a pivoting trigger that pushes a transfer bar to trip the sear.

Military and Commercial Pistols

ester-Molina's eight slide serrations appear in three groups, with three in the forward group, three in the middle and two in the rearmost group, see Figure E-3.

The hardwood grips are distinctive with nineteen vertical serrations or ridges. The grips are both wider and thicker than those of a Model 1911A1, so the pistol grip feels somewhat bulkier, see Figure E-4. The trigger guard is a bit narrower at the front than the Model 1911A1's. The slide stop detent serves also as the slide dismount cut. And a problem the Ballester-Molina shares with most of its contemporaries is having undersized sights. Otherwise, the operation and fieldstripping of the Ballester-

Fig. E-3. Above, Colt slide serrations; below, the slide serrations on the Ballester-Molina slide.

Molina pistol is quite similar to the Colt Model 1911A1.

The internal mechanical differences of the Ballester-Molina include a shorter hammer strut, a firing-pin stop without relief cuts on its sides and a larger-diameter safety lock pin. While none of these changes alter the Ballester-Molina pistol's handling, its parts will not interchange between a Ballester-Molina and an Argentine Modelo 1927 or U.S. Model 1911A1. A Ballester-Molina slide will fit loosely and function on a Colt or equivalent Argentine-made frame, but a Ballester-Molina frame is too wide to accept a Model 1911A1 slide.

Fig. E-4. Left, Colt walnut checkered grips; right, vertical serrations on the Ballester-Molina wood grips.

Model 1911, M1911A1

Fig. E-5. Above, the slide marking includes the name, "Ballester-Molina." Below, the name is "Ballester-Rigaud." After 1939, the latter was dropped. Note the absence of the slide dismount cut.

The Ballester-Molina is well-made, with a highly polished blue-black finish. While many pistols were marked **BALLESTER-RIGAUD** on the slide (Rorice Rigaud was the chief engineer of the team), that slide marking was not used after 1939 and all subsequent pistols were marked **BALLESTER-MOLINA**, see Figure E-5.

The right side of the slide may include an Argentine government crest just ahead of the slide serrations. Also on the right side of the slide, the name of an official Argentine military or police agency may appear.

Serial numbers were stamped inside the slide (visible only when removed from the receiver), on the barrel link, and on the left side of the mainspring housing, see Figure E-6. A number or other marking of the agency using the pistol may also appear on inside of the slide, on the center slide rail.

In addition to the standard .45-caliber service pistol, from 1940 to 1953 HAFDASA also produced smaller numbers of Ballester-Molinas

Military and Commercial Pistols

chambered in .22 Long Rifle. Identical in size and appearance to the .45-caliber weapon, these used a blowback bolt to accommodate the lower recoil of the rimfire cartridge. These guns were issued for training to Argentine military and police agencies. Compared to the .45-caliber service pistol, the .22s are rare today due to limited production.

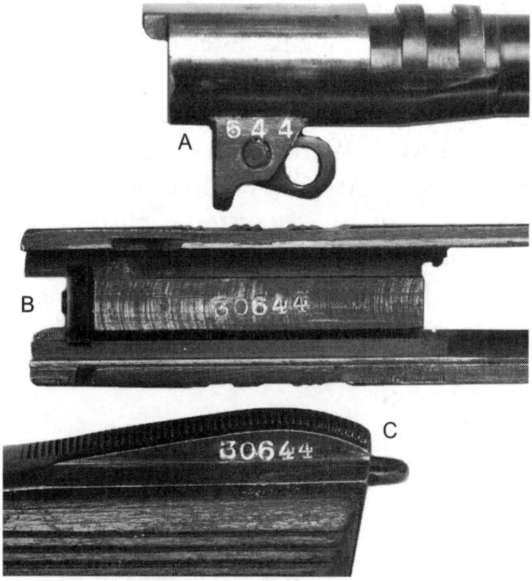

Fig. E-6. Serial numbers on the Ballester-Molina are found on: (A) the barrel link, (B), the inside of the slide, and (C) on the left side of the mainspring housing.

WORLD WAR II

The Argentine government issued the Ballester-Molina pistol, first to military units and then to various police forces. And while Argentina did manage to remain neutral during World War II, many Ballester-Molina pistols made it into the fighting.

In 1940, a British Purchasing Commission visited the Americas to buy war materials. Still reeling from their forced evacuation at Dunkirk, the British were buying every firearm they could find. The British Purchasing Commission was impressed with the Ballester-Molina. British military forces were well acquainted with its parent pistol, the Model 1911, having issued it to the Royal Air Force during and after World War I. The Commission purchased some 15,000 Ballester-Molina pistols (serial number prefix "B") and had them shipped to Great Britain.

A top-secret espionage and sabotage unit called Special Operations Executive (SOE) was put into the operation by the British government at the urging of Prime Minister Winston Churchill. Their brief was to operate as spies and saboteurs behind enemy lines. SOE operatives received many of the Ballester-Molinas when they were parachuted behind enemy lines in occupied Europe and Burma. The British also issued some 10,000 of the Ballester-Molina pistols to their 8th Army fighting in the North African desert against Italian and German forces. The pistols served well in the harsh desert conditions.

After World War II, Ballester-Molina manufacture and issue continued in Argentina before production was finally stopped in 1953. Exact figures have not been published, but the manufacturing certainly ran into the tens of thousands.

In the 1960s, the Pistola PD, a 9 mm Browning High Power pistol, began supplanting the Ballester-Molina and the Modelo 1927, see Figure E-7, at which point an unknown number of both older pistols were released for export. Ballester-Molinas did remain in limited service, particularly in naval and police hands, as late as the 1982 South Atlantic War, which Argentina and Britain fought over ownership

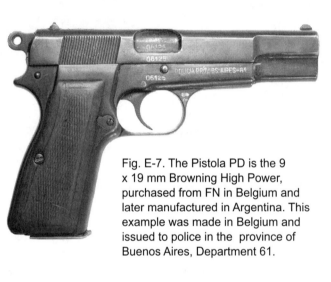

Fig. E-7. The Pistola PD is the 9 x 19 mm Browning High Power, purchased from FN in Belgium and later manufactured in Argentina. This example was made in Belgium and issued to police in the province of Buenos Aires, Department 61.

of the Falkland Islands. In the 1990s, Argentina released its remaining Ballester-Molina pistols from reserve stocks, and many of these were imported into the United States. Other commercial sales were made in Latin America.

Appendix F
Automatic Pistol, Caliber .45, Model 1911
Automatic Pistol, Caliber .45, Model 1911A1
U.S. Army Ordnance Department
Assigned Serial Numbers (s/n)
Annotated

The author and technical editors wish to thank Mr. Charles Clawson for providing collectors with the most-up-to-date information currently available regarding serial numbers in his monumental book, *Collector's Guide to Colt .45 Service Pistols, Model 1911 and 1911A1*.

Generally speaking, year of manufacture and shipping date for military pistols were the same. But during World War II, contracts overlapped from one year to the next and shipping dates for some pistols could have occurred in either year. The following table notes serial numbers in order of shipping dates, rather than strictly in the more familiar production date order. Any differences are described in the Quantity column in lined boxes and explained in Note 1.

The only way to be sure of the shipping date of a particular U.S. military pistol—or a commercial pistol for that matter—of Colt manufacture is to obtain a "Letter of Authenticity" from Colt's Manufacturing Company, LLC, as described in Appendix K. Unfortunately, such letters are not available from the other contractors, Springfield Armory, Remington Arms-UMC, Singer Manufacturing Company, Ithaca Gun Company, Remington Rand, and Union Switch & Signal.

The author cautions that such a letter from Colt does not authenticate the particular firearm, only that a firearm with that serial number was shipped on that date.

NOTE: Any minor differences in the serial number ranges shown in Tables 5-1, 5-13 and Appendix B are due to differing methods of evaluating serial number records and other data. There is no "official" serial number list.

Model 1911, M1911A1

Year	Manufacturer	Start Serial Number	End Serial Number	Military Service Destination	Quantity	Notes
				Model 1911 Production, U.S. Army Ordnance Department Contract		
		1	500	ARMY	500	Marked "MODEL OF 1911. U.S. ARMY"
		501	1000	NAVY	500	Marked "MODEL OF 1911. U.S. NAVY"
		1001	1500	ARMY	500	Marked "MODEL OF 1911. U.S. ARMY"
		1501	2000	NAVY	500	Marked "MODEL OF 1911. U.S. NAVY"
		2001	2500	ARMY	500	Marked "MODEL OF 1911. U.S. ARMY"
		2501	3500	NAVY	1000	Marked "MODEL OF 1911. U.S. NAVY"
		3501	3800	USMC	300	Marked "MODEL OF 1911. U.S. ARMY"
		3801	4500	ARMY	700	Marked "MODEL OF 1911. U.S. NAVY"
1912	Colt	4501	5500	NAVY	1000	Marked "MODEL OF 1911. U.S. NAVY"
		5501	6500	ARMY	1000	Marked "MODEL OF 1911. U.S. ARMY"
		6501	7500	NAVY	1000	Marked "MODEL OF 1911. U.S. NAVY"
		7501	8500	ARMY	1000	Marked "MODEL OF 1911. U.S. ARMY"
		8501	9500	NAVY	1000	Marked "MODEL OF 1911. U.S. NAVY"
		9501	10500	ARMY	1000	Marked "MODEL OF 1911. U.S. ARMY"
		10501	11500	NAVY	1000	Marked "MODEL OF 1911. U.S. NAVY"
		11501	12500	ARMY	1000	Marked "MODEL OF 1911. U.S. ARMY"
		12501	13500	NAVY	1000	Marked "MODEL OF 1911. U.S. NAVY"

Military and Commercial Pistols

Year	Manufacturer	Start Serial Number	End Serial Number	Military Service Destination	Quantity	Notes
1912, cont.	Colt, cont.	13501	17250	ARMY	3750	Marked "MODEL OF 1911. U.S. ARMY"
		17251	36400	ARMY	19150	
		36401	37650	USMC	1250	
		37651	38000	ARMY	350	
1913	Colt	38001	43800	NAVY	5800	Marked "MODEL OF 1911. U.S. NAVY"
		43801	43900	NAVY	100	Marked "MODEL OF 1911. U.S. NAVY" For USS NEW YORK
		43901	44000	NAVY	100	Marked "MODEL OF 1911. U.S. NAVY" For USS TEXAS
		44001	60400	ARMY	16400	
1914	Colt	60401	72570	ARMY	12170	
	Springfield	72571	81750	ARMY	9179	
1915	Springfield	81751	83855	ARMY	2104	Marked "MODEL OF 1911. U.S. ARMY"
		83856	83900	ARMY	45	
1914	Colt	83901	84400	USMC	500	
		84401	96000	ARMY	11600	
		96001	97537	NAVY	1537	Marked "MODEL OF 1911. U.S. NAVY"

Model 1911, M1911A1

Model 1911/1911A1 U.S. Army Ordnance Department Assigned Serial Numbers (s/n) Annotated, cont.						
Year	Manufacturer	Start Serial Number	End Serial Number	Military Service Destination	Quantity	Notes
1914, cont.	Colt, cont.	97538	102596	ARMY	5059	Marked "MODEL OF 1911. U.S. ARMY"
	Springfield	102597	107596	ARMY	5000	
		107597	109500	ARMY	1904	
1915	Colt	109501	110000	NAVY	500	Marked "MODEL OF 1911. U.S. NAVY" Last "NAVY" marked 1911 group
		110001	113496	ARMY	3496	
	Springfield	113497	120200	ARMY	6704	
		120201	120566	ARMY	366	**All subsequent 1911/1911A1 pistols Marked for "U.S. ARMY"**
	Colt	120567	125566	ARMY	5000	
1916	Springfield	125567	127130	ARMY	6704	
1917		127131	127978	ARMY	845	
1916		128617	133186	ARMY	4570	Apparently used as replacement s/ns when needed during 1916-1918
1916		133187	137400	ARMY	4214	1916, smallest 1911 production year
1917	Colt	137401	151186	ARMY	13786	
1916		151187	151986	USMC	800	Marked "MODEL OF 1911. U.S. ARMY" shipped out of sequence in 1916
1917		151987	185800	ARMY	33814	

Military and Commercial Pistols

		Model 1911/1911A1 U.S. Army Ordnance Department Assigned Serial Numbers (s/n) Annotated, cont.				
Year	Manufacturer	Start Serial Number	End Serial Number	Military Service Destination	Quantity	Notes
1917, cont.		185801	186200	USMC	400	Marked "MODEL OF 1911. U.S. ARMY" Transferred from Army
		186201	204986	ARMY	18786	
1918		204987	209586	ARMY	4600	
		209587	210386	USMC	800	
1917		210387	215386	ARMY	5000	Reserved for receivers
		215387	216186	USMC	800	
		216187	216586	ARMY	400	Marked "MODEL OF 1911. U.S. ARMY" Transferred from USMC
	Colt, cont.	216587	216986	USMC	400	
1918		216987	217386	USMC	400	Last direct USMC shipment
1917		217387	217800	ARMY	404	
		217801	223952	ARMY	6152	
1918		223953	223990	NAVY	38	
		223991	232000	ARMY	8010	Marked "MODEL OF 1911. U.S. ARMY"
		232001	233600	NAVY	1600	
		233601	573000	ARMY	319746	Not shipped in numeric order

Model 1911, M1911A1

Year	Manufacturer	Start Serial Number	End Serial Number	Military Service Destination	Quantity	Notes
Model 1911/1911A1 U.S. Army Ordnance Department Assigned Serial Numbers (s/n) Annotated, cont.						
1918	Rem-UMC	1	13381	ARMY	13381	Remington Arms-UMC was assigned their own s/n range
1919	Rem-UMC, cont.	13382	21676	ARMY	8295	Remington Arms-UMC was assigned their own s/n range.
	Colt	551000	629500	ARMY	76154	Production stopped after s/n 629500
Model 1911A1 Production, U.S. Army Ordnance Department Contract						
1924		700001	710000	General Stores	10000	Model 1911A1 production begins
1937		710001	711605	Army/Navy	1605	836 to the Navy, 769 to the Army
		711606	712349	Navy	744	Navy shipment
1938		712350	713645	General Stores	1296	Begin marking slides **MI9IIAI U.S. ARMY** to end of production, Smallest 1911A1 shipment year
1939	Colt	713646	717281	Navy	3636	Known as "1939 Navy"
1940		717282	721977	General Stores	4696	Mostly CSR inspected
1941		721978	756733	General Stores	34756	721978 –ca. 734000 blued, after ca. 734000 all Parkerized
1942		756734	793657	General Stores	36924	
		793658	797639	Navy	3982	Known as "1942 Navy"

Military and Commercial Pistols

Model 1911/1911A1 U.S. Army Ordnance Department Assigned Serial Numbers (s/n) Annotated, cont.						
Year	Manufacturer	Start Serial Number	End Serial Number	Military Service Destination	Quantity	Notes
1942, cont.	Colt, cont.	797640	800000	General Stores	2361	After #799441 pistols no longer shipped in numeric order. All s/n ranges following s/n 799441 are approximate
1941	Singer Mfg. Co.	S800001	S800500	Springfield to USAAF	500	Slides are marked "S. MFG. CO". Rarest 1911A1 manufacturer
NA	H&R Mfg. Co.	H800501	H801000	Order Canceled	0	None delivered, Order Canceled
1942		801001	856100	General Stores	55100 (1)	All s/n ranges following #799441 are approximate
	Colt	856101	862000	General Stores	5899 (1)	Approximate s/n ranges.
1943		862001	958100	General Stores	102,000	Approximate s/n ranges.
1941	RI Arsenal	856101	856300	RIA Rework	200	S/ns duplicated by Colt
1942	Augusta Arsenal	856301	856304	AA Rework	4	S/ns duplicated by Colt
	RI Arsenal	856305	856404	RIA Rework	100	S/ns duplicated by Colt
1943	Ithaca	856405	916404	General Stores	60000	S/ns duplicated by Colt

Model 1911, M1911A1

Model 1911/1911A1 U.S. Army Ordnance Department Assigned Serial Numbers (s/n) Annotated, cont.

Year	Manufacturer	Start Serial Number	End Serial Number	Military Service Destination	Quantity	Notes
1942	Remington Rand	916405	921700	General Stores	5295 (1)	Approximate s/n range. S/n duplicated by Colt
		921701	1041404	General Stores	125,000 (1)	Approximate s/n range s/n duplicated by Colt—921701-958100
1943	Union Switch & Signal	1041405	1096404	General Stores	55000	Colt duplicated s/ns 1088726-1092896
1943, cont.		1088726	1092896	General Stores	4171	Colt duplication s/ns of US&S s/ns 1088726 -1092896
	Colt	1096405	1154999	General Stores	58594 (1)	Approximate s/n range
1944		1155000	1208673	General Stores	112,269 (1)	Approximate s/n range
1943	Ithaca	1208674	1235000	General Stores	26326 (1)	Approximate s/n range
1944		1235001	1279673	General Stores	71,000 (1)	Approximate s/n range
unknown	Augusta Arsenal	1279674	1279698	AA Rework	25	Replacement Numbers
1943	Remington Rand	1279699	1363699	General Stores	84,000 (1)	Approximate s/n range

Military and Commercial Pistols

Year	Manufacturer	Start Serial Number	End Serial Number	Military Service Destination	Quantity	Notes
	Remington Rand	1363700	1441430	General Stores	161,732 (1)	Approximate s/n range
1944	Ithaca	1441431	1471430	General Stores	30,000	
	Remington Rand	1471431	1609528	General Stores	138,098	Approximate s/n range
	Colt	1609529	1719999	General Stores	110,470 (1)	Approximate s/n range
1945	Colt, cont.	1720000	1743846	General Stores	134,318 (1)	Approximate s/n range
1944	Remington Rand	1743847	1816641	General Stores	72,795	
	Ithaca	1816642	1845997	General Stores	29355 (1)	Approximate s/n range
1945		1845998	1890503	General Stores	73,862 (1)	Approximate s/n range
1944	Remington Rand	1890504	2031600	General Stores	141096 (1)	Approximate s/n range
1945		2031601	2075103	General Stores	184,600 (1)	Approximate s/n range

Model 1911/1911A1 U.S. Army Ordnance Department Assigned Serial Numbers (s/n) Annotated, cont.

Model 1911, M1911A1

						Model 1911/1911A1 U.S. Army Ordnance Department Assigned Serial Numbers (s/n) Annotated, cont.
Year	**Manufac- turer**	**Start Serial Num- ber**	**End Serial Number**	**Military Service Destination**	**Quantity**	**Notes**
1944	Ithaca	2075104	2110464	General Stores	35360 (1)	Approximate s/n range
		2110465	2134403	General Stores	59,300 (1)	Approximate s/n range
	Remington Rand	2134404	2244803	General Stores	110,400	
1945	Colt	2244804	2368781	General Stores	Approx. 119,450 (1)	Approximate s/n range
		2368782	2380013	Canceled	None (1)	
	Remington Rand	2380014	2465139	General Stores	85,126 (1)	Approximate s/n range
		2465140	2619013	Canceled	None (1)	
	Ithaca	2619014	2660318	General Stores	41,305 (1)	Approximate s/n range
		2660319	2693613	Canceled	None (1)	

1. Manufacture and/or shipping spanned the years shown in the boxed entry with an overlap of serial numbers at the end of the first year. The number in the first year is approximate but the total in the second year is the exact number shipped.

Appendix G
British Military and Commercial Proof Marks

It is a misconception among many collectors that arms used by Great Britain's military forces during World War I or World War II will show what were commercial proofs. True military-issue small arms, with the exception of many Lend-Lease weapons, will show British military markings. They will also show commercial proof marks if they were sold in commercial trade after having been released from service. Those pre-World War I and pre-World War II Model 1911 or 1911A1 pistols in .45 or .455 caliber that were sold privately by commercial dealers to individuals in the early stages of both wars will show the commercial proofs of the period. Firearms purchased by the British government for issue to the military will not show commercial proof marks unless those marks were applied after they were released from government service and before being sold on the commercial market in the United Kingdom, or to firms in the United Kingdom intending to export them to other countries, such as the United States.

The collector must be aware of the distinction between those Model 1911s and 1911A1s which were sold commercially in Great Britain and those acquired by the government for military service. Those distinctions are described in the following paragraphs.

British *military* firearms, from the period of World War I through the end of World War II, were marked with 1) the government property mark, the broad arrow; 2) with the proof mark which was the crossed pennants; 3) and with an inspector's mark, usually a crown with the initial(s) of the reigning monarch over the initial or number of the War Department inspector. The crossed pennants proof mark was also stamped on each major part of the firearm, see Figure G-1, G-2 (A), and Table G-1.

Additional marks found on many British 1911/1911A1 pistols are **NOT ENGLISH MAKE** and, if intended to be sold in commercial trade, **RE-LEASED BRITISH GOVT.** and the year, see Figure G-3. These marks

479

Model 1911, M1911A1

were applied after the pistols were declared surplus and released from military service.

NOTE: Firearms acquired by the British military before World War I will frequently show the broad arrow over "**WD**" for War Department.

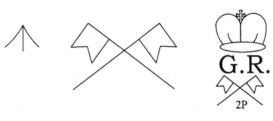

Fig. G-1. Markings signifying British military ownership, left to right: Broad Arrow; Crossed Pennants proof mark, and reigning monarch's crown and initials over crossed pennants above the inspector's identification.

Because of the need to put firearms into the hands of the British military or Home Guard in 1940-1941, many firearms sent from the United States (and possibly other countries) did not always go through either the proof testing or the military inspection program, initially. But by the war's end in 1945, virtually all that were issued to the troops or Home Guard had. Of course, those that may have been lost, stolen, or "borrowed" may not show these markings.

Fig. G-2. The broad arrow to the right (A) indicates that this Colt New Service was purchased in 1915 for use with British forces. The double broad arrow on the left (B) shows that it was released from military service.

The Model 1911/1911A1 was declared obsolete and surplus to military needs in 1947 and released for commercial sale. But some were also released by the British government prior to World War II; these will show two broad arrows, tip to tip indicating that the pistol was released from service, refer to Figure G-2, B. Also, commercial pistols that had been purchased by civilians and military personnel found their way into

Military and Commercial Pistols

commercial trade. All of the Model 1911/1911A1s sold after 1947 will show 1) the commercial markings of 1904, if released before 1925; 2) the commercial markings of 1925 if released by 1954; 3) or the commercial markings of 1955 if released in that year and after.

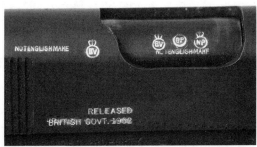

Firearms released from British military service from 1955 on will show markings consistent with the commercial proofing rules of 1955. However, and this cannot be empha-

Fig. G-3. Lend-Lease Model 1911A1s released from British military service after 1947 will show the legend, "RELEASED BRITISH GOVT." and the year.

sized enough, the presence of 1955 commercial proof marks on a firearm is not proof that the firearm was in British military service during World War II. The proof laws applied to all firearms sold from 1955 on, both commercial and military, just as the commercial proof marks of 1904 or 1925 were applied to all firearms sold after those years.

Only if the firearm shows the British military markings, the Broad Arrow and crossed pennants, can you be sure that it saw service in some branch of the British military, see Table G-1.

Table G-1 British Military Markings Found on Model 1911/Model 1911A1 Pistols *
Pre-World War I
Proof Mark
Broad Arrow (British military ownership)
WD (War Department)
May also show commercial proof marks of 1904, either London or Birmingham. See Table G-2.
World War I
Broad Arrow (British military ownership)

Model 1911, M1911A1

Table G-1, cont. British Military Markings Found on Model 1911/Model 1911A1 Pistols *
Crossed Pennants proof mark (proof mark)
1914-1916: Swallowtail pennants
1916-1918: Triangle pennants indicating proofing at Colt's Hartford, Connecticut
View Proof (inspection)
Crown/alphanumeric/E indicating inspection at RSAF Enfield Lock
Crown/G2/A indicating inspection at Colt's Hartford, Connecticut
World War II
U.S. civilian/business donations: Colt factory commercial markings
British Purchasing Commission: Broad arrow, Enfield inspection marking, no crossed pennants
Lend-Lease: U.S. property and Ordnance Department inspection markings. Not military
Australian purchase or British supplied: broad arrow within "D"
Canadian purchase or British supplied: Canadian broad arrow in "C"
* All British military M1911/1911A1s sold as surplus to military needs in commercial trade will show the Government commercial proof marks according to the schemes of 1925 or 1955, depending on when they were released. May also be marked "RELEASED BRITISH GOVERNMENT" and the year. Some Commonwealth pistol not marked.

BRITISH COMMERCIAL MARKINGS

British proof marks are found on numerous Model 1911s and Model 1911A1s. Great Britain established national proof laws in 1631 and they were administered by the first English gunsmith guild, The Armourers' Company. Initially, seven gunsmiths in this guild were charged with inspecting and maintaining the firearms of members of the citizens militia. Six years later, "The Master Wardens and Society to the Misterie of Gunmakers of the City of London"—later known as "The Worshipful Company of Gunmakers in the City of London"—was founded by "125 gunmakers." This organization established the first proof tests and was granted the right by the Crown to conduct all proof testing within an area encompassing the City of London and out to ten miles beyond its city limits. Over the years, the regulations regarding proofing grew to

Military and Commercial Pistols

encompass all major parts of a firearm. We are concerned here with the British proof rules of 1904, 1925 and 1955 as listed in Table G-2.

Table G-2
British Commercial Markings Found on Model 1911/Model 1911A1 Pistols

London	Birmingham
Proof Rules of 1904 (1904-1925)	
Proof Mark	
Crown over intertwined GP—barrel	Crown over BP—barrel
View Mark	
Crown over V on barrel, receiver, and slide	Crown over BV—barrel, receiver, and slide
Proof Rules of 1925 (1926-1954)	
Proof Mark	
Crown over intertwined GP within a circle—barrel	Crown over BP within a circle—barrel
View Mark	
Crown over V in circle—barrel, receiver, and slide	Crown over BV within a circle—barrel, receiver, and slide
Nitro Proof	
Arm upraised with Sword over NP within a circle—barrel	Crown over NP within circle—barrel
Viewer's Proof	
Not applicable	Crossed scepters with initials and/or numbers on right left and bottom
NOT ENGLISH MAKE stamped on all firearms not manufactured in Great Britain — 1925-1955 only	
Proof Rules of 1955 (1955 to Present)	
Proof Mark	
Crown over intertwined GP—receiver and slide	Crown over BNP—receiver and slide
Nitro Proof	
Arm upraised with Sword over NP within a circle—barrel .45" (or .455") .900" 7 TONSPER □"	Crown over BNP .45" (or .455") .900" 7 TONSPER □"

Model 1911, M1911A1

Appendix H
Prefixes and Suffixes for the Model 1911/1911A1 and Variations

During a long period of manufacture a variety of prefixes and suffixes were used to identify various lines of Model 1911/1911A1 production. The best known are variations on the abbreviation for number to signify pistols manufactured to fulfill U.S. Army Ordnance Department and U.S. Navy contracts, "C" for commercial production, and "W" for production in .455 Webley caliber. The 1968 Gun Control Act in the United States required in-depth record keeping beyond that for internal accounting purposes. In 1970, Colt changed its serial numbering system to include other prefixes and suffixes to identify more closely the individual lines of pistols. All prefixes and suffixes used by Colt, Remington Arms-UMC, Springfield Armory, Singer, Ithaca, Remington Rand and Union Switch & Signal are listed in Table H-1, below.

Table H-1
Model 1911/1911A1 Serial Number Prefixes and Suffixes

Prefix	Suffix	Manufact-urer	Model and/or Serial Number or Year Range
None		Colt	.22 ACE, All pre-World War II production
None		Colt	Special Army Model (March 1911 Test, 15 manufactured)
None		Colt	Super .38 Automatic Pistol
C		Colt	Commercial Model 1911/1911A1 (C1-C240,227
	C	Colt	Commercial M1911A1 (240,228C-336,169C)
CLW		Colt	Lightweight Commander (aluminum receiver) Series 70 (1969-1983)
CS		Colt	Super .38 Automatic Pistol, Series 70
FA		Colt	Officer's Model ACP Mk IV
FC		Colt	Commander, Nickel (1983+)
FG		Colt	.45 Automatic Pistol (1983+)
FL		Colt	Commander series (1984+)

Military and Commercial Pistols

Prefix	Suffix	Manufacturer	Model and/or Serial Number or Year Range
	**Table H-1, cont.** **Model 1911/1911A1 Serial Number Prefixes and Suffixes**		
FN		Colt	Gold Cup National Match Pistol .45 ACP (1983+)
GO		Rock Island Arsenal	General Officer M15 Pistol
	H	Colt	.38 Special Conversion Kit
	LW	Colt	Lightweight Commander (aluminum receiver, 1949-1968)
	NM	Colt	Gold Cup National Match Automatic Pistol (1957-1970)
	NMR	Colt	Super 38 National Match Automatic Pistol (1946-1960)
	MS	Colt	Gold Cup National Match Automatic Pistol (small number in 1961
No.		Colt	Colt Model 1911 (s/n # 1-4,500)
Nº		Colt	Colt Model 1911/1911A1 (s/n #4,501-EOP)
		Springfield Armory	All production
		Ithaca	All production (see Nº I below)
		Remington Rand	Model 1911A1, s/n # 916,405 to 955,000-1,015,499
		Union Switch & Signal	All production
Nº I		Ithaca	Some early production, rare
NO.		Remington Arms-UMC	All production
		Remington Rand	955,001 to 1,015,499-EOP
Nº S		Singer	All production
	O	Colt	.38 Special Conversion Kit
SM		Colt	.22 Service Model ACE
U		Colt	.22-.45 and .45-.22 Conversion Kit

485

Model 1911, M1911A1

Prefix	Suffix	Manufact-urer	Model and/or Serial Number or Year Range
W		Colt	Model 1911 Automatic Pistol, .455 Webley caliber
X		Any	U.S. Ordnance Department-issue replacement serial number
70B		Colt	.45 Automatic Pistol, Series 70 (1981 ((?))-1983+)
70BS		Colt	Colt Commander Automatic Pistol (blue finish), Series 70
70G		Colt	.45 Automatic Pistol, Series 70 (1970-1976)
	G70	Colt	.45 Automatic Pistol, Series 70 (1976-1979)
70L		Colt	9 mm Automatic Pistol, Series 70
70N		Colt	Gold Cup National Match .45 (1970-1980)
	N70	Colt	Gold Cup National Match .45 (1980-1983)
70S		Colt	Super .38 Automatic Pistol, Series 70
70SC		Colt	Colt Commander Automatic Pistol (nickel finish), Series 70
80BS		Colt	Colt Commander Automatic Pistol, Series 80

APPENDIX I
MODEL 1911/1911A1/SERIES 70/80 SLIDE MARKINGS

Model 1911 (Military), Colt, Slide, Left

Colt, slide, left. s/n 1-83,855. **Patent** and **address** blocks in serif type.

Colt, slide, left, s/n 83,856-247,290. August 19, 1913 **patent** added.

Colt, slide, left, s/n 247,291-EOP. **Patent** and **address** marks in sans serif type.

Colt, slide, left s/n 1-20,000. Colt **logotype**—rampant colt in a circle—behind grasping grooves, or slide serrations.

Colt, slide, left, s/n ca. 20,001-275,000 to 280,000. Colt **logotype**—rampant colt without a circle—behind grasping grooves, or slide serrations.

NOTE: Slide marking photographs are from the collections of Karl Karash and North Cape Publications, Inc., unless otherwise noted.

Model 1911, M1911A1

Colt, slide, left, s/n 275,001-280,000 to 625,500. Colt **logotype** located between patent and address blocks.

MODEL 1911 (MILITARY), COLT, SLIDE, RIGHT

Colt, slide, right, s/n 1-180,000. **Model** marking in serif type face.

Colt, slide, right, s/n 180,001-260,000. **Model** marking in sans serif type face with letters and numbers 0.09 inch high.

Colt, slide, right, s/n 260,001-629,500 and 700,001-712,349. **Model** marking in sans serif type face with letters and numbers 0.11 inch high.

Colt, slide, right, **U.S. Navy** marking in type face with serifs, letters and number 0.09 inch high.

Military and Commercial Pistols

MODEL 1911/1911A1 COLT (COMMERCIAL), SLIDE MARKINGS, RIGHT

Colt, slide, right, s/n C1-C130,000. **Commercial** model marking.

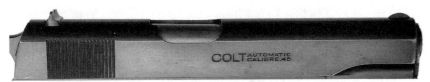

Colt, slide, right, s/n C130,001-C221.000. **Commercial** model marking.

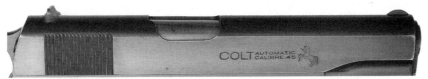

Colt, slide, right, s/n C220,001-272,500C. **Commercial** model marking.

Colt, slide, right, s/n 275,001C to mid-1970s. Non-National Match **commercial** marking.

Colt, slide, right, Series 70/80 non-National Match **commercial** marking.

Model 1911, M1911A1

Colt, slide, right, Series 80 and M1991 **commercial** model marking.

MODEL 1911/1911A1 COLT (COMMERCIAL), SLIDE MARKINGS, LEFT

Colt, slide, left, s/n C1-C6,500. **Patent** and **address** markings in a type face with serifs. This was the same marking used from s/n 1-83,855 on military pistols.

Colt, slide, left, s/n C6,501-C130,000. **August 19, 1913 patent added.**

Colt, slide, left, s/n C130,001-336,169C. **Patent** and **address** blocks rearranged into two lines of sans serif type. Logotype moved to right side.

Colt, slide, left, **Series 70**

Military and Commercial Pistols

Colt, slide, left, **Series 80**.

Colt, slide, left, **Model 1991A1** series.

NATIONAL MATCH, COLT (PRE-WORLD WAR II), SLIDE MARKINGS

Colt, slide, left, Pre-World War II National Match. Model, name and caliber in **sans serif** type.

Colt, slide, left, Pre-World War II National Match. Patent and address blocks in two lines of **sans serif** type.

Colt, slide, right, **Post-World War II National Match (Gold Cup)**.

Model 1911, M1911A1

Colt, slide, left, **Post-World War II National Match (Gold Cup)**.

COLT, SUPER .38 MODEL AUTOMATIC PISTOL, SLIDE MARKINGS

Colt, slide, right, **Pre-World War II Super .38 Automatic Pistol**. The left side used the s/n C156,001-C215,018 address and patent marking.

COLT, ACE AND SERVICE ACE, SLIDE MARKINGS

Colt, slide, Right, **Pre-World War II ACE** .22 Caliber pistol.

Colt, slide, right, **Pre-World War II Service ACE** .22 caliber pistol.

COLT .22-.45 CONVERSION UNIT, SLIDE MARKINGS

Colt, slide, Left, **Pre-World War II ACE and Service ACE** .22 Caliber pistols.

Military and Commercial Pistols

Colt, slide, right, 1946-1955 **.22 caliber conversion unit**.

Colt, slide, left, 1946-1955 **.22 caliber conversion unit**.

COLT, COMMANDER, SLIDE MARKINGS

Colt, slide, right, **Lightweight Commander** marking, pre- Series 70.

Colt, slide, left, **Lightweight Commander** marking, pre-Series 70.

Colt, slide, left, **Commander** marking, Series 70.

493

Model 1911, M1911A1

MODEL 1911, SPRINGFIELD ARMORY, SLIDE MARKINGS

Springfield Armory, slide, right, all production. **Model** marking in sans serif type face.

Springfield Armory, slide, left, all production. **Patent** and **address** markings in sans serif type face.

MODEL 1911, REMINGTON ARMS-UMC SLIDE MARKINGS

Remington Arms-UMC, slide, right, all production. **Model** marking in sans serif

Remington Arms-UMC, slide, left, all production. **Patent** and **address** markings in sans serif type.

MODEL 1911, NORTH AMERICAN ARMS, SLIDE MARKINGS

North American Arms, Ltd., slide, left, all production. Right side left blank. Address marking in sans serif type.

494

Military and Commercial Pistols

MODEL 1911A1, ITHACA GUN COMPANY, SLIDE MARKINGS

Ithaca, slide, right, s/n 906,000-916,400 and a few as late as 1,208,674-1,208,700. All other Ithaca slides are left blank on the right side.

Ithaca, slide, left, all production.

MODEL 1911A1, REMINGTON RAND, SLIDE MARKINGS

Remington Rand, slide, left, s/n 916,405-930,000. **Address** 1.35 inches long. Right side left blank.

Remington Rand, slide, left, s/n 930,001-1,020,000 with overlap at both ends of the range. Address with **U.S.A.** added

Remington Rand, slide, left, s/n 1,000,000-EOP. After s/n 1,020,000 used exclusively. **Address** 1.20 inches long.

Model 1911, M1911A1

MODEL 1911A1, UNION SWITCH & SIGNAL, SLIDE MARKINGS

Union Switch & Signal Company, slide, left, all production. Right slide left blank.

UNIQUE SLIDE MARKINGS

A.J. Savage slide. The contract was canceled in late 1918 before finished pistols could be manufactured. Some slides were later used as replacement parts.

This slide may or may not be original Harrington & Richardson production from their canceled 1941 Education Contract. It is included here for informational purposes only. The slide was mounted on an unnumbered Colt M1911A1 receiver that had been imported by Century Arms International as part of a shipment of miscellaneous arms. Fred Buswell collection.

APPENDIX J
DISASSEMBLY/ASSEMBLY PROCEDURE
MODEL 1911/1911A1

John M. Browning designed the Model 1911 for, among other characteristics, ease of "takedown" for cleaning. Accordingly, there are two levels of assembly/disassembly: "takedown" for cleaning and routine maintenance, and "complete disassembly" for repair and refurbishment. Pistols should be fieldstripped and cleaned after every shooting session. Complete disassembly should be very infrequent unless the pistol receives heavy use.

Always wear safety glasses. Always clean the bore with a brass bristle brush from the rear to avoid damaging the lands at the muzzle. Do not use stainless steel bore brushes. Use a good grade of cleaning solvent, and apply a *light* coat of oil with a cleaning patch to the interior and exterior of the barrel and all other parts. Copper and lead fouling should be removed depending on the degree of buildup your barrel experiences. There are a number of good kits available for this purpose from most gun and sporting good stores.

Wipe the outside surfaces of any firearm with a soft cloth impregnated with silicone oil to remove fingerprints, dust and any airborne pollution. After cleaning, apply an occasional coat of lemon oil to oil-finished wood stocks, or wax to resin-impregnated stocks. Ivory, stag, mother-of-pearl, or exotic wood stocks should be washed with a mild soap solution, dried thoroughly and thinly coated with a good grade of auto wax containing silicone.

Needless to say, all firearms and ammunition must be stored in securely locked containers.

NOTE: All directions are given from the shooter's point of view with the pistol held properly in the hand unless otherwise noted. When disassem-

Model 1911, M1911A1

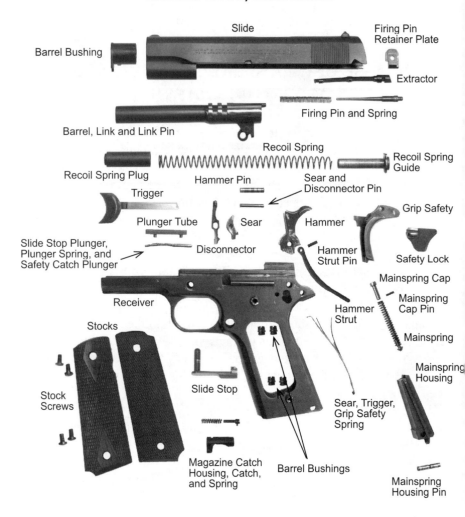

Slide

Firing Pin
Retainer Plate

Barrel Bushing

Extractor

Firing Pin and Spring

Barrel, Link and Link Pin

Recoil Spring

Recoil Spring
Guide

Recoil Spring Plug

Hammer Pin

Sear and
Disconnector Pin

Trigger

Grip Safety

Plunger Tube

Sear

Hammer

Slide Stop Plunger,
Plunger Spring, and
Safety Catch Plunger

Disconnector

Hammer
Strut Pin

Safety Lock

Receiver

Mainspring Cap

Mainspring
Cap Pin

Stocks

Hammer
Strut

Mainspring

Stock
Screws

Slide Stop

Mainspring
Housing

Sear, Trigger,
Grip Safety
Spring

Magazine Catch
Housing, Catch,
and Spring

Barrel Bushings

Mainspring
Housing Pin

When disassembling the Model 1911/1911A1 according to the instructions on the following pages, use this as a guide to part names.
Do not force any part and do not use a screwdriver or other blade to
separate parts, particularly the stocks from the receiver.

Clean powder residue from all parts. Check carefully in all
crevices. When reassembling, lightly oil all parts to prevent rust and
corrosion and to assure smooth, flawless operation.

498

Military and Commercial Pistols

bling any firearm, lay the parts on a clean surface in the order in which they were removed.

FIELDSTRIPPING
Begin by following the first rule of firearms handling: **assume all firearms are loaded**. Always check to see that they are not.

1. Remove the **magazine** by pressing the magazine release on the right side of the pistol, see Figure J-1.

2. Draw the slide back and look into the **ejector port** on the top right side of the slide to make sure that there is no cartridge in the breech, see Figure J-2. On Series 70 pistols, draw the slide all the way back so that the Accurizor bushing edges past the barrel shoulder and can be turned.

3. Push in on the **recoil spring plug** under the barrel and turn the **barrel bushing** to your left. Use a finger to control the recoil spring plug and recoil spring to prevent it from flying out.

4. Ease out the **recoil spring plug** and **recoil spring** out through the front of the **recoil spring housing**, see Figure J-3.

5. Cock the **hammer** and push the **slide** back until the **slide stop** can be raised into the slide dismount cut (small notch to rear), see Figure J-4.

6. The leg of the **slide stop** passes through the **receiver** from left to right. Push on the end of the slide stop leg from the right and remove it from the receiver.

7. Turn the pistol upside down and move the **slide** forward and off the **receiver**.

8. With the slide upside down, turn the **barrel bushing** in the opposite direction and pull out from the slide, see Figure J-5.

9. Remove the **recoil spring** and **recoil spring guide** by pulling it up and back out of the slide, see Figure J-6.

Model 1911, M1911A1

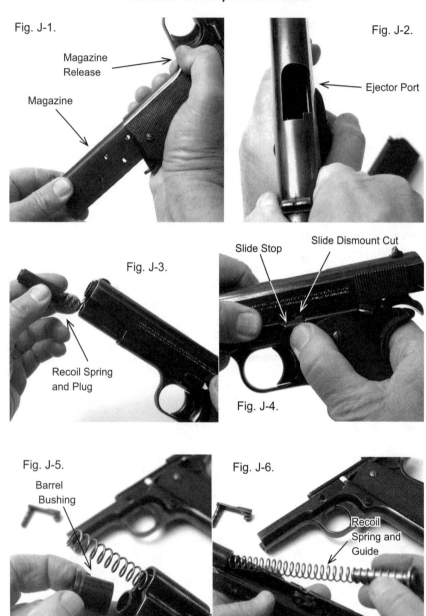

Fig. J-1.

Magazine Release

Magazine

Fig. J-2.

Ejector Port

Fig. J-3.

Recoil Spring and Plug

Slide Stop

Slide Dismount Cut

Fig. J-4.

Fig. J-5.

Barrel Bushing

Fig. J-6.

Recoil Spring and Guide

500

Military and Commercial Pistols

10. Push the **barrel link** forward and remove the barrel from the slide. This completes the fieldstripping procedure. Before reassembling, make certain the barrel is clean and unobstructed. If the pistol will not be used any time soon, apply a *light* coating of oil with a clean patch to the bore and outside of the barrel, also to the slide, both inside and out, and all other parts.

To Reassemble

11. Insert the **barrel** through the front of the slide until the locking lugs engage with the slide, see Figure J-7.

12. Hold the slide upside down. Insert the **barrel bushing** into the **barrel bushing seat** and turn it to your right.

13. Insert the **recoil spring guide** and **recoil spring** through the rear of the **recoil spring housing**.

14. With the barrel link lying forward along the barrel, and your thumb pressing down slightly on **the recoil spring guide** to hold it and the **barrel link** in place, slide the **receiver** onto the **slide** from the front, see Figure J-8.

15. Slide the **receiver** back slightly to free the **barrel link**, then forward. Line up the **slide dismount cut** with the rear of the **slide stop**. Press the **slide stop** down past the **slide stop plunger**—taking care not to scratch the side of the **receiver**—and through the **barrel link** and into its hole on the other side of the receiver, see Figure J-9.

16. Place the **recoil spring plug** on the **recoil spring** and press down with the tip of your index finger until it is below the **barrel bushing**. Move the barrel bushing to your right so that it captures the **recoil spring plug**, see Figure J-10.

CAUTION: the recoil spring exerts between eighteen and twenty-four pounds of pressure and can cause severe eye damage. Never point the recoil spring assembly directly at your face when assembling or disassembling the pistol. Always control the recoil plug and spring with your finger when the assembly is under tension.

Model 1911, M1911A1

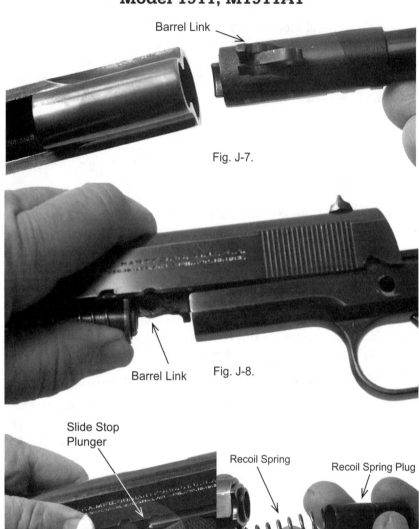

Barrel Link

Fig. J-7.

Barrel Link   Fig. J-8.

Slide Stop
Plunger

Recoil Spring   Recoil Spring Plug

Slide Stop

Fig. J-9.   Fig. J-10.

Military and Commercial Pistols

COMPLETE DISASSEMBLY

With the pistol fieldstripped, the **slide** can be disassembled as follows:

17. Use a pointed tool to press in on the rear of the **firing pin** until the **firing pin stop** can be moved down in its track, see Figure J-11. Shift the tool up to control the **firing pin spring** as the firing pin stop moves past it.

18. Remove the **firing pin** and its **firing pin spring**.

19. Use a screwdriver to remove the **extractor** by prying outward, see Figure J-12.

20. To remove the **rear sight** (only if damaged and must be replaced), drive it out from left to right using a flat-faced brass punch of the proper size.

21. Do not attempt to remove the **front sight**. If it must be replaced, it should be done by a competent gunsmith.

Reassembly of the Slide
The procedure is the reverse of the disassembly procedure.

Disassembly of the Receiver
With the pistol fieldstripped, the **receiver** can be disassembled as follows:

22. Remove the **stock screws** holding the stocks in place. With the screws out, reach your index finger into the magazine well and gently push the **stocks** up and off the **stock screw bushings**. Do not insert a screwdriver or other tool between the **stock** and **receiver** to pry them off, see Figure J-13.

23. It is not a good idea to remove the **stock screw bushings** unless absolutely necessary. If you must, use a screwdriver of the proper size so that the slots are not damaged. Use Loctite when replacing them. Take care not to crossthread the bushings when replacing them.

24. With the hammer down, remove the **mainspring housing pin** by pushing it out to the right with a non-marring tool, see Figure J-14.

Model 1911, M1911A1

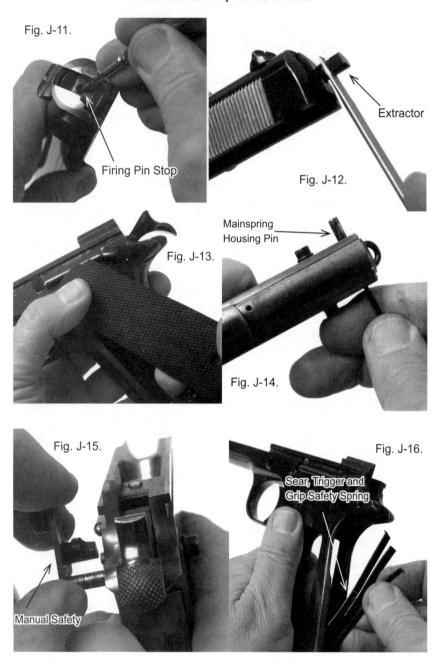

Fig. J-11.

Firing Pin Stop

Extractor

Fig. J-12.

Fig. J-13.

Mainspring
Housing Pin

Fig. J-14.

Fig. J-15.

Fig. J-16.

Sear, Trigger and
Grip Safety Spring

Manual Safety

Military and Commercial Pistols

25. Remove the **mainspring housing assembly** from the receiver by sliding it down and off.

26. Pull the **hammer** back slightly and push in on the leg of the **thumb safety** on the right side of the receiver. Wriggle both the thumb safety and hammer until the manual safety slides out of the receiver to the left, see Figure J-15.

27. Remove the **grip safety**.

28. Remove the **sear**, **trigger**, and **grip safety spring**, see Figure J-16.

29. Push out the **hammer pin** from the right and remove the **hammer**.

30. Push out the **sear and disconnector pin** and remove the **sear** and **disconnector**.

31. Insert a small screwdriver into the slotted head of the **magazine catch spring guide**. Push in on the **magazine catch** so that it protrudes from the right side of the **receiver** and turn the screwdriver carefully counterclockwise, see Figure J-17. Remove the **magazine catch** from the right.

32. Disassemble the **magazine catch** by turning the slotted head clockwise and drawing out the **magazine catch spring guide** and **spring**, see Figure J-18.

CAUTION: The magazine catch is under spring tension.

33. Push the **trigger** back until it can be drawn out the rear of the receiver.

34. Remove the **slide stop plunger** assembly by drawing it out of the **plunger tube** to the rear, see Figure J-19. Note that the forward end (slide stop plunger) has a rebate. This prevents it from falling out of the plunger tube. Reinsert with this end forward. Note also the slight bend or kink in the spring. Do not attempt to straighten it.

35. To disassemble the **mainspring housing**, use a small flat-face punch to remove the **mainspring cap pin**, see Figure J-20.

Model 1911, M1911A1

Fig. J-17.

Magazine Catch
Assembly

Fig. J-18.

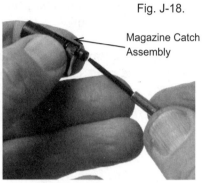

Magazine Catch
Assembly

Fig. J-19.

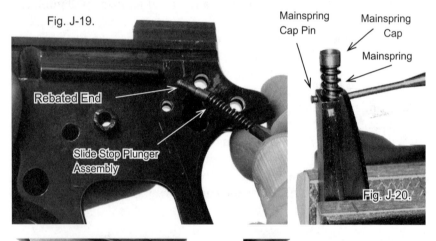

Rebated End

Slide Stop Plunger
Assembly

Mainspring
Cap Pin

Mainspring
Cap

Mainspring

Fig. J-20.

Fig. J-21.

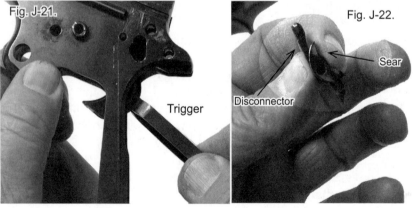

Trigger

Fig. J-22.

Sear

Disconnector

Military and Commercial Pistols

CAUTION: The mainspring is under significant tension and will fly out. Be sure to control it at all times and never allow it to point at your face.

36. Remove the **mainspring** and its **mainspring cap** and **mainspring housing pin retainer**.

37. Do not remove the **plunger tube**. If it must be removed, have it done by a competent gunsmith. Always replace with a new plunger tube.

38. Do not attempt to remove the **ejector** as it is pinned in place. If it must be removed, have it done by a competent gunsmith.

Reassembly of the Receiver
Before reassembly, clean and *lightly* oil all parts including the inside and outside of the receiver.

39. Grip the **mainspring housing** in a padded vise and use a flat-face punch to force the **mainspring cap** and **mainspring** down far enough to insert the mainspring cap pin.

40. Reinsert the **trigger** through the rear of the receiver. You may want to apply a *slight* bit of light lubricating grease to the side rails only, see Figure J-21.

41. Reassemble the **magazine catch** by inserting the **magazine spring guide** into the **spring**. Insert the assembly into the **magazine catch** and turn the slotted head counterclockwise.

42. Insert the assembled **magazine catch** into the **receiver**. Push in on the **magazine catch** so that it rises slightly above the right side of the **receiver** and turn the slotted head clockwise.

43. Assemble the **sear** and **disconnector** with the curved end of the **sear** pointing up and the flat bottom of the **disconnector** down and forward, see Figure J-22. Slide the **assembly** into the rear of the **receiver** with the **disconnector** protruding through the top of the frame and its flat is against the **trigger bar**. Insert the **sear** and **disconnector pin**, see Figure J-23.

Model 1911, M1911A1

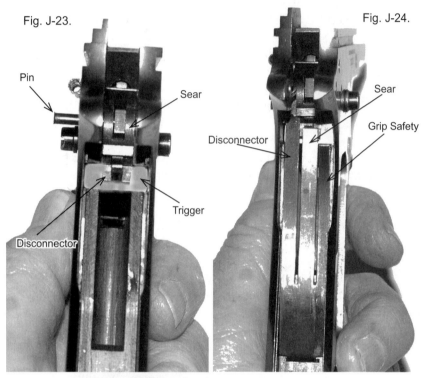

Fig. J-23.

Pin

Sear

Disconnector

Trigger

Disconnector

Fig. J-24.

Sear

Grip Safety

Fig. J-25.

Grip Safety

Military and Commercial Pistols

44. Slide the **hammer** into place and insert the **hammer pin**.

45. Place the **sear**, **trigger**, and **grip safety spring** into its slot at the bottom rear of the **receiver**, see Figure J-24. Make sure that the left tip (bent at a right angle) presses against the **sear** and the middle leaf against the **disconnector and trigger**. Slide the **mainspring housing** on just far enough to hold the mainspring in place.

46. Place the **grip safety** into the vertical opening at the rear of the **receiver**, see Figure J-25.

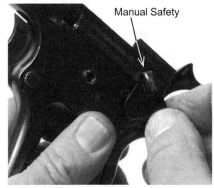

Manual Safety

Fig. J-26.

47. Insert the leg of the **manual safety** through the holes in the **receiver tang** and the **grip safety**.

48. With the **hammer** in the half-cock position, turn the **manual safety** down while pressing inward so that it passes the **safety catch plunger** and seats between the **hammer** and **sear**, see Figure J-26.

49. With the **hammer** in the down position, slide the **mainspring housing** fully into position and insert the **mainspring housing pin** at the bottom of the grip, see Figure J-27.

50. Cock the **hammer** and while controlling it with your thumb, pull the **trigger** to lower it. This procedure assures that you have reassembled the receiver correctly.

51. Reattach the **stocks**.

Magazine Disassembly
The magazine may be disassembled for cleaning. Lubricate light-

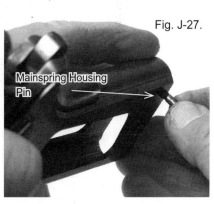

Fig. J-27.

Mainspring Housing Pin

Model 1911, M1911A1

ly after cleaning and before reassembly. Wipe the inside dry before reassembling.

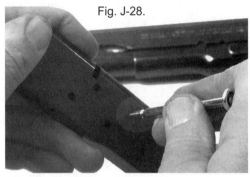

Fig. J-28.

52. Use a non-marring tool to press the **follower** down past the fourth viewing hole.

53. Insert a rod or screwdriver through the fourth view hole to hold the **spring** in place, see Figure J-28.

54. Turn the **magazine** upside down and shake to allow the **follower** to drop down. Lift up by the front lip, twist slightly and draw out, see Figure J-29.

55. Place your hand over the top of the **magazine** and ease out the tool holding the **spring**. Remove the **spring**.

56. Model 1911/1911A1 magazine **base plates** are pinned or welded in place. Removing the base plate will probably damage it or the magazine body.

To reassemble, place the **spring** in the **magazine body**. Place the flat back of **the magazine follower** on top of the **spring** and slide it back and tip down until the **follower** clears the magazine lips. Use a small screwdriver to pull the to front end of the spring forward until it snaps into place.

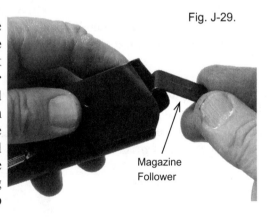

Fig. J-29.

Magazine
Follower

NOTE: The magazine spring has a short coiled end or L-shaped loop at the top. The coil or loop faces forward.

510

APPENDIX K
COLT LETTERS OF AUTHENTICITY

Colt's Manufacturing Company, LLC, offers an archival service that will provide a letter describing a particular firearm manufactured by Colt from a wide range of models, from the Model 1851 Navy revolver to modern Colt rifles and shotguns. The archive staff will search company records and issue a letter on the Colt's factory letterhead containing the serial number and any information found in the company records; this usually includes: the serial number, caliber, barrel length, type of finish, type of stocks, any special features listed, name of the purchaser, date of shipment, factory order number, and number of guns in the shipment.

The information sources are company records; the collector must keep in mind that all entries until recently were made by hand and may not contain all the data describing the subject firearm.

The current cost for letters of authentication for the Model 1911/1911A1 and current variations is $100.00. Additional charges are added if special features such as engraving, inlays, etc. are involved as additional staff time is required for verification. Letters are generally delivered with three to six months.

An expedited service is available whereby the collector can telephone the archivist and receive the information within three days. An additional fee is applied.

To obtain a letter of authentication, supply the serial number and model of the firearm in question in a letter together with the current fee to: Colt's Manufacturing Company LLC, Customer Service Department, P.O. Box 1868, Hartford, CT 06144-1868, U.S.A.

Current pricing and information can be obtained from the company Web site at http://www.coltsmfg.com/cmci/historical.asp.

The collector should be aware that a Colt letter does not prove a particular firearm is original as it left the factory; it only notes that a particular serial number was listed in the Colt records. A firearm could bear a specific serial number in question and still be a counterfeit. Or, it may have been refinished or altered with major and minor parts changed after it was shipped from the Colt factory.

APPENDIX L
BIBLIOGRAPHY

Books

A Century of Achievement, Colt's Patent Firearms Manufacturing Company, 1937.

Angier, R.H. *Firearms Blueing and Browning,* The Stackpole Company, Harrisburg, PA, 1936.

Askins, Col. Charles. "The .45 Auto With Pershing in Mexico," *America: The Men and Their Guns That Made Her Great,* edited by Craig Boddington, Petersen Publishing Company, Los Angeles, CA, 1981.

Bady, Donald B. *Colt Automatic Pistols,* 2nd Edition, Revised and Enlarged, Borden Publishing Company, Alhambra, CA, 1973.

Chemical Cross Reference, Lindsay Publications, Bradley, IL 60915, 2003.

Clawson, Charles W. *Colt .45 Service Pistols, Models of 1911 and 1911A1,* Charles W. Clawson, Fort Wayne, IN 46885, 1991.

Crowell, Benedict. "Chapter XI. Pistols and Revolvers," *America's Munitions, 1917-1918.* Government Printing Office, Washington, 1919.

Duguid CMG, A. Fortescu, Col. *A Question of Confidence: The Ross Rifle in the Trenches,* Service Publications, PO Box 33071, Ottawa, ON K2C 3Y9, 1999.

Goddard, William H.D. *The Government Models: The Development of the Colt Model 1911,* Andrew Mowbray Publishers, Woonsocket, RI, 02895, 1988.

Grant, Ellsworth L. *The Colt Armory: A History of the Colt Armory in Hartford, 1855-1980.* Andrew Mowbray Publishers, Woonsocket, RI, 02895, 1982.

Greeley, Horace, IV. *The Colt U.S. General Officers' Pistol,* Andrew Mowbray Publishers, PO Box 460, Woonsocket, RI, 02895, 1989.

Hackley, F.W., W.H. Woodin, E.L. Scranton. *History of Modern U.S. Military Small Arms Ammunition, Vol. 1, 1880-1939,* Macmillan Company, 1967.
Harrison, Jesse C. *U.S. Pistols and Revolvers 1909-1945,* The Arms Chest, Oklahoma City, OK 73150, 4th edition, 1993.

Military and Commercial Pistols

Harrison, Jesse C. *U.S. Military Markings, 1900-1965,* The Arms Chest, Oklahoma City, OK 73150, 1993.

Hatcher, J.S. *Textbook of Pistols and Revolvers.* Small-Arms Technical Publishing Company, Plantersville, SC, 1935.

Hoffschmidt, E. J. *Know Your .45 Auto Pistols, Model 1911 & A1,* Blacksmith Corporation, Southport, CT, 1974.

Jenkins, Bill. *U.S. Military Match and Marksmanship Automatic Pistols,* Andrew Mowbray Publishers, Woonsocket, RI, 02895, 2005.

Jinks, Roy G. *History of Smith & Wesson*, Beinfeld Publishing, Inc., North Hollywood, CA, 1977.

Kuhnhausen, Jerry. *The Colt .45 Automatic, A Shop Manual, Volume I* , Heritage-VSP Gun Books, McCall, ID 83868, 1990.

Kuhnhausen, Jerry. *The U.S. M1911/1911A1 Pistols and Commercial M1911 Type Pistols, A Shop Manual, Volume II*, Heritage-VSP Gun Books, McCall, ID 83868, 1990.

Meadows, Edward Scott. *U.S. Military Automatic Pistols, Volume I, 1894-1920,* Richard Ellis Publications, Inc., Moline, IL 61265, 1993.

Meadows, Edward Scott. *U.S. Military Holsters and Pistol Cartridge Boxes,* Taylor Publishing Company, Dallas, TX, 1987.

Morse, D.R. and M.T. *Production Statistics: U.S. Arms Makers, From ArmaLite to Winchester*, Firing Pin Enterprizes, Phoenix, AZ 85060, 1997.

Mullin, Timothy J. *American Beauty: The Prewar Colt National Match Government Model Pistol,* Collector Grade Publications, Cobourg, Ontario, Canada K9A 4W5, 1999.

Murphy, Bob. *Colt New Service Revolvers*, World-Wide Gun Report, Inc., Aledo, IL 61231, 1985.

Nofi, Albert A. *Marine Corps Book of Lists*, Da Capo Press, Cambridge, MA 02142, 3rd edition, 2001.

Office of the Chief of Military History, U.S. Army. *United States Army in World War II, Special Studies, The Ordnance Department: Planning Munitions for War,* U.S. Government Printing Office, Washington, D.C., 20402, 1955.

Model 1911, M1911A1

Pate, Charles W. *U.S. Handguns of World War II: The Secondary Pistols and Revolvers,* Andrew Mowbray Publishers, Woonsocket, RI, 02895, 1998.

Potocki, John. *The Colt Model 1905 Automatic Pistol,* Andrew Mowbray Publishers, Woonsocket, RI, 02895, 1998.

Sahr, Robert C. "Inflation Factors for Years 1665 to Estimated 2013," revised February 2003, Political Science Department, Oregon State University, Corvallis, OR 97331.

Severn, James E. *Colt Firearms, 1836-1958.* Published by the Author, Santa Ana, CA, 1954.

Smith, W.H.B. *The Book of Pistols and Revolvers,* Stackpole Company, Harrisburg, PA, 4th edition, 1960.

Stratton, Charles R. *British Enfield Rifles, Volume 1, SMLE (No. 1) Rifles, Mk I and Mk III,* North Cape Publications, Inc., PO Box 1027, Tustin, CA 92781, 1997.

Stratton, Charles R. *British Enfield Rifles, Volume 4, Pattern 1914 and U.S. Model of 1917 Rifles,* North Cape Publications, Inc., PO Box 1027, Tustin, CA 92781, 2000.

Wilson, R. K. *Textbook of Automatic Pistols.* T.G. Samworth, The Stackpole Company, Harrisburg, PA, 1924.

Wilson, R. L. *The Book of Colt Firearms,* Blue Book Publications, Inc., Minneapolis, MN 55425, 1993. (This is a revised edition of Robert Q. Sutherland's landmark study of Colt firearms, first published in 1971 by the author.)

Wilson, R. L. *The Book of Colt Engraving,* Wallace Beinfeld Publications, Inc., Los Angeles, CA, 1974.

Correspondence

"Approval of Slocum, Avrum & Slocum Laboratories Company, New York City, for the manufacture of Caliber .45, Model of 1911 Automatic Pistol." From Chief of Production Division to Chief of Procurement Division, Ordnance Department, U.S. Army, August 24, 1918.

"Parco Lubrite is a trade name originally used by the Parker Corporation." From John Donofrio, Chemetall Oaktite Corporation, February 18, 2008.

"Remington-UMC Model 1911 .45 Automatic Pistols Cited in Ordnance Dept. and Other Records." From Franklin B. Mallory, Chief Researcher, Springfield Research Service,

Military and Commercial Pistols

to Roy Marcot, February 23, 1994.

"Serial Numbers of .45 Colt Automatic Pistols Manufactured Under Contract P4537-11338Sa." From A. M. Mattice, Advisory Engineer, Remington Arms Company, Inc., Cunard Building, 25 Broadway, New York City to Major Lee O. Wright, Ord. Dept, U.S.A., Assistant, Office of the Chief of Ordnance, War Department, Washington, D.C., July 26, 1923.

Magazine and Journal Articles and Other Sources

Crossman, Colonel Jim. "Trials of the .45," *American Rifleman,* National Rifle Association, Fairfax, VA 22030, May 1985.

Johnston, Gary Paul. "A Mystery Remington-UMC 1911 Pistol," *American Rifleman,* February 2000.

Karash, Karl. *M1911/1911A1/Government Models, Photographic Images: Pistols, Model 1911, 1911A1, and Government Models, The Karl Karash Collection,* 2004 on Compact Disc. Available from North Cape Publications, Inc., PO Box 1027, Tustin, CA 92781. $19.95 plus $2.95 postage. Phone 800 745-9714 to order.

Marcot, Roy. "Remington Rand M1911A1 Pistols," *Journal of the Remington Society,* 3rd Quarter, 2000.

Maze, Robert G. "His Majesty's Government Models," *American Rifleman,* Volume 155, No. 7, July 2007. Also at http://www.nrapublications.org/TAR/KingColt2.asp in greater detail.

Ordnance Department Publications

FM 23-35, Basic Field Manual, Automatic Pistol, Caliber .45 M1911 and M1911A1, War Department, Government Printing Office, Washington, D.C., 1940.

FM 23-35/AFM 50-17, Pistols and Revolvers, Department of the Army and the Air Force, Government Printing Office, July 1960.

Description of the Automatic Pistol, Caliber .45, Model of 1911, with Rules for Management, Memoranda of Trajectory and Description of Ammunition, Ordnance Department Publication No. 1866, Washington, D.C., 1912.

Description of the Automatic Pistol, Caliber .45, Model of 1911, with Rules for Management, Memoranda of Trajectory and Description of Ammunition, Ordnance Department Publication No. 1866, Washington, D.C., 1914.

Model 1911, M1911A1

Description of the Automatic Pistol, Caliber .45, Model of 1911, with Rules for Management, Memoranda of Trajectory and Description of Ammunition, Ordnance Department Publication No. 1866, Washington, D.C., 1915.

Description of the Automatic Pistol, Caliber .45, Model of 1911, with Rules for Management, Memoranda of Trajectory and Description of Ammunition, Ordnance Department Publication No. 1866, Washington, D.C., 1917.

Ordnance Field Service Base Shop Data, Pistol, CAL. 45 M1911A1 (Automatic), B.S.D.-P-1, Rock Island Arsenal, Sept. 1942.

"Report of Board on Tests of Revolvers and Automatic Pistols," *Annual Report of the Chief of Ordnance for 1907*, Washington, D.C., 1907.

Small Arms Firing Manual, 1913, Office of the Chief of Staff, War Department, Government Printing Office, Washington, D.C., 1914.

Small Arms Firing Regulations, U.S. Navy, 1917, Government Printing Office, Washington, D.C., 1916.

Specifications Governing the Manufacture and Inspection of Pistol and Revolver Ball Cartridges, Caliber .45, Model of 1911 for the Automatic Pistol, Model 1911, Double-Action Revolver, Model 1917, No. 514, Government Printing Office, Washington, D.C., 1917.

Technical Regulations No. 1400–45A, *Ordnance Maintenance—Infantry and Aircraft Armament, Pistols and Revolvers*. War Department, Washington, D.C., December 13, 1927.

Technical Manual 9-1005-211-12. *Pistol, Caliber .45, Automatic, M1911A1, With Holster, Hip (1005-673-7965) and Pistol, Caliber .45, Automatic, M1911A1, With Holster, Shoulder (1005-561-2003)*, Headquarters, Department of the Army. Washington, D.C., September 1968 and February 1976.

Technical Manual 9-1295. *Ordnance Maintenance, Cal. .45 Automatic Pistol, M1911 and M1911A1*, War Department, Washington, D.C., September 1947.

Technical Manual 9-1904. *Ammunition Inspection Guide*, War Department, Washington, D.C., March 1944.

Technical Manual 9-2205. *Fundamentals of Small Arms*, Department of the Army, Washington, D.C., 1942.

Military and Commercial Pistols

Training Regulations No. 320-15, March 3, 1924 for Automatic Pistol, Calibre .45, Model of 1911, Washington, D.C., 1924.

Department of the Army Publications
Instructions to Bidders and Specifications Governing The Manufacture of the United States Rifle, Caliber .30 Model 1903, Ordnance Department, U.S. Army, Government Printing Office, Washington, D.C., July 1, 1916.

TM 43-0001-27. *Army Ammunition Data Sheets, Small Caliber Ammunition, FSC 1305*, Headquarters, Department of the Army, April 1994.

About the Author

Joe Poyer is the author of more than 400 magazine articles on firearms, the modern military, military history and personal security. He has written and published twelve novels with worldwide sales exceeding five million copies and authored or coauthored nine nonfiction books on the modern military from other publishers.

He is the editorial director and publisher of North Cape Publications®, Inc., which publishes the "For Collectors Only®" and "A Shooter's and Collector's Guide" series of books for firearms collectors and shooters. In these series, he has written or coauthored: *The .45-70 Springfield*; *U.S. Winchester Trench and Riot Guns, and Other U.S. Combat Shotguns*; *The M1 Garand, 1936 to 1957*; *The SKS Carbine*; *The M14-Type Rifle*; *The SAFN-49 Battle Rifle*; *The Swedish Mauser Rifles*; *The M16/AR15 Rifle*; *The Model 1903 Springfield Rifle and Its Variations*; *The American Krag Rifle and Carbine*; *Swiss Magazine Loading Rifles, 1869 to 1958*; *The AK-47 and AK-74 Kalashnikov Rifles and Their Variations;* and *The Model 1911 and Model 1911A1 Military and Commercial Pistols.*

Mr. Poyer has served as editor of the following magazines: *Safe & Secure Living*; *International Military Review*; *International Naval Review* and as field editor for *International Combat Arms*. He is currently at work on a new book in the "For Collectors Only" series, *The Colt Double Action Military Pistols.*

Mr. Poyer was the on-camera Military Affairs Analyst and Reporter for a major television station in Los Angeles, California. He also imported the very fine L1A1A inch pattern FAL rifles from Australia in the late 1980s.

Model 1911, M1911A1

About the Technical Adviser and Editor

Karl Karash is the technical adviser for this book, He is a well-known collector of 20th-century U.S. military small arms, especially the 1911/1911A1 pistol. He was the original author of the 1911/1911A1 section of the *Standard Catalog of Military Firearms*. He is also listed as a contributor to other books on the 1911/1911A1 pistol as well as to the best informational Website (www. coolgunsite.com) on the 1911/1911A1 pistol. Author of a photo Compact Disc, *M1911/1911A1/Government Models, Photographic Images: Pistols, Model 1911, 1911A1, and Government Models, The Karl Karash Collection,* containing over 5,000 unretouched, high- resolution images (in JPG format) of Model 1911/1911A1 pistols, hundreds of images of commercial Government Model pistols, as well as accessories and tools. (The CD is available from North Cape Publications.) This CD is not intended to be a showcase, but a tool for beginners and advanced collectors alike to see what original pistols look like without make-up. Much of Karl's time is spent trying to help new collectors avoid the pitfalls and predators of collecting as well as encouraging new collectors to become interested in the history of 20th-century U.S. small arms. Karl is an avid collector and student of M1 Carbines and M1 Garands, as well as being an engineer and machinist.

Craig Riesch is the editor for this book. He is a well-known collector and scholar of U.S. military small arms. He is the author of *U.S. M1 Carbines, Wartime Production* and is the coauthor of *The .45-70 Springfield* and *The M1 Garand, 1936 to 1957*. He also edited *The American Krag Rifle and Carbine, Swiss Magazine Loading Rifles, 1869 to 1958,* and *The Model 1911 and Model 1911A1 Military and Commercial Pistols,* all in the "For Collectors Only®" series plus *The AK-47 and AK-74 Kalashnikov Rifles* in the "Shooter's and Collector's" series. Both series are guides to antique and collectible modern firearms identification and verification.

Mr. Riesch has spent a great deal of time studying U.S. military firearms and is consulted by many collectors for authentication of military and civilian arms. He has been a collector himself for over forty years. Mr. Riesch is a U.S. Army combat veteran and served in Vietnam during the period of the Tet Offensive. He worked for 33 years as a product operations manager for a major defense company.

PUBLICATIONS AVAILABLE FROM
NORTH CAPE PUBLICATIONS®, INC.

The books in the "For Collectors Only®" and "A Shooter's and Collector's Guide" series are designed to provide the firearms collector with an accurate record of the markings, dimensions and finish found on an original firearm as it was shipped from the factory.

For Collectors Only® Series

The Model 1911 and 1911A1 Military and Commercial Pistols, by Joe Poyer ($35.95). The first book on the Model 1911/1911A1 in over fifteen years. Provides a complete part-by-part by serial number range for both military and commercial models as well as several foreign models. Serial number charts are extensive and cover each variation individually. Additional charts compare military and serial numbers by year of manufacture and provide an annotated list of military serial numbers. All markings—factory inspection, military acceptance, and factory address and patent markings—are discussed and illustrated.

M1911/1911A1/Government Models, Photographic Images: Pistols, Model 1911,1911A1, and Government Models, *The Karl Karash Collection*, 2004.
Karl Karash has produced a portfolio on Compact Disk of over 5,000 color photographs of Model 1911/1911A1 pistols, both military and commercial, which is available from North Cape Publications, Inc. This collection is an invaluable tool for researching the M1911/M1911A1 Pistol. A total of 205 pistols are shown full size in right and left views, and in close-ups of all significant parts and markings. Available from North Cape Publications, Inc., PO Box 1027, Tustin, CA 92781. $19.95 plus $2.95 postage.

The .58- and .50-Caliber Rifles and Carbines of the Springfield Armory, 1865–1872, by Richard A. Hosmer ($19.95). This book describes the .58- and .50-caliber rifles and carbines that were developed at the Springfield Armory between 1865 and 1872 and which led ultimately to the selection of the famed ".45-70 trapdoor."

Serbian and Yugoslav Mauser Rifles, by Branko Bogdanovic ($19.95). Thousands of Yugoslav Mauser rifles have been imported into North America in the last two decades and Mr. Bogdanovic's book will help the collector and shooter determine which model he or she has, and its antecedents. Every Mauser that found its way into military service in Serbia/Yugoslavia is listed and described.

Model 1911, M1911A1

Swiss Magazine Loading Rifles, 1869 to 1958, by Joe Poyer ($19.95). A complete part-by-part description for the Vetterli, Schmidt-Rubin, and K-31 rifles in all their variations by serial number range, plus a history of their development and use, their cleaning, maintenance, and how to shoot them safely and accurately.

The American Krag Rifle and Carbine (2nd edition, revised), by Joe Poyer, edited by Craig Riesch ($22.95). A part-by-part description of the first magazine repeating arm adopted for general service in American military history.

The Model 1903 Springfield Rifle and Its Variations (2nd edition, revised and expanded), by Joe Poyer ($22.95). Includes every model of the Model 1903 from the ramrod bayonet to the Model 1903A4 Sniper rifle. Every part is described by serial number range, markings and finish.

The .45-70 Springfield (4th edition, revised and expanded), by Joe Poyer and Craig Riesch ($19.95), covers the entire range of .45-caliber "trapdoor" Springfield arms, including bayonets, tools and accoutrements.

U.S. Winchester Trench and Riot Guns and Other U.S. Combat Shotguns (2nd edition, revised), by Joe Poyer ($16.95). Describes the elusive and little-known "Trench Shotgun" and all other combat shotguns used by U.S. military forces.

U.S. M1 Carbines, Wartime Production (5th edition, revised and expanded), by Craig Riesch ($19.95), describes the four models of M1 Carbines from all ten manufacturers. Complete with codes for every part by serial number range.

The M1 Garand, 1936 to 1957 (4th edition, revised and expanded), by Joe Poyer and Craig Riesch ($19.95). This book covers such important identification factors as manufacturer's markings, proof marks, final acceptance cartouches stampings and heat treatment lot numbers plus detailed breakdowns of every part in minute detail.

Winchester Lever Action Repeating Firearms, by Arthur Pirkle
      Volume 1, **The Models of 1866, 1873 & 1876** ($19.95)
      Volume 2, **The Models of 1886 and 1892** ($19.95)
      Volume 3, **The Models of 1894 and 1895** ($19.95)
These famous lever action repeaters are completely analyzed part-by-part by serial number range in this first new series on these fine weapons in twenty years.

Military and Commercial Pistols

The SKS Carbine (3rd revised and expanded edition), by Steve Kehaya and Joe Poyer ($16.95). The SKS Carbine "is profusely illustrated, articulately researched and covers all aspects of its development as well as . . . other combat guns used by the USSR and other Communist bloc nations." Glen Voorhees, Jr., *Gun Week*.

British Enfield Rifles, by Charles R. Stratton (each volume, $16.95)
> Volume 1, **SMLE (No. 1) Mk I and Mk III** (2nd edition, revised)
> Volume 2, **Lee-Enfield No. 4 and No. 5 Rifles** (3rd Edition, revised)
> Volume 4, **Pattern 1914 and U.S. Model of 1917 Rifles** (2nd edition, revised)

The British Army's famed rifles are analyzed in detail on a part-by-part basis, complete with all inspector's and military markings.

The Mosin-Nagant Rifle (4th revised and expanded edition), by Terence W. Lapin ($19.95). A comprehensive volume covering all aspects and models from the Imperial Russian rifles to the Finnish, American, Polish, Chinese, Romanian and North Korean variations. Includes part-by-part descriptions of all makers plus all variants such as carbines and sniper rifles.

The Swedish Mauser Rifles (2nd edition), by Steve Kehaya and Joe Poyer ($19.95). A complete history of the development and use of the Swedish Mauser rifles is provided as well as a part-by-part description of each component. All 24 models are described and a complete description of the sniper rifles and their telescopic sights is included. All markings, codes, regimental and other military markings are charted and explained. A thorough and concise explanation of the Swedish Mauser rifle, both civilian and military.

A Shooter's and Collector's Guide Series

The AK-47 and AK-74 Kalashnikov Rifles and Their Variations (2nd edition, revised and expanded), by Joe Poyer ($22.95). The AK-47 and its replacement, the AK-74, are examined on a part-by-part basis to show the differences between various types of receivers, other parts, and the AK and AKM models. Also contains a detailed survey of all models of the Kalashnikov rifle from the AK-47 to the AK-108.

The M16/AR15 Rifle (3rd edition, revised and expanded), by Joe Poyer ($22.95). This 155-page, profusely illustrated, large-format book examines the development, history, and current and future use of the M16/AR15. It describes in detail all civilian AR15 rifles and takes the reader step-by-step through the process of accurizing the AR15 into an extremely accurate target rifle.

Model 1911, M1911A1

The M14-Type Rifle (3rd edition, revised and expanded), by Joe Poyer ($19.95). A study of the U.S. Army's last and short-lived .30-caliber battle rifle. Also includes the National Match M14 rifle, the M21 and M25 sniper rifles, civilian semiautomatic match rifles, receivers, parts and accessories and the Chinese M14s. A guide to custom-building a service-type rifle or a match-grade, precision rifle.

The SAFN-49 Battle Rifle, by Joe Poyer ($14.95). This detailed study of the SAFN-49 provides a part-by-part examination of the four calibers in which the rifle was made, a description of the SAFN-49 Sniper Rifle and its telescopic sights, plus maintenance, assembly/disassembly, accurizing, restoration and shooting. A new exploded view and section view are included.

Collector's Guide to Military Uniforms
Campaign Clothing: Field Uniforms of the Indian War Army
Volume 1, **1866–1871** ($12.95)
Volume 2, **1872–1886** ($14.95)
Lee A. Rutledge has produced a unique perspective on the uniforms of the Army of the United States during the late Indian War period following the Civil War. He discusses what the soldier really wore when on campaign. No white hats and yellow bandanas here.

A Guide Book to U.S. Army Dress Helmets, 1872–1904, by Mark Kasal and Don Moore ($16.95). From 1872 to 1904, the men and officers of the U.S. Army wore a fancy, plumed or spiked helmet on all dress occasions. As ubiquitous as they were in the late 19th century, they are extremely scarce today. Kasal and Moore have written a step-by-step, part-by-part analysis of both the Models 1872 and 1881 dress helmets and their history and use. Profusely illustrated with black-and-white and color photographs of actual helmets.

All of the above books can be obtained directly from North Cape Publications®, Inc., P.O. Box 1027, Tustin, CA 92781 or by calling Toll Free 1-800 745-9714. Orders may also be placed by Fax (714 832-5302) or via e-mail to ncape@ix.netcom.com. CA residents add 7.75% sales tax. Current rates are any two books: Media Mail (7-21 days) $3.95, add $0.95 for each additional book. Priority Mail: 1-2 books $5.95 or 3-10 books, $10.50. International Rates on request to E-mail address: ncape@ix.netcom.com. Visit our Internet Website at http://www.northcapepubs.com. Our complete, up-to-date book list can always be found there. All book prices and postage rates subject to change.